# HIKE LIST

# 60 Hikes within 60 MILES

## ST. LOUIS

### INCLUDING SULLIVAN, POTOSI, AND FARMINGTON

### SECOND EDITION

## Steve Henry

**MENASHA RIDGE PRESS**
Birmingham, Alabama

Library of Congress Cataloging-in-Publication Data

Henry, Steve.
    60 hikes within 60 miles, St. Louis: including Sullivan, Potosi, and Farmington/
Steve Henry.—2nd ed.
        p. cm.
    ISBN 13: 978-0-89732-612-4
    ISBN 10: 0-89732-612-1
        1. Hiking—Missouri—Saint Louis Region—Guidebooks. 2. Saint Louis Region
(Mo.)—Guidebooks. I. Title. II. Title: Sixty hikes within sixty miles, St. Louis.

GV199.42.M82S754 2006
796.5109778'56—dc22                                     2006046749

Cover design by Grant M. Tatum
Text design by Karen Ocker
Cover photo copyright © Alamy/Richard Wong
Author photo (page ix) © by Glenn Hoffmeister
All other photos by Steve Henry
Maps by Steve Jones and Steve Henry

Menasha Ridge Press
P.O. Box 43673
Birmingham, AL 35243
www.menasharidge.com

Thanks to all the park folks and volunteers who built these
spectacular trails. May all who hike these paths appreciate the
beautiful results of their labor as much as I do.

# TABLE OF CONTENTS

# TABLE OF CONTENTS

# ACKNOWLEDGMENTS

Thanks first to all those who work and volunteer in the parks, conservation departments, and national forests in the St. Louis area. Due to their vision and hard work, St. Louisans are blessed with miles and miles of beautiful trail only an hour or two from the metro area. Furthermore, they're always happy to answer questions—even those from guidebook authors who barge into their offices five minutes before quitting time, wearing muddy boots, and smelling kind of gamy.

I also owe much to all my friends and family. No matter how dirty, sweaty, and scratched-up I was from exploring the wildlands around St. Louis, they still opened their doors to me. Thanks to Chuck, for lending me office space and giving me a flexible work schedule while researching these trails, and to Sharon, for all the computer advice. Thanks also to the folks at Menasha Ridge Press, who were patient with me, and somehow formed a mountain of material into a coherent and readable book. May our guidebook bring you miles of smiles in the hills, hollows, glades, and valleys of eastern Missouri and western Illinois.

# FOREWORD

Welcome to Menasha Ridge Press's *60 Hikes within 60 Miles,* a series designed to provide hikers with information needed to find and hike the very best trails surrounding cities usually underserved by good guidebooks.

Our strategy is simple: First, find a hiker who knows the area and loves to hike. Second, ask that person to spend a year researching the most popular and very best trails around. And third, have that person describe each trail in terms of difficulty, scenery, condition, elevation change, and all other categories of information that are important to hikers. "Pretend you've just completed a hike and met up with other hikers at the trailhead," we tell each author. "Imagine their questions, be clear in your answers."

An experienced hiker and writer, author Steve Henry has selected 60 of the best hikes in and around the St. Louis metropolitan area, ranging from walks through the open meadows and marshes of August A. Busch Memorial Conservation Area to bushwhacking treks out to Green's Cave along the Meramec River. From urban hikes that make use of parklands to aerobic outings in national forests, Henry provides hikers (and walkers) with a great variety of hikes—and all within roughly 60 miles of St. Louis.

You'll get more out of this book if you take a moment to read the Introduction that explains the trail profiles. The "Topographic Maps" section will help you understand how useful topos will be on a hike, and will also tell you where to get them. And though this is a "where-to," not a "how-to" guide, those of you who have not hiked extensively will find the Introduction of particular value.

As much for the opportunity to free the spirit as to free the body, let Steve Henry's hikes elevate you above the urban hurry.

All the best,
—The Editors at Menasha Ridge Press

# ABOUT THE AUTHOR

Steve Henry grew up on a farm in the rolling hills of central Kansas, spending much of his youth working under the blue skies of the plains. After earning bachelor's degrees in marketing and agricultural economics at Kansas State University, he served a sentence of seven years in the offices of a large insurance company. Missing the outdoor life, he left the corporate world in 1985 to cycle across the continent twice, including one trek from Alaska to Key West. Since then he has led bicycle and backpack tours, contributed articles to outdoor publications and Web sites, and written *Mountain Bike! The Ozarks* and *The Best in Tent Camping: Missouri and the Ozarks*. He heads for the mountain and desert West whenever he can shake himself loose from the Midwest, and always looks forward to fall and winter hiking, camping, biking, and canoeing in the Ozarks. When not roaming the outdoors by foot, bike, or canoe, Steve sees the country from the driver's seat of a Peterbilt 379.

# PREFACE

St. Louisans are so lucky. There are miles and miles of trail in eastern Missouri and western Illinois, ranging from rugged all-day treks to short jaunts perfect for an evening walk. These trails explore a wide range of scenery, wandering through forests, river valleys, piney ridges, deep hollows, prairies, glades, wetlands, and several rugged canyons. Best of all, we Midwesterners can enjoy them year-round. When the glamour destinations in the western states are buried under feet of snow, we can still hit the trail.

In fact, winter is the favorite hiking season for many folks, including me. The forest is gray-brown, but bright cedars and pines stand out like green candles. Shorter days mean less time to hike, but the winter sunshine is deep and rich. The bugs are gone, there's no humidity, and the days are often autumn-like. The trees are bare, exposing scenic vistas obscured by greenery during the warm months. And bitterly cold weather means still more beauty. Waterfalls and streams freeze into fantastic ice sculptures, seeps from rock layers form icicle mustaches along cliff faces, and the snow squeaks pleasantly underfoot. After ice storms, the forest glitters as if encrusted with diamonds. The trees crack and groan in the wind, pelting you with tinkling showers of ice crystals as they shed their frozen jackets. And since lots of folks are intimidated by the cold, you'll have all this beauty to yourself!

Good as winter is, you can start arguments over which season, spring or fall, is the best time to hike. Those "first breath of spring" days in early March are delightful. Wildflowers start blooming, and the new leaves are an incredibly bright green when the buds first pop. Redbuds tinge the hillsides pink, and after the flowering dogwoods bloom the forest floor is carpeted with white petals. The songbirds return, and in wetlands the symphony of frogs belting out their mating calls is entrancing. Spring rains fill the streams, and all the waterfalls and cascades come to life. Don't let rain keep you off the trail—it's worth getting a bit damp just to enjoy the noisy streams, and leaves and mosses along the trail glow a bright, iridescent green when soaked by spring showers.

On the other hand, fall hiking is hard to beat. The temperatures moderate, the bugs disappear, the heat and humidity of summer are gone, and the colors are incredible. I like hiking just after the leaves have fallen. Then, even on cloudy days, yellow leaves carpeting the forest floor make the whole landscape glow as if lit from beneath. The trail is crunchy with leaves and acorns, and the air is crisp and sweet. Only two drawbacks mar fall hiking: once the leaves are down it's harder to find the trail when hiking less-traveled paths, and in November and December hunters take to the

Winter wandering on the Lakeshore Trail at Council Bluff Lake

woods. Hiking more-popular trails can solve the former problem, and choosing hikes in state and county parks, where hunting is prohibited, takes care of the latter one. And avoid Department of Conservation properties during hunting season; almost all of these are popular hunting destinations.

Summer isn't a fun time to hike around St. Louis. The trails are hot, humid, overgrown, and buggy. Still, occasional cool fronts sometimes bring respites and hiking early in the morning can be delightful. If you're really adventurous and determined to hike in summer, check the calendar for the full moon and do some night hiking. Most conservation areas are open until 10 p.m., national forest trails have no time limitations, and if you're camping in one of the state parks you can wander their trails from your campsite. It's fun to explore the woods in the moonlight, listening to the owls and coyotes as you go.

Whatever season you choose, you'll find hikes of all lengths and difficulties in this guide. I focused more on true hikes as opposed to walks, though there are several short, paved hikes included in the book. Since I used the edge of the metro area as my starting point for the 60-mile radius from town, some hikes are beyond 60 miles from the Arch. As you scan the table of contents you'll note several trails a bit farther than 60 miles, no matter how you cut it. These trails are some of the best hikes in the two-state area, so I included them anyway. My yardstick for choosing hikes was this: If you could drive to a trail, do the hike, and easily drive home again the same day, it went in the book. Had I stuck religiously to the 60-mile limit, you'd miss out on such treasures as Mina Sauk Falls, the Castor River Shut-Ins, and the beautiful Mississippi River overlooks at Trail of Tears State Park.

You're also getting quite a few more than 60 hikes. Many of the parks described in this guide offer more than one trail—in some cases six or more routes in one trail system—totaling more than 100 hikes. That's why you'll see wide ranges in estimated hiking times in some chapters. In general, trail-difficulty ratings are an inexact science. This book's ratings were determined by the Sierra Club's system, which is based solely on distance and altitude

Crossing Bidwell Creek on a wintry day, John J. Audubon Trail

change. Because of this, a short, rugged trail that will really work you over could receive an easier rating, while a longer, flatter hike might receive a tougher one. Furthermore, the multiple-trail chapters mentioned above get tougher ratings because of their total distance, even though they may include short hikes deserving easier ratings. Don't take the ratings as gospel—read the text to get a feel for how tough a given hike really is, and whether there's a shorter option more suited to your time and energy.

Multiple trail systems make some of the hiking recommendations (see pages xiv–xx) look strange, too. Since one trail system may have hikes of several lengths, you'll see the same park listed in several distance categories. Also, remember that hiking recommendations are somewhat subjective. My beautiful hike may be your boring one, and vice versa. Several times I've thought a trail somewhat unimpressive, only to later hear others rave about how great it was. Also, the "Hikes Good for Young Children" category doesn't mean its trails are cakewalks. All hikes in that category are short, but may include stretches of rugged trail and occasional stream crossings. After all, kids love to climb boulders and play in water, so trails with these features are perfect for kids.

The maps in the book are good ones, but trail maps from the parks and forest service are more detailed. These are often found at trailheads and park offices, and many are available in printable format on the Internet. Since trail systems sometimes undergo changes, don't be surprised to occasionally find different trails or markings from those described in the text. Reroutes take place, flooding forces adjustments, new trails may be added to a network, or different marking systems may be adopted. Also, in the text you'll often read of trails marked with carsonite posts. In case you're not familiar with these, they're the flat, flexible, fiberglass posts often used to mark trails. Most hikes are well marked and easy to follow, and those that aren't are noted in the text.

Though I rarely get lost, I always carry a map and compass or GPS with me on an unfamiliar trail, and I recommend you do the same. If you lose your way, simply backtrack to the last known marker on the map, orient yourself with your compass, and you're all set. If you somehow lose the trail completely, your compass will guide you on a heading to the nearest road. With a GPS it's really simple—if you set a waypoint before leaving the trailhead you can use the trackback feature to find your way back.

Another hiking essential is a good pair of hiking boots. The most scenic trails are often the most rugged, and good footwear makes hiking them more enjoyable. Waterproof boots, either Gore-Tex or treated leather, are preferred. They let you splash dry-footed through the

Breached dam on the St. Francis River

many shallow streams and wetlands you'll cross on these hikes. Also helpful on stream crossings and rugged trails, especially when it's rainy or icy, is a good hiking staff. You can usually find a stick along the trail that serves the purpose, but the new lightweight, telescoping, metal ones are superb.

I recommend carrying a camera, pair of binoculars, magnifying glass, and a couple of field guides on your hikes. They'll slow you down, but in a good way. You'll find yourself spotting birds, identifying wildflowers, photographing bluffs and waterfalls, thus being drawn more deeply into the landscape and experiencing the natural world in a more satisfying way. Hiking is more enjoyable if you know a bit about the territory you're wandering through. Without an understanding of what's behind nature's beauty, hiking through scenic landscapes is like reading a travel book in a foreign language—you'll like the pretty pictures, but you'll miss out on the fascinating story in the text.

Powder Valley Nature Center and Shaw Nature Reserve are two destinations perfect for developing your knowledge of western Illinois and eastern Missouri's natural beauty. Powder Valley's visitor center is a superb place to study the area's flora and fauna, and Shaw's Whitmire Wildflower Garden will give you a leg up on identifying wildflowers and trees. Both places sell a wide range of field guides, and while you're at Powder Valley you can subscribe to the Department of Conservation's magazine, *Missouri Conservationist*. Free for all residents of Missouri, it's full of informative nature articles and features on places to go on the DOC's vast array of landholdings.

Whether you know a little or a lot about the natural world, you'll find much beauty along the hikes in this guidebook. I hope you enjoy hiking these paths as much as I do, and get out on the trail often. May you surprise flocks of turkeys, spot bald eagles, meander through carpets of wildflowers, splash through clear cascades, and picnic on scenic, cedar-studded bluffs.

Hope to see you out there!
—*Steve Henry*

# HIKING RECOMMENDATIONS

# HIKING RECOMMENDATIONS

# HIKING RECOMMENDATIONS

# HIKING RECOMMENDATIONS

# HIKING RECOMMENDATIONS

# HIKING RECOMMENDATIONS

## ▶ TRAILS FOR TRAIL RUNNERS

## ▶ MULTIUSE TRAILS (mountain bikes, inline skates, horses, etc.)

*Note:* Trails may be open to some, but not all, of the above listed uses.

# HIKING RECOMMENDATIONS

## ▶ MULTIUSE TRAILS (continued)

23. Cuivre River State Park (page 100)
25. Graham Cave State Park (page 107)
27. Klondike Park (page 114)
29. Lost Valley Trail (page 122)
30. Matson Hill Park (page 126)
31. Quail Ridge County Park (page 129)
33. Berryman Trail (page 138)
34. Council Bluff Lake (page 142)
38. Johnson Shut-Ins State Park (Goggins Mountain Trail) (page 157)
40. Meramec Conservation Area (page 165)
48. John J. Audubon Trail (page 199)
50. Crane Lake Trail (page 207)
56. St. Francois State Park (Pike Run Trail) (page 231)
57. St. Joe State Park (page 235)
58. Trail of Tears State Park (Peewah Trail) (page 238)

## ▶ HISTORIC TRAILS

4. Columbia Bottom Conservation Area (page 27)
17. Route 66 State Park (page 75)
25. Graham Cave State Park (page 107)

## ▶ GOOD WINTER HIKES (open space with warming sunshine, streams with spectacular ice formations)

3. Chubb Trail (Castlewood Loop) (page 23)
4. Columbia Bottom Conservation Area (page 27)
10. Howell Island Conservation Area (page 49)
17. Route 66 State Park (page 75)
18. Fults Hill Prairie Nature Preserve (page 80)
19. Little Grand Canyon (page 83)
21. Piney Creek Ravine Nature Preserve (page 91)
29. Lost Valley Trail (page 122)
35. and 36. Green's Cave Bushwhacks (pages 146 and 150)
37. Hughes Mountain Natural Area (page 154)
38. Johnson Shut-Ins State Park (Shut-Ins Trail) (page 157)
39. Lower Rock Creek (page 161)
45. Shaw Nature Reserve (page 185)
46. Taum Sauk Mountain State Park (page 190)
47. Amidon Memorial Conservation Area (page 196)
52. Hickory Canyons Natural Area (page 216)
53. Pickle Springs Natural Area: Trail Through Time (page 219)
55. Silver Mines–Millstream Gardens Trail (page 227)
59. Valley View Glades (page 242)

# INTRODUCTION

Welcome to the new edition of *60 Hikes within 60 Miles: St. Louis*! If you're new to hiking, or even if you're a seasoned trailsmith, take a few minutes to read the following introduction. We'll explain how this book is organized and how to get the best use of it.

## ▶ THE MAPS

### THE OVERVIEW MAP AND OVERVIEW-MAP KEY

Use the overview map on the inside front cover to assess the exact locations of each hike's primary trailhead. Each hike's number appears on the overview map, on the map key facing the overview map, and in the table of contents. Flipping through the book, a hike's full profile is easy to locate by watching for the hike number at the top of each page.

The book is organized by region as indicated in the table of contents. A map legend that details the symbols found on trail maps appears on the inside back cover.

### TRAIL MAPS

Each hike contains a detailed map that shows the trailhead, the route, significant features, facilities, and topographic landmarks such as creeks, overlooks, and peaks.

## ▶ GPS COORDINATES

This book includes GPS coordinates in two formats: latitude–longitude and Universal Transverse Mercator (UTM). Latitude–longitude coordinates tell you where you are by locating a point west (latitude) of the 0° meridian line that passes through Greenwich, England, and north or south of the 0° (longitude) line that belts the Earth, aka the Equator. Included for each hike are GPS coordinates that indicate a trailhead, parking area, visitor center, or other key orienting feature. The coordinates were plotted using DeLorme's topographic mapping program TopoUSA.

Topographic maps show latitude–longitude as well as UTM grid lines. Known as UTM coordinates, the numbers index a specific point using a grid method. The survey datum used to arrive at the coordinates in this book is WGS84 (versus NAD27 or WGS83). For readers who own a GPS unit, whether handheld or onboard a vehicle, the latitude–longitude or UTM coordinates provided on the first page of each hike may be entered into the GPS unit. Just make sure your GPS unit is set to navigate using WGS84 datum.

Most trailheads, which begin in parking areas, can be reached by car, but some hikes still require a short walk to reach the trailhead from a parking area. In those cases a handheld unit is necessary to continue the GPS navigation process. That said, however, readers can easily access all trailheads in this book by using the directions given, the overview map, and the trail map, which shows at least one major road leading into the area. For those who enjoy using the latest GPS technology to navigate, the necessary data has been provided to get you to either a park entrance or

# INTRODUCTION

trailhead area. A brief explanation of the UTM coordinates from Hike 44, Ozark Trail: Courtois Section (page 181), follows:

| | |
|---|---|
| UTM Zone | 15S |
| Easting | 655398 |
| Northing | 4214285 |

The UTM zone number **15S** refers to one of the 60 vertical zones of the UTM projection. Each zone is 6 degrees wide. The easting number **655398** indicates in meters how far east or west a point is from the central meridian of the zone. Increasing easting coordinates on a topo map or on your GPS screen indicate that you are moving east, while decreasing easting coordinates indicate you are moving west. The northing number **4214285** references in meters how far you are from the equator. Above and below the equator, increasing northing coordinates indicate you are traveling north, while decreasing northing coordinates indicate you are traveling south. To learn more about how to enhance your outdoor experiences with GPS technology, refer to Russell Helms's *GPS Outdoors: A Practical Guide for Outdoor Enthusiasts* (Menasha Ridge Press).

## ▶ HIKE DESCRIPTIONS

Each hike profile contains seven key items: an "In Brief" description of the trail, a Key At-a-Glance Information box, GPS coordinates, directions to the trailhead, a trail map, a hike description, and information on nearby activities when applicable. Combined, the maps and information provide a clear method to assess each trail from the comfort of your favorite reading chair.

### IN BRIEF

As the name implies, this is a concise "taste of the trail." Think of this section as a snapshot focused on the historical landmarks, beautiful vistas, and other interesting sights you may encounter on the trail.

### KEY AT-A-GLANCE INFORMATION

The information boxes give you a quick idea of the specifics of each hike. There are 12 basic elements covered.

**LENGTH** The length of the trail from start to finish. There may be options to shorten or extend the hikes, but the mileage corresponds to the described hike. Consult the hike description to help decide how to customize the hike for your ability or time constraints.

**CONFIGURATION** A description of what the trail might look like from overhead. Trails can be loops, out-and-backs (that is, along the same route), figure eights, or balloons. Sometimes the descriptions might surprise you.

# INTRODUCTION

**DIFFICULTY** The degree of effort an "average" hiker should expect on a given hike. For simplicity, difficulty is described as "easy," "moderate," or "difficult."

**SCENERY** Rates the overall environs of the hike and what to expect in terms of plant life, wildlife, streams, and historic buildings.

**EXPOSURE** A quick check of how much sun you can expect on your shoulders during the hike. Descriptors used are self-explanatory and include terms such as shady, exposed, and sunny.

**TRAFFIC** Indicates how busy the trail might be on an average day, and if you might be able to find solitude out there. Trail traffic, of course, varies from day to day and season to season.

**TRAIL SURFACE** Indicates whether the trail is paved, rocky, smooth dirt, or a mixture of elements.

**HIKING TIME** How long it took the author to hike the trail. Estimated times are based on an average pace of 2 to 3 mph, adjusted for the ease or difficulty of the hike's terrain. Hikes with widely ranging time estimates describe trail networks with hiking options of varying lengths. Keep in mind that if you're a birder, wildflower lover, amateur geologist, or a doze-on-rocks type like the author, hike times will be quite a bit longer.

**ACCESS** Notes time of day when hike route is open, days when it is closed, and when permits or fees are needed to access the trail. When possible, directions to hikes begin from the nearest interstate exit off highways leading from St. Louis. Directions to trails far from expressways start from nearby towns or major highway intersections.

**MAPS** Which map is the best, or easiest to read (in the author's opinion) for this hike, and where to get it.

**FACILITIES** What to expect in terms of restrooms, phones, water, and other niceties available at the trailhead or nearby.

**SPECIAL COMMENTS** Provides you with those extra details that don't fit into any of the above categories. Here you'll find information on trail hiking options and facts such as whether or not to expect a lifeguard at a nearby swimming beach.

## DIRECTIONS
These, along with the trail map, will help you locate each trailhead.

## DESCRIPTIONS
The trail description is the heart of each hike. Here, the author provides a summary of the trail's essence as well as a highlight of any special traits the hike offers. Ultimately, the hike description will help you choose which hikes are best for you.

## NEARBY ACTIVITIES
Not every hike will have this listing. For those that do, look here for information on nearby sights of interest.

# INTRODUCTION

## ▶ WEATHER

While any time is fine for hiking in the St. Louis area, spring and fall are most folks' favorite seasons. The first warm breath of spring brings wildflowers, and seasonal rains bring the streams to life—waterfalls and cascades are everywhere in April and May. October brings spectacular fall colors, along with crisp, cool days free of bugs and humidity. Winter is my favorite time to hike: no bugs, no heat and humidity, and best of all, no foliage. Vistas obscured by greenery in the warm months open up in winter. And when it's really cold, the streams, waterfalls, and seeps create incredible ice formations. Summer, with its heat and humidity, is a tough time to hike around St. Louis. Get out early in the morning, or try something really unique—choose a park open after sunset and hike by the light of the full moon.

### DAILY TEMPERATURES BY MONTH
### ST. LOUIS, MISSOURI (degrees Fahrenheit)

|      | JAN | FEB | MAR | APR | MAY | JUN |
|------|-----|-----|-----|-----|-----|-----|
| MIN  | 21  | 27  | 36  | 47  | 57  | 66  |
| MAX  | 38  | 44  | 55  | 67  | 77  | 85  |
| MEAN | 30  | 35  | 46  | 57  | 67  | 76  |

|      | JUL | AUG | SEP | OCT | NOV | DEC |
|------|-----|-----|-----|-----|-----|-----|
| MIN  | 71  | 69  | 60  | 48  | 37  | 26  |
| MAX  | 90  | 88  | 80  | 68  | 54  | 42  |
| MEAN | 80  | 78  | 70  | 58  | 45  | 34  |

## ▶ WATER

How much is enough? Well, one simple physiological fact should convince you to err on the side of excess when deciding how much water to pack: A hiker working hard in 90-degree heat needs approximately 10 quarts of fluid per day. That's 2.5 gallons—12 large water bottles or 16 small ones. In other words, pack along one or two bottles even for short hikes.

Some hikers and backpackers hit the trail prepared to purify water found along the route. This method, while less dangerous than drinking untreated water, comes with risks. Purifiers with ceramic filters are the safest. Many hikers pack along the slightly distasteful tetraglycine-hydroperiodide tablets to de-bug water (sold under the names Potable Aqua, Coughlan's, and others).

Probably the most common waterborne "bug" that hikers face is giardia, which may not hit until one to four weeks after ingestion. It will have you living in the bathroom, passing noxious rotten-egg gas, vomiting, and shivering with chills. Other parasites to worry about include E. coli and cryptosporidium, both of which are harder to kill than giardia.

# INTRODUCTION

For most people, the pleasures of hiking make carrying water a relatively minor price to pay to remain healthy. If you're tempted to drink "found water," do so only if you understand the risks involved. Better yet, hydrate prior to your hike, carry (and drink) six ounces of water for every mile you plan to hike, and hydrate after the hike.

## ▶ THE TEN ESSENTIALS

One of the first rules of hiking is to be prepared for anything. The simplest way to be prepared is to carry the "Ten Essentials." In addition to carrying the items listed below, you need to know how to use them, especially navigation items. Always consider worst-case scenarios like getting lost, hiking back in the dark, broken gear (for example, a broken hip strap on your pack or a water filter getting plugged), twisting an ankle, or a brutal thunderstorm. The items listed below don't cost a lot of money, don't take up much room in a pack, and don't weigh much, but they might just save your life.

**Water:** durable bottles and a water treatment like iodine or a filter

**Map:** preferably a topo map and a trail map with a route description

**Compass:** a high-quality compass

**First-aid kit:** a good-quality kit including first-aid instructions

**Knife:** a multitool device with pliers is best

**Light:** a flashlight or headlamp with extra bulbs and batteries

**Fire:** windproof matches or lighter and fire starter

**Extra food:** you should always have food in your pack when you've finished hiking

**Extra clothes:** rain protection, warm layers, gloves, warm hat

**Sun protection:** sunglasses, lip balm, sunblock, sun hat

## ▶ FIRST-AID KIT

A typical first-aid kit may contain more items than you might think necessary. These are just the basics. Prepackaged kits in waterproof bags (Atwater Carey and Adventure Medical make a variety of kits) are available. Even though there are quite a few items listed below, they pack down into a small space:

Ace bandages or Spenco joint wraps

Antibiotic ointment (Neosporin or the generic equivalent)

Aspirin or acetaminophen

Band-Aids

Benadryl or the generic equivalent, diphenhydramine (in case of allergic reactions)

Butterfly-closure bandages

Epinephrine in a prefilled syringe (for people known to have severe allergic reactions to such things as bee stings)

Gauze (one roll)

Gauze compress pads (a half dozen 4- by 4-inch pads)

Hydrogen peroxide or iodine

# INTRODUCTION

*First-aid kit contents (continued)*

Hydrogen peroxide or iodine

Insect repellent

Matches or pocket lighter

Moleskin/Spenco "Second Skin"

Sunscreen

Whistle (it's more effective in signaling
    rescuers than your voice)

## ▶ TOPO MAPS

The maps in this book have been produced with great care and, used with the hiking directions, will direct you to the trail and help you stay on course. However, you will find superior detail and valuable information in the U.S. Geological Survey's 7.5-minute-series topographic maps. Topo maps are available online in many locations. A well-known free service is located at **www.terraserver.microsoft.com** and another free service with fast click-and-drag browsing is located at **www.topofinder.com**. You can view and print topos of the entire United States from these Web sites, and view aerial photographs of the same area at terraserver. Several online services such as **www.trails.com** charge annual fees for additional features such as shaded-relief, which makes the topography stand out more. If you expect to print out many topo maps each year, it might be worth paying for shaded-relief topo maps. The downside to USGS topos is that most of them are outdated, having been created 20 to 30 years ago. But they still provide excellent topographic detail.

Digital topographic-map programs such as DeLorme's TopoUSA enable you to review topo maps of the entire United States on your PC. You can also download GPS data gathered while hiking into the software and plot your own hikes.

If you're new to hiking, you might be wondering, "What's a topographic map?" In short, a topo indicates not only linear distance but elevation as well, using contour lines. Contour lines spread across the map like dozens of intricate spider webs. Each line represents a particular elevation, and at the base of each topo a contour's interval designation is given. If the contour interval is 20 feet, then the distance between each contour line is 20 feet. Follow five contour lines up on the same map, and the elevation has increased by 1,00 feet.

Let's assume that the 7.5-minute series topo reads "Contour Interval 40 feet," that the short trail we'll be hiking is two inches in length on the map, and that it crosses five contour lines from beginning to end. What do we know? Well, because the linear scale of this series is 2,000 feet to the inch (roughly two and three-quarters inches representing 1 mile), we know our trail is approximately four-fifths of a mile long (2 inches are 2,000 feet). But we also know we'll be climbing or descending 200 vertical feet (five contour lines are 40 feet each) over that distance. And the elevation designations written on occasional contour lines will tell us if we're heading up or down.

In addition to the outdoor shops listed in the Appendix, you'll find topos at major universities and some public libraries, where you might try photocopying the

# INTRODUCTION

ones you need to avoid the cost of buying them. But if you want your own and can't find them locally, visit the U.S. Geological Survey Web site at **topomaps.usgs.gov.**

## ▶ HIKING WITH CHILDREN

No one is too young for a hike in the outdoors. Be mindful, though. Flat, short, and shaded trails are best with an infant. And toddlers who have not quite mastered walking can still tag along, riding on an adult's back in a child carrier. Use common sense to judge a child's capacity to hike a particular trail, and always count that the child will tire quickly and need to be carried.

When packing for the hike, remember the child's needs as well as your own. Make sure children are adequately clothed for the weather, have proper shoes, and are protected from the sun with sunscreen. Kids dehydrate quickly, so make sure you have plenty of fluid for everyone. To assist an adult with determining which trails are suitable for youngsters, a list of hike recommendations for children is provided on page xvi.

## ▶ GENERAL SAFETY

No doubt, potentially dangerous situations can occur outdoors, but as long as you use sound judgment and prepare yourself before hitting the trail, you'll be much safer in the woods than in most urban areas of the country. It is better to look at a backcountry hike as a fascinating chance to discover the unknown rather than a chance for potential disaster. Here are a few tips to make your trip safer and easier.

- Always carry food and water whether you are planning to go overnight or not. Food will give you energy, help keep you warm, and sustain you in an emergency situation until help arrives. You never know if you will have a stream nearby when you become thirsty. Bring potable water or treat water before drinking it from a stream. Boil or filter all found water before drinking it.

- Stay on designated trails. Most hikers get lost when they leave the path. Even on the most clearly marked trails, there is usually a point where you have to stop and consider which direction to head. If you become disoriented, don't panic. As soon as you think you may be off-track, stop, assess your current direction, and then retrace your steps back to the point where you went awry. Using a map, a compass, and this book, and keeping in mind what you have passed thus far, reorient yourself and trust your judgment on which way to continue. If you become absolutely unsure of how to continue, return to your vehicle the way you came in. Should you become completely lost and have no idea of how to return to the trailhead, remaining in place along the trail and waiting for help is most often the best option for adults and always the best option for children.

# INTRODUCTION

- Be especially careful when crossing streams. Whether you are fording the stream or crossing on a log, make every step count. If you have any doubt about maintaining your balance on a foot log, go ahead and ford the stream instead. When fording a stream, use a trekking pole or stout stick for balance and face upstream as you cross. If a stream seems too deep to ford, turn back. Whatever is on the other side is not worth risking your life.

- Be careful at overlooks. While these areas may provide spectacular views, they are potentially hazardous. Stay back from the edge of outcrops and be absolutely sure of your footing; a misstep can mean a nasty and possibly fatal fall.

- Standing dead trees and storm-damaged living trees can pose a real hazard to hikers and tent campers. These trees may have loose or broken limbs that could fall at any time. When choosing a spot to rest or a backcountry campsite, look up.

- Know the symptoms of hypothermia. Shivering and forgetfulness are the two most common indicators of this insidious killer. Hypothermia can occur at any elevation, even in the summer, especially when the hiker is wearing lightweight cotton clothing. If symptoms arise, get the victim shelter, hot liquids, and dry clothes or a dry sleeping bag.

- Take along your brain. A cool, calculating mind is the single most important piece of equipment you'll ever need on the trail. Think before you act. Watch your step. Plan ahead. Avoiding accidents before they happen is the best recipe for a rewarding and relaxing hike.

## ▶ ANIMAL AND PLANT HAZARDS

### TICKS

Ticks like to hang out in the brush that grows along trails. Hot summer months seem to explode their numbers, but you should be tick-aware during all months of the year. Ticks, which are arthropods and not insects, need a host to feast on in order to reproduce. The ticks that light onto you while hiking will be very small, sometimes so tiny that you won't be able to spot them. Primarily of two varieties, deer ticks and dog ticks, both need a few hours of actual attachment before they can transmit any disease they may harbor. Ticks may settle in shoes, socks, hats, and may take several hours to actually latch on. The best strategy is to visually check every half-hour or so while hiking, do a thorough check before you get in the car, and then, when you take a posthike shower, do an even more thorough check of your entire body. Ticks that haven't attached are easily removed but not easily killed. If you pick off a tick in the woods, just toss it aside. If you find one on your body at home, dispatch it and then send it down the toilet. For ticks that have embedded, removal with tweezers is best.

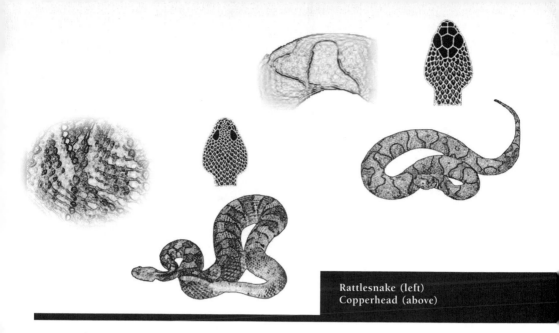

Rattlesnake (left)
Copperhead (above)

## SNAKES

Venomous snakes aren't a big problem for hikers in the St. Louis area, but they're definitely out there. Copperheads, with populations scattered throughout the bi-state area, are the most common. Rattlesnakes, though rare, are occasionally sighted in the St. Louis area and the Ozarks. You may spot cottonmouth water moccasins in bottomlands in the southern reaches of the bi-state area. Look out for snakes sunning themselves on the trail on cool days or shading up under trailside shrubbery during summer heat. Unless they're torpid from the cold weather, snakes will sense your footfalls before you reach them and move away. Wearing boots with ankle-high uppers will usually protect you if a poisonous snake strikes.

## POISON IVY/POISON OAK/POISON SUMAC

Recognizing poison ivy, oak, and sumac and avoiding contact with them is the most effective way to prevent the painful, itchy rashes associated with these plants. Poison ivy ranges from a thick, tree-hugging vine to a shaded groundcover, three leaflets to a leaf; poison oak occurs as either a vine or shrub, with three leaflets as well; and poison sumac flourishes in swampland, each leaf containing 7 to 13 leaflets. Urushiol, the oil in the sap of these plants, is responsible for the rash. Usually within 12 to 14 hours of exposure (but sometimes much later), raised lines and/or blisters will appear, accompanied by a terrible itch. Refrain from scratching, because bacteria under fingernails can cause infection and you will spread the rash to other parts of your body. Wash and dry the rash thoroughly, applying a calamine lotion or other product to help dry the rash. If itching or blistering is severe, seek medical attention. Remember that oil-contaminated clothes, pets, or hiking gear can easily cause an irritating rash on you or someone else, so wash not only any exposed parts of your body but also clothes, gear, and pets.

## MOSQUITOES

Although it's very rare, individuals can become infected with the West Nile virus by being bitten by an infected mosquito. Culex mosquitoes, the primary varieties that can transmit West Nile

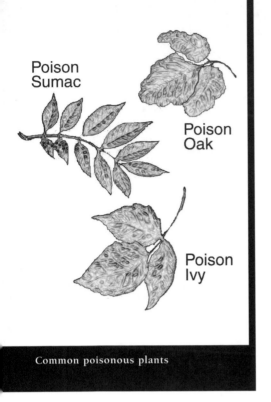

Poison
Sumac

Poison
Oak

Poison
Ivy

Common poisonous plants

virus to humans, thrive in urban rather than natural areas. They lay their eggs in stagnant water and can breed in any standing water that remains for more than five days. Most people infected with West Nile virus have no symptoms of illness, but some may become ill, usually 3 to 15 days after being bitten.

Anytime you expect mosquitoes to be buzzing around, you may want to wear protective clothing, such as long sleeves, long pants, and socks. Loose-fitting, light-colored clothing is best. Spray your clothing with insect repellent, remembering to follow the instructions on the product label and to take extra care with children.

## ▶ THE BUSINESS HIKER

If you're in the St. Louis area on business as a resident or visitor, these hikes include many quick getaways perfect for a long lunch escape or an evening hike to unwind from a busy day at the office or convention. Instead of staying cooped up inside, head out to one of the many parks and conservation areas on the fringes of the metro area and combine lunch with a relaxing walk.

Little Creek Nature Area is an ideal escape in the north suburbs, and Cliff Cave County Park offers quick hikes in the southern ones. In west St. Louis County Queeny, Castlewood, and Babler parks are nearby, and if you can sneak away for several hours you could get in a few miles on the Lost Valley, Lewis and Clark, or Matson Hill Trails in St. Charles County. Those working along Interstate 44 in southwest St. Louis County have it made—Forest 44 Conservation Area, Route 66 State Park, the Chubb Trail, and Powder Valley Nature Center are only a few of the many excellent hiking areas scattered along this scenic highway corridor. With this guidebook, you can devise well-planned getaways from an hour to all day.

## ▶ TRAIL ETIQUETTE

Whether you're on a city, county, state, or national park trail, always remember that great care and resources (from nature as well as from your tax dollars) have gone into creating these trails. Treat the trail, wildlife, and fellow hikers with respect.

Here are a few general ideas to keep in mind while on the trail.

1. Hike on open trails only. Respect trail and road closures (ask if not sure); avoid possible trespass on private land; obtain all permits and authorization as required. Also, leave gates as you found them or as marked.

2. Leave no trace of your visit other than footprints. Be sensitive to the dirt beneath you. This also means staying on the trail and not creating any new ones. Be sure to

pack out what you pack in. No one likes to see the trash someone else has left behind.

3. Never spook animals. An unannounced approach, a sudden movement, or a loud noise startles most animals. A surprised snake or skunk can be dangerous to you, to others, and to itself. Give animals extra room and time to adjust to your presence.

4. Plan ahead. Know your equipment, your ability, and the area in which you are hiking—and prepare accordingly. Be self-sufficient at all times; carry necessary supplies for changes in weather or other conditions. A well-executed trip is a satisfaction to you and to others.

5. Be courteous to other hikers or bikers you meet on the trails.

# Hikes in
# ST. LOUIS
# METRO AREA

# BABLER STATE PARK

## KEY AT-A-GLANCE INFORMATION

**LENGTH:** 17.5 miles on 5 trails

**CONFIGURATION:** Network of interconnecting loops

**DIFFICULTY:** Easy on Hawthorne, Virginia Day, Woodbine, and Dogwood Trails; moderate–hard on Equestrian Trail

**SCENERY:** Forested hills interlaced with deep hollows and occasional rock outcroppings

**EXPOSURE:** Shady throughout

**TRAFFIC:** Light on weekdays, moderately busy on weekends

**TRAIL SURFACE:** Natural surface mix of packed earth and gravel

**HIKING TIME:** 1 hour or less on Hawthorne, Woodbine, Virginia Day, and Dogwood trails; 3–4 hours on Equestrian.Trail

**ACCESS:** Park gate opens at 7 a.m. daily; closes at 6 p.m., November–March; closes at 9 p.m., April–October

**MAPS:** The visitor center has a free trail map; a $3 orienteering map shows trails and topography; Eureka and Weldon Spring USGS topos

**FACILITIES:** Visitor center, restrooms, water, shelters, campground, picnic areas, swimming pool

**SPECIAL COMMENTS:** Pets must be leashed

## ▶ IN BRIEF

Nestled against suburban St. Louis, Babler State Park is perfect for early-morning trail runs before your workday begins and ideal for evening getaway hikes to unwind from a stressful day.

## ▶ DESCRIPTION

Babler State Park is a beautiful enclave on the western edge of the St. Louis metropolitan area. Babler was once an isolated spot in the hinterlands of the city. Not anymore—the metro area has grown around it in recent years, leaving Babler an incredibly beautiful oasis of forested hills in the midst of mushrooming subdivisions. Now this 2,500-acre semiwilderness jewel is an easily accessible getaway for the hundreds of thousands of residents in this growing urban center.

The park is named for Edmund Babler, an early-20th-century St. Louis doctor known for providing care to the needy. Edmund's brother Jacob, a successful self-made businessman, donated the original 900 acres for Babler Park and lobbied the Civilian Conservation Corps to build it. Handsome buildings, shelters, bridges, and the huge stone park entrance showcase the CCC's rustic log-and-stone handiwork. Upon his death, Jacob Babler also willed $2.5 million to the park for maintenance, guaranteeing the park's development for future St. Louisans.

Jacob and Edmund's legacy has evolved into one of the prettiest urban parks in the Midwest. Babler has something for everyone—besides miles of hiking, biking, and equestrian trails, there's an

## GPS TRAILHEAD COORDINATES (PARK ENTRANCE)

| | |
|---|---|
| UTM ZONE (WGS84) | 15S |
| EASTING | 702944 |
| NORTHING | 4276123 |
| LATITUDE-LONGITUDE | |
| NORTH | N38° 36' 37.5128" |
| WEST | W90° 40' 9.0520" |

## ▶ DIRECTIONS

Babler State Park is located in Wildwood. From Interstate 44, take Exit 264 for Eureka and MO 109. Follow MO 109 8 miles north to MO BA–Babler Park Drive. Turn left on MO BA and drive 1 mile to the park entrance.

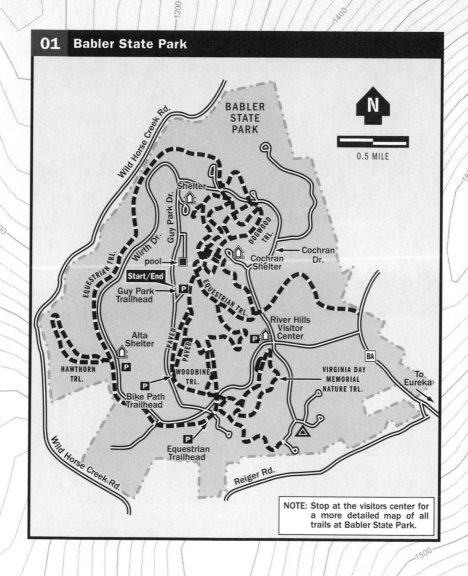

**BABLER STATE PARK**

N

0.5 MILE

Wild Horse Creek Rd.

Guy Park Dr.

Shelter

DOGWOOD TRL.

Wirth Dr.

pool

Cochran Shelter

Cochran Dr.

EQUESTRIAN TRL.

Start/End

Guy Park Trailhead

EQUESTRIAN TRL.

River Hills Visitor Center

Alta Shelter

PAVED

PAVED

BA

HAWTHORN TRL.

WOODBINE TRL.

VIRGINIA DAY MEMORIAL NATURE TRL.

To Eureka

Bike Path Trailhead

Equestrian Trailhead

Wild Horse Creek Rd.

Reiger Rd.

NOTE: Stop at the visitors center for a more detailed map of all trails at Babler State Park.

Olympic-size swimming pool for cooling off after summer hikes, courts for basketball, volleyball, and tennis, and playgrounds for the kids. Want to relax and picnic after your hike? There are hundreds of shady picnic sites, along with several large shelters that can be rented for group events. And if you enjoy Babler so much that you don't want to go home, you can pitch your tent in the park's fully equipped campground and stay a night or two.

Start your day in Babler with a visit to the River Hills Visitor Center, where you'll find a small gift shop, maps, information board, and naturalists describing the park's history and the contributions of the Babler family. Microscopes are set up for examining samples of minerals, plants, and bird feathers found in Babler.

CCC bridge at Babler State Park

Large glass cases house a diorama of the park's plants and animals, and other displays showcase fish species inhabiting Bonhomme and Wild Horse creeks. My favorite visitor-center attraction is the huge viewing window where, with binoculars provided by the park, you can watch the Babler's resident birds chow down at a set of feeders. I once saw a young white-tailed buck, his antlers in velvet, grazing on the slope just below the feeders.

Counting the bike path, you'll have six trails to choose from at Babler. While the paved bike path is pretty tame, it's perfect for campers overnighting in the park. It begins near the back of the campground and meanders 2 miles northwest to the Guy Park trailhead, connecting to all but one of the park's other trails along the way. This smooth, easily graded hike is the perfect route for novices and walkers looking for an easy way to explore the woods.

The 2-mile Virginia Day Memorial Nature Trail, whose trailhead is across the road from the visitor center, is the first hike you'll come to as you enter Babler. Named for a volunteer naturalist who spent her later years sharing her love of the natural world with the park's visitors, this loop trail explores the hollow and ridge between the campground and visitor center. You can also access this hike from the Equestrian trailhead, or from the campground via a 0.75-mile hike on the bike path. This easy trail even has a 0.6-mile short loop at its northern end that's perfect for small children. The Virginia Day is marked with red arrows for counterclockwise travel, and passes through patches of ferns and mayapples, under the boughs of several peaceful cedar groves, and travels along dry washes that come to life during cloudbursts, making this a fun-but-somewhat-muddy hike during rainstorms. You'll have several climbs and descents between the ridge and the hollow it overlooks, but grades are easy and the treadway is smooth on this laid-back hike in the woods.

The second hike you'll come to as you enter Babler is the Equestrian Trail, a half mile southwest of the visitor center. Though you can access three trails from the Equestrian trailhead here—Virginia Day, the Equestrian Trail, and the paved bike path—you'll be better off to start your hike from the Guy Park trailhead, where there's water and a paved parking lot, leaving the gravel lot open for horse trailers. To reach Guy Park trailhead, continue 0.1 miles southwest to Guy Park Drive and follow it a half mile north to the Guy Park trailhead.

Though some hate hiking where the horses roam, I think the Equestrian Trail, which includes half the trail miles in the park, best shows off Babler State Park's beauty. Counting the spur trail out to MO BA, this horse path wanders 8.5 miles and connects to all four hiking trails and the bike path. It passes through two stone-lined tunnels under the park road, delightfully cool respites on a hot summer hike. Bring your lunch on this trail, too—on the western side of the loop your hike will parallel Wirth Drive for a 1-mile stretch that's studded with picnic sites.

Except for a few short stretches that get very muddy when wet, the trail's rock, gravel, and packed-earth tread is excellent. This trail's width is another nice feature: it's wide enough throughout its length to allow side-by-side hiking and thus allows for better conversation as you wander through the woods. Though it would make an excellent path for trail running, it's best if joggers stay away to avoid conflict with equestrians. Should you meet horses while hiking, stand quietly to the downhill side of the trail and let them pass. If horse traffic begins to get on your nerves, simply skip off onto a hiking path at one of the many intersection points along the bridle path. Equestrian traffic at Babler is heaviest on weekends.

The Equestrian Trail is the hilliest hike in the park, but you'll be well rewarded for your efforts. The trail winds through deep hollows and climbs to breezy ridgetops with occasional views of the surrounding country, especially after fall, when autumn clears the heavy summer foliage that usually obscures Missouri vistas. Several hollows harbor old-growth forest, where groves of trees with trunks one to two feet thick tower over the path. Especially impressive is a deep, dark hollow just uphill from the swimming pool, where an oak more than three feet thick stands next to the trail. In the northern part of the Equestrian Trail you'll see an ancient sycamore, five to six feet thick at the base, that's been blasted by lightning or wind. Though its branches are scattered on the forest floor all around it, this old-timer still survives, with patches of grass growing from crotches high above the ground. My favorite highlight on the Equestrian Trail is on the loop's eastern side, just below the Cochran Shelter. There, above a deep hollow, the trail hugs a 100-foot-long, 15-foot-tall rock wall with large boulders scattered along its base.

The 1.75-mile Woodbine Trail, marked with blue arrows on carsonite posts, and the 2-mile Dogwood Trail, marked with green arrows, also start at Guy Park trailhead. Both are loop hikes with spur trail access, and are primarily packed dirt and gravel. The Woodbine Trail is the easiest hiking route in the park and uses the paved bike path for nearly a quarter of its length. From Guy Park, it parallels the bike path, then climbs east into the woods onto a ridge, which it follows to the bike path for its return to Guy Park. It has climbs that'll get you breathing heavily, and is excellent for trail running. My favorite feature on the Woodbine is a huge tree fallen over the bike path, with a section sawed out for trail passage. It's three feet thick at the bole on the uphill side of the trail, and its remains stretch more than 100 feet down the hill on the opposite side.

Though considered the toughest trail in Babler, the Dogwood Trail isn't really very difficult. It has several climbs over its 2-mile length, but none is exceedingly long or strenuous by Ozark hiking standards. Since the Dogwood crosses or shares treadway with the Equestrian Trail several times, there are a few confusing spots. But studying a map and following the trail markers will keep you on the right path. The Dogwood bounces between the park's moist bottomland and breezy ridges, winding across many tributary hollows along its route. Where the Dogwood approaches the park center with its pool and ball fields, you'll find the trail's highlight—a delightful spring bubbling from under a 20-foot rock ledge. This spot is especially captivating during rain, when a waterfall cascades down the slope above and pours over the rock ledge into the cool spring pool.

The 1.25-mile Hawthorn Trail, located at the Alta Shelter on the western side of Babler on Wirth Drive, is my favorite of the park's four hiking trails. It's the most remote, has an excellent packed-earth-and-gravel treadway, and isn't a hard hike at all. It's an elongated loop on the spine of a fingerlike ridge that extends northwest from Wirth Drive, sloping gently down to its farthest reach, then swinging back to climb gently back to the trailhead. At the turnaround there's a nice rock outcropping and an overlook above Wild Horse Creek Road. My favorite feature on the Hawthorn is a quarter mile down its northeast leg. There you'll find the most amazing tree. About six feet up, three long slits evenly spaced around its hollow trunk spread upward and outward, coming back together 25 feet above the ground. These gashes make the tree look like a blown-out straw, and if you were skinny enough you could crawl into this cavity. I'm amazed that a tree so weakened could survive for so long on a windy Missouri ridgetop without being blown down. When you finish your hike on the Hawthorn, check out the impressive Civilian Conservation Corps log-and-stone construction of the Alta Shelter next to the trailhead. Huge circular fireplaces, heavy log benches, stout rock walls—you'll find yourself booking your next family reunion or company picnic at this beautiful CCC legacy on the western ridge of Babler State Park.

These are all the trails in Babler, but for easy walking don't overlook the park roads. On the quiet weekdays or early weekend mornings in Babler, walkers and runners love to explore the park's ridges and hollows on its 7 miles of winding and beautiful asphalt drives. Wherever you hike, keep an eye peeled for stunning displays of wildlife in this enclave so close to the city. While hiking at Babler I've seen deer, coyotes, groundhogs, raccoons, opossum, hawks, barred owls, several varieties of woodpeckers, and countless songbirds.

▶ **NEARBY ACTIVITIES**

Rockwoods Reservation, a few miles south on MO 109, offers still more hiking trails and another fascinating visitor center (see page 70). Kids will enjoy Six Flags Over Mid-America amusement park in nearby Eureka. And the many restaurants scattered throughout suburban St. Louis east of Babler await your posthike hungries.

# CASTLEWOOD STATE PARK

## ▶ IN BRIEF

While exploring Castlewood State Park's trails you'll hike through lush, flower-decorated bottomlands, admire panoramic views from bluffs towering above the Meramec River, and wander past the ruins of abandoned resorts that once graced this riverside landscape.

## ▶ DESCRIPTION

Castlewood State Park is one of St. Louis's most popular hiking destinations, and when you hit the park's trails you'll see why. On its 1,779 acres along 5 miles of the Meramec River you'll hike wooded bottomlands, climb onto spectacular bluffs above the stream, wander along forested ridges, and meander along Keifer Creek, a pretty little brook that bisects the park as it flows into the Meramec. You can explore this wonderland in the city's suburbs on five excellent trails. Since some hikes are flat and easy while others are rugged and steep, Castlewood has a hike for nature lovers of any age or physical condition.

It wasn't always so peaceful and unspoiled in this riverside enclave. Between the First and Second World Wars, Castlewood was a popular, hard-partying resort area. The landscape was crowded with hotels, clubs, bathhouses, stores, a post office, and a train depot where the Missouri Pacific Railroad unloaded thousands of visitors. More folks arrived by car, boat, or on foot, and

## ▶ DIRECTIONS

From the Big Bend Road exit off I-270, drive west 5 miles on Big Bend Road to Reis Road. Go 1 mile south on Reis Road to Keifer Creek Road. Turn left on Keifer Creek Road and immediately enter the park. Hikes can start from the visitor center, the trailhead next to the Keifer Creek bridge, a small parking lot just east of the railroad tracks, or from the boat-ramp picnic area.

## ⓘ KEY AT-A-GLANCE INFORMATION

**LENGTH:** 13 miles on 5 trails

**CONFIGURATION:** Network of interconnecting loops

**DIFFICULTY:** Easy

**SCENERY:** Lush bottomlands and spectacular bluff overlooks along the Meramec River

**EXPOSURE:** Mostly shady, with exposed stretches in river-bottom meadows and bluff overlooks

**TRAFFIC:** Medium-heavy on most trails; light traffic on Cedar Bluff and Stinging Nettle loops

**TRAIL SURFACE:** Packed earth on river-bottom trails; mixture of packed earth, gravel, and rock on ridgetop trails, with several steep, rocky, and rooty sections

**HIKING TIME:** 1 hour–all day, depending upon trail choices

**ACCESS:** Open 7 a.m.–half-hour after sunset

**MAPS:** Trail map available at visitor center; Manchester USGS topo

**FACILITIES:** Water, restrooms, picnic areas, shelters, playground, visitor center, boat ramp

**SPECIAL COMMENTS:** Pets on leash; no removal of flowers, plants, rocks, or other articles without written permission; watch for mountain bikers

**GPS TRAILHEAD COORDINATES (PARK ENTRANCE)**

| | | |
|---|---|---|
| UTM ZONE (WGS84) | | 15S |
| | EASTING | 713868 |
| | NORTHING | 4270073 |
| LATITUDE-LONGITUDE | | |
| | NORTH | N38° 33' 12.1886'' |
| | WEST | W90° 32' 44.4585'' |

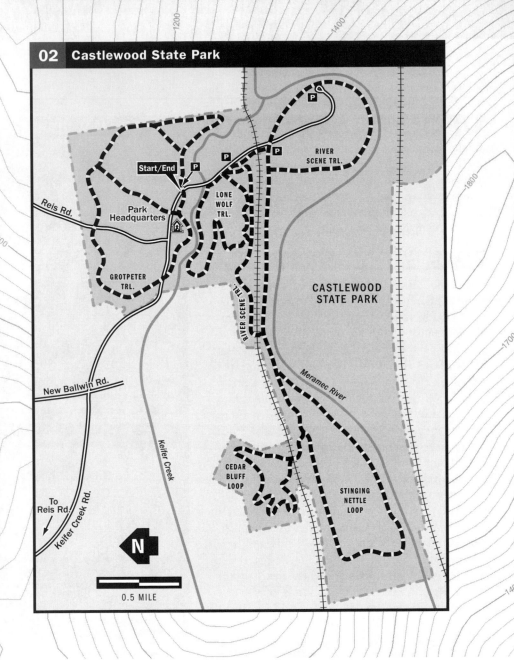

weekend crowds often reached 10,000. They spent their weekends swimming, canoeing, sunbathing, and playing games by day, and dancing and surreptitiously enjoying Prohibition home brew by night. It's hard to imagine the revelry that once took place in now-peaceful Castlewood, so stop at the visitor center as you enter the park. There you can read information boards and check out photos of the park's wilder days, when boats and swimmers choked the river and parties kept the hills and hollows alive far into the night.

The party crowds are long gone, leaving Castlewood to the more down-to-earth wildlife. The park's natural habitats include the river, its gravel bars and bottomland forest, a floodplain, prairielike meadows, hillside woodlands, exposed stone bluffs, and the small stream environment of Keifer Creek. Geese, ducks, kingfishers, and blue herons hunt and forage along the river. Hawks soar along the bluffs towering over the Meramec, and numerous songbirds flit through the trees. Hike at dusk and you'll hear barred owls calling in the evening hush. Several varieties of woodpeckers live among Castlewood's trees. Deer, turkeys, and coyotes also range through the park.

Animals in this suburban park are somewhat acclimated to human activity, letting you sometimes get closer looks at them than in wilder settings. On an early spring hike on the River Scene Trail, I watched a pileated woodpecker banging away at a riverside tree, hacking out its nesting hole, leaving a scattering of splinters at the base of the tree. I was only 25 feet away, and it ignored me completely. On an early-morning outing I was enjoying a midhike nap on the bluff section of the River Scene Trail when I heard something running through the dry leaves behind me. I turned over quietly and saw three coyotes trotting past, oblivious to my presence 50 feet uphill from their path.

Spring is a great time for wildflower lovers to explore the riverside trails at Castlewood. The moist bottomlands along the River Scene and Stinging Nettle trails are carpeted with spring beauties, wild sweet William, violets, dogwoods, and red-buds. Bluebells, my favorite Missouri wildflower, put on an unbelievable display in the floodplain along the River Scene Trail.

Because it showcases all the park's habitats, most hikers choose the River Scene Trail as the best hike in Castlewood. Starting from the trailhead across from the first park shelter, the River Scene climbs quickly to a panoramic overlook of the Meramec River. It then turns west and follows a rugged cliff edge for more than a half mile, then follows a descending bluffline over a long series of wooden staircases and platforms. You'll be treated to spectacular vistas all along the way, looking across the river valley toward Lone Elk County Park and the Castlewood Loop of West Tyson County Park's Chubb Trail on the south side of the Meramec. At the western end of the River Scene Trail a crumbling staircase descends to river level, where ghostly, cracked, and broken foundations stand next to the railroad track. These are ruins from the park's resort days. The store, post office, and train depot were located here, and the stairs led up to the clubs and hotels that once dotted the hillside. After the ruins, the River Scene takes a tunnel under the railroad and turns east to follow the Meramec back to the boat-launch picnic area, then returns to the trailhead along the park road.

As you exit the tunnel on the River Scene Trail you'll see another path to the right, heading upstream along the river. This is the spur to the Stinging Nettle Loop, a level, 3-mile hike in the Meramec River's floodplain. The spur to the loop is a wonderful ramble along the river's edge, often so close to the stream that a slip would mean taking an unexpected swim. In times of flood the river might carve away chunks of the trail, causing temporary closures while park staff reroute the path. Once the spur reaches the loop, the trail becomes tamer; but it's still a nice walk through moist bottomland forest. Watch for the trail's namesake stinging nettles—they're everywhere on the forest floor along the path. The Stinging Nettle Loop is very muddy during or after rain, and takes a long time to dry out.

The 2-mile Cedar Bluff Loop breaks off the north side of the Stinging Nettle Loop 0.2 miles west of the spur trail junction. It's not marked, so look sharp for a trail heading north toward the tracks. This spur passes under the railroad through a low tunnel leading to the Cedar Bluff Loop's beginning on the north side of the tracks. The Cedar Bluff Loop is the park's getaway hike. It's so far back that few people use it, so you'll likely have the trail to yourself. This beautiful hike winds through wooded hills and will challenge you with a couple of stiff climbs, then reward you with a quarter-mile hike along a breezy ridgetop with scenic views.

The Lone Wolf Trail explores the back side of the ridge separating Keifer Creek from the Meramec. It starts at the trailhead across from the first park shelter and shares treadway with the River Scene Trail to the first overlook. It then parallels the River Scene Trail for nearly half a mile, wiggling through the woods just downslope from the River Scene before swinging away to the north where the wooden steps begin. From there, the Lone Wolf Trail is a secluded single-track path winding along the shoulders of a hollow, with several vistas overlooking the park's central valley. It eventually descends to Keifer Creek, then swings east and follows that pretty stream back to the trailhead.

The Grotpeter Trail also follows Keifer Creek for a while. It's a 3-mile loop with two cutoff trails that form a 1.5-mile inner loop. Since it avoids a grade that's rugged, rocky, and steep, novice hikers should choose the inner loop. Hikes on the Grotpeter can begin in several places, but the best starting point is the visitor center parking lot. One of the cutoff trails forming the inner loop heads uphill across from the visitor center, and the main loop heads east and west from the parking area. On the Grotpeter, you'll hike along Keifer Creek for a mile in a mix of bottomland woods and scrubby meadows, then climb to the ridge forming the park's northern boundary. After a 1-mile hike along the ridge, you'll descend back to the park's central valley. It's best to hike the Grotpeter in a counterclockwise direction so that the trail's steepest grade is a descent.

Markings are sparse or nonexistent on the trails in Castlewood, but it's not hard to find your way around there. There's almost always another hiker or mountain biker in this popular park who can help you out, and the river and roads will help keep you within park boundaries. While I only describe 13 miles of hiking at Castlewood, park literature says there are 15.5 miles of trails. The other 2.5 miles are on the Castlewood Loop on the south side of the river. They're part of the Chubb Trail (see following profile) in West Tyson County Park.

# CHUBB TRAIL

## ▶ IN BRIEF

The Chubb Trail and its companion paths offer everything a good hike should have—from challenging climbs and descents from windy ridges and cool, calm hollows to easy meanders next to the Meramec River, where you'll spot lots of wildlife.

## ▶ DESCRIPTION

The Chubb Trail wanders through a scenic landscape on the Meramec River's south shore, exploring three beautiful parks on its 7-mile run. West Tyson County Park is the trail's western terminus, and Lone Elk County Park anchors the east end. Between the two county parks, the 3-mile Castlewood Loop explores an undeveloped tract of Castlewood State Park. But you don't need to hike this entire point-to-point trail to see its beauty. Side trails let you break the Chubb into treks from 2.5 miles to 14 miles. Even shorter hikes can be found on the Chinkapin and Buck's Run trails in West Tyson County Park.

The variety of terrain along the Chubb makes it one of the best hikes in the St. Louis area. In its western reaches the trail winds among

## ▶ DIRECTIONS

To reach the West Tyson County Park trailhead, drive west on I-44 to Exit 266, Lewis Road. Turn right, drive 100 yards to the park entrance, and then go right into the park. The Chubb trailhead is the first left off the park road. The trailhead for the Flint Quarry, Ridge, Chinkapin, and Buck Run trails is at the end of the park road.

To reach the Lone Elk Park trailhead, drive west on I-44 to Exit 272, MO 141. Go west on the North Outer Road from MO 141 and follow it into Lone Elk Park. Three miles after leaving MO 141, reach the Chubb trailhead, just past the World Bird Sanctuary, where the fenced portion of Lone Elk Park begins.

## ⓘ KEY AT-A-GLANCE INFORMATION

**LENGTH:** 7 miles on Chubb; side trails add 5 additional miles

**CONFIGURATION:** Out-and-back; side trails create shorter loop options

**DIFFICULTY:** Moderate to difficult, depending upon route choices

**SCENERY:** Forested hills with rocky outcrops, windy highlands, and several beautiful stretches next to the Meramec River

**EXPOSURE:** Shady throughout

**TRAFFIC:** Moderate-heavy

**TRAIL SURFACE:** Mixture of packed earth, gravel, and rock; some sections very rocky and rooty

**HIKING TIME:** 3 hours–all day, depending upon route choices

**ACCESS:** Open from 8 a.m.–30 minutes after sunset

**MAPS:** Trail map available from St. Louis County Parks; Manchester USGS topo

**FACILITIES:** Restrooms, picnic sites, picnic shelters, and water available in the parks on either end of the trail; water, restrooms, and cold drinks available at World Bird Sanctuary's visitor center

**SPECIAL COMMENTS:** Watch for mountain bikes and equestrians on weekends; pets must be leashed

### GPS TRAILHEAD COORDINATES (WEST TYSON PARK TRAILHEAD)

| | |
|---|---|
| UTM ZONE (WGS84) | 15S |
| EASTING | 710400 |
| NORTHING | 4264829 |
| LATITUDE-LONGITUDE | |
| NORTH | N38° 30' 25.1793'' |
| WEST | W90° 35' 13.3018'' |

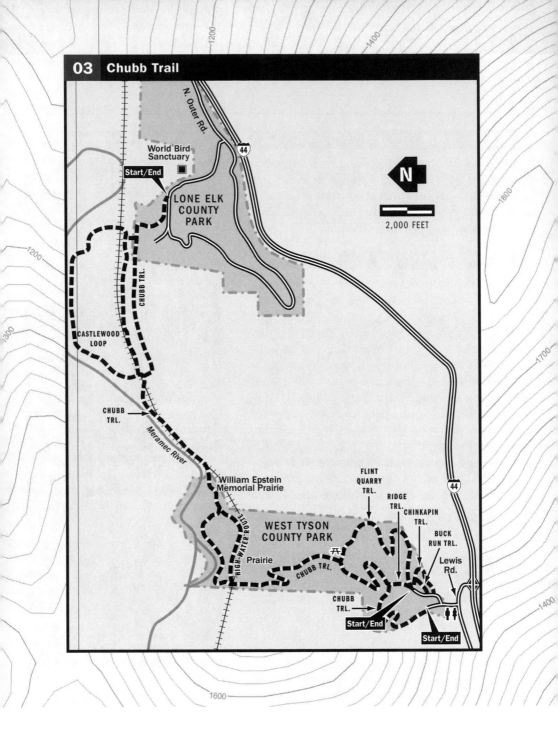

the rugged Crescent Hills of West Tyson Park, twisting and turning over mossy, rugged rock ledges, challenging you with one long climb and several short, steep ones. When the terrain finally eases next to the Meramec River, the character of the landscape changes dramatically. You'll cross the William Epstein Memorial Prairie, glimpsing a remnant of the 55,000 acres of grasslands that once covered much of St. Louis County. Next the trail winds among huge trees in a moist bottomland for 2 miles to intersect with the Castlewood Loop. The Castlewood Loop explores another wide-open prairie landscape and more river-bottom forest. The Castlewood Bluffs tower over the Meramec River to the north, contrasting beautifully with the gentle landscape south of the river.

The diverse landscape through which the Chubb wanders attracts a wide variety of wildlife. You'll see herons, kingfishers, geese, and a variety of ducks on the river, and pileated, downy, and red-bellied woodpeckers that inhabit the forest. Turkeys are thick along the Meramec. Even if you don't see them you'll probably spot their tracks in muddy patches of the trail. Barred owls are common here. And in winter, keep a sharp eye on riverside trees—you might spot an eagle perched over the Meramec. When packing your field guides for this hike, don't bring just the bird book. The hillsides, bottomlands, and prairies grow a fine crop of wildflowers, too.

Unless you arrange a shuttle, the Chubb Trail is an out-and-back hike totaling 14 miles, not including the Castlewood Loop, which adds another 2 to 3 miles. Luckily, you can use the three trailheads, the Castlewood Loop, and two side trails in West Tyson Park to break the Chubb into shorter options. Two of these originate from West Tyson's Chubb trailhead. The longest is a 13-mile hike following the Chubb Trail to the Castlewood Loop, going around the loop, then returning to the trailhead. Another option follows the Chubb to its junction with the Flint Quarry Trail, follows the Flint Quarry Trail to the Ridge Trail, follows the Ridge Trail back to the Chubb, then follows the Chubb back to the trailhead for a 4.5-mile hike. You can also start these hikes from West Tyson's lower trailhead, knocking 2 miles off each one.

Options from the West Tyson end of the Chubb require steep, rugged hiking through the Crescent Hills. Easier hikes on the Chubb start from the Lone Elk trailhead. Except for the ascent and descent to the parking area, you'll have gentle bottomland hikes that are perfect for laid-back hikers or trail runners. Both options from Lone Elk use the Castlewood Loop.

From the Lone Elk trailhead, the Chubb goes downhill and veers west along the railroad tracks on a narrow dirt road. Just as the descent ends, look for a trail heading north. It goes through a culvert under the tracks and connects with the Castlewood Loop. Taking this spur, hiking the loop, and returning to the trailhead gives you a 4-mile hike.

For a 6-mile hike, do not turn right initially and cross the tracks but continue west along the Chubb. It parallels the railroad (on your right) for another mile, then turns north across the tracks to intersect with the Castlewood Loop. Hiking the loop and returning to the trailhead from here makes 6 miles. You could add miles to either of these options by hiking the Chubb farther west.

Trail markings on the Chubb varied last time I hiked it, but they were there when I needed them. Intersections are marked with square wooden posts with arrows, either routed into the post or on plastic strips fixed to the post. On the Castlewood Loop, where it's easier to get lost, directional posts are spaced along the trail for clockwise travel. On the West Tyson end of the park there are few posts, but since the trail is easy to follow you won't miss them.

If you're new to this trail, the Chubb trailhead on the western end is a nice place to start. The shelter there has interpretive displays describing the area's history and natural landscape. The first 3 miles from the trailhead are rough, rugged, and beautiful. You'll bounce across rough hollow washes, wind through little cedar groves, and stair-step over rock layers, sometimes going right through them on narrow gaps. Near the 1-mile point you'll follow a rock wall for 200 yards before intersecting with the Ridge Trail. It's a short path connecting the Chubb to the Flint Quarry Trail and the lower West Tyson trailhead.

From its junction with the Ridge Trail, the Chubb starts climbing. There'll be a few breaks in the ascent, but most of the way you'll climb over more rock ledges and hollows. A mile after leaving the Ridge Trail you'll top out on a knob and intersect with the Flint Quarry Trail. There, at the top of a long hill, you'll find something hikers often dream of but rarely get—a picnic table!

To loop back to one of the West Tyson trailheads, take the Flint Quarry Trail from this junction. It's named for the flint you'll tread on for the next half mile or so. Native Americans once came to the Crescent Hills to gather this material for arrowheads, spear points, and tools. The Flint Quarry Trail heads east from the intersection, follows the rolling spine of a ridge for a half mile, then heads south along the chain-link fence of the Tyson Research Center. It eventually swings southwest, runs through a grove of cedars, follows a 6-foot-high mossy rock wall for 100 yards, then descends back to West Tyson Park, ending on a road. A short hike left on the road leads to West Tyson's lower trailhead. To the right you'll see the Ridge Trail, which leads back to the Chubb.

Hiking the Chubb all the way to Lone Elk, you'll skip the Flint Quarry Trail and descend from the picnic site at the intersection. It's downhill all the way to the river bottom, winding through woods and over rock outcroppings. The most spectacular of these is called "The Stairs" by mountain bikers, and when you see them you'll know why. Many can ride down them, but few can climb them. The descent ends at the William Epstein Memorial Prairie and its interpretive display. You can explore the prairie on 1.3 miles of mown paths.

After leaving the prairie, the Chubb follows the Meramec River for 2 miles. It's level and gentle but can be really muddy if it has rained recently. At the 5-mile point you'll come to the Castlewood Loop. Turn left, pass two old farm buildings, and break out of the trees into a riverside prairie. You'll follow the edge of the prairie for 0.75 miles, walking through grasses reaching above your waist, angling to the Meramec River and hiking next to it. When the prairie ends, wind through the woods for another half mile, still paralleling the river and its impressive bluffs. When the trail makes a looping turn and heads west again, look for a trail going south toward the railroad tracks. It goes through a tunnel under the tracks to join the Chubb Trail a half mile from its end at Lone Elk Park.

The Castlewood Loop continues another mile west to rejoin the Chubb, following an old road for the last half mile. To finish the hike from West Tyson to Lone Elk, cross to the south side of the tracks and go east on the narrow road paralleling the railroad. One mile down this road you'll pass the tunnel shortcut to the Castlewood Loop, and the climb to the trailhead begins. About 200 yards into the climb, the trail breaks right off the old road onto single-track, then winds another half mile to the Lone Elk trailhead. If you miss the turn onto single-track, you'll soon T into the World Bird Sanctuary's gravel road. Turn right and walk back to the trailhead.

# COLUMBIA BOTTOM CONSERVATION AREA

## ▶ IN BRIEF

At Columbia Bottom, you can hike to the Confluence of the Mississippi and Missouri Rivers, just downstream from the site of Lewis and Clark's 1803–04 winter camp.

## ▶ DESCRIPTION

Columbia Bottom Conservation Area, purchased in 1997, is one of Missouri's newest conservation areas. Its 4,318 acres nestle into the elbow at the junction of the Mississippi and Missouri rivers. The confluence of these mighty rivers is located just downstream from the site of Lewis and Clark's 1803–04 winter camp near Wood River, where their party rested and made preparations for their historic two-year adventure. One of the Department of Conservation's goals in managing Columbia Bottoms is restoration of the area to resemble its appearance at the time of Lewis and Clark's journey. A variety of habitats are being developed, including wetlands, marshes, sloughs, river-bottom forest, and bottomland prairie.

Start your exploration of Columbia Bottom at the area's excellent visitor center. Completed in 2004, its displays are the perfect way to familiarize yourself with the conservation area and what's going on within its borders before hitting the trail. You can pick up maps there, look over a series of nature and historic displays about Columbia Bottom, and sit in on an interpretive talk if you land there at the right time (check the DOC newsletter, "Making Tracks," for schedule and info). Interpretive stops scattered across the grounds add still

## ▶ DIRECTIONS

From the Riverview Drive exit on I-270, drive 3 miles north to the entrance of Columbia Bottom Conservation Area. The spur to the loop begins at the visitor center; the main loop begins at the river access.

## ⓘ KEY AT-A-GLANCE INFORMATION

**LENGTH:** 8 miles

**CONFIGURATION:** Loop with spur

**DIFFICULTY:** Easy

**SCENERY:** Wetland prairies, riverside forest, views of Mississippi River

**EXPOSURE:** Shady on River's Edge Trail; open on Confluence Trail

**TRAFFIC:** Light on weekdays, busy on weekends

**TRAIL SURFACE:** Packed earth on River's Edge Trail, gravel and asphalt on Confluence Trail

**HIKING TIME:** 1–3 hours

**ACCESS:** Open 6 a.m. daily; closes at 10 p.m. April–September; closes at 7 p.m. October–March

**MAPS:** Area maps available at visitor center; Columbia Bottom USGS topo

**FACILITIES:** Parking, picnic sites, visitor center, restrooms, boat ramp, interpretive displays

**SPECIAL COMMENTS:** Pets must be leashed

**GPS TRAILHEAD COORDINATES (VISITOR CENTER)**

| | | |
|---|---|---|
| UTM ZONE (WGS84) | 15S | |
| EASTING | 744718 | |
| NORTHING | 4299645 | |
| LATITUDE-LONGITUDE | | |
| NORTH | N38° 48' 41.7865'' | |
| WEST | W90° 10' 53.7157'' | |

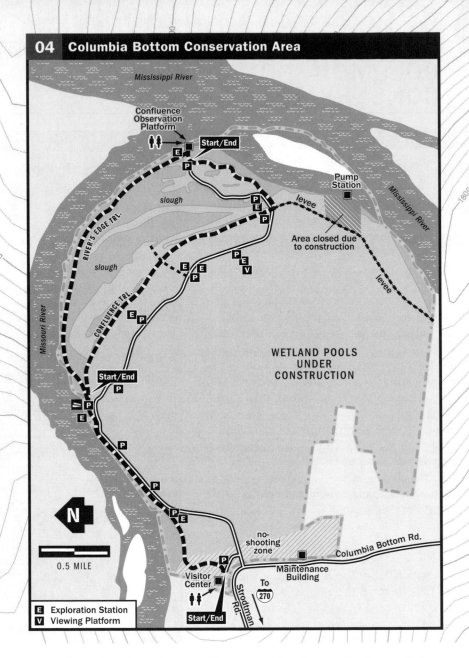

Mississippi River

Confluence
Observation
Platform

Start/End

E

P

Pump
Station

slough

Mississippi River

RIVER'S EDGE TRL.

levee

P E

P

slough

Area closed due
to construction

levee

P E V

E E

P

CONFLUENCE TRL.

Missouri River

E

P

Start/End

P

WETLAND POOLS
UNDER
CONSTRUCTION

E

P

N

P

0.5 MILE

P E

no-
shooting
zone

Columbia Bottom Rd.

P

Maintenance
Building

Visitor
Center

To
270

Strodtman Rd.

E Exploration Station
V Viewing Platform

Start/End

more information about the area. There are eight of these displays in Columbia Bottom. Only four of them are accessible via the trail, though, so you'll have to do the driving tour if you want to see them all before your hike.

These interpretive stops are beautifully done. Each is wheelchair accessible, consists of two concrete stands decorated with mosaics related to its subject, and displays several signboards full of information describing the site you're visiting. They describe the area's habitats and the DOC's methods for managing each one. You'll learn about backwater sloughs, bottomland prairies, how the area's managed agriculture helps wildlife populations, how the river action sculpts the land, and more. I enjoy the little fun facts and nature Q & A on each display. I didn't know that a patch of wetland the size of one interpretive sign holds up to 100,000 aquatic invertebrates for waterfowl feeding, for example, or that a square yard of bottomland prairie contains as much as 25 miles of roots.

With its varied habitats, Columbia Bottom is a wonderful place for wildlife viewing—a rarity on the edge of a major metro area. You'll probably see Missouri's ubiquitous deer and turkeys while hiking to the Confluence, and in the woods along the River's Edge Trail you'll spot a variety of songbirds. Herons and other shorebirds stalk the sloughs, pools, and riversides, and eagles are often sighted here in winter. Spring and fall feature thousands of migrating ducks, geese, and other waterfowl.

I like the open vastness of Columbia Bottom, especially on a weekday or during winter, when few other folks are around. While the trails are flat and lack the scenic bluffs, overlooks, and forests of the typical Ozarks hike, the wide-open expanse of grasslands fringed with a belt of trees along

Interpretive display along the Confluence Trail

the river is very pleasing to the eye. Your view runs for several miles, broken only by scattered clumps of trees and the occasional tall building or smokestack in the far distance. I also enjoy the distant views of the Chain of Rocks Bridge just south of Columbia Bottom. Once a busy part of Old Route 66, it's now a pedestrian- and bike-only crossing of the Mississippi, with downriver views of the St. Louis skyline.

Two trails explore Columbia Bottom Conservation Area. The 4.75-mile Confluence Trail runs from the visitor center to the Missouri-Mississippi junction, and the 3-mile River's Edge Trail follows the Missouri from the Confluence back to the river access. You can cover both trails on a 9.5-mile loop hike by starting from the visitor center and hiking the Confluence Trail to the Confluence Overlook. Then, after checking out the Confluence, follow the River's Edge Trail back to its junction with the Confluence Trail next to the river access, and retrace your steps 1.8 miles back to the visitor center. If you have less time and energy, park at the river access and hike both trails as a 6-mile loop, skipping the Confluence Trail segment between the river access and the visitor center.

Whichever option you choose, I recommend hiking outbound on the Confluence Trail and returning via the River's Edge Trail, saving the more wilderness-like hiking for last. The Confluence Trail is a gravel hiking/biking path that follows a gently curving course through the open bottomlands for most of its length, hitting four of the interpretive displays along the way. It enters riverside woods in its last half mile before the Confluence.

At the Confluence you'll find restrooms, an overlook platform with benches, and the largest of the conservation area's outdoor interpretive displays. This one focuses on historical facts such as the rivers as highways, explorers who followed these water routes, and maps showing the location of Lewis and Clark's 1803–04 winter camp. These diagrams show how wild the rivers once were, constantly changing their courses over time—lines representing Lewis and Clark's outbound and return routes vary from one another, and the winter camp, located near the confluence at that time, was several miles north of where you now stand. The display is topped off with a pole marking history-making flood levels, with the 1993 flood mark 15 feet above the display's concrete base.

Your return trip on the River's Edge Trail will be a sharp contrast to your outbound hike. You'll switch from open hiking on a gravel prairie trail to a winding dirt path in deep woods next to the Missouri River. Just as the name implies, for most of its length you'll be right on the edge of the stream with constant views of the river. If the water's low there'll be a monstrous sandbar next to you for much of the hike, and the heavy riverside woods will keep you shaded on hot summer hikes. In some places the trees and vines are so thick you'll walk through a green tunnel. If you like cold weather, hit the River's Edge Trail on winter days when the temperatures have been well below freezing for a week or two. The Missouri will be covered with ice floes, and from the trail you'll hear the river hiss, groan, crack, and crunch as the floes collide on their way to the Mississippi.

▶ **NEARBY ACTIVITIES**

Check out the Chain of Rocks Bridge at the intersection of I-270 and Riverview Drive. Open to pedestrian and bike traffic only, this restored bridge is the old Route 66 link across the Mississippi River.

# CLIFF CAVE COUNTY PARK

## ▶ IN BRIEF

With its extensive network of short trails, Cliff Cave is an excellent place for quick evening hikes. You'll wander past sinkholes and a small lake, and admire the Mississippi River from a scenic bluff overlook.

## ▶ DESCRIPTION

Most of the trails in Cliff Cave are smooth, packed earth on level terrain. The few rocky stretches are in the northeast tract of the park, where the trail follows rocky bluff edges for a short way. Sinkholes are scattered thickly across the landscape in the southwest tract of Cliff Cave. The trails wind among them, often on causeway-like paths between these conical depressions. A few of them hold water in small ponds, and one of them is slowly swallowing an abandoned car.

The sinkholes feed the park's namesake cave, which wanders for almost 2,000 feet beneath the park. Several of the sinkholes are back entrances to the cave. The main entrance is just up the road from the parking area. A stream gurgles from the cavern's mouth and flows past mossy green rocks and a stone retaining wall. The cave is open to exploration by permit only. Don't enter the cave without one, and never enter when it's raining. The many sinkholes quickly drain runoff into the cave, causing sudden flooding in its passages. At these times the little stream at the cave's mouth becomes a roaring torrent.

A spaghetti bowl of trails—that's Cliff Cave's trail system. Tightly packed into 222 acres of forest, this intricate network defies exact mapping and measuring. It's kind of like a spiderweb tossed over the landscape. Maps of the trail system are an

## ▶ DIRECTIONS

From I-255, drive 1.6 miles south on Telegraph Road to Cliff Cave Road. Turn left and follow Cliff Cave Road 1.5 miles to the park.

## ⓘ KEY AT-A-GLANCE INFORMATION

**LENGTH:** 5 miles

**CONFIGURATION:** Network

**DIFFICULTY:** Easy

**SCENERY:** Forests, sinkholes, bluff views of Mississippi River

**EXPOSURE:** Shady

**TRAFFIC:** Light

**TRAIL SURFACE:** Packed earth, roots, few rocky sections

**HIKING TIME:** 1-3 hours

**ACCESS:** Open 8 a.m.–half-hour after sunset

**MAPS:** Oakville USGS topo; hand-drawn map available at trailhead

**FACILITIES:** Parking, picnic site

**SPECIAL COMMENTS:** Pets must be on leash; no cave exploration without permit

**GPS TRAILHEAD COORDINATES (PARK ENTRANCE)**

| | | |
|---|---|---|
| UTM ZONE (WGS84) | 15S | |
| EASTING | 736460 | |
| NORTHING | 4260287 | |
| LATITUDE-LONGITUDE | | |
| NORTH | N38° 27' 34.4427'' | |
| WEST | W90° 17' 23.9509'' | |

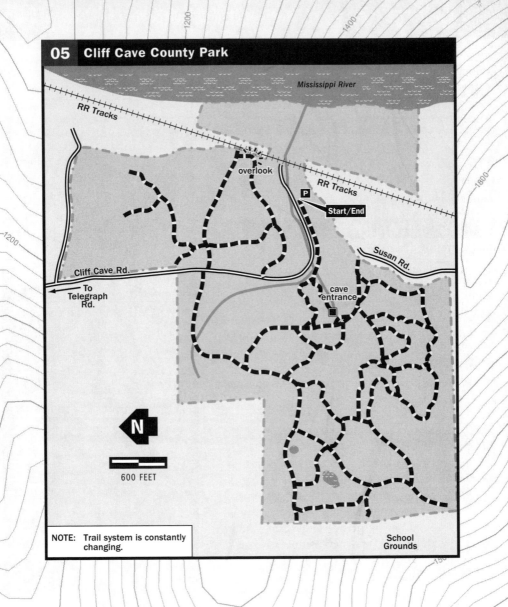

Mississippi River

RR Tracks

overlook

P

RR Tracks

Start/End

Susan Rd.

Cliff Cave Rd.

To
Telegraph
Rd.

cave
entrance

N

600 FEET

NOTE: Trail system is constantly
changing.

School
Grounds

approximation, and trails here change often as people explore new routes. Other than a few painted blazes and arrows from mountain bike races held in the park, there are no markings to guide you. Even so, it's hard to get lost in Cliff Cave Park. Subdivisions line the park's north and south borders, a school bounds the west, and Cliff Cave Road and the Mississippi River form the eastern edge. In this 222-acre park, you'll never be more than a quarter mile from one of these boundaries.

Though the park is small and its trails unmarked, Cliff Cave is a wonderful place to hike. The terrain is generally level, but the trails twist and wind among the sinkholes like a roller coaster, making quick climbs and descents. Its packed-earth trails are excellent for trail running, and options for short hikes make it a wonderful place to bring children. It's also an ideal place for cold winter hikes, when you want to admire white landscapes or glittering ice-coated forests but can't be out for long distances or periods of time.

The county-parks department's Web site (**www.stlouisco.com/parks**) estimates 3.5 miles of trail in Cliff Cave, but it's probably closer to 5 or 6. About 1 mile of trail is in the northeast tract of the park. To enter this tract, walk up the park road from the parking area, round the curve, and choose either of two trails leading east from the road. It's worth exploring this smaller part of Cliff Cave just to see the bluff overlook on its east edge, where you'll overlook the Mississippi from a wide ledge. From the ledge, the trail curves west along the bluff, overlooking the parking lot and cave entrance.

Most of Cliff Cave's trails are in the southwest tract of the park. There are two entrances to this part of Cliff Cave. If you hike the northeast tract first, there's a path leading from that tract across Cliff Cave Road and into the southwest tract. It heads west along a little stream, turns south to cross the stream, passes a 1950s-vintage car body, and enters the network from the north. If you want to hike the southwest tract first, walk from the parking area up to the trail leading to the cave. A few steps off the road there's a fork in the trail, with the left fork leading to the cave entrance. The right fork crosses the cave stream and angles northwest uphill to the trail system, with nice views of the cave entrance as it climbs.

It's impossible to tell you how to find your way around Cliff Cave's complex—but very enjoyable—system of trails. Just get in there and get to know the place, and you'll soon know this pretty little enclave like your backyard.

## ▶ NEARBY ACTIVITIES

Cave-exploration permits are available for $4. Contact St. Louis County Parks at (314) 615-4FUN.

# RUSSELL E. EMMENEGGER NATURE PARK

## KEY AT-A-GLANCE INFORMATION

**LENGTH:** 1.75 miles

**CONFIGURATION:** Loop

**DIFFICULTY:** Very easy

**SCENERY:** Creeks, forested hills, views over Meramec River valley

**EXPOSURE:** Shady

**TRAFFIC:** Medium

**TRAIL SURFACE:** Packed earth, sawdust, short paved section

**HIKING TIME:** One half-hour

**ACCESS:** Open sunrise–sunset

**MAPS:** Kirkwood USGS topo; park map available at Powder Valley Nature Center

**FACILITIES:** Water, restrooms, picnic shelter

**SPECIAL COMMENTS:** Pets on leash; no collecting of plants, rocks, or other natural objects

### GPS TRAILHEAD COORDINATES (PARK ENTRANCE)

| UTM ZONE (WGS84) | 15S |
|---|---|
| EASTING | 723818 |
| NORTHING | 4269470 |

| LATITUDE–LONGITUDE | |
|---|---|
| NORTH | N38° 32' 43.8289'' |
| WEST | W90° 25' 54.4736'' |

## IN BRIEF

Emmenegger's short trail is a nice evening jaunt after a hard day on the job. You'll explore a peaceful hollow and view overlooks of the Meramec River.

## DESCRIPTION

Russell E. Emmenegger Nature Park is named for the man who in 1975 donated his property for this pretty little green space. The Nature Park is a joint venture between the City of Kirkwood and the Missouri Department of Conservation. Included in Emmenegger's 95 acres is the Missouri Department of Conservation's 14-acre Possum Woods Conservation Area.

Before Mr. Emmenegger obtained this pretty landscape, it was owned by Edwin Lemp of the Lemp brewing family. The mansion he built on his property, named Cragwold, still stands on the Meramec River bluffs outside the park's northern boundary. Lemp kept exotic animals such as buffalo, llama, and yak on his property. Tall fences used to contain the animal pens can still be seen at the park's northern boundary. Check the bulletin board at the park entrance. There you can read a *St. Louis Post-Dispatch* article on the park and its interesting history.

The 1.5-mile trail in Emmenegger Nature Area is a short loop perfect for evening hikes or trail running. There are two accessible paved loops near the trailhead, and the remainder is mulch or natural surface. Future plans are to connect Emmenegger with Kirkwood's Greentree Park and the envisioned

## DIRECTIONS

From I-44 and Lindbergh Road, drive a half mile south on Lindbergh to Watson Road. Drive a half mile west to Geyer Road. Go a short distance north on Geyer, cross I-44, and turn left on Cragwold Road. Follow Cragwold 1 mile, cross I-270 and T into Stoneywood Road. Turn left and drive a half mile to Emmenegger Park.

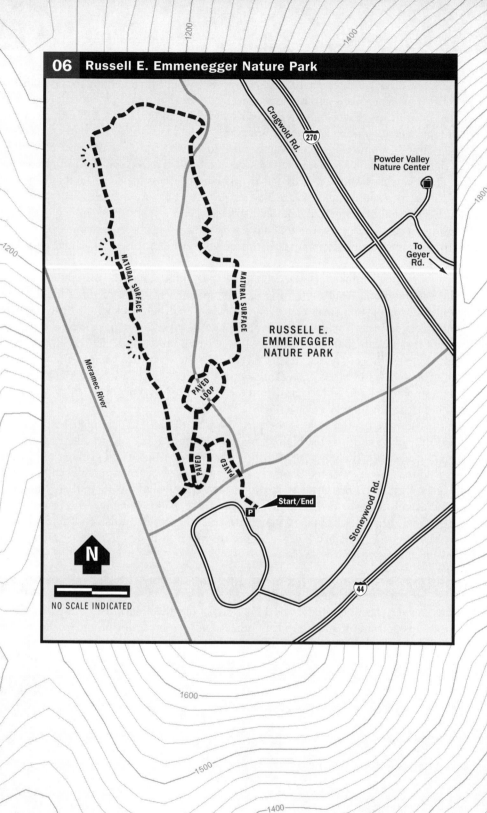

Cragwold Rd.

270

Powder Valley
Nature Center

To
Geyer
Rd.

NATURAL SURFACE

NATURAL SURFACE

RUSSELL E.
EMMENEGGER
NATURE PARK

Meramec River

PAVED LOOP

PAVED

PAVED

Start/End

P

Stoneywood Rd.

44

N

NO SCALE INDICATED

Meramec River Greenway, a 108-mile route that would eventually hook up with the Ozark Trail. Since plans also call for connecting the Ozark Trail to the Ozark Highlands Trail in Arkansas, maybe one day you can start hiking in Emmenegger Nature Area and not quit until you reach Fort Smith, Arkansas!

But I suppose I should come back to Earth, and just tell you about the 1.5 miles you can hike right now. From the trailhead, a paved spur leads north across a creek to the westernmost of the two 0.1-mile accessible loops at Emmenegger Nature Park's south end. If you're like me, preferring to save the best scenery for last, turn right and hike the trail counterclockwise. On the other hand, hiking clockwise results in gentler ascents. The trail has few markings—just a few carsonite posts with arrows—but it's next to impossible to lose your way on this well-defined path in a small area.

Traveling counterclockwise, you'll hike part of both paved loops, then break off the east loop and head north. The path is mulched in the sometimes-muddy bottomland, following a small creek valley a half mile. There's usually a little water in the creek, and you'll splash across it at the loop's upper end. After crossing the creek you'll break west, climb steeply, then T into a trail on a ridge. The official trail goes left along the ridge. The path to the right leads a few yards to some old foundations and the remains of Mr. Lemp's exotic-animal fence. There's a nice overlook ledge at the top of the climb, with expansive views across the Meramec River Valley—and lots of industry, but I'll take any overlook I can get!

The next quarter mile is the prettiest part of the walk through Emmenegger Nature Park. You'll hug the bluff above the Meramec River and wander past several small glades. You'll enjoy several more vistas over the valley and clamber over some rugged rock steps. After the last glade the trail eases away from the river and into the woods, then levels out at the west end of the accessible loops. From there, the trailhead is only a short way to the left on the paved walk. A natural surface trail goes west from the end of the paved loop. Take it, and in a few yards you'll find a bench overlooking the Meramec River—the perfect place to hang out before ending your hike at Emmenegger Nature Park.

▶ **NEARBY ACTIVITIES**

The Powder Valley Nature Center, 11715 Cragwold Road, is a fascinating place, and has maps and information on many other conservation areas around St. Louis. For information, call (314) 301-1500.

# FOREST 44 CONSERVATION AREA

## ▶ IN BRIEF

In Forest 44 Conservation Area you'll be mystified by the "losing stream," a creek that disappears beneath a rock layer, only to emerge as a spring several hundred yards downstream.

## ▶ DESCRIPTION

When it purchased the land in 1990, the Department of Conservation saved Forest 44's 985 acres from encroaching development. Forest 44 and its neighboring untrammeled landscapes of West Tyson County Park, Lone Elk County Park, Route 66 State Park, and the private Tyson Research Center form a green preserve of more than 2,000 acres in southwest St. Louis County. Forest 44's hillsides were once logged, and its valleys were cultivated by farmers. A couple of big trees near the beginning of the Dogwood Ridge Trail mark an old homestead. You can read a bit of Forest 44's history on the DOC Web site in an article entitled "Growing Up on Forest 44."

This beautifully recovering area has forest, prairies, and several hollows emptying into Williams Creek, the stream flowing along Forest 44's eastern edge. Flowering dogwoods and redbuds decorate the forest in spring, and you'll likely see deer and turkeys while hiking the area. Its mix of open spaces and forest makes it great for birding, too. Hawks, owls, several varieties of woodpecker, and lots of songbirds are seen here. A friend who hikes often in Forest 44 has seen herons in Williams Creek, and once spotted a mink along the stream.

### ℹ KEY AT-A-GLANCE INFORMATION

**LENGTH:** 12+ miles

**CONFIGURATION:** Network

**DIFFICULTY:** Easy-moderate

**SCENERY:** Wooded hills and hollows, small prairie, a disappearing stream

**EXPOSURE:** Mostly shaded

**TRAFFIC:** Light

**TRAIL SURFACE:** Packed earth and gravel

**HIKING TIME:** 1-5 hours

**ACCESS:** Open 4 a.m.-10 p.m.

**MAPS:** Manchester USGS topo; area map available from Missouri Department of Conservation

**FACILITIES:** Parking, toilets

**SPECIAL COMMENTS:** Pets must be leashed

## ▶ DIRECTIONS

From the intersection of I-44 and MO 141, go 1 mile west on Meramec Station Road (the south service road) to Hillsboro Road. Turn left and follow Hillsboro Road a half mile to the trailhead for Forest 44.

### GPS TRAILHEAD COORDINATES (TRAILHEAD)

| | | |
|---|---|---|
| UTM ZONE (WGS84) | 15S | |
| EASTING | 716753 | |
| NORTHING | 4267238 | |
| LATITUDE-LONGITUDE | | |
| NORTH | N38° 31' 37.7921" | |
| WEST | W90° 30' 48.5463" | |

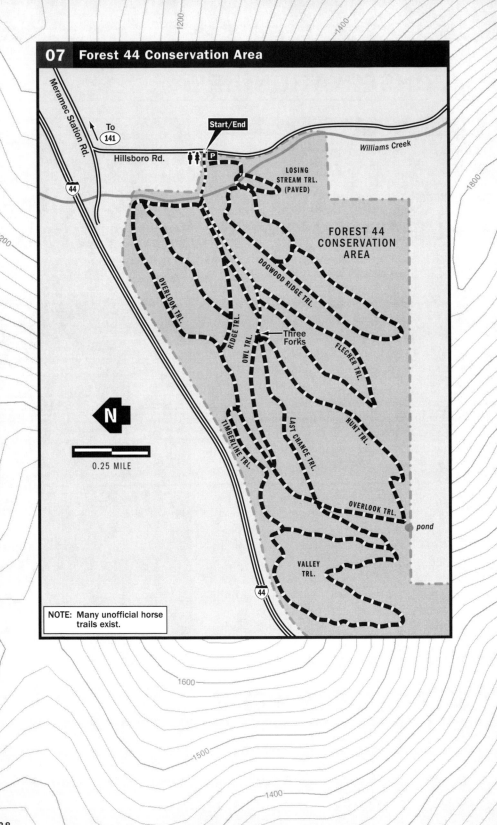

To
141

Meramec Station Rd.

Start/End

Hillsboro Rd.

Williams Creek

44

P

LOSING
STREAM TRL.
(PAVED)

FOREST 44
CONSERVATION
AREA

OVERLOOK TRL.

DOGWOOD RIDGE TRL.

RIDGE TRL.

OWL TRL.

Three
Forks

FLECHER TRL.

N

0.25 MILE

TIMBERLINE TRL.

LAST CHANCE TRL.

HUNT TRL.

OVERLOOK TRL.

pond

44

VALLEY
TRL.

NOTE: Many unofficial horse
trails exist.

You may lose your way now and then while hiking Forest 44. It's a popular equestrian area, and the riders have cut lots of unofficial paths between the maintained trails. Maps of the area don't show all these, nor do they show the area's official trails quite accurately. Many of the routes have names and markings, but they're not consistent. To counteract this, at most intersections the DOC places carsonite posts bearing arrows and the notation "To Parking." All hollows and creeks lead to Williams Creek near the trailhead, further helping you find your way to the parking lot. The hum of I-44's traffic along the north boundary of Forest 44 is a final reference point. It's not too hard to find your way around in Forest 44, though. After several hikes here you'll learn the lay of the land, and will enjoy exploring this pretty landscape.

One route you can't get lost on is the Losing Stream Trail, a 0.6-mile paved path from the trailhead. It leads to all other trails in the area and passes a prairie, a wetland, and a spring. From one of its bridges you'll see where the stream "loses" itself. It disappears beneath a ledge, then wells up as a spring several hundred yards downstream. This accessible trail crosses the losing stream twice in its short—but scenic—run.

The Dogwood Ridge Trail is a 2.5-mile loop off the western side of the Losing Stream Trail. It's a long, narrow loop with a cutoff path dividing it in half. On its northwestern side you'll hike along prairie meadows and may spot deer or turkey from a viewing stand built along the trail. A couple of big trees at the northeastern end of the prairie are all that's left from a farmstead that once stood here. At its southwestern end, the loop angles up a hillside, then follows a ridge back to the Losing Stream Trail. As you'd expect from the trail's name, lots of white dogwood blooms decorate this hike in spring.

From the north end of the Dogwood Ridge Trail you'll see a gravel road on the other side of the meadow. This road follows the valley back to Forest 44's horse trails. The first path you'll come to is the Flecher Trail, a loop extending southwest off the road. It's similar to the Dogwood Ridge Trail—it follows a prairie edge to the south, then climbs onto a ridge and follows it back north to the road. Just past the Flecher Trail the road ends at a place I call Three Forks, since three paths lead away from there. Called the Hunt, Last Chance, and Owl trails, they lead west onto a ridge and T into the Overlook Trail, which runs along the ridge back to the trailhead.

When you reach Three Forks, you'll be about 1 mile from the trailhead. Taking the Hunt Trail, the leftmost of the three paths, you'll follow the hollow bottom for a while, then climb west onto a ridge. There you'll be at the south end of Forest 44, turning right onto the Overlook Trail at its southwestern end. You'll be 0.8 miles from Three Forks and 1.8 miles from the trailhead. Following the Overlook Trail along the ridge to Williams Creek, then back to the trailhead, makes a loop hike of just under 4 miles.

Approximately 0.35 miles after joining the Overlook Trail, you'll come to an intersection. The trail to the right is the upper end of the Last Chance, which runs 0.6 miles downhill to Three Forks. The path to the left is the Valley Trail, which explores an unmarked and wild area of Forest 44. The Valley Trail is a 2.6-mile loop with a cutoff shortening it to 1.4 miles, but few markings make this somewhat confusing route hard to follow. Still, it's a pretty area to explore. You can't get too lost on the Valley Trail, but stay alert—I-44 is its northern boundary, and the traffic hum can be your directional beacon.

A quarter mile past the Last Chance junction, the Overlook Trail intersects with the upper end of Owl Trail. A right turn here leads a half mile downhill to Three Forks. Another quarter mile down the Overlook, the Timberline Trail comes in from the left—this is where you'd come up if you hike the Valley Trail. Just beyond the Timberline Trail you'll see a trail to the right, with a "To Parking" sign. This is the Ridge Trail, and while it's a shortcut to the trailhead, it doesn't save much distance. It is more peaceful, though. The next 0.7 miles on the Overlook Trail is next to I-44, overlooking the highway at several points. Though the traffic is noisy, the road cut opens up views of the West County skyline.

Much of the Overlook Trail's 0.7-mile run along I-44 is downhill. It levels out next at Williams Creek, then turns south to head up the hollow. Just after the turn there's a trail to the right, heading southeast and steeply uphill. It runs a half mile over to the Ridge Trail. From this junction, it's a short run along the creek to the gravel road to Three Forks. Turn left on the road, and you'll cross the creek and head back to the trailhead along the north edge of a prairie. Or you can hike straight ahead through the grass to the Dogwood Ridge Trail, follow it to the Losing Stream Trail, and hike its paved path back to the parking area.

## ▶ NEARBY ACTIVITIES

Other good trails are nearby in Greensfelder (page 45), Lone Elk (page 55), and West Tyson county parks. The World Bird Sanctuary near Lone Elk Park is a must-see for anyone interested in birds of prey. Visit **www.worldbirdsanctuary.org** for more information.

# GREEN ROCK TRAIL

## ▶ IN BRIEF

In its scenic wanderings over the rugged, wooded hills of southwest St. Louis County, the Green Rock Trail introduces you to three of the metro area's outstanding natural areas—Rockwoods Reservation, Greensfelder County Park, and Rockwoods Range.

## ▶ DESCRIPTION

The Green Rock Trail was designed and built in the mid-1960s by Boy Scout Troop 594 from St. Louis Country Day School. Now maintained by the Greater St. Louis Area Boy Scout Council, the Green Rock is one of the finest woods walks to be found in a large metropolitan area. It explores Rockwoods Range, Greensfelder County Park, and Rockwoods Reservation, three of St. Louis's prettiest green spaces. Though the Green Rock has

## ▶ DIRECTIONS

To reach the northern trailhead, drive west from St. Louis on I-44 to Exit 264, Eureka–MO 109. Turn right and drive north 4 miles to the Rockwoods Reservation entrance on Woods Road. Turn left and go 0.1 miles to Glencoe Road. Turn right and follow Glencoe Road 1.5 miles to the visitor center parking lot. Trailhead is in the grassy area south of the parking lot, near a maintenance area.

To reach the southern terminus of the Green Rock, drive west on I-44 to Exit 261, Allenton Road–Six Flags. Drive west on Fox Creek Road, which is I-44's north outer road. Shortly after the road curves north away from I-44, 1.5 miles down Fox Creek, you'll see the trailhead and parking area on the left.

You can also park at the Greensfelder Memorial Picnic Area in Greensfelder County Park (page 90), and hike the middle sections of the Green Rock from there.

## ⓘ KEY AT-A-GLANCE INFORMATION

**LENGTH:** 10 miles

**CONFIGURATION:** Point-to-point

**DIFFICULTY:** Moderate–hard

**SCENERY:** Forested hills and hollows with occasional vistas

**EXPOSURE:** Shaded throughout

**TRAFFIC:** Light

**TRAIL SURFACE:** Mixture of packed earth and gravel, with numerous short rocky and rooty sections

**HIKING TIME:** 5–7 hours

**ACCESS:** Open sunrise–half hour after sunset

**MAPS:** Available at visitor center in Rockwoods Reservation or from Greater St. Louis Area Boy Scout Council; Eureka USGS topo

**FACILITIES:** Restrooms, water, and visitor center at Rockwoods Reservation at north end of trail; water also available in Greensfelder Park along middle reaches of the Green Rock via short side hikes

**SPECIAL COMMENTS:** No pets on Rockwoods Reservation portion of the trail, allowed only on leash for remainder; no gathering of flowers or edible plants; heavy equestrian use of Greensfelder Park portion of Green Rock

### GPS TRAILHEAD COORDINATES (ROCKWOODS ENTRANCE)

| UTM ZONE (WGS84) | 15S |
|---|---|
| EASTING | 705329 |
| NORTHING | 4270169 |
| LATITUDE-LONGITUDE | |
| NORTH | N38° 33' 22.5398'' |
| WEST | W90° 38' 36.8398'' |

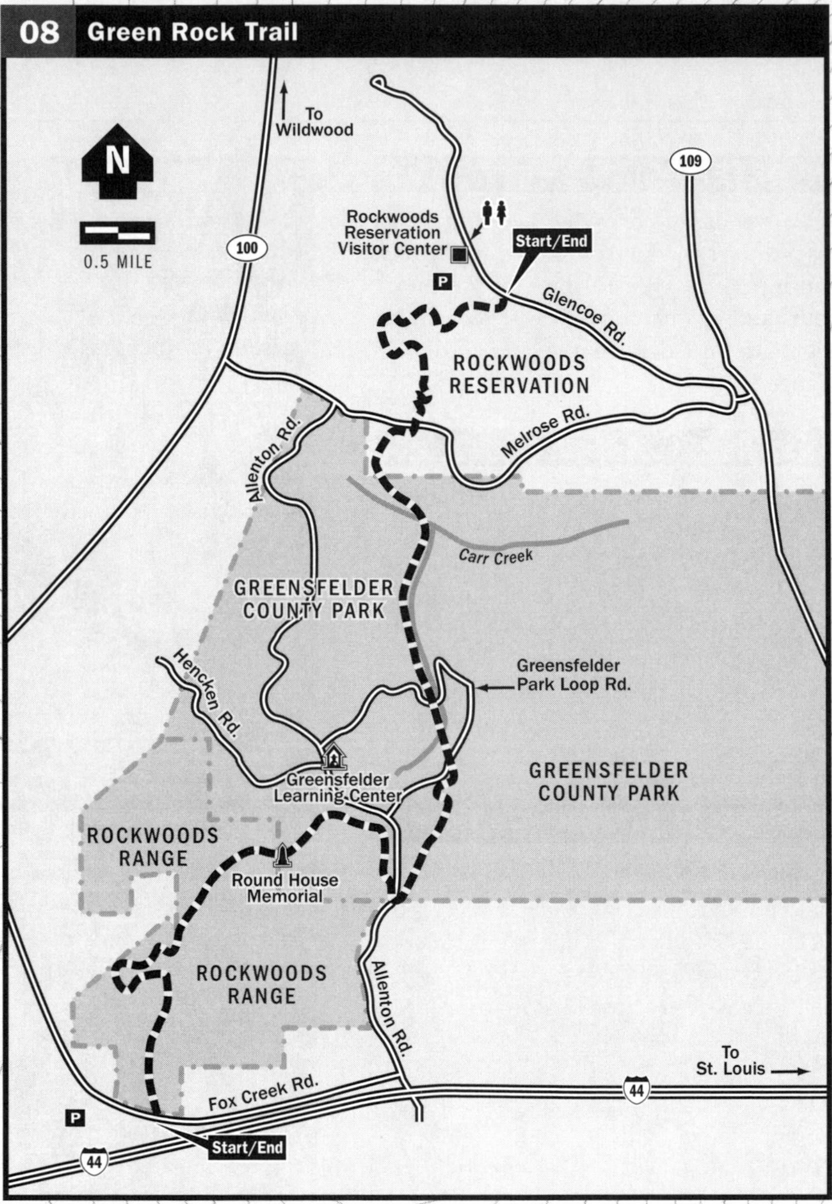

**N**

0.5 MILE

To
Wildwood

109

Rockwoods
Reservation
Visitor Center

Start/End

P

Glencoe Rd.

100

ROCKWOODS
RESERVATION

Melrose Rd.

Allenton Rd.

Carr Creek

GREENSFELDER
COUNTY PARK

Greensfelder
Park Loop Rd.

Hencken Rd.

Greensfelder
Learning Center

GREENSFELDER
COUNTY PARK

ROCKWOODS
RANGE

Round House
Memorial

ROCKWOODS
RANGE

Allenton Rd.

To
St. Louis

44

P

Fox Creek Rd.

Start/End

44

relatively few spectacular features like panoramic vistas or impressive bluffs, the remote feel of this trail so close to a major city makes hiking it a wonderful experience. The Green Rock feels so surprisingly like true wilderness that it'll be a mental jolt the few times you cross roads or pass behind one of the few houses near the trail.

Like the Appalachian Trail, the Green Rock is marked with rectangular white paint blazes on trailside trees and occasional posts with yellow "Green Rock Trail" signs. Confusing points occur on trail stretches in Greensfelder Park, where the Green Rock has numerous intersections with hiking paths there. Carry a map of Greensfelder and consult it frequently while in the park, and you'll have little trouble finding your way. Conventional wisdom says the path is marked for travel south to north, but I find the markings easy to follow from north to south, too. I prefer starting at the north end in Rockwoods Reservation, where I can get maps, water, and trail information, and then finish the hike near I-44 for a quick trip to a nearby eatery. Others like hiking south to north and topping off their hike with a picnic at the pretty sites in Rockwoods Reservation.

The Green Rock has several stiff climbs and a few rocky stretches, but that's one of the reasons it feels more like a wild Ozark trail than an urban ramble. The rocky sections are few and short, so trail running or hiking the Green Rock is a dream for those who want a little workout with their training or nature wanderings. On the Green Rock you'll hike along ridges, descend side hills and switchbacks to deep hollows, travel along dry washes that become cooling brooks with cascades and low waterfalls during summer thunderstorms, and enjoy shady wanderings through the thick forest that covers almost the entire trail.

I like to start my hike with a stop at the visitor center in Rockwoods Reservation. There you'll find information on the history of the area, and the critters, flowers, and woodlands you'll check out on your hike. There are several preserved specimens, including a bobcat, a hawk, and several owls and songbirds, as well as live exhibits of snakes, turtles, and lizards. Maps of Rockwoods Reservation and Range are available here, and you can fill your water bottles and get trail information from the rangers, too.

The trail begins at a signboard south of the visitor center, heads into the woods, crosses a bridge over Hamilton Creek, and swings uphill to the southwest. Just before the climb you'll pass a huge tree almost four feet thick at its base. A few steps uphill is the stump of another forest monster. Moss and forest plants are growing in the rotted center of this old stump, helping in the process of decomposition. The climb tops out after a quarter mile, drops into a hollow, and climbs onto another ridge. Here, at the half-mile point, you'll climb through a rock layer and travel on it for a short way, with boulders and stone outcroppings scattered all about you on the nose of the ridge. Then the trail swings south to follow the ridge for an easy half mile, with a deep hollow to your left and hints of views through the trees. The path then crosses the ridge to the left and quickly descends into a deep hollow where two streams join, with small boulders and rock outcroppings scattered everywhere. The trail then leaves the hollow and begins a quarter-mile climb, wiggling and twisting through close-spaced trees and rocks, just like the classic Ozark trails found farther south. Much of the trail is like this, and it's a tribute to the excellent design and hard work of the scouts who built the Green Rock.

After one more descent and a short, stiff climb, the trail crosses Melrose Road, marking almost 2 miles. After an easy half-mile cruise along a ridge, the trail enters Greensfelder Park and makes a rugged descent over a pretty series of rock layers on a boulder-strewn slope. At the bottom of the descent lies a nice reward—the start of a long, mostly level hike in the bottomlands of Carr Creek. For the next 1.5 miles you'll meander with the creek among immense trees reaching for the sky. For the last mile, the Green Rock shares the route with the Eagle Valley horse trail in Greensfelder, complete with equestrian jumps and a nice little picnic site that's perfect for a mid-hike picnic break.

Watch closely for the fork where the Green Rock breaks off the Eagle Valley Trail. It's about a quarter mile south after the paved scenic drive crossing in Greensfelder, and isn't marked with official Green Rock trail markers. To make matters worse, if you miss the turn you'll come to an old Green Rock marker from before the trail was rerouted, and you could end up hiking a long way before realizing your mistake. Look for a narrow trail starting uphill to the east, marked only with a carsonite post with hiker symbols and no-horses symbols.

From its fork off the Eagle Valley Trail, the Green Rock climbs a quarter mile to cross the scenic drive again, marking the halfway point of your hike. In the mile after the scenic drive you'll face one descent and challenging climb before reaching several antennae that mark the highest point on the trail. Just south of the towers is a confusing tangle of trails, but plentiful blazes will keep you on the right path. If you don't cross Allenton Road and swing west within a half mile following the towers, you've taken the wrong path.

Shortly after the towers, the Green Rock joins the DeClue Trail in Greensfelder Park and follows it across Allenton Road. It rolls over numerous little ups and downs that are great for your heart rate before hitting a gravel road a mile from the Allenton Road crossing. I found no markings here, but turning left and following the road keeps you on the right path. A quarter mile down this road is the Round House Memorial, where A. P. Greensfelder, whose namesake park you're hiking through, once had—you guessed it—a round house. Take a break to read the interpretive signs at this fascinating site before hitting the trail once more.

Two trails lead away from the memorial, and neither is marked. Don't take the one at the far end of the memorial that looks like an old woods road—it's the Round House Loop in Rockwoods Range. The Green Rock is a single-track path leaving the memorial about a third of the way down the north side of the parking area. It's about 2.5 miles to the Fox Creek trailhead from here, on a secluded narrow path with several climbs and descents. I especially enjoy the Green Rock's final half mile, where it wanders along an intermittent creek. Several impressive rock ledges span the stream to form exquisite little waterfalls during or just after storms, complete with rock ledges and steps to sit on and dangle your feet in before ending your adventure on the Green Rock.

# GREENSFELDER COUNTY PARK

## ▶ IN BRIEF

The metro area is rapidly growing around this pretty green space, but it feels as wild as ever. Hiking is just one way to explore Greensfelder's forested hills. All trails in the park are open to equestrians, and two routes are open for mountain biking.

## ▶ DESCRIPTION

With 1,724 acres of rugged hills and hollows, Greensfelder is the largest of St. Louis County's parks. It's named for A. P. Greensfelder, a conservationist who donated land for nearby Rockwoods Range. The Round House Memorial, located just off Allenton Road, is where Greensfelder built an oval-shaped country home in 1928. Displays at the memorial describe this unique house and the accomplishments of its owner. You can visit the memorial via a 750-yard walk down a gravel road from the Round House Memorial parking lot on Allenton Road.

Greensfelder combines the adjoining Rockwoods Range and Rockwoods Reservation to form a 4,955-acre green space in southwest St. Louis County. In this semiwild area you'll see lots of wildlife, especially deer, turkeys, and numerous birds. I once walked up behind an inattentive coyote on the Eagle Valley Trail. You can explore this pretty landscape on seven trails ranging from 1 to 3.5 miles in length. In addition to the designated trails, several miles of unofficial paths cut by equestrians lace the area.

## ℹ KEY AT-A-GLANCE INFORMATION

**LENGTH:** 15 miles on 7 interconnecting trails, ranging in length from 1 to 3.5 miles

**CONFIGURATION:** Network

**DIFFICULTY:** Moderate

**SCENERY:** Forested hills with occasional vistas

**EXPOSURE:** Shady

**TRAFFIC:** Heavy on Eagle Valley and Deer Run trails; light to moderate on all others

**TRAIL SURFACE:** Packed earth, gravel, and rock

**HIKING TIME:** 1-2 hours on any individual trail; by stringing several trails together, you could hike all day at Greensfelder

**ACCESS:** Open sunrise–half-hour after sunset

**MAPS:** Eureka USGS topo; park map available from county parks in Clayton

**FACILITIES:** Water, restrooms, campground, picnic sites, stable, playgrounds

**SPECIAL COMMENTS:** Expect heavy horse traffic, especially on Eagle Valley and Deer Run trails

## ▶ DIRECTIONS

Drive southwest on I-44 to Exit 261, Six Flags–Allenton Road. Drive 2 miles north on Allenton Road to the park. Some good starting places include the Learning Center, the Round House Memorial, or the equestrian parking lot and the campground.

**GPS TRAILHEAD COORDINATES (PARK ENTRANCE)**

UTM ZONE (WGS84)   15S
    EASTING   701843
    NORTHING   4267144

LATITUDE-LONGITUDE
    NORTH   N38° 31' 47.3609''
    WEST   W90° 41' 3.9008''

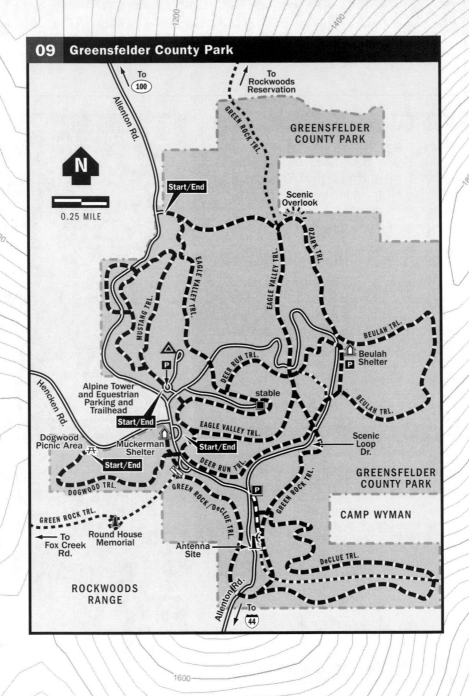

N

0.25 MILE

To 100

To Rockwoods Reservation

GREENSFELDER COUNTY PARK

Allenton Rd.

GREEN ROCK TRL.

Start/End

Scenic Overlook

EAGLE VALLEY TRL.

MUSTANG TRL.

EAGLE VALLEY TRL.

OZARK TRL.

BEULAH TRL.

Beulah Shelter

DEER RUN TRL.

stable

BEULAH TRL.

Alpine Tower and Equestrian Parking and Trailhead

Hencken Rd.

Start/End

EAGLE VALLEY TRL.

Scenic Loop Dr.

GREENSFELDER COUNTY PARK

Dogwood Picnic Area

Muckerman Shelter

Start/End

DEER RUN TRL.

Start/End

DOGWOOD TRL.

GREEN ROCK TRL.

GREEN ROCK TRL.

CAMP WYMAN

GREEN ROCK/DeCLUE TRL.

GREEN ROCK TRL.

Round House Memorial

To Fox Creek Rd.

Antenna Site

DeCLUE TRL.

ROCKWOODS RANGE

Allenton Rd.

To 44

Greensfelder is a nice place to hike, but route-finding can be a little confusing until you get to know the place. The unofficial paths tangle things somewhat, and inconsistent markings along the trails add to the confusion. The starting points of all trails are marked with signs giving trail names and distances, but markings along the trails themselves are sporadic or nonexistent. Most intersections aren't well marked, and the area map isn't completely accurate, either. I also found differing stated trail lengths on maps and trail signs. For all that, finding your way around Greensfelder isn't too hard. Trail segments are short, so even if you lose your way you'll soon run into Allenton Road, the Scenic Loop, or a well-traveled path like the Eagle Valley Trail. The confusion adds to the adventure of exploring Greensfelder. And after a few hikes you'll get a feel for the landscape and understand the trail system like your own backyard.

The 3.5-mile Eagle Valley Trail follows wide gravel paths for much of its length, so it's a good choice for your first hike at Greensfelder. It's like the backbone of the trail system, running from the campground, around the stables, and past the Learning Center. From the Learning Center it descends to Carr Creek, then veers north to follow it a mile to the northern reaches of the park. In Carr Creek's bottomland you'll pass numerous equestrian obstacles. At the end of its northern run along the creek, the Eagle Valley turns west, climbs a short way, then turns south on rough single-track. After about a half mile on single-track, it nudges the northern end of the Mustang Trail, then climbs steeply onto a ridge. On the ridge it once again becomes a wide gravel path and goes south to return to the campground.

The 0.75-mile Ozark Trail is another wide gravel path that's easy to follow. On its run from the northeast corner of the Eagle Valley Trail to the Beulah Shelter, this point-to-point route passes a splendid overlook with a picnic table—an ideal rest stop. To make a loop from the Beulah Shelter, combine the Ozark Trail and parts of the Eagle Valley and Deer Run trails to make a 2-mile hike. This loop could be extended further by tacking on the 1.8-mile Beulah Trail. It explores the hollow east of the Beulah Shelter and has a long descent and climb. Both the Beulah Trail and Beulah Shelter are named for a mule whose owner donated funds for this nice picnic site.

Like the Eagle Valley Trail, the 2.5-mile Deer Run Trail is a loop exploring the central part of Greensfelder. It shares trail with the Eagle Valley on the loop around the stables. It's confusing to follow in places, so it'll require some perseverance and patience to hike it. Starting from the Experiential Learning Center, the trail follows Allenton Road south to the Scenic Loop, then turns to follow the scenic loop to the Beulah Shelter. Where it intersects with the Beulah Trail, there's a fork. The left fork angles downhill to Carr Creek. The right fork crosses the scenic Loop, goes past the Beulah Shelter, then crosses back to the inside of the Scenic Loop. It then veers west, goes through a rugged glade-restoration area, and descends to Carr Creek. After crossing the Eagle Valley next to the creek, it climbs incredibly steeply to the stables, where it Ts into the west side of the Eagle Valley Trail. A left turn leads around the stable and back to the Experiential Learning Center.

The Mustang Trail is a 1.3-mile loop in the western part of Greensfelder. It leaves the Alpine Tower parking area next to the campground and follows a spur trail north into the woods. From where the Mustang Trail's loop begins, the right fork descends into a secluded hollow with an incredibly wild feel. There's usually a little water in the hollow and lots of rock outcroppings and fallen timber. It's one of the wildest places in the park. At the northern end of the loop, the Mustang touches the western side of the Eagle Valley Loop, then veers west to climb steeply to Allenton Road. It then follows the road most of the way back to the Alpine Tower, with a short side loop option on a tiny triangle of park land on the west side of Allenton Road.

The Dogwood and DeClue trails explore the southern end of the park. The 2.5-mile DeClue Trail isn't quite a loop, but can be made into one by hiking a small segment of the Green Rock Trail, which passes through Greensfelder County Park. Park at the picnic area just south of the Scenic Loop, and hike the road up to the antenna site. A short way up the road you'll see a sign for the DeClue Trail. Turn left, and a few steps down the path you'll cross the Green Rock. Turn right and follow the Green Rock for a quarter mile. Don't veer off an old road breaking left—that used to be the DeClue, but it's not anymore. Stick with the Green Rock until it's almost to Allenton Road. Go left at the fork next to Allenton Road on the single-track trail heading east. The DeClue follows the southern park boundary for a mile, with screams from Six Flags's roller coaster riders as background noise. Then it swings north, crosses an old road, and winds into a deep hollow before climbing steeply back to the antenna site.

The Dogwood Trail starts from the Dogwood Picnic Area and runs 1.1 miles east to the Muckerman Shelter. It's a point-to-point hike, so you'll have to either backtrack or hike back to the Dogwood Picnic Area on Hencken Road. A side trail from its eastern end leads several yards south to the Round House Memorial access road. A short way down the gravel road leading to the Round House, you'll intersect the Green Rock Trail. A sign at the junction says it's also the DeClue Trail, and it's an option for extending your hike. A 1-mile hike east on this trail goes to the Green Rock–DeClue junction near the antenna site.

## ▶ NEARBY ACTIVITIES

Additional hiking opportunities are available nearby at West Tyson and Lone Elk (page 55) county parks, and the Green Rock Trail passes through Greensfelder County Park (page 45).

# HOWELL ISLAND CONSERVATION AREA

## ▶ IN BRIEF

Howell Island is an easy hike on an isolated 2,500-acre island in the Missouri River. Its varied habitats make it a wonderful place for birding, wildlife watching, and wildflower walks.

## ▶ DESCRIPTION

Howell Island, a 2,500-acre, 4-mile-long island between the Missouri River and Centaur Chute, is an isolated wildland in western St. Louis County. Parts of this low-lying bottomland flood during high-river stages, keeping the area wild. The island is directly across the Missouri River from Weldon Spring and August A. Busch conservation areas. Howell Island and its neighboring public lands comprise a 17,000-acre green space in the rapidly expanding suburbs of St. Louis and St. Charles counties.

Howell Island is a land of diverse habitats. The wide Missouri flows down its northwest side, and narrow Centaur Chute flows along the southeast bank. Though the island was heavily logged before the Department of Conservation bought it in 1978, tall stands of cottonwood, sycamore, willow, and other river-bottom tree species have grown back to cover much of the island. Some parts of the

## ▶ DIRECTIONS

Go west on US 40–I-64 to Exit 16, Long Road and Chesterfield Airport Road. The ramp curves south over the highway and becomes Long Road. At the first light, turn right onto Chesterfield Airport Road, and follow it for 2 miles to a Phillips 66 convenience store. Bear left onto Olive Street Road and continue west past Rombach's Farm. After 2 miles, Olive Street becomes North Eatherton Road, and begins zigzagging along the levee. Another 2 miles after leaving the Phillips 66 convenience store, you'll see the Howell Island parking area on the right.

### ❶ KEY AT-A-GLANCE INFORMATION

**LENGTH:** 7 miles

**CONFIGURATION:** Loop

**DIFFICULTY:** Easy

**SCENERY:** Lush forest, heavy thickets, wildlife food plots, marshes, chutes on the Missouri River

**EXPOSURE:** Even mix of shady and exposed trail

**TRAFFIC:** Light

**TRAIL SURFACE:** Packed earth on old roads

**HIKING TIME:** 2–4 hours

**ACCESS:** Open 4 a.m.–10 p.m.

**MAPS:** Weldon Spring USGS topo; area map available from DOC offices at Busch Conservation Area

**FACILITIES:** Trailhead parking

**SPECIAL COMMENTS:** Pets must be leashed; don't try to cross Centaur Chute when it's under water. In summer, stop at nearby Rombach's Farm on your way out. They have delicious sweet corn, tomatoes, melons, and other good stuff fresh from the farm.

### GPS TRAILHEAD COORDINATES (PARKING AREA)

| UTM ZONE (WGS84) | 15S |
|---|---|
| EASTING | 701919 |
| NORTHING | 4281956 |
| **LATITUDE-LONGITUDE** | |
| NORTH | N38° 39' 47.4647'' |
| WEST | W90° 40' 45.3215'' |

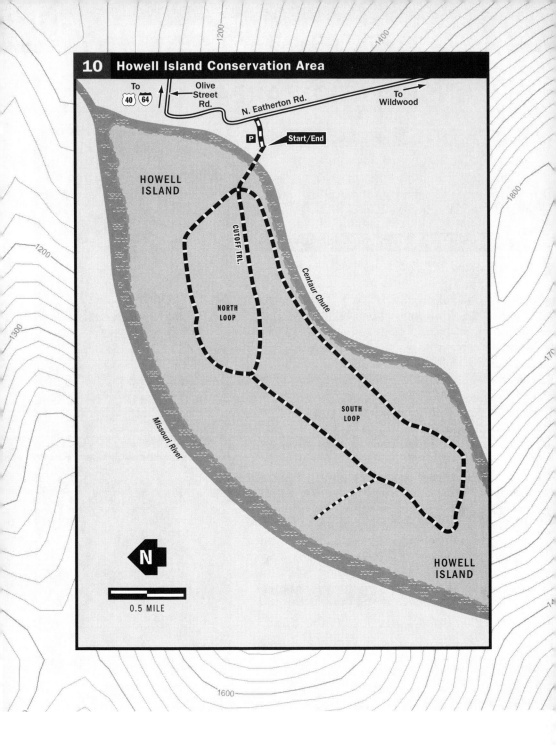

**10  Howell Island Conservation Area**

forest understory are clear and open, while others are tight thickets of undergrowth. Open fields managed for wildlife food production cover approximately
one-third of the island, and field edges contain habitats of prairie grasses and
shrubs. During high-river stages, some of the landscape turns into marsh.

These varied habitats make Howell Island an excellent place for wildlife study. The woods are crawling with deer, turkeys, squirrels, and other small mammals and reptiles. On spring evenings choruses of frogs belting out their mating calls will serenade your sunset hikes. In winter you'll spot eagles on the island; they'll be soaring overhead or roosting in trees above the river. Unless the river's deep and flowing fast, you'll spot geese and ducks in the quiet backwaters of Centaur Chute. On one early-morning hike I spotted cardinals, chickadees, nuthatches, kingfishers, goldfinches, and various woodpecker species.

You can explore Howell Island on a level 7-mile loop. A cutoff trail divides the hike into a 3.7-mile north loop and a 6-mile south loop. The hiking is so easy here you probably won't need the cutoff trail. Trail markings are plastic squares with hiker symbols emblazoned on them; mile markers help you gauge your progress. The only land access to Howell Island is a concrete causeway across Centaur Chute. When the causeway is under water, as often happens during spring rains, the island's only access is by boat. Don't attempt to cross the causeway when it's under water. Don't cross even if flows are just an inch or two over the causeway—the river might be rising, and you could be stranded when you finish hiking.

The trail's a nice soft footpath on an old road. Its wide, grassy surface is excellent for trail running or walking side-by-side with a friend and chatting. Winter is my favorite season to hike Howell Island. The river is usually low enough to clear the causeway, and any muddy sections freeze solid. Leaves are gone, so you can spot wildlife more easily in the trees and thickets, and there are no bugs. Spring also offers nice hiking—birds and frogs are singing their mating songs, and wildflowers are blooming—but seasonal rains often bring muddy trails and high water that covers the causeway. Summer hikes are usually hot, with lots of mosquitoes. Fall's great, as it is everywhere in Missouri, but many hunters come to Howell Island during deer season.

Hiking the loop counterclockwise, you immediately enter wooded thickets. The first mile of the north loop is the only part of the hike where you'll hear traffic. Once you bend west and away from North Eatherton Road, the only sound of civilization you'll hear is the occasional takeoff from nearby Spirit of St. Louis Airport. Part of the north loop is on an elevated road, passing through lowlands that are marshy if there's been rain or river flooding.

You'll come to the cutoff trail 2 miles into the loop, shortly after entering a mile-long field of crops and grasslands. Trekking this field is a pleasure on winter hikes—the sun warms you, and you can see the Missouri River bluffs over in Weldon Spring Conservation Area. When you re-enter the woods at the field's southern end, look for an old road heading west. You can follow it until it fades out, then pick your way through thick woods to reach the Missouri River across from Weldon Spring. The brush is thick, so do this only if you're comfortable finding your way in overgrown places.

Three-tenths of a mile after leaving the big field, you'll see another trail fork. The correct choice is the left fork. From there the trail winds through forests and occasional wildlife food plots, bending gradually to the northeast. You'll parallel Centaur Chute the last 1.5 miles to the trailhead, usually with a band of trees between you and the stream. In one scenic spot you'll walk on the chute's bank for a short way, with nice views up and down the stream. You'll likely spot geese or ducks feeding up and down the chute on this last stretch of your hike.

# LITTLE CREEK NATURE AREA

## KEY AT-A-GLANCE INFORMATION

**LENGTH:** 3 miles

**CONFIGURATION:** Network of interconnecting loops

**DIFFICULTY:** Very easy

**SCENERY:** Trails at Little Creek explore forested hills and hollows, a prairie, and a creek bottomland. From the trailhead you'll have a nice view of the downtown St. Louis skyline.

**EXPOSURE:** Shady, with several open areas

**TRAFFIC:** Medium

**TRAIL SURFACE:** Packed earth

**HIKING TIME:** 1–2 hours

**ACCESS:** Visitor center open 9 a.m.–4 p.m. weekdays; trails open all week

**MAPS:** Florissant USGS topo; trail map available at visitor center

**FACILITIES:** Restrooms, water, visitor center

**SPECIAL COMMENTS:** Pets must be leashed; no collecting of rocks, plants, or any other natural features; no smoking on the grounds

## GPS TRAILHEAD COORDINATES (PARK ENTRANCE)

| | |
|---|---|
| UTM ZONE (WGS84) | 15S |
| EASTING | 735322 |
| NORTHING | 4295003 |
| LATITUDE–LONGITUDE | |
| NORTH | N38° 46' 20.5779'' |
| WEST | W90° 17' 28.6051'' |

## IN BRIEF

Little Creek Nature Area features a beautiful network of trails built and maintained by the students and teachers of the Ferguson-Florissant School District. In addition to the usual hills, hollows, and streams, Little Creek's trails take you past a restored log cabin and an overgrown graveyard.

## DESCRIPTION

As public lands go, Little Creek Nature Area is truly unique. It's not under the control of a park system, a conservation department, or any traditional land-management agency. Little Creek belongs to the Ferguson-Florissant School District, and the property is maintained by students and faculty. The district bought the land in 1968 to enhance its outdoor science program. Since then they've developed a microsize working farm, built classrooms, designed a visitor center in the old farmhouse, and nurtured a small wildland behind the complex.

On Little Creek's 97 acres, thousands of students learn land stewardship, biology, and environmental sciences. They also study animals on the nature area's farm, where chickens, pigs, goats, and sheep are raised. Sheep-shearing days are held in May, when students learn how sheep are shorn, how the wool is carded, and how it's spun into material. The students also do land-maintenance projects, planting windbreaks, handling prairie burns, and—happily for us hikers—constructing an incredibly well-built trail system, complete with wooden bridges named after wild critters that might roam Little Creek.

## DIRECTIONS

Little Creek Nature Area is located at 2955 Dunn Road, in Florissant. Dunn Road is the north service road for I-270, and Little Creek is halfway between the Elizabeth/Washington and West Florissant Road exits.

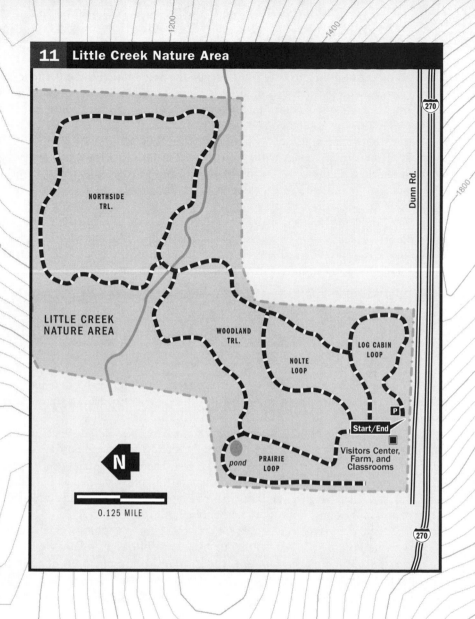

NORTHSIDE
TRL.

LITTLE CREEK
NATURE AREA

WOODLAND
TRL.

NOLTE
LOOP

LOG CABIN
LOOP

Dunn Rd.

270

pond

PRAIRIE
LOOP

Start/End

Visitors Center,
Farm, and
Classrooms

270

N

0.125 MILE

The trail system consists of five overlapping loops. Every intersection is clearly marked with color-coded arrows on posts, but there are no markings between the junctions. The 0.3-mile Log Cabin Loop, marked with yellow at the junctions, goes past—you guessed—a log cabin. Though it was brought in from somewhere else, it was restored on the site where a log cabin stood in the mid-1900s. Perhaps it belonged to the Pohlman family, whose overgrown, 1800s-era graveyard you'll pass farther out on the Log Cabin Loop.

The Log Cabin Loop is a noisy hike, right next to busy I-270. As you move to the back of the property you'll escape the noise entirely. The 0.4-mile Nolte Loop, marked with green arrows at intersections, is much quieter. It goes north from the farm, descends into a hollow full of huge trees, then turns back south and climbs up to T into the Log Cabin Loop.

The Nolte shares part of its path with the Woodland Trail. At 0.8 miles, the Woodland Trail, marked with red arrows at intersections, is the second longest trail at Little Creek. For most of its length the path lives up to its name, traveling through deep woods. It parallels Little Creek on its northern reaches and goes past Frog Pond just before joining with the Nolte.

The Woodland Trail shares its western portion with the 0.4-mile Prairie Loop, marked with black arrows at intersections. The Prairie Loop travels through open areas with views of the city all around, so it doesn't feel very wild. Still it's an interesting walk. It passes an interpretive display of a windbreak planted by the students in 1987 and another on prairie-restoration work. Also, it was on the Prairie Loop that I once watched a sharp-shinned hawk nab a songbird one winter day and hunker in the sun under a tree to enjoy its meal.

The 1-mile Northside Trail is the longest loop in Little Creek. It meanders along the creek for a fourth of its length, then makes a winding loop through the hills at the north end of the nature area. The Northside Loop, deep in the property's back side, is the most peaceful and wild hike at Little Creek. By the time you hike back to the Northside Trail, walk around the loop, and make your way back to the trailhead, you'll have hiked 2 miles.

If you can, come to Little Creek during normal business hours. The visitor center is open then, and you can get maps of the trail system. The center houses a fascinating display assembled by the St. Louis Science Center. There's an excellent set of exhibits about prehistoric societies, focusing on the Mound Culture that once flourished in the St. Louis area. There are maps and drawings of a typical village, and artifacts like pottery shards, projectile points, stone tools, household items, and figurines.

While at the visitor center, ask for a copy of the pamphlet "Some Historical Notes on the Little Creek Wildlife Area," by John Albin. Albin's family bought this property in 1930, when it was rural countryside along old Route 66. His short account of growing up in the once-bucolic area is a fun read. His story about finding Native American artifacts goes well with the exhibits, and his notes about Route 66's hobos are fascinating.

## ▶ NEARBY ACTIVITIES

A few miles east of Little Creek Nature Area is the historic Chain of Rocks Bridge, where old Route 66 crossed the Mississippi. The once-abandoned bridge has been restored as a pedestrian and bicycle path and ties into a whole network of bicycling routes.

# LONE ELK COUNTY PARK

## ▶ IN BRIEF

While exploring Lone Elk Park on the White Bison Trail, you'll probably hike right past the park's elk and deer herds, and in the neighboring World Bird Sanctuary you'll see eagles, owls, and myriad other birds. Bring your camera and binoculars!

## ▶ DESCRIPTION

Lone Elk County Park, where you'll hike past elk and deer and view bison from the park's scenic drive, wasn't always such a peaceful place. During World War II and the Korean Conflict, property that's now within Lone Elk and the neighboring Tyson Research Center and West Tyson County Park was an ammunition storage and testing site. Earth and concrete bunkers held munitions, armed guards roamed the area, and the hills echoed with the sound of gunfire from ammo testing. Between the wars, St. Louis County bought the land, and elk, bison, and deer were introduced to the area as part of the short-lived Tyson Valley Park. The army reacquired the land during the Korean Conflict, removed the buffalo, and left the elk and deer to roam the landscape. When a bull in rut rammed one of their vehicles, though, the army decided to shoot the elk herd.

Even with all that ammo at their disposal, the army missed one elk. And when the county bought the land in the early 1960s to again develop a park, employees spotted a majestic bull living secretively in the park's hollows. Unseen by humans for nearly ten years, he was named the "Lone Elk," and eventually became the park's namesake. Students in the Rockwoods School District, fired up over the sad plight of the lonely elk, teamed with the Lions Club

## ▶ DIRECTIONS

From I-44, take Exit 272 for Valley Park–Fenton–MO 141. Access the North Outer Road and drive 2 miles west to the park entrance.

## ⓘ KEY AT-A-GLANCE INFORMATION

**LENGTH:** 3.25 miles, with optional 0.5-mile hike at the World Bird Sanctuary

**CONFIGURATION:** Loop

**DIFFICULTY:** Easy

**SCENERY:** Wooded hills and deep hollows around a small lake

**EXPOSURE:** Shady throughout

**TRAFFIC:** Medium

**TRAIL SURFACE:** Packed earth and gravel

**HIKING TIME:** 1–2 hours

**ACCESS:** Park open from 8 a.m.–sunset; World Bird Sanctuary open 8 a.m.–5 p.m.

**MAPS:** Available from County Parks in Clayton; Manchester USGS topo

**FACILITIES:** Restrooms, water, picnic sites, picnic shelters

**SPECIAL COMMENTS:** No pets—they'll chase or spook the elk and deer. Nor should you closely approach these unpredictable wild animals.

**GPS TRAILHEAD COORDINATES (PARK ENTRANCE)**

| UTM ZONE (WGS84) | 15S |
| --- | --- |
| EASTING | 715303 |
| NORTHING | 4267609 |
| LATITUDE-LONGITUDE | |
| NORTH | N38° 31' 51.0786'' |
| WEST | W90° 31' 47.9643'' |

N

0.25 MILE

LONE ELK
COUNTY PARK

CASTLEWOOD
STATE PARK

World Bird
Sanctuary

North Outer Rd.

44

Park Rd.

CHUBB TRL.
(TO WEST
TYSON)

shelter

Start/End

P

shelter

Park Rd.

Park Rd.

44

1200

1400

1800

1700

1300

1200

1600

1500

1500

1400

1300

1200

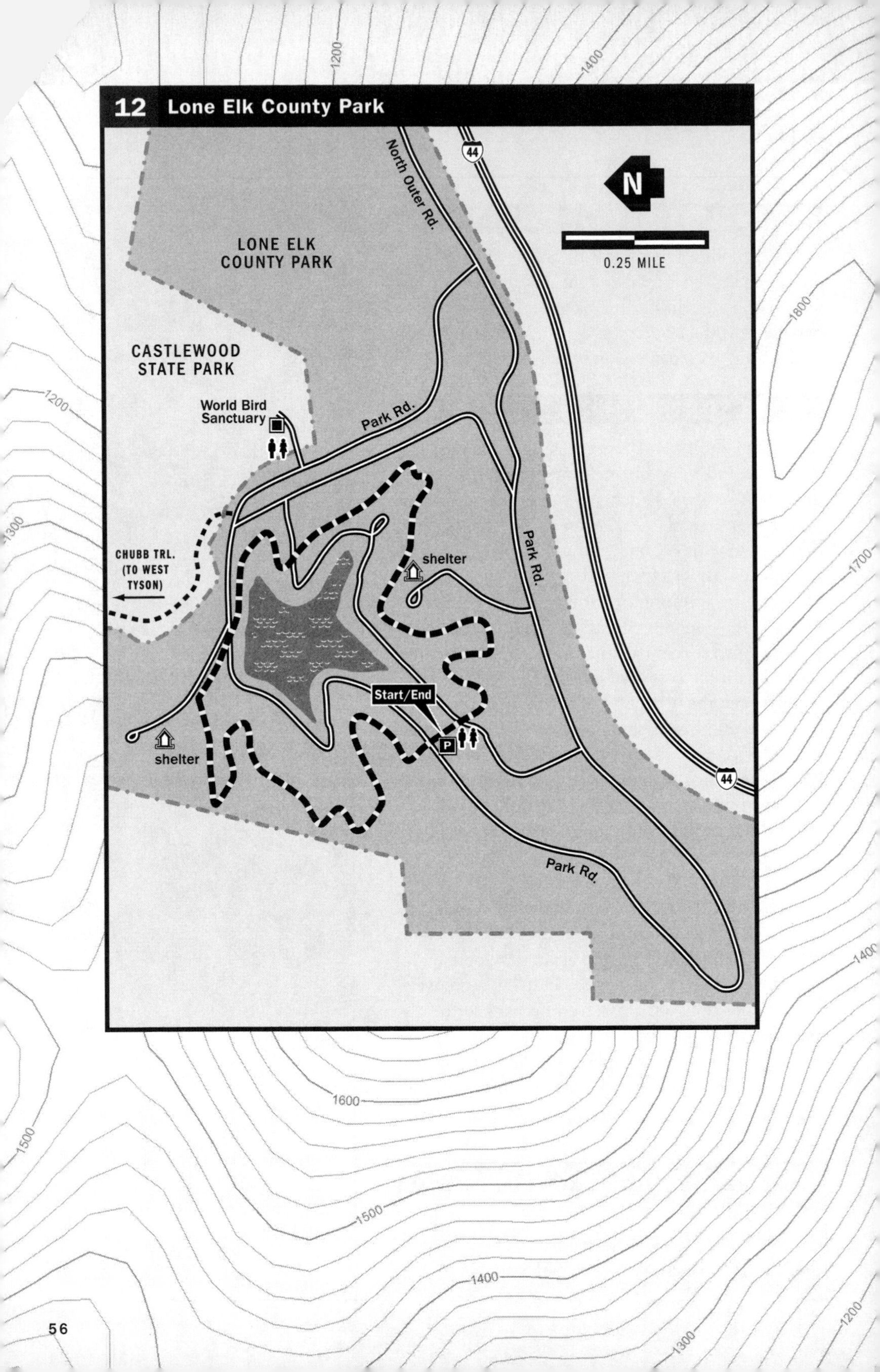

to raise money to buy additional elk for the new park. In 1966, a half-dozen elk imported from Yellowstone National Park were released in the park, and a bison herd was added to St. Louis's new wildlife park in the early 1970s.

Elk, bison, and deer aren't the only wildlife on display for your visit to Lone Elk. The World Bird Sanctuary, an educational organization dedicated to rescuing and preserving threatened species and their habitat, is on Lone Elk's entrance road. The sanctuary has restrooms, water, cold drinks, and a fascinating visitor center where you can closely observe raptors, tortoises, and several species of snakes.

The sanctuary has an easy half-mile hike that's a perfect warm-up for the trail in Lone Elk. It begins at the end of the pedestrian-only gravel drive leading from the parking lot past enclosures housing eagles, owls, and other birds. If your timing is right, you can watch the owls chow down on mice, too. This easy trail wanders a quarter mile to the Meramec River bottomlands, passing bird-feeding stations along the way. One of the stations has a photography and viewing blind, so bring your camera and binoculars. You can make this one-way hike into a loop by following the gravel road at the bottom of the hill back to the sanctuary entrance. Whatever option you choose, you'll hike just over a half mile. On a winter hike on the sanctuary's trail I once spotted an eagle perched above the Meramec—quite a contrast to the injured and recovering eagles in captivity back up the hill.

The 3.25-mile White Bison Trail in Lone Elk is longer and tougher, but even more packed with wildlife. You'll probably hike within a few yards of deer and elk, and during mating season you'll hear the bulls bugling. On your way to the trail, stop at the observation tower near the park entrance to survey the landscape you'll explore on the White Bison. The trail starts from either end of the parking lot at the Lone Elk visitor center west of the park lake. Marked with brown signs bearing white bison silhouettes and the word "Trail," it's a single-track path circumnavigating the lake. You'll often hear the lake's geese and ducks honking and quacking as you wander the surrounding hills. The White Bison Trail is a hilly path. But since ascents are gently graded, hikers of all fitness levels will enjoy this easy trail.

For no particular reason, I prefer hiking the White Bison clockwise. Starting from the north end of the old visitor center parking lot, look for a White Bison Trail sign at the base of the hill overlooking the picnic area. Cross a little bridge past the sign and start climbing gently northeast. There are nice vistas of the lake along the trail, especially during winter when the trees are bare. From several high points you'll catch glimpses of the Meramec River bluffs far to the north. As you wind through the hills and hollows above the lake you'll soon notice the trail surface on north- and east-facing slopes is packed earth that gets sloppy when wet, while south- and west-facing slopes are gravelly and offer firm hiking surfaces in all kinds of weather.

The first 1.25 miles wind over the landscape between the old visitor center and the Whitetail Shelter. At the 1-mile point there's an easy place to lose your way. You'll have just completed a looping turn on a short stretch of old road that leaves you heading west toward the boundary fence. Just after a trail marker the path breaks north off the old road and swings back east. Since there's no arrow on the marker, it's easy to miss this turn and continue hiking the road to the park boundary, where you'll mistakenly follow an unofficial path north along the fence, cross a dry wash, then follow an open meadow to the Whitetail Shelter. If you do make this mistake, just follow the paved road south 100 yards from the shelter and you'll rejoin the White Bison where it hits the paved road just south of the dry wash.

The trail turns south and follows the shelter access road 0.1 mile to the park's loop road, then crosses the loop road next to the lake's dam. Here you'll see another path breaking right to follow the water's edge. While not an official trail, it's a nice lakeside shortcut that rejoins the White Bison after a quarter-mile hike along the lake. The White Bison ascends from the road crossing, passes through a small boulder field, and loops around a thumb of the lake below the observation tower. After intersecting with the shortcut trail, it crosses the park road and enters Elk Hollow.

The remaining 1.5 miles of the White Bison Trail are my favorite part of the hike. Though you can see and hear park roads from most parts of the White Bison, this last stretch is, with a few exceptions, farther from park roads and feels more isolated. The trail wanders up and down the sides of several of deep, forested hollows and crosses intermittent streams. Since elk and deer often hang out on this side of the park, you may get to hike with the wild critters on this last stretch of the White Bison. The deer often won't move until you're within five yards of them. Don't approach any of the animals too closely. They should be respected as the unpredictable wild creatures that they are. Use your binoculars for close examination of the magnificent antlered elk that live along the trail.

Your hike on the White Bison ends at the south end of the visitor center parking lot. If you want to do a few more miles, go to the trailhead on the park entrance road near the World Bird Sanctuary and hike the Castlewood Loop. It's part of the spectacular Chubb Trail (page 23), a path that explores three parks along the Meramec River.

# POWDER VALLEY NATURE CENTER

## ▶ IN BRIEF

Short, easy trails, excellent interpretive displays, and an awesome nature center make Powder Valley the perfect place for outdoor enthusiasts of all ages to explore and learn about the natural world.

## ▶ DESCRIPTION

The tame trails surrounded by urban subdivisions at Powder Valley don't offer long hikes and a wilderness experience, but this is still a wonderful place to visit. Quickly accessible from anywhere in the southern half of the St. Louis metro area, it's the perfect place for a quick evening hike, a brief lunchtime escape to the woods, a short getaway from winter-induced cabin fever, or an easy and educational walk with the kids. Paved trails make it easy to roll that stroller along, though you may huff and puff a little if you choose to push it up the hills on the Hickory Ridge and Broken Ridge trails. For a break you can relax at one of the many benches scattered liberally along the trails at Powder Valley.

Powder Valley's big attraction lies in its outdoor-education opportunities. You may end up spending as much time in the nature center as you do on the trail. It's full of fascinating exhibits, including many interactive displays for the kids. Nature-photography exhibits usually line the hallways. Comfortable armchairs sit before a huge wall of windows, looking out on a set of feeders where hundreds of birds fight for their daily grub. Sometimes raccoons climb to the feeders and join the competition. At another display, you look deep into a pool containing native Missouri turtles,

## ℹ KEY AT-A-GLANCE INFORMATION

**LENGTH:** 2.2 miles on 3 short trails

**CONFIGURATION:** Loops

**DIFFICULTY:** Very easy

**SCENERY:** Wooded hills and hollows

**EXPOSURE:** Shady throughout

**TRAFFIC:** Heavy

**TRAIL SURFACE:** Paved

**HIKING TIME:** 2 hours

**ACCESS:** Trails open 8 a.m. daily; close 8 p.m. during Daylight Savings Time, 6 p.m. during Standard Time; nature center open 8 a.m.–5 p.m.

**MAPS:** Trail map available at nature center; Kirkwood USGS topo

**FACILITIES:** Water, restrooms, phone, cold drink machine at trailhead

**SPECIAL COMMENTS:** No pets; no trail running; no removal of plants, rocks, or other natural objects

## ▶ DIRECTIONS

From I-44 and Lindbergh Road, drive a half mile south on Lindbergh to Watson Road. Drive a half mile west on Watson to Geyer Road. Go a short distance north on Geyer, cross over I-44, and turn left onto Cragwold Road. Follow Cragwold 1 mile to Powder Valley Nature Center.

## GPS TRAILHEAD COORDINATES (PARK ENTRANCE)

| | |
|---|---|
| UTM ZONE (WGS84) | 15S |
| EASTING | 724125 |
| NORTHING | 4270209 |
| LATITUDE-LONGITUDE | |
| NORTH | N38° 33' 7.5152'' |
| WEST | W90° 25' 40.9462'' |

**13** Powder Valley Nature Center

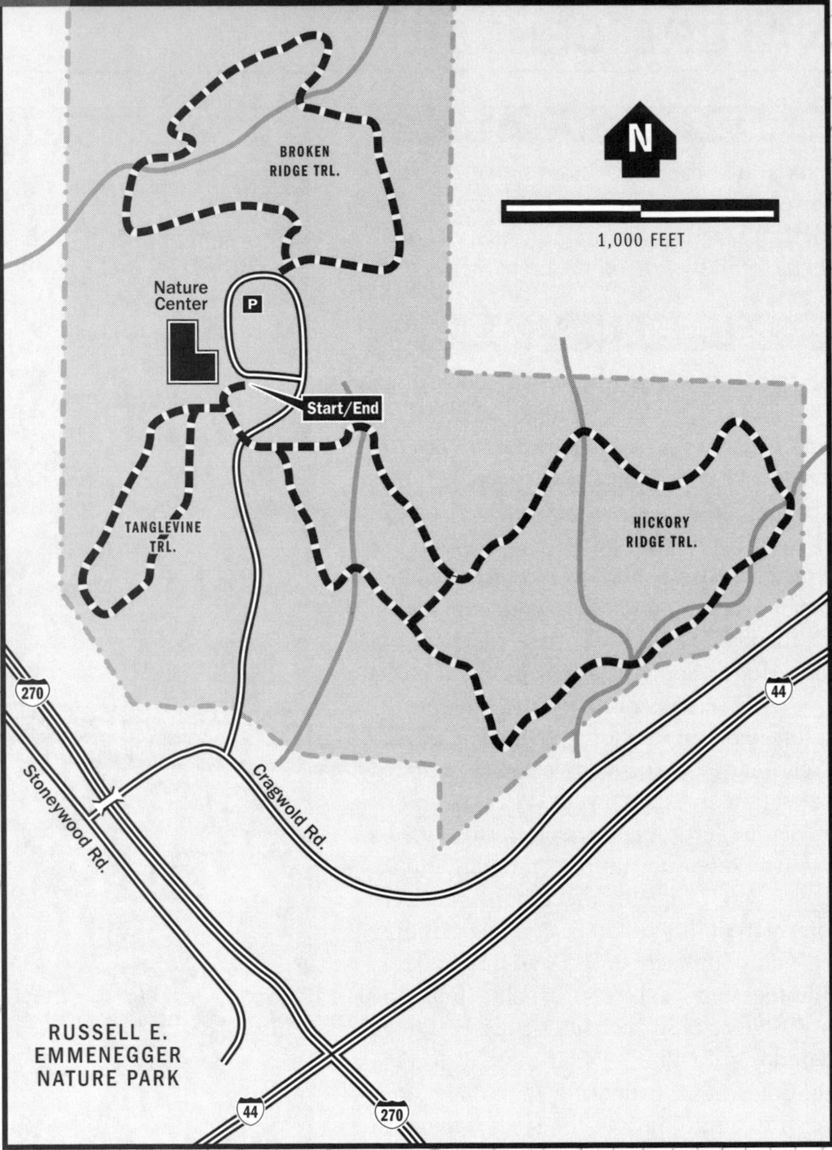

BROKEN RIDGE TRL.

N

1,000 FEET

Nature Center

P

Start/End

TANGLEVINE TRL.

HICKORY RIDGE TRL.

270

44

Stoneywood Rd.

Cragwold Rd.

44

270

RUSSELL E. EMMENEGGER NATURE PARK

then go to the center's lower level and examine them close-up through the pool's glass sides. My favorite exhibit is the glass-encased indoor beehive, where transparent tubes leading from the building's wall give bees access between the hive and the outdoors. It's fascinating to watch them coming and going, and stumbling all over each other in seeming confusion as they build honeycombs and make honey in the glass-walled hive.

This nature center is the perfect stop to study up on Missouri outdoors before venturing onto wilder trails further south in the Ozarks. In the gift shop you'll find trail guides and identification books for Missouri birds, flowers, trees, and other flora and fauna. There are even tapes for identifying birds and frogs by their calls. Free flyers are available on such topics as owls, snakes, spiders, frogs, wildflowers, and the like. Handouts also cover such topics as land improvement for wildlife and birdhouse construction. Maps for other conservation areas in the St. Louis region are available at the shop, along with a wide variety of nature gifts perfect for birthdays, Christmas, or your own wall or bookshelf. The center even has a library with hundreds of nature and natural science books, complete with tables and a quiet study area.

The easiest hike at Powder Valley is the Tanglevine Trail. It starts from a trailhead at the south end of the parking lot and building complex, where you'll find water, restrooms, soda and juice machines, a shelter, and an interesting photo display of birds you might see in Powder Valley. The wheelchair-accessible Tanglevine is really just a level and paved 0.3-mile walk, made interesting with interpretive signboards along the trail. You'll learn to make sense of Missouri's tangled underbrush by studying such exhibits as "Know Your Vines," "Backyard Café," and "Backyard Waste or Backyard Habitat?"

The Hickory Ridge Trail, the longest and hilliest hike in Powder Valley, begins from the same trailhead as the Tanglevine. It's a 1.2-mile hike that can be shortened to a half mile via a cutoff trail. A 0.1-mile spur leading south from the trailhead crosses Powder Valley's entrance road on an elevated bridge to join the loop. One steep climb and several smaller hills will challenge you on this trail, but benches at scenic spots offer plenty of comfortable breaks. On the Hickory Ridge, you'll see boulders and rock outcroppings, hike next to a pretty little stream, cross creeks and dry washes on wooden bridges, and pass through Powder Valley's Savannah Restoration Area.

The 0.7-mile Broken Ridge Trail starts from the opposite end of the parking lot from the other two trails. You'll see its sign at the north end of the parking lot as you drive into Powder Valley. It's just another nice paved walk in the woods, with two easy hills to climb and benches at scenic spots. On the Broken Ridge you'll get a lesson on Missouri forests. Signs scattered along the path identify trees, specify their normal height ranges, and describe their uses. You'll learn that mockernut hickory, considered the finest of all hickories, is the one used for tool handles and athletic equipment, and that sassafras leaves are used not only for tea but also for root beer.

Don't blow off Powder Valley because its hikes are so short and easy. Take advantage of Powder Valley Nature Center's educational opportunities, and the understanding of nature you develop will enhance your and your children's hiking experiences all over the Ozarks. Hiking through natural beauty without knowing much about it is like flipping through a book in a foreign language—you can admire the pretty pictures, but you'll miss the fascinating story written in the text. Visits to Powder Valley will teach you how to read the story all around you as you wander through the outdoors.

## ▶ NEARBY ACTIVITIES

Additional hiking can be accessed at nearby Russell E. Emmenegger Nature Park (page 34), just across I-270 from Powder Valley, and at Greensfelder (page 45), West Tyson, and Lone Elk (page 55) county parks a few miles west on I-44. Laumeier Sculpture Park (**www.laumeier.com**), with easy walks past fascinating outdoor artwork, is just to the south of Powder Valley. Nearby downtown Kirkwood has several excellent bakeries, restaurants, and coffee shops for your posthike enjoyment (**www.ci.kirkwood.mo.us**).

# QUEENY PARK

## ▶ IN BRIEF

Queeny Park, a green oasis in the heart of west St. Louis County's burgeoning suburbs, offers wonderful hiking, trail-running, and cross-country-skiing opportunities on a laid-back trail system suitable for nature lovers of all levels.

## ▶ DESCRIPTION

Though Queeny Park's landscape has been developed for nearly two centuries, this urban jewel first became a park only 25 years ago. The Jarville House, located near the park's current trailhead, was built in 1853 by John Mathias Hyacinthe Renard. For the next 120 years, the Jarville House and the surrounding land served as a country estate for several well-to-do families. The last of these was Edgar M. Queeny, president of the Monsanto Company, who expanded the landholding to 570 acres, updated old buildings, and added new ones. Queeny sold the property to a real estate company in 1962 in order to raise money for Barnes Hospital. In the late 1960s, St. Louis County authorized a bond issue to buy the estate. Aided by a $1 million pledge from Queeny's widow, Ethel, the purchase was made and Queeny Park was dedicated in late 1974.

The Jarville House was remodeled and expanded in 1990, when the American Kennel Club moved its Dog Museum to St. Louis and the Queenys' old carriage house became the museum's gift shop. Touring the museum and gift shop is an excellent way to end your hike in Queeny Park. Picnic shelters and lots of open picnic sites dot the park's center, and several lakes offer fishing. The

## ▶ DIRECTIONS

From I-64–US 40, drive 2 miles south on Mason Road to Queeny Park. Trailhead parking is on the western side of Mason Road, next to the Dog Museum and Queeny Barn at 1721 Mason Road.

### ℹ KEY AT-A-GLANCE INFORMATION

**LENGTH:** 7 miles on 6 trails

**CONFIGURATION:** Network of interconnecting trails

**DIFFICULTY:** Easy–moderate

**SCENERY:** Wooded hills with scattered meadows and small prairies

**EXPOSURE:** Mostly shaded paths in the woods with several wide-open stretches through grassy meadows

**TRAFFIC:** Heavy

**TRAIL SURFACE:** Mostly dirt and vehicle-width gravel roads interspersed with short paved sections and occasional stretches of single-track

**HIKING TIME:** 2–3 hours for the Hawk Ridge Trail; 1 hour or less for all other trails

**ACCESS:** Open 7 a.m.–half-hour after sunset

**MAPS:** Available at Dog Museum or at county parks office in Clayton; Kirkwood and Creve Coeur USGS topos

**FACILITIES:** Water, restrooms, picnic areas, shelters, playground, swimming pool, rec complex, fishing lakes, museum

**SPECIAL COMMENTS:** Keep an eye peeled for mountain bikers and equestrians with whom you'll share Queeny's trails

**GPS TRAILHEAD COORDINATES (PARK ENTRANCE)**

| | | |
|---|---|---|
| UTM ZONE (WGS84) | 15S | |
| | EASTING | 718882 |
| | NORTHING | 4276996 |
| LATITUDE–LONGITUDE | | |
| | NORTH | N38° 36' 52.1899'' |
| | WEST | W90° 29' 9.6552'' |

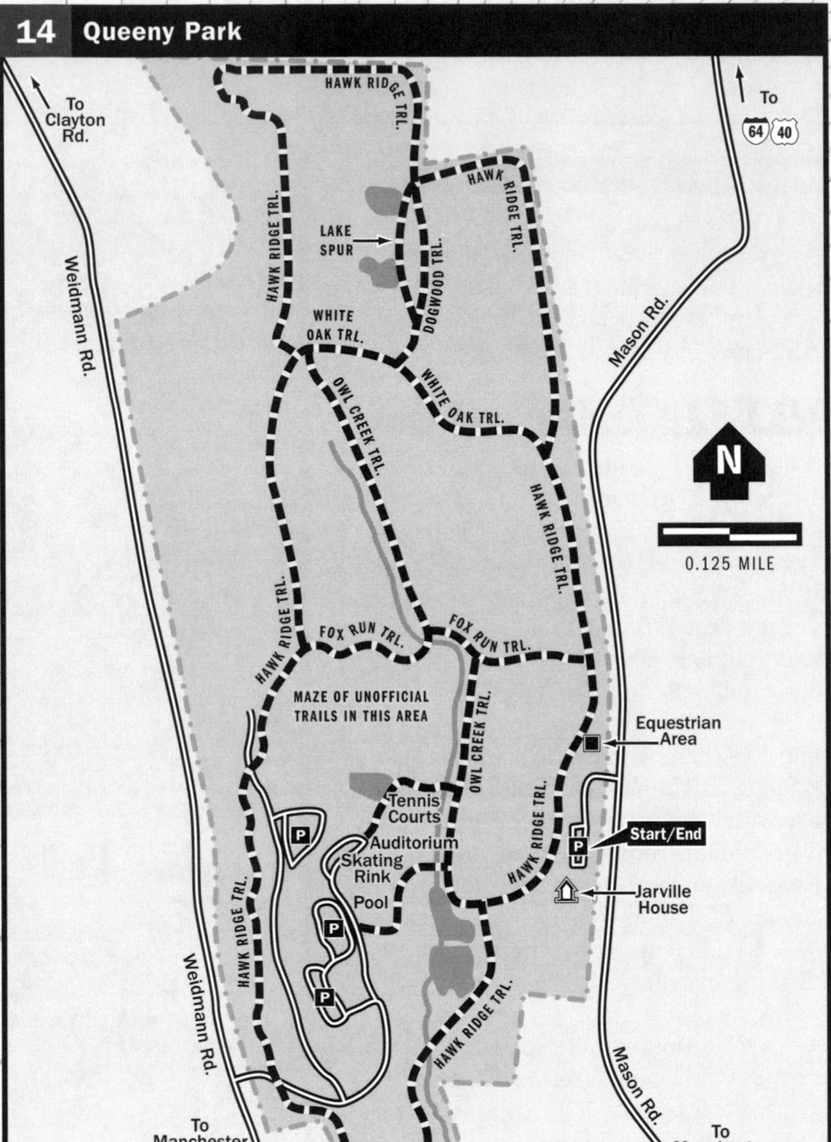

To Clayton Rd.

To 64 40

HAWK RIDGE TRL.

HAWK RIDGE TRL.

Weidmann Rd.

LAKE SPUR

DOGWOOD TRL.

WHITE OAK TRL.

WHITE OAK TRL.

OWL CREEK TRL.

Mason Rd.

HAWK RIDGE TRL.

N

0.125 MILE

HAWK RIDGE TRL.

FOX RUN TRL.

FOX RUN TRL.

MAZE OF UNOFFICIAL TRAILS IN THIS AREA

OWL CREEK TRL.

Equestrian Area

P

Tennis Courts

Auditorium

Skating Rink

Pool

HAWK RIDGE TRL.

P

P

HAWK RIDGE TRL.

P P Start/End

Jarville House

Weidmann Rd.

HAWK RIDGE TRL.

HAWK RIDGE TRL.

To Manchester Rd.

Mason Rd.

To Manchester Rd.

Greensfelder Recreation Complex in the middle of Queeny has tennis courts, an indoor ice-skating rink, an outdoor roller-skating rink, an Olympic-size pool, and a playground. In summer, the St. Louis Symphony holds the Queeny Pops Concerts at the rec complex. What a deal! Where else could you end a hike by relaxing to the strains of fine symphonic music? If you want to stick to the outdoor atmosphere, arrange for your group to enjoy one of the park staff's hayrides and bonfires after your hike.

The long hike in Queeny Park is the 4.5-mile Hawk Ridge Trail. Roughly following the park perimeter, this loop hike connects the park's other five trails. These other routes are point-to-point hikes cutting across the loop formed by the fairly long Hawk Ridge, letting you choose shorter loop options if you aren't up to the entire perimeter hike. Most trails at Queeny Park are wide, smooth, and well graded, making them popular trail-running or cross-country skiing routes. Horseback riding is another popular activity at Queeny, so be on the lookout for equestrians while hiking here. When meeting horses, move to the downhill side of the trail and stand quietly while they pass.

Traveling in a clockwise direction, the Hawk Ridge Trail leaves the Jarville House trailhead on a paved path that heads southwest. It descends to the park center near the Corporate Picnic Area, where you'll find restrooms and water. The trail swings south, passes a couple of ponds, and crosses a creek on a covered bridge. Several single-track paths break left into the woods. They don't really go anywhere, but are fun short hikes in the undergrowth—a nice contrast to the wide, paved path of the southeast part of the Hawk Ridge Trail. Sporadic trail markings and several side trails make route-finding in this southern half of the Hawk Ridge confusing at times. Any sidetracks you end up on will soon fade or hit the park boundary, so you won't be lost for long. Just retrace your steps back to the main trail and continue.

The vaguest part of the loop begins just past the covered bridge, where the pavement ends and the trail breaks south, crosses the eastern end of a long, grassy picnic area, and heads into the woods along a brook. You'll soon come to a fork, where you should bear right. The left fork wanders through the woods for a quarter mile before ending at private property. The right fork swings west and parallels the south boundary of Queeny, crosses a sawdust-covered path that would take you north to the grassy picnic area, pushes through some undergrowth, then appears to end at the back of a subdivision. Turn north here, follow the open grassy area until you cross the park's west entrance road, then look for the trail in the trees at the open field's western edge. You'll intersect several horse trails along the way and have numerous opportunities to choose the wrong one, but eventually you'll hit a paved path leading north past a house. Just past the house, the trail becomes gravel again, passes a bench, then comes to the junction with the Fox Run Trail.

After the Fox Run junction it's much easier to find your way. Most intersections in the wilder north part of Queeny are marked, and fewer side trails exist to confuse you. You could turn east from this junction and follow the Fox Run Trail across the park and back to the trailhead, enjoying a wooded descent, hiking along a stream, and ascending past the park nursery on your way back to the Jarville House and the trailhead. Continuing north on the Hawk Ridge takes you into the less-developed north half of Queeny. This stretch of trail passes a 240-year-old white oak before reaching the junction with the Owl Creek and White Oak trails.

The Owl Creek Trail heads southeast from this junction. It descends to the park's bottomlands, passing several trees with signboards identifying the trees and describing their characteristics and uses. It intersects with the Fox Run Trail in the bottomlands, joins it for a while, then leaves it to continue south behind some old corrals. After the corrals, the Owl Creek joins a paved trail coming from the Greensfelder Recreation Complex and continues south along a creek, ending at the Corporate Picnic Shelter. The White Oak Trail goes east from the junction with the Hawk Ridge and Owl Creek trails and wanders through quiet forests for a half mile before rejoining the Hawk Ridge Trail on the eastern side of Queeny Park.

The Hawk Ridge continues north, passes through an equestrian trials area, then enters my favorite part of the park—the open, peaceful high prairie in the northern end of Queeny. It's a high, open meadow with tall grasses that sway and rustle in the wind, and expansive views of the sky that are great for admiring sunrises and sunsets. Benches are scattered about for relaxing and enjoying this surprisingly quiet, empty space in the busy suburbs. In the prairie area's northwest corner, park staff maintain an experimental flowering meadow. There you'll see purple cornflower, black-eyed Susan, Indian blanket, Indian paintbrush, and many more colorful wildflowers. The trail follows the perimeter of this beautiful grassland for a mile before reentering the forest in the northeast part of the park.

Immediately after reentering the woods, the Hawk Ridge intersects with the Dogwood Trail. The Dogwood heads 0.3 miles south to a T intersection with the White Oak Trail, passing a 180-year-old hickory along the way. The Lake Spur breaks off the Dogwood Trail and goes to a couple of small lakes. You'll walk right across the dam of one of these pools in the woods. These quiet pools in the woods are peaceful spots, perfect for a midhike picnic.

From its intersection with the Dogwood Trail, the Hawk Ridge heads east in thick forest that contrasts wonderfully with the wide-open prairie it recently explored. Much of it follows the park boundary, looking into the backyards of homes abutting Queeny, but it's still a secluded and quiet hike. Several short and stiff climbs will challenge you on this part of the Hawk Ridge before you swing south past junctions with the White Oak and Fox Run trails, pass through a natural area with identified trees, then parallel Mason Road back to the trailhead near the Jarville House and the AKC Dog Museum.

Sound confusing? Well, with sporadic markings and numerous unofficial side trails, the trail system at Queeny can be quite a tangle for first-time visitors to the park. Queeny is a small place, though, bounded by roads and subdivisions, so you can't get too lost. It doesn't take very long to get to know the place, either. After a few hikes in this urban hideaway, you'll learn the lay of the land and will love wandering Queeny's fascinating maze of trails.

# ROCKWOODS RANGE

## ▶ IN BRIEF

Compared with the popular Rockwoods Reservation next door, Rockwoods Range is a quiet and relatively undiscovered 1,400 acres of near-wilderness in the busy suburbs of St. Louis.

## ▶ DESCRIPTION

Rockwoods Range is a bit of wilderness in the booming suburbs of southwest St. Louis County. Hiking this 7-mile system feels more like being deep in the Ozarks than rubbing elbows with a sprawling metropolitan center. Furthermore, Rockwoods Range is relatively undiscovered compared with the more-popular trails in nearby Rockwoods Reservation and Greensfelder and West Tyson county parks. It's one of the great escapes in the immediate St. Louis area.

Rockwoods Range's 1,388 acres became part of Missouri's public lands in 1943, when A. P. Greensfelder donated the land to the Missouri Department of Conservation. One of the first members of the state's Conservation Commission, Greensfelder was instrumental in the creation of Rockwoods Reservation in 1938 and also donated property for Greensfelder County Park. Thanks to his farsighted efforts, these three contiguous tracts of once-isolated landscape form a 4,955-acre green-space getaway in the St. Louis suburbs. While hiking in Greensfelder's legacy, you'll enjoy lush woodlands, rock outcroppings,

## ▶ DIRECTIONS

From I-44, take Exit 261, Allenton Road–Six Flags. Drive west on Fox Creek Road, which is I-44's north outer road. At 1.5 miles down Fox Creek, shortly after the road curves north away from I-44, you'll see the south trailhead and parking area on the left. The north trailhead is an additional 2.5 miles north on the east side of Fox Creek Road.

## ⓘ KEY AT-A-GLANCE INFORMATION

**LENGTH:** 7 miles

**CONFIGURATION:** 3-mile loop with 2 spurs

**DIFFICULTY:** Easy–moderate

**SCENERY:** Forested ridges and hollows

**EXPOSURE:** Shady throughout

**TRAFFIC:** Light

**TRAIL SURFACE:** Packed earth and gravel with several rugged and rocky sections

**HIKING TIME:** 2–3 hours

**ACCESS:** Open sunrise–half-hour after sunset

**MAPS:** Maps available at the Rockwoods Reservation headquarters north of Eureka; Eureka USGS topo

**FACILITIES:** None

**SPECIAL COMMENTS:** Pets on leash only; watch for horses on this popular equestrian trail; no cutting or removal of vegetation, except for collection of nuts, berries, fruits, and mushrooms for personal consumption

**GPS TRAILHEAD COORDINATES (SOUTH TRAILHEAD)**

| UTM ZONE (WGS84) | 15S |
|---|---|
| EASTING | 700444 |
| NORTHING | 4264214 |
| LATITUDE-LONGITUDE | |
| NORTH | N38° 30' 13.5149'' |
| WEST | W90° 42' 4.6724'' |

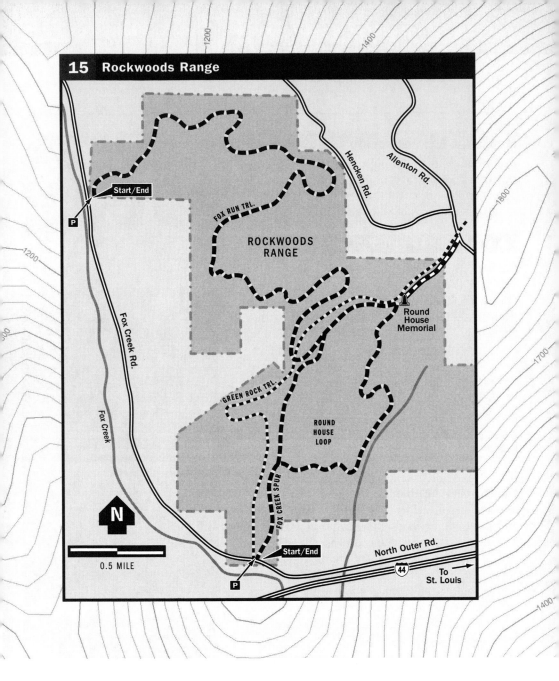

## 15  Rockwoods Range

sinkholes, and rocky intermittent streams. The Green Rock Trail connects Rockwoods Range to neighboring Greensfelder Park and Rockwoods Reservation to form a 40-mile trail network through this expansive landscape of forested hills and hollows.

Hikes in Rockwoods Range follow a network of three trails—the Fox Creek Spur, the Round House Loop, and the Fox Run Trail. The Round House is the heart of this trail system, and the other two trails are spurs leading from their trailheads to the Round House Loop. The Fox Creek Spur is nothing fancy, just a steady 0.6-mile climb from the south trailhead to the southwest reaches of the Round House Loop. It's the easy access if all you want to do is hike the Round House and then head home.

The 3.5-mile Fox Run Trail is the fancy one. My favorite hike in Rockwoods Range, the Fox Run is narrow, crooked, filled with lots of ups and downs, and really lost and wild feeling. Since it's a long point-to-point spur to the Round House that can't be made into a loop, Fox Run is the least-used trail on Rockwoods Range—and that's exactly why you should hike it. From the north trailhead you'll climb steeply at first on the Fox Run, then ease into a gentle uphill for a quarter mile. You'll then level out to run along a ridge for a half mile, make a sharp descent followed by a steep climb onto a neighboring ridge, and follow its spine for nearly a mile. A couple of benches on this ridgeline run are perfect for admiring vistas of the surrounding countryside, especially in winter when the trees are bare. You'll leave the ridge a short way past the second bench, do several quick ups and downs over side hollows feeding into Fox Creek, cross the Green Rock Trail, and climb onto a ridge to join the Round House Loop on its northwest side.

The Round House Loop is named for A. P. Greensfelder's country home, which was designed with a circular floor plan. It once stood in what is now Greensfelder Park, adjacent to the park's boundary with Rockwoods Range. The site is now called the Round House Memorial and has interpretive displays in a landscaped open space in the woods. You can access the Round House Loop from the memorial rather than hiking in on the Fox Creek Spur or Fox Run Trail. Just go to Greensfelder Park, park in the picnic area with the Round House Memorial sign, and hike a quarter mile southwest on the closed gravel road to the memorial. You'll see the Round House Loop at the west end of the memorial.

The Round House Loop has almost as much variety as the Fox Run Trail, but is a little more laid back. Still, it'll challenge you. It has a 0.4-mile climb, a corresponding descent, and lots of shorter ups and downs along the ridge on the north and west sides of the loop. Hiking clockwise from the memorial, you'll descend 0.4 miles, winding through a beautiful grove of cedars along the way. When the trail levels out you'll swing west to follow a rocky, intermittent stream 0.3 miles, then turn north to start the long climb to the junction with the Fox Creek Spur. From the junction you'll follow a rolling ridgeline all the way back to the Round House Memorial. The Round House Loop is a wide trail that's perfect for side-by-side walking with a companion, and not bad for trail running. Just watch for loose rocks in the treadway while trotting along the Round House Loop.

Markings are poor to nonexistent on these trails, so bring a map with you when you hike Rockwoods Range. The Green Rock Trail cuts through the Range, making things still more confusing. The Green Rock's southern terminus is at the south trailhead, and it's easy to mistake it for the Fox Creek Spur. The Department of Conservation map is a good one; it shows all the trails and topo lines for the area and will keep you on the right path. If you do get lost, just follow any creek or dry wash downstream and you'll come out of the woods on Fox Creek Road.

# ROCKWOODS RESERVATION

## KEY AT-A-GLANCE INFORMATION

**LENGTH:** 9.5 miles on 5 separate trails

**CONFIGURATION:** Loops

**DIFFICULTY:** Easy

**SCENERY:** Forested ridges, steep-sided hollows, rugged boulders and rock outcroppings, historic mine and quarry sites, and a beautiful spring and spring-fed creek

**EXPOSURE:** Except for Prairie Trail, all hikes are well shaded

**TRAFFIC:** Moderate

**TRAIL SURFACE:** The Wildlife Habitat Trail and a mile of Trail among the Trees are paved; remainder is a mishmash of packed earth, gravel, and rock ledges; steepest sections traversed by wooden staircases

**HIKING TIME:** 1 hour or less for each trail; longer hikes available by combining several trails

**ACCESS:** Open sunrise–half-hour after sunset

**MAPS:** Trail map available at visitor center; Eureka USGS topo

**FACILITIES:** Water, restrooms, picnic sites, visitor center

**SPECIAL COMMENTS:** No pets; warning signs at all trailheads recommend leaving no valuables in car due to a spate of break-ins

## GPS TRAILHEAD COORDINATES (ROCKWOODS ENTRANCE)

| UTM ZONE (WGS84) | 15S |
| --- | --- |
| EASTING | 705329 |
| NORTHING | 4270169 |
| **LATITUDE-LONGITUDE** | |
| NORTH | N38° 33' 22.5398" |
| WEST | W90° 38' 36.8398" |

## IN BRIEF

With scenic hikes from 300 yards to 4 miles on surfaces ranging from easy pavement to winding and steep single-track through the woods, Rockwoods Reservation has a trail for hikers of all skill levels.

## DESCRIPTION

Hiking through the beautiful forested hills of Rockwoods Reservation, you'll have a tough time imagining this landscape as it appeared in the early 20th century. After a period of homesteading in the early 19th century, the attractive ridges and valley explored by Rockwoods' trails were logged bare in the late 1800s. They were further denuded by decades of extensive limestone quarrying that ended in the 1930s. Steam trains once hissed and whistled in this now-peaceful valley, hauling limestone along a narrow-gauge rail spur connecting the mines with the main rail line in Glencoe. In the valley's mining heyday, Rockwoods was the site of a small town with a school, post office, general store, housing for the miners and their families, and an orchard.

Mining ended in 1938, when the Glencoe Mining Company went belly-up and the land was purchased by the Missouri Department of Conservation. On your hikes through this once ravaged landscape, you'll see signs of past abuse—building foundations, rugged piles of overburden, remnants of the old railroad, an abandoned limestone kiln, and Cobb Cavern, a deep cave carved out by the Glencoe Mining Company when open-pit mining

## DIRECTIONS

Drive west from St. Louis on I-44 to Exit 264, Eureka–MO 109. Turn right and drive north 4 miles to Rockwoods Reservation entrance on Woods Avenue. Turn left on Woods Avenue and go 0.1 miles to Glencoe Road. Turn right and follow Glencoe Road for 1.5 miles to the visitor-center parking lot.

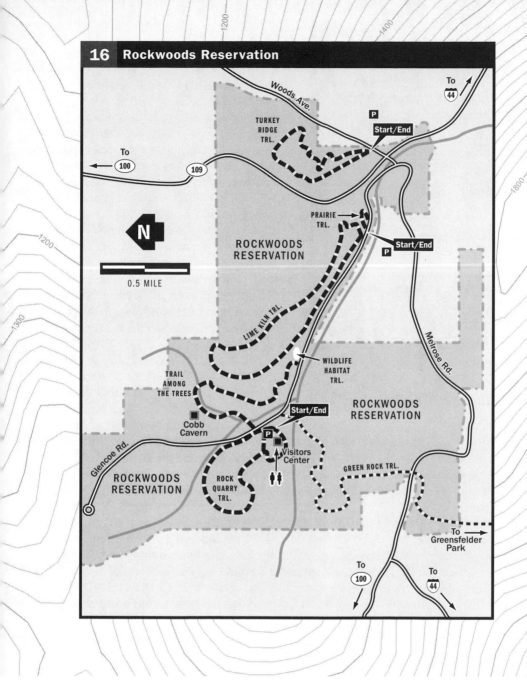

# 16  Rockwoods Reservation

TURKEY RIDGE TRL.

To 44

P Start/End

To 100

109

N

0.5 MILE

ROCKWOODS RESERVATION

PRAIRIE TRL.

P Start/End

LIME KILN TRL.

WILDLIFE HABITAT TRL.

Melrose Rd.

TRAIL AMONG THE TREES

ROCKWOODS RESERVATION

Glencoe Rd.

Cobb Cavern

Start/End

P

Visitors Center

ROCK QUARRY TRL.

GREEN ROCK TRL.

To Greensfelder Park

ROCKWOODS RESERVATION

To 100

To 44

became unproductive. Under the stewardship of Rockwoods's staff, this once-blasted moonscape has become a forested wonderland where wildlife roam and wildflowers grow, with trails wandering through land scattered with fascinating rock ledges and overgrown artifacts of Rockwoods's past.

If you like knowing the history and natural features of the lands you roam, start your hike at the visitor center. There you'll find displays of old mining tools,

Abandoned kiln, Lime Kiln Trail

pictures of the reservation's mining days, and four maps that describe Rockwoods's landscape during the area's homestead, logging, mining, and conservation periods that will enable you to recognize the crumbling ruins along the trails. There are also exhibits of park wildlife, including preserved specimens of a bobcat, owls, a hawk, several songbirds, and live turtles, lizards, and snakes. Some artifacts, like bones, antlers, and pelts, can be picked up and handled. While you're there get a park map, interpretive booklets for the self-guiding sections found on several of Rockwoods's trails, and the flyer "A Brief History of Rockwoods Reservation," by Steve Wyatt, which gives an excellent overview of the area from prehistoric times to the present.

The first hike you'll reach upon entering Rockwoods is the Turkey Ridge Trail. Its trailhead is at the park entrance on the eastern side of MO 109 on Woods Road. Though it has few spectacular features, the Turkey Ridge is a nice 2-mile walk in the woods with a single-track, packed-earth-and-gravel treadway that's wonderful for trail running. It ascends for most of its first half mile through rock layers, passing lots of the "Swiss Cheese" rocks that are so prevalent in the parklands of southwest St. Louis County. After topping out, the trail crosses a ridge, then descends into a hollow with a majestic grove of tall trees with trunks one to two feet thick. It then climbs gently out of the hollow, leveling out on a ridge at the 1-mile point near the first of four trailside benches scattered along the last mile of the hike. The remainder of the hike is level or gently descending, passing through a stately grove of pines before returning to the trailhead.

Half a mile up Glencoe Road is the second trailhead in Rockwoods, providing access for the Prairie and Lime Kiln trails. The Prairie Trail is a 500-yard hike through a restored prairie that'll only take a few minutes. The information board at the trailhead is an interesting read. It lists the plants that you'll see on your walk, explains the natural factors that led to the development of prairies, and describes human activities that have caused these grasslands' decline in the years since our arrival.

The Lime Kiln Trail is a 3.25-mile hike that'll make you work a little harder than the flat Prairie Trail. Since it's the most hilly, rocky, and rugged trail in Rockwoods, the Lime Kiln is my favorite trail in the reservation. It's named for the massive, abandoned stone kiln near the trailhead; 40 feet tall and 20 feet square at the base, the kiln was built in 1856. It was used to burn limestone at over 800°F, turning it into powder for mortar. An interpretive sign at its base tells the story of this ghostly behemoth in the woods.

I like hiking the Lime Kiln counterclockwise. The trail heads east from the kiln on a level wooded path next to the prairie, then swings north and climbs for a half mile, ascending through several rock layers and a delightful cedar grove. Next comes a pleasant mile-long jaunt along an undulating ridgeline traveling northwest; then the trail swings south and descends into a deep hollow. A fallen tree paralleling the trail makes a handrail for crossing the dry wash in the hollow, or a nice bridge when the stream's running. In the next half mile, the trail meanders among more rock outcropping and ledges and passes several clumps of daffodils. Since patches of daffodils or iris in otherwise wild forests usually mark old homesites, you're probably near someone's yard from the old miner's village. Paralleling Glencoe Road after the flower patch, the trail comes to a beautiful spring bubbling from under a rock ledge. It parallels the watercress-lined spring stream, a wonderfully green slash across the landscape even in winter, for a quarter mile before veering away to return to the Lime Kiln trailhead.

Parking for the 300-yard Wildlife Habitat Trail is 0.75 miles up Glencoe Road from the Lime Kiln trailhead. This paved trail isn't much of a hike, but is interesting when walked with the interpretive booklet available from the visitor center. With numbered stops corresponding to explanations in the booklet, it's a nice trail for educating you or your kids about the natural world.

Rockwoods' remaining two hikes, the 2.25-mile Rock Quarry Trail and the 1.5-mile Trail among the Trees, start from the visitor center and can be hiked as a 3.75-mile loop. Before hiking, pick up the booklets "Meet the Trees" and "Trail among the Trees," which are usually available at boxes at the trailheads. The Rock Quarry Trail has quiz boxes on trailside trees in its first mile. You can use your booklet to identify the tree, then open the box and see if you're right. The Trail among the Trees wanders among old mine sites, with numbered interpretive points matching explanations in the booklet.

The Rock Quarry Trail starts at the south end of the grassy area near the visitor center. You'll climb for much of the first half mile, passing lots of neat rock outcroppings and trees with quiz boxes and ID tags, topping out on the ridge above the visitor center. A trail fork to the right leads 0.15 miles downhill to the visitor center, so take the left fork to continue the loop. You'll enjoy a nice half mile along the ridge, then descend steeply into a fascinating hollow. Lots of mossy rock outcroppings and boulders leftover from the mining days are scattered all over the valley sides, and across the hollow is a cliff with a deep alcove blasted into its base. A little farther on, you'll see the spur to Cobb Cavern's entrance and pass several abandoned foundations before reaching the Rock Quarry Trail's end on Glencoe Road just north of the visitor center.

To continue the loop, cross the road to the paved beginning of the Trail among the Trees. It goes through the center of the abandoned mine site in its first half mile, passing an old stone wall, dynamite-blasted rock faces, monstrous boulders, and remnants of the old railroad. The first 0.1 mile is paved, then you'll cross Hamilton Creek on stepping stones and ascend a 47-step staircase to a bench above the stream. The main trail goes right, but take the spur to the left to a cliff at the base of which, if you look hard, you'll find a cave entrance. It's known as Bathtub Cave, because to enter you must let yourself down just as you do when taking a bath. This dry cave has two small rooms about ten feet square, with three-foot-high ceilings—not recommended for the claustrophobic.

From the cave spur, the now-unpaved main trail wanders among several interpretive sites in a rocky and rugged hollow, then heads for the hills at about the half-mile mark. The trail climbs over the next quarter mile with several breaks for level stretches or short descents, returning to pavement partway through the climb. It then follows a breezy ridge for nearly a half mile to a rocky overlook that's best in winter when foliage is gone and you can see the park below you and the ridge across the valley. After the overlook the path is unpaved again for a short reach through several rugged ledges, then it's a gentle descent along the last quarter mile to Glencoe Road just south of the visitor center.

▶ **NEARBY ACTIVITIES**

Additional hiking opportunities await you at Babler State Park (page 14), the Green Rock Trail (page 41), Rockwoods Range (page 70), and Lone Elk (page 55) and West Tyson county parks. At Lone Elk you can check out free-roaming bison and elk.

# ROUTE 66 STATE PARK

## ▶ IN BRIEF

In Route 66 State Park, you'll see man and nature working together to bring a once-destroyed landscape back to life. Once an environmental nightmare, this new state park is an example of nature's ability to heal herself. You can explore this gentle landscape on laid-back paved and gravel trails.

## ▶ DESCRIPTION

Old Route 66, designated a US Highway in 1926, is probably better known and more popular now than when it was still in existence. John Steinbeck called it the "Mother Road" in his literary classic *The Grapes of Wrath*. Also known as the "Main Street of America," this gone-but-not-forgotten highway once ran through Route 66 State Park. The visitor center and park headquarters are in an old roadhouse that once sold gas, served meals, and rented rooms to travelers. The bridge into the park once carried Route 66's traffic.

Strangely, this park wouldn't exist if not for the double-punch of a great flood and one of the country's biggest environmental disasters. Most of the park's land was once part of Times Beach, a small town on the Meramec River. Like Route 66, Times Beach was born in 1926, when the *St. Louis Times* bought 400 acres on the Meramec, broke it into lots, and offered them for $67.50 to anyone who would buy a six-month subscription to the paper. Most buyers used their lots as weekend getaways, but as St. Louis grew and commuting became commonplace, Times Beach evolved into a true community.

In 1982, a December flood inundated the town, damaging almost every one of its homes.

## ▶ DIRECTIONS

Drive west on I-44 to Exit 266, Lewis Road. Turn right and follow Lewis Road a quarter mile to the park.

## KEY AT-A-GLANCE INFORMATION

**LENGTH:** 7 miles

**CONFIGURATION:** Loop, with shortcut connectors and side trails

**DIFFICULTY:** Easy

**SCENERY:** Forests, meadow grasslands, riverbanks

**EXPOSURE:** Open; occasional shade in groves

**TRAFFIC:** Medium–heavy

**TRAIL SURFACE:** Some parts paved, some gravel

**HIKING TIME**: 1–3 hours

**ACCESS:** Open 7 a.m.–half-hour after sunset

**MAPS:** Manchester USGS topo; trail map available at visitor center

**FACILITIES:** Water, toilets, picnic shelters, phone, visitor center

**SPECIAL COMMENTS:** Pets must be leashed. Leftover segments of old Route 66 are scattered along I-44. Pick up a guidebook at the visitor center and head west to discover some of this fading bit of America's history.

### GPS TRAILHEAD COORDINATES (TRAILHEAD)

| | | |
|---|---|---|
| UTM ZONE (WGS84) | 15S | |
| EASTING | 709746 | |
| NORTHING | 4264622 | |
| LATITUDE–LONGITUDE | | |
| NORTH | N38° 30' 19.0188'' | |
| WEST | W90° 35' 40.4830'' | |

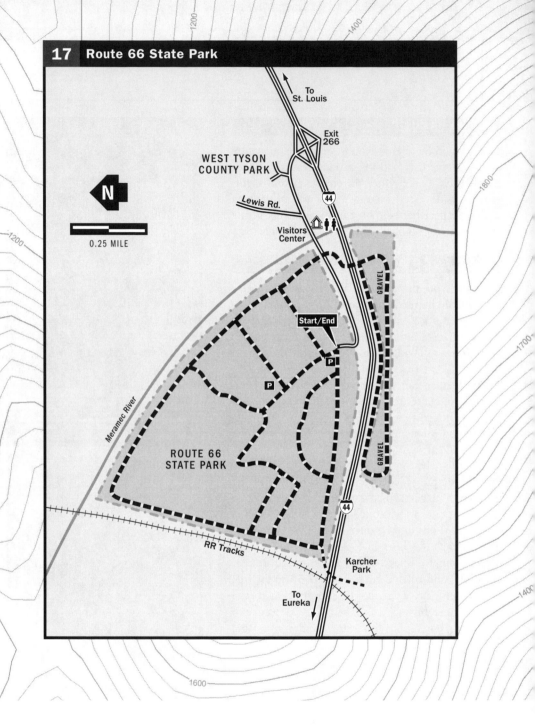

To
St. Louis

Exit
266

WEST TYSON
COUNTY PARK

Lewis Rd.

44

N

0.25 MILE

Visitors
Center

Start/End

P

P

GRAVEL

GRAVEL

Meramec River

ROUTE 66
STATE PARK

44

RR Tracks

Karcher
Park

To
Eureka

On top of the flood came news that waste oil sprayed on the town's streets to control dust contained dioxin, making the entire city an environmental hazard. The government bought out everyone in the city, razed the homes, and brought in an incinerator. In 1996 and 1997, hundreds of thousands of tons of soil were burned to neutralize the toxic threat. The low hills in the park are piles of burned soil, and the park's marshes and pools are the pits dug for dirt to cover the mounds.

As it turns out, one of the nation's worst environmental disasters became a successful environmental-restoration story. Missouri's Department of Natural Resources took over Times Beach's 409 acres in 1997 and opened Route 66 State Park in 1999. It's a piece of land come back from the dead, and it's great to see. In this slowly healing landscape you'll find meadows of tall grass, marshes full of cattails, riverside habitat along the Meramec River, and patches of forest left over from Times Beach's residential yards. Missouri's usual plethora of wildflowers is here, too—supplemented by iris and other species carried over from residential landscaping.

Wildlife is thick in this formerly hazardous parkland. You'll see deer while wandering around Route 66, and they're so tame they'll sit in the grass as you wander by, only their heads and necks extending above the lush meadows. In spring, when the marsh ponds are full, it's a wonderful place for birding. On one hike I spotted turkeys, a hawk, a red-headed woodpecker, herons, geese, several ducks, an egret, red-winged blackbirds, an eastern bluebird, kingfishers, an eastern kingbird, and a family of killdeer that skittered down the trail in front of me. Eagles are sometimes spotted here, too.

Route 66 has around 7 miles of trail, including the park road that ties the system together. The road is paved, one-way, and not very busy, so it's not annoying to hike where the cars can go, too. A 1.7-mile gravel loop is south of I-44, and the rest of the paths are north of the interstate. While most of the trails north of the highway are paved, about 1.5 miles are gravel. Not all the trails in this new park were finished when this book was written, but the map shows all the paths to be completed in the near future. In the southwest corner of Route 66, a side trail goes under the highway to Eureka's Karcher Park and connects to that city's trail system.

Route 66's trails are perfect for trail running, cross-country skiing, and hiking side-by-side with a friend. It's an ideal destination for evening hikes after work, too. The paved path along the Meramec River has picnic tables tucked into the woods above the river, so bring lunch or dinner with you when you visit Route 66. The noise from I-44 is a little distracting, but several rows of trees planted next to the highway will soon grow tall enough to reduce the racket. Even now the back half of the park is quiet and peaceful.

No trip to Route 66 State Park is complete without stopping at the visitor center in the old roadhouse. It has an excellent gift shop full of Route 66 memorabilia, history, route guides for traveling what's left of the old road, and nature field guides. There's an incredible set of exhibits about Route 66 and Times Beach in the center, too. The center houses a 1929 road map of Missouri, Burma Shave jingles on cards scattered throughout the hall, copies of old roadhouse menus, and a handmade Route 66 quilt that depicts the old highway winding over piney mountains, across cactus-studded deserts, past teepees, an old-fashioned curio shop, and a man riding a jackrabbit. There's even a photo of St. Louis's most famous "No-Tell Motel," a one-time Route 66 landmark. Taken just before the motel was demolished, the caption reads, "It's Check-Out Time at Coral Courts—No More One-Night Stands." There's lots more to see, so don't you check out of this park until you check out the visitor center.

# Hikes in
# ILLINOIS

# FULTS HILL PRAIRIE NATURE PRESERVE

## KEY AT-A-GLANCE INFORMATION

**LENGTH:** 1.6 miles

**CONFIGURATION:** Loop

**DIFFICULTY:** Very easy

**SCENERY:** Hillside prairies with expansive views of the Mississippi River valley

**EXPOSURE:** Even mix of shady forest and exposed grassland

**TRAFFIC:** Light

**TRAIL SURFACE:** Packed earth

**HIKING TIME:** 1 hour

**ACCESS:** Open dawn–dusk

**MAPS:** Renault USGS topo

**FACILITIES:** Parking, 1 picnic site

**SPECIAL COMMENTS:** Pets must be leashed

### GPS TRAILHEAD COORDINATES (PRESERVE ENTRANCE)

UTM ZONE (WGS84)  15S
EASTING  746501
NORTHING  4226782

LATITUDE–LONGITUDE
NORTH  N38° 9' 18.9363''
WEST  W90° 11' 12.1895''

## ▶ IN BRIEF

When you think of prairie lands, do you envision low hills and a sea of grass extending to the horizon? Come to Fults Hill and explore a hillside prairie. This place will make you stop to catch your breath—from both steep climbs on the trail and expansive bluff views of the Mississippi River Valley.

## ▶ DESCRIPTION

Fults Hill is definitely not your typical prairie. Don't expect the low swells of central Illinois or northern Missouri prairies in this nature preserve. This is a hillside prairie, and like other hill grasslands in Illinois, it survived only because it was too steep to farm. Fults Hill Prairie Nature Preserve is more than prairie, too. Its diverse landscape includes forest, glades, and steep bluffs. Kidd Lake Marsh Natural Area, directly across Bluff Road from Fults Hill, adds a wetland landscape to the mix. Kidd Lake is a remnant of American Bottoms, a huge marshland that once stretched for miles along the Illinois side of the Mississippi River.

The different habitats at Fults Hill and Kidd Lake attract a wide variety of wildlife. Warblers migrate through the area in spring, and several species of hawk come by in the fall. You may spot an eagle here during winter. Turkey vultures often soar over the bluffs. Herons, egrets, geese, and many duck species inhabit and forage Kidd Lake's marsh—you can observe them through binoculars

## ▶ DIRECTIONS

From the intersection of IL 3 and IL 156 in Waterloo, go one block west on IL 156–Park Street to Lakeview Drive. Turn south, and follow Lakeview out of town. It becomes Maeystown Road, and goes through Maeystown 9 miles later. Two miles beyond Maeystown, turn left onto Bluff Road and drive 6 miles to Fults Hill Prairie Nature Preserve.

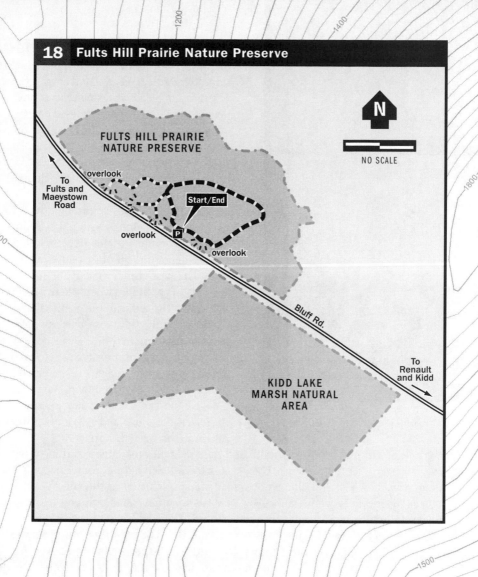

**FULTS HILL PRAIRIE NATURE PRESERVE**

N

NO SCALE

overlook

To Fults and Maeystown Road

Start/End

overlook

P

overlook

Bluff Rd.

To Renault and Kidd

**KIDD LAKE MARSH NATURAL AREA**

from the bluffs on Fults Hill. On spring evenings you'll enjoy a chorus of frogs belting out their mating songs. Muskrats live in the marsh, too—those domelike structures in the marsh are their houses.

The trail is marked with green carsonite posts with hiker symbols. No matter which way you go from the trailhead, you'll start off with a tough climb. To the north the trail ascends a steep, packed-earth slope with water bars. Head southeast, and you face more than 200 wooden steps onto the bluff, but the staircase is the easier way to go. It also saves the best overlooks for the end of your hike. When the stairs end, the trail continues up steeply, and you'll see the first of several side trails running a few yards west to rock-ledge viewpoints over Kidd Lake Marsh. From this steep bluff you'll look straight down on traffic rolling up and down the appropriately named Bluff Road.

Descending to one of Fults Hill Prairie's bluff overlooks

For several hundred yards you'll parallel the bluff, with lots of vistas over the Mississippi River valley. Veer left and come to a fork. The right fork leads to a small hill prairie, and the left fork—the main trail—climbs easily on a narrow ascending ridge spine for the next 200 yards, topping out on a high ridge. Turn left and follow this wooded ridge for the next 0.75 miles, with occasional glimpses of the river valley through the trees. While you're peering southwest through the woods, note the deep amphitheater-like hollow to your left. For much of this ridgetop run you'll be walking on the lip of this huge bowl.

The best vistas come at the northwestern end of the ridge, where there's a fork in the trail. The official trail breaks left and descends off the ridge, but take the right fork first. It leads a quarter mile to a steep hillside prairie with beautiful expansive views of the Mississippi River valley—an excellent spot for picnicking or napping in tall, rustling grasses. You can see for miles up and down the river bottoms, and Missouri's wooded hills line the western horizon.

The main trail fork turns south and descends into the largest and most impressive hill prairie on the preserve. The grass is thick, deep, and decorated with a sprinkling of wildflowers, and clumps of sumac shine bright red in the fall. While not as high as the previous overlook, the view here is stupendous, and only gets better as you hike a descending grassy ridge toward the bluff. The trail forks a short way down the ridge, with the left fork leading back to the trailhead. The right fork continues west on the grassy ridge and descends another 100 yards, with spectacular views over the Mississippi valley all the way. Near the end of the ridge the trail forks yet again, with each path leading to a ledge overlook above Bluff Road. My favorite is the left one, where I can hang out on a cedar-lined rock shelf wide enough to hold a small bus.

From the fork above the overlooks, it's only a quarter mile to the trailhead on the main trail, descending steeply all the way. You'll cut through a thin band of trees and emerge into another patch of incredibly steep hillside prairie with expansive views, then reenter the woods and drop quickly to the trailhead.

Fults Hill's short trail is ideal for a summer evening getaway. At the end of your hike, relax at one of the overlooks, watching birds on the marsh and admiring a Mississippi River valley sunset.

▶ **NEARBY ACTIVITIES**

Before or after your hike, check out picturesque Maeystown. Founded in the 1850s, it features a couple of old stone one-lane bridges and lots of historical stone buildings, including a bar and restaurant, a general store, and a sweet shop with the product I always search out after a hike—ice cream!

# LITTLE GRAND CANYON

## ▶ IN BRIEF

Little Grand Canyon is a little-known hideaway that's worth the drive from St. Louis. You'll hike down stone steps cut in steep, fantastically eroded slick-rock chutes into a moist bottomland guarded by 300-foot cliffs. Your reward for climbing out of the canyon's depths is a panoramic view of the Mississippi River valley and the distant Missouri hills.

## ▶ DESCRIPTION

Unless you compare it to its namesake natural wonder, Little Grand Canyon is anything but little. The creek that sculpts this box-canyon jewel drops 350 feet in its 1-mile run to the nearby Big Muddy River, carving a breathtaking landscape on its way to the Mississippi River floodplain. Tall hardwoods grace the canyon floor and the hillsides above, and the moist bottomland is lousy with wildflowers in spring. In October, fall colors contrast brightly with the buff stone of the canyon cliffs.

With its varied habitat of forest, canyon, moist bottomland, riverside bluff, and open floodplain, Little Grand Canyon attracts a wide variety of wildlife. Songbirds pass through on their spring and fall migrations, and several species of woodpeckers flit among the trees in this lushly wooded

## ▶ DIRECTIONS

From Chester, drive 26 miles south on IL 3 to Towne Creek Road and turn left. This turn is 2 miles past the IL 149 turnoff, and there'll be a sign pointing to Sand Ridge and Little Grand Canyon. Follow Towne Creek Road 6.5 miles to Hickory Ridge Road. Turn right on Hickory Ridge Road, and follow it 6.5 miles to the trailhead. About 4 miles down this last 6.5-mile stretch there's a four-way stop with a really confusing signpost with more street names than there are roads. Following a brown sign for Little Grand Canyon, turn at the four-way and continue 2.5 miles down Hickory Ridge Road to the trailhead.

## ⓘ KEY AT-A-GLANCE INFORMATION

**LENGTH:** 3.6 miles

**CONFIGURATION:** Loop

**DIFFICULTY:** Easy

**SCENERY:** Towering rock walls, fantastically eroded sandstone canyons, craggy bluffs, and moist bottomlands

**EXPOSURE:** Shaded throughout

**TRAFFIC:** Medium

**TRAIL SURFACE:** Asphalt on steep approaches to the canyon, packed earth and gravel on the canyon floor, rugged and rocky on trails into and out of the canyon

**HIKING TIME:** 2–3 hours

**ACCESS:** Area open 6 a.m.–10 p.m.

**MAPS:** Gorham USGS topo; trail map available at forest service office in Murphysboro

**FACILITIES:** Parking, picnic sites, toilets

**SPECIAL COMMENTS:** Exercise caution on hazardous cliffs and slippery sandstone steps. Though this trail's difficulty rating is easy, be prepared for steep and rugged grades into and out of the canyon.

### GPS TRAILHEAD COORDINATES (TRAILHEAD)

| UTM ZONE (WGS84) | 16S |
| --- | --- |
| EASTING | 288884 |
| NORTHING | 4173098 |
| LATITUDE-LONGITUDE | |
| NORTH | N37° 40' 50.9142'' |
| WEST | W89° 23' 38.6560'' |

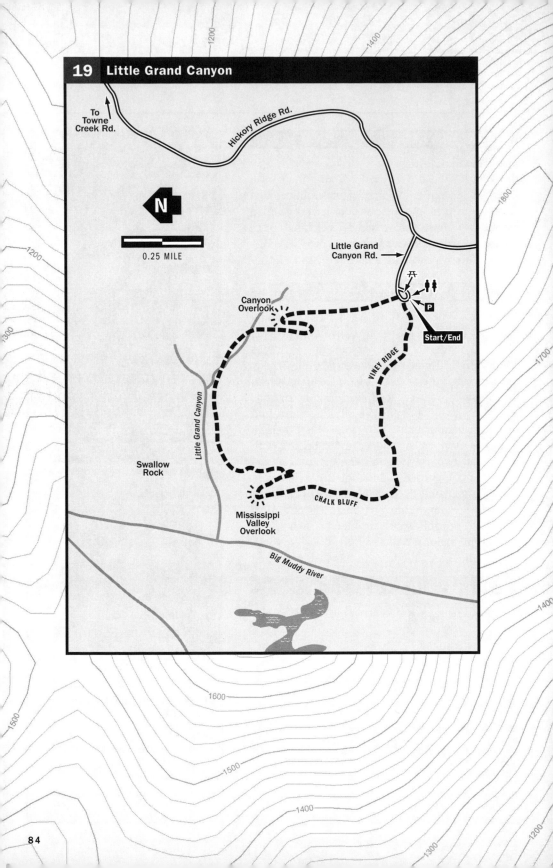

# 19 Little Grand Canyon

To Towne Creek Rd.

Hickory Ridge Rd.

N

0.25 MILE

Little Grand Canyon Rd.

Canyon Overlook

Start/End

P

VINEY RIDGE

Little Grand Canyon

Swallow Rock

CHALK BLUFF

Mississippi Valley Overlook

Big Muddy River

canyon. Deer are often spotted here, along with the occasional fox, bobcat, and mink. The exposed rock layers of the canyon walls have hundreds of crevices and grottos that attract reptiles and amphibians to this moist, cool canyon, while hawks and vultures soar above the cliffs.

This trail is a good hike in either direction, but traveling counterclockwise saves the best overlook for last—a nice reward for your climb out of the canyon. Marked with white paint blazes, the trail starts north from the parking area and heads downhill on an asphalt path. A half mile down the trail is the canyon overlook, a sneak peek at things to come. There the pathway becomes packed earth and switchbacks to the south, descending toward a narrow side canyon on your right. Believe it or not, you're going to drop into that sandstone trough and scramble down it into the Little Grand Canyon.

Mississippi Valley Overlook, Little Grand Canyon

This stretch is an incredible descent through a 200-yard-long sandstone sculpture, accented with bright green moss. It's rare that a trail even comes near a spectacular feature like this, and here you get to hike down the middle of one! Rough steps are hewn from the rock in steep spots, making your scramble down the trough a bit easier. If it has rained recently you'll have to work your way carefully over and around waterfalls and cascades on the slippery rock bottom. In its last 25 yards the chute slopes 40 degrees over smoothly eroded rock layers with four evenly spaced pothole waterfalls in the otherwise-uniform slope.

After bottoming out in Little Grand Canyon, the trail breaks west and follows an intermittent stream, crossing it several times on a packed-earth-and-gravel path. Layered sandstone cliffs tower above, riddled with grottos and crevices. You'll follow the canyon for about 0.75 miles, curving slowly to the south. The first half mile is in dense forest, then the woods thin as you approach the canyon mouth. You'll be near the Big Muddy floodplain when dead trees begin to appear. The bluff on your right is Swallow Rock, and Chalk Bluff rises vertically on the left.

Just before reaching the canyon mouth, the trail breaks south and angles up the hollow below Chalk Bluff. The trail steepens quickly and enters another exquisite mossy sandstone chute similar to the one you followed down into the canyon. For a second time you'll clamber up steep ledgy rocks and over carved rock steps, and dodge waterfalls and cascades that threaten to fill your boots. Halfway up is a particularly enchanting spot—a fork in the chute, with twin waterfalls splashing into a pool—if you're lucky enough to be here when the streams are flowing. A fallen tree spanning this narrow sandstone gap high overhead reminds me of slot-canyon hiking in southern Utah.

When you pop up out of the chute, the trail switches back north, tops out on Chalk Bluff, and leads you along the cliff edge for a quarter mile. You'll be hiking on a ledge above the mossy sandstone trough you just scrambled up, and ahead will be the main stem of the Little Grand Canyon. This quarter mile run ends at the panoramic vista of the Mississippi Valley overlook. You'll be standing on the point of Chalk Bluff, the cliff you admired while hiking the canyon below. Across the mouth of the Little Grand Canyon, Swallow Rock towers above the canyon floor. A hazy 7 miles to the west are the Missouri hills. From the overlook it's a 1.1-mile hike back to the trailhead on gravel and asphalt, with several benches scattered here and there. You'll wiggle through the woods on a narrow twisting ridge spine all the way, with deep hollows to the left and right.

Though the trail is short, allow plenty of time to admire the scenery on this spectacular hike. And bring your field guides, binoculars, and camera to Little Grand Canyon. Its lush and varied landscape is a wonderful place for nature study.

## ▶ NEARBY ACTIVITIES

Nearby Piney Creek Ravine Nature Preserve (page 91) is another fantastic natural area. Also, Pomona Natural Bridge is an incredible rock span at a Shawnee National Forest picnic site near Pomona, and should not be missed. Just south of Little Grand Canyon is the Pomona Winery, the northernmost of five wineries on the Shawnee Hills Wine Trail (**www.shawneewinetrail.com**). Exploring southern Illinois and sampling its wines on this scenic driving tour is a wonderful finale to a day in the outdoors.

# PERE MARQUETTE STATE PARK

## ▶ IN BRIEF

Located near the confluence of the Illinois and Mississippi rivers, Pere Marquette State Park's trails have spectacular vistas across the valleys of these two mighty streams. Pere Marquette's extensive trail system offers hikes of various lengths, and you can finish off your day in the outdoors with dinner at the beautiful Pere Marquette Lodge.

## ▶ DESCRIPTION

Just getting to Pere Marquette State Park is a scenic undertaking. With the Mississippi on one side and bluffs on the other, Illinois's Great River Road is an enthralling drive. Pere Marquette State Park is named for Father Jacques Marquette, a French missionary who was one of the first Europeans to explore the confluence. His arrival in 1673 is commemorated at the Pere Marquette Memorial a mile east of the park.

With 8,000 acres of riverside hills, Pere Marquette is one of Illinois's largest parks. Its first 2,600 acres were acquired in 1932. The Civilian Conservation Corps worked in the park during the 1930s, building trails, shelters, bridges, and lookouts. While you'll admire the CCC's moss-covered stonework at the park's overlooks, their most impressive project was the park's beautiful lodge. Locally quarried stone was used for the lodge's construction, but its monstrous timbers are Douglas fir and western cedar from Oregon. The fireplace in the main room is 50 feet tall and weighs an estimated 700 tons. Illinois prison inmates built the lodge furniture.

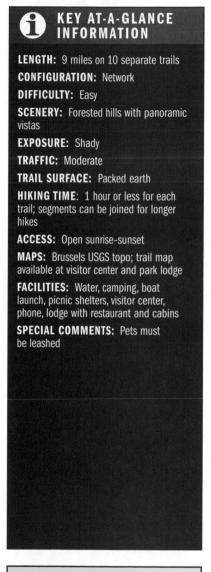

### ⓘ KEY AT-A-GLANCE INFORMATION

**LENGTH:** 9 miles on 10 separate trails

**CONFIGURATION:** Network

**DIFFICULTY:** Easy

**SCENERY:** Forested hills with panoramic vistas

**EXPOSURE:** Shady

**TRAFFIC:** Moderate

**TRAIL SURFACE:** Packed earth

**HIKING TIME:** 1 hour or less for each trail; segments can be joined for longer hikes

**ACCESS:** Open sunrise-sunset

**MAPS:** Brussels USGS topo; trail map available at visitor center and park lodge

**FACILITIES:** Water, camping, boat launch, picnic shelters, visitor center, phone, lodge with restaurant and cabins

**SPECIAL COMMENTS:** Pets must be leashed

**GPS TRAILHEAD COORDINATES (PARKING AREA)**

| UTM ZONE (WGS84) | 15S |
| EASTING | 712808 |
| NORTHING | 4316631 |
| LATITUDE-LONGITUDE | |
| NORTH | N38° 58' 22.1479'' |
| WEST | W90° 32' 36.5839'' |

## ▶ DIRECTIONS

From Alton, drive 22 miles northwest on IL 100, the Great River Road. The park is 5 miles past Grafton. Hikes can start from the visitor center and various points on the park road.

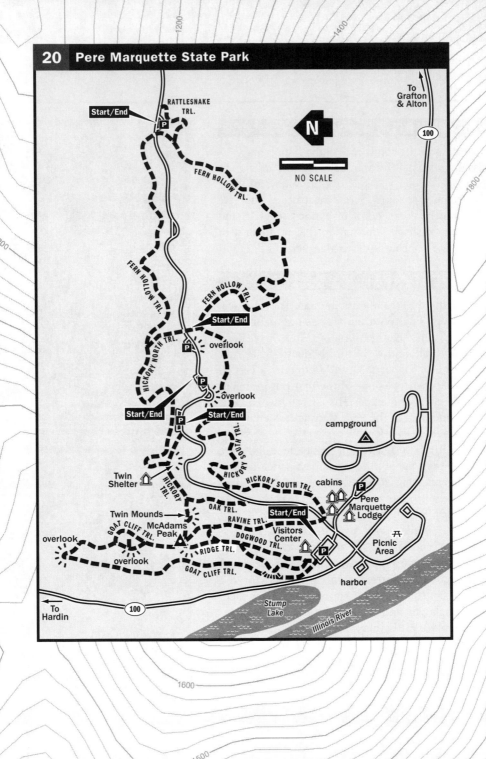

Start/End

RATTLESNAKE TRL.

To Grafton & Alton

100

N

NO SCALE

FERN HOLLOW TRL.

FERN HOLLOW TRL.

FERN HOLLOW TRL.

Start/End

HICKORY NORTH TRL.

overlook

overlook

Start/End

Start/End

campground

HICKORY SOUTH TRL.

HICKORY SOUTH TRL.

cabins

P

Pere Marquette Lodge

Twin Shelter

HICKORY TRL.

OAK TRL.

Twin Mounds

GOAT CLIFF TRL.

McAdams Peak

RAVINE TRL.

Start/End

Visitors Center

Picnic Area

overlook

DOGWOOD TRL.

P

overlook

RIDGE TRL.

GOAT CLIFF TRL.

harbor

To Hardin

100

Stump Lake

Illinois River

Recently renovated, the lodge is Pere Marquette's crown jewel. It has an indoor swimming pool, saunas, a cocktail lounge, and a dining room known for an incredible Sunday buffet. Expansive windows in the main hall and dining room look out across the Illinois River. A weekend at Pere Marquette, relaxing in the lodge between hikes on the park's trails, is the perfect getaway. Or just show up on Sunday, have a nice brunch, then work off that wonderful buffet by hiking up to Pere Marquette's overlooks.

The park visitor center, opened in 1997, was built to match the rustic lodge. Trail maps and a relief map of the park are located there, along with the "Father Marquette" mural. There's a 270-gallon aquarium with native fish, and there are exhibits on area history and geology. Pick up one of the park's bird checklists for your hike, too. More than 230 species have been spotted here—and the overlooks and trails are great places to spot them. Eagles are often seen here in winter, and the park holds Bald Eagle Days from December through March. The park plans other events throughout the year, including owl programs, wetland hikes, and fall-color walks. Check out Pere Marquette's excellent Web site for an event listing (**dnr.state.il.us/ lands/landmgt/parks/r4/peremarq.htm**).

While the park's trail map doesn't show topographic features, it's a must for keeping track of where you are on the trail system. Ten interconnected trails ramble through Pere Marquette, each with its own unique blaze. The map is keyed to these blazes and lists the length of each segment—a perfect tool for choosing hike lengths to match your time and energy. By putting together trail segments of various lengths, you'll design hikes ranging from a half mile to 8 miles. Markings on the trail are excellent: blazes are kept freshly painted, and many intersections are marked with signs and arrows. Except for steep sections in the western end of the trail system, all the paths in Pere Marquette are wonderful for trail running.

Trails in the western part of the park are shorter, more scenic, and therefore more popular. The longer trails in the eastern part of the park have a wilder, more secluded flavor. The Dogwood Trail is a half-mile loop from the visitor center. It features lots of steps and has an alcove overlook built into the bluff face. The Goat Cliff Trail is a 1.5-mile segment of trail that, when combined with the Dogwood Trail, makes a very scenic 2-mile loop from the visitor center. It angles up the hillside on the west end of the trail system, passing several boulders and following a cliff face for a short way. Along its fishhook-shaped route, the Goat Cliff Trail passes three overlooks and a couple of hillside prairies before ending at McAdams Peak.

McAdams Peak, 791 feet high and 372 feet above the river, is the most scenic overlook in the park. A CCC shelter with a double-deck viewing platform looks west across the Illinois and Mississippi rivers. McAdams Peak is also a trail hub, where three other paths break south and east. The Hickory Trail heads east from McAdams, passing the Twin Mounds overlook and the Twin Shelter on its half-mile run to the park road. The Ridge Trail goes a quarter mile straight south, connecting the Goat Cliff Trail to the Dogwood. The Ravine Trail also heads south, dropping down 60 or 70 stone steps, and follows a narrow defile on its half-mile run. It intersects the park road behind the lodge, and across the road the 1.5-mile Hickory South Trail angles southeast.

From here begin longer loop options, using the more-isolated trails in the eastern part of the network. Combining the Hickory South, Hickory North, Hickory, and Ravine trails makes a 3-mile loop. Add the Fern Hollow and Rattlesnake trails to the eastern end of the loop, and you'll hike 6.25 miles. Tack on the Goat Cliff–Dogwood–Ridge loop, and you'll have an 8.25-mile hike covering almost every bit of trail in Pere Marquette. Sound confusing? It's not as long as you carry the park map with you.

The 1.5-mile Hickory South Trail goes along a stream for a short way, then angles up to follow the hillside beneath the park road overlooks. There'll be two side trails to the park road along the way. Just east of the Flagpole Overlook, you'll reach the 2.5-mile Fern Hollow Trail. A trail going left here cuts across to Hickory North and the 3-mile loop option. Continue on the Fern Hollow Trail for the 6.25-mile option. The most isolated trail in the park, Fern Hollow's south half winds among peaceful moist hollows, where you'll see—you guessed it—lots of ferns. At 1.5 miles after leaving Hickory South, the Fern Hollow Trail angles north to cross the park road. Just before the road crossing, the Rattlesnake Trail heads east off the Fern Hollow. The 0.75-mile Rattlesnake makes a roller-coaster run to intersect the park road east of Lover's Leap overlook. It passes some pretty nice rock walls along the way.

To hook back up with the Fern Hollow Trail after hiking the Rattlesnake, walk 0.4 miles west on the road. You'll rejoin the Fern Hollow just 100 yards from where you left it on the Rattlesnake Trail. On its 1-mile run from here to the Hickory North Trail, the Fern Hollow Trail travels along a steep wooded slope with a deep hollow on the right. Once on Hickory North, you'll drop into a deep hollow, then hike up a mossy rock-bottom stream for a short way, where moss-green rock formations and little waterfalls and cascades lie hidden in a deep, dark hollow. When you leave the hollow, you'll climb steeply onto a ridge and T into the Hickory Trail. The Twin Shelter, with still more scenic vistas, is a few yards to the left. To close your loop, go right on the Hickory Trail and follow it a quarter mile to McAdams Peak, then follow the Ridge Trail back to the visitor center.

This trail system may sound confusing, but when you get out there with a map you'll see it's fairly straightforward. Well-marked trails with lots of cutoffs and connectors make possible a wide array of loop options. Best of all, whatever path you choose could eventually lead to the lodge, where good food and cold adult beverages await!

### ▶ NEARBY ACTIVITIES

The 20-mile Sam Vadalabene Bike Trail runs from Pere Marquette to Alton, traveling along the Mississippi River much of the way. Nearby Grafton has a winery, antique shops, and ice-cream stands (**www.grafton.il.us**).

# PINEY CREEK RAVINE NATURE PRESERVE

## ▶ IN BRIEF

Piney Creek Ravine's secretive canyons hide the biggest display of prehistoric petroglyphs and pictographs in Illinois. When you descend into the enchanting canyons at Piney Creek, you'll be awed by the natural beauty that inspired the ancients' creativity.

## ▶ DESCRIPTION

Piney Creek Ravine Nature Preserve is a captivating and bewitching place. Nature's beauty abounds in the preserve. Impressive rock walls tower above clear streams that flow noisily over ledges and drift quietly through deep pools. Mossy boulders line the creeks, which roar to life after rainfall, creating mesmerizing cascades and falls. One waterfall pours off a 75-foot-long ledge with a deep overhang, free-falling ten feet to the rocks below, then cascading another ten feet over rock layers to the streambed. Shading this beauty are groves of shortleaf pines—one of only two stands of these handsome evergreens found growing naturally in the state.

A fascinating display of ancient pictographs and petroglyphs adds a dash of intrigue and mystery to Piney Creek's beauty. Located beneath an overhang that shielded the prehistoric artists from the elements, these haunting works of art depict

## ⓘ KEY AT-A-GLANCE INFORMATION

**LENGTH:** 2.25 miles

**CONFIGURATION:** Loop with spur

**DIFFICULTY:** Very easy

**SCENERY:** Pine-studded canyons, impressive rock formations, streams, prehistoric rock art

**EXPOSURE:** Even mix of shady and exposed terrain

**TRAFFIC:** Light

**TRAIL SURFACE:** Packed earth and gravel, with several steep, rocky, and rugged sections

**HIKING TIME:** 2–3 hours

**ACCESS:** Area closed from dusk–dawn

**MAPS:** Welge USGS topo

**FACILITIES:** Parking, picnic table, trash can at trailhead

**SPECIAL COMMENTS:** Pets must be leashed; dangerous cliff areas exist; no collecting of artifacts; no carving, chalking, painting, or otherwise defacing of prehistoric rock art

## ▶ DIRECTIONS

From Chester, drive 14 miles south on IL 3 to Hog Hill Road, where a sign points left to Piney Creek Nature Preserve, 7 miles down the road. Follow Hog Hill Road east 4 miles to Rock Crusher Road. Continue east 2.5 miles on Rock Crusher Road to Piney Creek Road. Turn left and follow Piney Creek Road 1.5 miles to the trailhead. From IL 4 in Campbell Hill, take Rock Crusher Road 6.5 miles west to Piney Creek Road, and then turn right 1.5 miles to Piney Creek Ravine's parking area.

**GPS TRAILHEAD COORDINATES (TRAILHEAD)**

| | |
|---|---|
| UTM ZONE (WGS84) | 16S |
| EASTING | 267998 |
| NORTHING | 4196964 |
| LATITUDE-LONGITUDE | |
| NORTH | N37° 53' 26.3187'' |
| WEST | W89° 38' 17.9626'' |

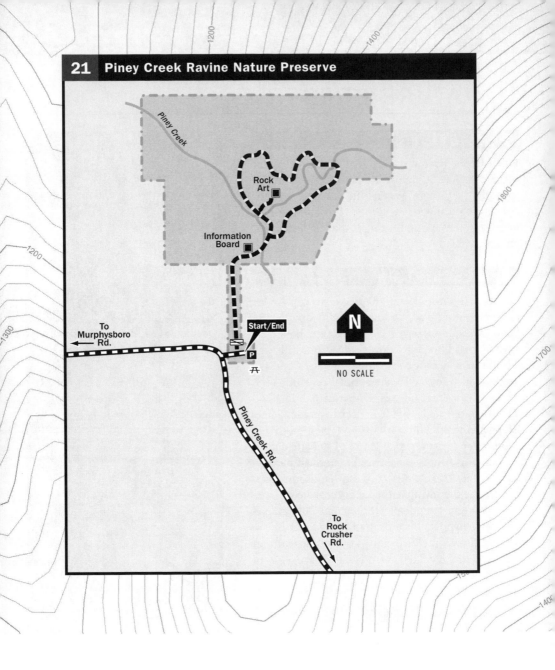

deer, birds, snakes, hands, and human figures. They form the largest collection of prehistoric rock art in Illinois and date from AD 500–1550. Some were pecked out with sharp rocks, while others were painted on the canyon wall using minerals mixed with animal fat.

The coolest thing about Piney Creek is its contrast with the surrounding countryside. On your drive to the trailhead, you might think you're in the wrong place, with nothing in view except corn and soybean fields, broken by the occasional pasture, woodlot, or distant church steeple. The first part of the

Rock Art at Piney Creek

hike will be no different—you'll walk a grass path between two fencerows with a pasture on one side and a field on the other that's pretty in its own way, but not the amazing scenery you just read about. When the fencerow on the right ends, you'll see a trail signboard near a grove of trees to the northwest, with a map of the hike and an interpretive display. This is the official beginning of the trail.

The trail heads northeast into the woods behind the signboard, marked with green carsonite posts with white arrows on a brown background. The path drops downhill from the treeline, crosses a footbridge, bounces up over a low ridge, and crosses a stream on a wide and shallow rock trough. This expanse of rock continues downstream to a spectacular ledge waterfall, which is really impressive during or just after rainstorms. A few steps past the crossing at a Y, the trail's 1.25-mile loop begins, and a sign points left to the rock art. I like taking a left here and hiking the trail clockwise, seeing the rock art first.

Going clockwise from the fork, you'll descend quickly into the canyon of Piney Creek. Look sharp to your left—partway down you'll pass the ledge waterfall, with its deep underhang. The ancients must have crawled back under the ledge's 15- to 20-foot overhang to look out through the falls and into the ravine. You'll descend parallel to this creek 100 yards or so, bottoming out in the ravine where the waterfall stream joins Piney Creek. This is an impressive spot. Rock walls tower behind you, to your left, and straight ahead, running hundreds of feet up and down the ravine. The stream, with its pools and cascades, stretches up and down the canyon. On freezing winter days, ice formations festoon the wall, and in summer mosses, ferns, and wildflowers decorate the area.

You'll splash across Piney Creek, jump up onto a low bench, and immediately hit the spur to the rock art. It's a short hike to the right along one of the cliff faces. When you reach the rock-art panel, you'll immediately see why the artists chose this spot. An overhang protects their outdoor studio, and an immense chunk of wall that long ago broke away from the cliff forms an extended backrest for admiring their creations, planning works yet to come, holding ceremonies, or simply kicking back to enjoy a beautiful spot. It's a good place for you to do the same. Interpretive signboards at the base of the cliff help you contemplate what's here. Unfortunately, years of graffiti are here, too, carved in the 130 years since the ravine was discovered in the 1870s. Please don't add yours to the collection.

From the rock-art spur, the trail continues downstream until the rock walls end, then breaks north to climb out of the ravine. You'll soon be paralleling the cliff above the rock-art panel, heading upstream above Piney Creek. For a quarter mile, you'll hike this ridge, with enticing views of an attractive S-curve in Piney Creek. The trail skirts the edge of this natural amphitheater, drops steeply into the ravine just above the serpentine curve, and crosses the creek on an immense slab of rock. A captivating place to explore, the stream floor is solid rock for several hundred yards up and down the ravine. Over the eons, Piney Creek has carved troughs, overhangs, waterfalls, and pools in the sandstone, all lightly decorated with moss and lichen. Ledgy canyon walls rise steeply above the creek, reflected in the pools below. You'll want to spend some time here, photographing, admiring, and stretching out on the sandstone ledges and benches.

After crossing Piney Creek the trail climbs a bit to an unmarked intersection. A short hike left goes back to the creek, where you'll see another waterfall 200 feet upstream. A few steps farther up the trail there's a second intersection, where a side trail leads past an overlook of that waterfall to a stream crossing at the edge of Piney Creek's boundary. After the second intersection the trail climbs gently, levels out above the serpentine curve, and meanders through the forest back to the parking lot spur, passing several final vistas of Piney Creek Ravine along the way.

Though the trail at Piney Creek is short, bring your camera and allow several hours to explore this incredible hideaway. It's like a tiny slice of rugged Ozark hills, magically transported to Illinois farm country. Bring your field guides and binoculars, too—the varied habitats in and around Piney Creek attract a wide variety of birds and other critters. Reptiles and amphibians love the rock walls and streams, and the moist environment encourages a diverse array of plants and wildflowers. Make a point of coming here during or after rain, when the streams and falls will be roaring.

### ▶ NEARBY ACTIVITIES

After hiking Piney Creek's short trail, you'll have plenty of time to check out additional local natural wonders at the Shawnee National Forest's Little Grand Canyon (page 83).

# Hikes in the
# WEST/NORTHWEST
## of the
# ST. LOUIS AREA

# AUGUST A. BUSCH MEMORIAL CONSERVATION AREA

## GPS TRAILHEAD COORDINATES (PARKING AREA)

| | |
|---|---|
| UTM ZONE (WGS84) | 15S |
| EASTING | 695884 |
| NORTHING | 4286476 |
| LATITUDE–LONGITUDE | |
| NORTH | N38° 42' 18.8700'' |
| WEST | W90° 44' 50.2286'' |

## ▶ IN BRIEF

Busch Conservation Area, a diverse landscape with easy trails that explore a wide variety of habitats, is an excellent hiking destination for novice hikers and families introducing young children to nature's wonders.

## ▶ DESCRIPTION

Like so many scenic enclaves in Missouri, Busch Conservation Area is the resurrection of a once heavily developed landscape. Farmers homesteaded this land from the early 1800s, wresting a living from these gentle hills for the next 150 years. In 1941 the government took over the area and built a plant for manufacturing TNT. The plant was demolished in the 1980s, but many of the 100 bunkers built to safely store the explosives still exist in the wildlife area. You'll pass many of these reminders of the area's wartime past on your hikes and drives in the Busch Conservation Area. In 1947, the Department of Conservation, with the aid of a $7,000 donation from Mrs. August Busch in memory of her husband, was able to purchase the land from the government.

Under the DOC's management, this old ammo-production site has become perhaps the best place in the St. Louis area to admire Missouri's plants and animals. An incredible array of wildlife lives in or migrates through Busch Conservation Area. More than 30 lakes dot the landscape, ranging from tiny ponds of a few hundred square yards to the expansive 182-acre Lake 33. Waterfowl are attracted by rich feeding areas and nesting boxes that dot the lakes year-round.

## ▶ DIRECTIONS

From the Weldon Spring–Defiance exit off US 40–Interstate 64, drive southwest 1 mile on MO 94 to MO D. Go 2 miles west on MO D to August A. Busch Memorial Conservation Area.

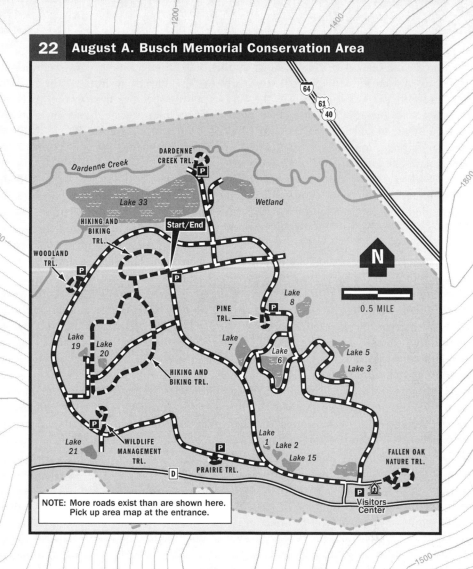

**DARDENNE CREEK TRL.**

Dardenne Creek

Lake 33

Wetland

**HIKING AND BIKING TRL.**

Start/End

**WOODLAND TRL.**

N

0.5 MILE

Lake 8

**PINE TRL.**

Lake 19

Lake 20

Lake 7

Lake 6

Lake 5

Lake 3

**HIKING AND BIKING TRL.**

Lake 21

**WILDLIFE MANAGEMENT TRL.**

Lake 1

Lake 2

Lake 15

**FALLEN OAK NATURE TRL.**

**PRAIRIE TRL.**

Visitors Center

64
61
40

NOTE: More roads exist than are shown here.
Pick up area map at the entrance.

Busch Conservation Area's numerous ponds also attract blue herons, sand-pipers, and other shorebirds. If you like to do more than just look at the wildlife, check into the area's managed hunts. Or bring your fishing pole—the lakes are stocked with bass, bluegill, crappie, several varieties of catfish and sunfish, and more. The visitor center has licenses and rental boats, and will direct you to the lake managed for the fish species you're after.

Busch Conservation Area is much more than lakes. Developed habitats here include oak–hickory woodland, a pine plantation, prairie, forest edge, and fields planted with attractive food sources for numerous birds and animals. This wide variety of habitats attracts myriad wild critters for you to study and admire on your wanderings. Hundreds of songbirds live in the woods and prairies or pass through on their annual migrations. Coveys of quail will scare you out of your boots if you inadvertently jump them from the brush at the trail's edge. Hawks watch over the landscape from perches next to the fields, and eagles are sometimes spotted by visitors during winter. You might see owls at dawn and dusk, or startle them from their hiding places during the day. Beaver live in the park's ponds and waterways. And the woods and grasslands are crawling with deer, turkey, and coyotes.

You'll better enjoy your time at Busch Conservation Area if you hit the visitor center before starting your exploration. Maps are available there, as well as self-guided tour booklets for the 8.7-mile Auto Tour and the Fallen Oak Nature Trail. The center has maps for many other conservation areas in Missouri, and an excellent set of interpretive displays that'll educate you on the plants and critters you'll see on your hikes. There's also a nature gift shop with trail guides, plant-, animal-, and bird-identification books, and a wide selection of gifts for the nature lover. If the center is closed, you can still pick up maps from the information box on the entrance road.

After leaving the center, head to the eastern end of the parking lot and begin your hike on the paved surface of the 0.7-mile Fallen Oak Nature Trail. With its inter-pretive exhibits, self-guiding trail booklet, and tree-identification tags, the Fallen Oak is a good educational follow-up to the visitor center. A wide variety of trees here attracts a host of birds to this part of the wildlife area. A viewing station lets you peek through a slotted wall to watch birds chow down at feeding stations. Birdhouses are hidden in the forest above the trail. A wooden bridge spans a deep wash that comes powerfully alive during storms. Benches offer you breaks when you need them. And pavement, a cutoff option, and only a couple of gradual climbs make the Fallen Oak an easy hike.

Following the Auto Tour will take you to most of Busch's other trails and give you a wonderful introduction to the historical and natural attractions in the area along the way. You'll pass a TNT storage bunker and a 200-year-old cemetery before reaching the Pine Trail at Station 4 of the Auto Tour. This 0.2-mile trail isn't much of a hike, but don't skip this pleasant walk through a pine plantation. The scent along the path can be wonderful, and the breeze sighing through these tall evergreens is possibly the most peaceful sound in the world. I enjoy laying on my back on the pine-needle bed to watch the stately pines sway in the wind.

The 0.4-mile Dardenne Creek Trail is near Station 5 on the Auto Tour. Though the trail is sometimes overgrown, muddy, and hard to follow, it's a neat place to check out a marsh-and-stream-stabilization project on Dardenne Creek. With its combina-tion of forest, marsh, grassy meadow, and streamside habitats, the area along this trail is an excellent birding spot. A developed wetland nearby, complete with wooden view-ing platforms, offers a great look at Busch's waterfowl during seasonal migrations.

At Auto Tour Station 7 you'll find the Woodland Trail, a 0.2-mile hike through an oak-hickory forest. This easy walk through a common Missouri habitat passes two ponds from which you'll hear spring peeper serenades on the year's first warm days. The 0.4-mile Wildlife Management Trail at Auto Tour Station 8 is a quick lesson in habitat development for wildlife. On this short hike you'll see two ponds, forest, for-est edge, prairie, intermittent streams, and brush piles. Auto Tour Station 10 is the

Prairie Trail, a 0.2-mile path wending through grasses up to six feet tall. I like walking the Prairie Trail on windy days, when its grasses whisper and swish in the breeze. It's nice on calm days, too, when you can hear birds, bugs, and critters rustling stealthily in the thick grasslands.

After warming up and learning about the area on these short hikes, you'll be ready for the Hiking and Biking Trail, the conservation area's longest hike. Located on B Road southwest of Lake 33, this 3.2-mile trail covers the landscape south of the lake on two loops joined by a short connector. This easy hike is marked for counterclockwise travel with markers at each mile. You'll pass lots of haunting old ammo bunkers, some with cedars growing from their sides and roofs. The trail follows a combination of old bunker-access roads, wildlife-area maintenance roads, and a short portion of one of the conservation area's gravel drives. With easy grades and wide treadways, this path is perfect for trail running and cross-country skiing. The north loop has nice views of Lake 33. The south loop crosses the dam of Lake 19 and passes an overgrown pond that's turned into a slough full of snags and cattails— a great place for spotting herons, kingfishers, woodpeckers, and other birds.

Ask the folks about Busch's interpretive programs. They schedule such fascinating events as Owl Prowls, Spring Peeper Walks, Autumn Color Hikes, and much more. Contact them for a program schedule or to plan a separate event for your organized group.

### ▶ NEARBY ACTIVITIES

The Lewis and Clark Trail, one of the best hikes in the St. Louis area, is just to the southeast (page 117). A series of wineries awaits your posthike relaxation in the towns along MO 94 between Defiance and Dutzow.

# CUIVRE RIVER STATE PARK

## KEY AT-A-GLANCE INFORMATION

**LENGTH:** 38 miles of trail on hikes ranging from 1–8 miles

**CONFIGURATION:** Series of interconnected loops

**DIFFICULTY:** Moderate on Cuivre River, Big Sugar Creek, and Lone Spring Trails; easy or very easy on all others

**SCENERY:** Forested hills and hollows, serpentine creeks, prairies, bluff overlooks on the Cuivre River

**EXPOSURE:** Shaded; exposed areas on Blazing Star, Prairie, and Lakeside trails

**TRAFFIC:** Moderate

**TRAIL SURFACE:** Packed earth, some gravelly and rugged sections

**HIKING TIME:** 4–5 hours on Cuivre River, Big Sugar Creek, and Lone Spring Trails, unless cutoff trails are used to shorten each loop; 1 hour or less on all other trails

**ACCESS:** Open 6 a.m.–10 p.m.

**MAPS:** Okete USGS topo; trail map available at visitor center

**FACILITIES:** Water, restrooms, campground, picnic shelters, playground, swimming, phone, visitor center

**SPECIAL COMMENTS:** Pets on 10-foot leash

### GPS TRAILHEAD COORDINATES (VISITOR CENTER)

| UTM ZONE (WGS84) | 15S |
| --- | --- |
| EASTING | 679276 |
| NORTHING | 4319404 |
| LATITUDE–LONGITUDE | |
| NORTH | N39° 0' 19.0814'' |
| WEST | W90° 55' 46.5085'' |

## IN BRIEF

In Cuivre River State Park's 6,394 acres of rugged, Ozark-like terrain, you can explore 38 miles of trail with loop hikes ranging from 1 to 8 miles in length. Along the way you'll see clear streams, springs, bluff overlooks, glades, and patches of tall-grass prairie.

## DESCRIPTION

Cuivre River State Park's landscape is a wooded island in the rolling farm country of northeastern Missouri. Part of the Lincoln Hills, an area that escaped heavy glaciation, Cuivre River's 6,394 acres feature the ridges, hollows, gravelly streams, and bluff overlooks common to the southern part of the state. Many plants and animals living here are found nowhere else in northern Missouri.

Though it didn't become a park until 1946, Cuivre River got its start in the 1930s. The Civilian Conservation Corps and Works Progress Administration worked here, developing the landscape as a federal recreation demonstration area. They built roads, bridges, group camps, and parts of the extensive trail system you'll be hiking. At the park's visitor center you'll find historical displays on the CCC and WPA, background on prehistoric human activity, a variety of nature-oriented displays, and a slide show. An aerial photo shows how the park truly is a wooded island in an agricultural landscape, and a relief map previews the topography of the trails.

The park includes the 1,165-acre Big Sugar Creek Wild Area, the 1,102-acre North Woods

## DIRECTIONS

Drive 14 miles north from Wentzville on US 61 to the Troy–MO 47 exit. Go 3 miles east on MO 47 to MO 147. Turn left onto MO 147 and follow it 2 miles to the park's visitor center. Map available there has directions to trailheads.

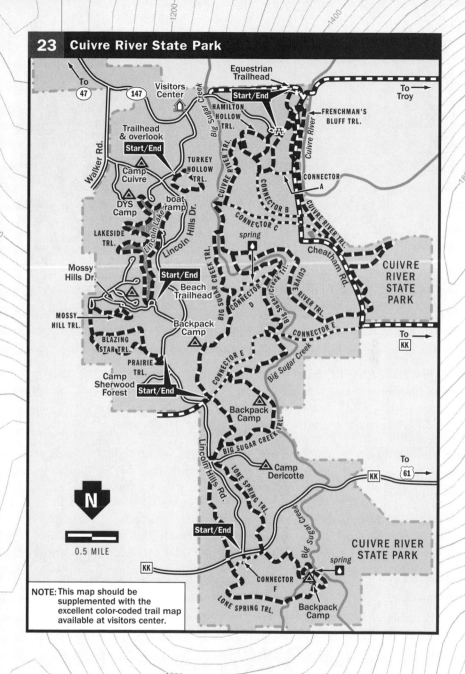

# 23 Cuivre River State Park

To 47

147

To Troy

Equestrian Trailhead

Start/End

Visitors Center

FRENCHMAN'S BLUFF TRL.

HAMILTON HOLLOW TRL.

Trailhead & overlook
Start/End

Big Sugar Creek

Cuivre River

TURKEY HOLLOW TRL.

CONNECTOR A

Walker Rd.

Camp Cuivre

boat ramp

CUIVRE RIVER TRL.

CONNECTOR B

CONNECTOR C

CUIVRE RIVER TRL.

DYS Camp

Lincoln Lake

Lincoln Hills Dr.

spring

Cheatham Rd.

CUIVRE RIVER STATE PARK

LAKESIDE TRL.

Start/End

Beach Trailhead

BIG SUGAR CREEK TRL.

CONNECTOR D

CUIVRE RIVER TRL.

BIG SUGAR CREEK TRL.

To KK

Mossy Hills Dr.

MOSSY HILL TRL.

Backpack Camp

CONNECTOR E

CONNECTOR E

Big Sugar Creek

BLAZING STAR TRL.

PRAIRIE TRL.

Camp Sherwood Forest

Start/End

Backpack Camp

To 61

BIG SUGAR CREEK TRL.

Camp Dericotte

KK

N

0.5 MILE

Lincoln Hills Rd.

LONE SPRING TRL.

Start/End

KK

spring

CUIVRE RIVER STATE PARK

CONNECTOR F

Big Sugar Creek

Backpack Camp

LONE SPRING TRL.

**NOTE:** This map should be supplemented with the excellent color-coded trail map available at visitors center.

View of Lincoln Lake from the
Lakeside Trail

Wild Area, and the 1,782-acre Lincoln Hills Natural Area. On Cuivre River's trails you'll explore a wide variety of habitat. The Prairie and Blazing Star trails go through tall-grass prairie and savanna. The Big Sugar Creek, Cuivre River, Lone Spring, and Frenchman's Bluff trails wander through deep hollows and forests, cross small creeks, and climb to spectacular bluff overlooks. There's even a 4-mile shoreline hike around Lincoln Lake on the Lakeside Trail.

The Lakeside Trail is the easiest hike in the park. It starts from either the beach or the boat launch, staying level all the way around the lake. For most of its length it follows the shore, with views of the lake's blue waters. In several places, ledges next to the water make perfect spots to soak your feet and admire the view. In quiet coves, look for herons stalking their prey, or turtles sunning themselves on logs. Monstrous grass carp hang out in the shallows near the beach, kicking up quite a wake when you startle them. There aren't any markings on the Lakeside Trail, but with the lake as your landmark you won't need any.

Cuivre River State Park has several more easy hikes. One of these is the Turkey Hollow Trail, a 1-mile jaunt off the park entrance road. The trail itself isn't much—just a nice walk in the woods with few steep grades—but it's a nice warm-up hike or a good walk with children. The 1-mile Mossy Hill Trail is much the same. It's a pleasant short hike from the park campground. The 2-mile Blazing Star Trail is better. It wanders among several hollows and across tall-grass prairies, with bright wildflowers scattered all about. A connector leads over to the campground and the Mossy Hill Trail to extend your hike to 3 miles. A side trail heading down-hollow from the southwest corner of the Blazing Star's loop leads to a couple of gated cave entrances. All of these short hikes are marked at intersections with carsonite posts bearing directional arrows.

Two other short trails, the 1-mile Hamilton Hollow and 2-mile Frenchman's Bluff trails, start from the picnic area 1 mile west of the visitor center. The Hamilton Hollow Trail is an easy and not-too-interesting ramble along wooded hillsides into and out of Hamilton Hollow. Frenchman's Bluff heads west from the picnic area, crosses the Cuivre River Trail, climbs onto its namesake bluff at a spectacular overlook above the Cuivre River, then follows the river for a half mile.

Both the Hamilton Hollow and Frenchman's Bluff trails connect to the Cuivre River Trail—the most scenic hike in the park. Three connectors cut across the Cuivre River Trail, dividing this 8-mile loop into shorter hiking options of 1.5, 2.8, and 4 miles. No matter which hike you choose, you'll enjoy at least a half mile along Frenchman's Bluff, with its panoramic view over farm fields on the western side of the Cuivre River. The loop begins from the equestrian camp, but you can access it from the picnic area via the Hamilton Hollow or Frenchman's Bluff Trails. It's marked with red blazes and carsonite posts with red arrows. All connectors are marked with white blazes. It's marked for clockwise travel, but going counterclockwise saves your bluff overlook for last. On the loop's eastern side you'll hike next to Sugar Creek for a mile, and wander for 2 miles along spectacular Frenchman's Bluff on the west.

The Big Sugar Creek Trail, marked with blue plastic blazes and arrows for clockwise travel, explores the center of the park. Its trailhead is on Lincoln Hills Road, 1.5 miles south of MO KK. Two connector trails, marked in white, divide this 7-mile trail into three loops. The north and middle loops are each 4 miles, and the south loop is 2.75 miles. Since there's no trailhead on the south loop, it must be combined with the middle loop for a 5.25-mile hike. The Big Sugar Creek Trail winds through deep hollows and along breezy ridges, crossing Big Sugar Creek twice in the southern loop. All three loops parallel Big Sugar Creek at some point. The prettiest spot along the trail is on the middle loop, where a spectacular bluff overlook with benches and a panoramic view await you. Connector D, divider between the middle and south loops, passes a pretty spring. If you're really ambitious, follow Connector E to the Cuivre River Trail and its spectacular views from Frenchman's Bluff.

The 6-mile Lone Spring Trail, marked with yellow arrows for clockwise travel, is a favorite. Horses aren't allowed there, the grades aren't too steep, and there are few rugged areas to slow your progress. Connector F divides the Lone Spring Trail into a pair of 3-mile loops. The north loop features an exquisite little spring seeping from beneath a rocky ledge and flowing into Big Sugar Creek. The trail crosses the low cliff above the spring, and a side trail descends to its quiet pool. A backcountry campsite near the spring makes the north loop popular with backpackers. A connector trail runs 0.2 miles from the southern tip of the Lone Spring Trail to the north end of the Big Sugar Creek Trail. The trailhead for the Lone Spring Trail is at the junction of Lincoln Hills Road and MO KK. A spur trail leads north from the trailhead to the middle of Connector F.

# ENGELMANN WOODS NATURAL AREA

## KEY AT-A-GLANCE INFORMATION

**LENGTH:** 2 miles

**CONFIGURATION:** Loop with spur access trail

**DIFFICULTY:** Very easy

**SCENERY:** Forested hills with occasional views of surrounding ridges and bottom-lands along the Missouri River

**EXPOSURE:** Shady throughout

**TRAFFIC:** Light

**TRAIL SURFACE:** Packed earth

**HIKING TIME:** 1–2 hours

**ACCESS:** Open 4 a.m.–10 p.m.

**MAPS:** Map available at trailhead; Labadie USGS topo

**FACILITIES:** None

**SPECIAL COMMENTS:** Pets on leash; no picnicking allowed; no collection of any vegetation, nuts, or fruits. Check out Head's Store in St. Albans, an old general store left over from the area's rural days. Just drive through town; you can't miss it. They have great sandwiches!

## ▶ IN BRIEF

Engelmann Woods is a wonderful short hike through deep woods comprising one of Missouri's few remaining old-growth forest landscapes.

## ▶ DESCRIPTION

Engelmann Woods is a beautiful outdoor secret in the St. Louis area. Located on 145 acres overlying a hollow that opens onto the Labadie Bottoms along the Missouri River, Engelmann protects a small remnant of the old-growth forest that once covered the hills up and down the Missouri. Majestic trees nearly 200 years old and reaching 100 feet into the forest canopy shade you on your wanderings among Engelmann's breezy ridges and quiet hollows.

Private landowners donated these forested hollows to the Missouri Botanical Garden in the 1940s. The Department of Conservation purchased Engelmann Woods in the early 1980s and designated it a natural area soon afterward. Engelmann Woods is also a wildlife refuge, so it's a hike on which you needn't avoid the yearly fusillades that occur during deer and turkey seasons. You'll likely see deer as you hike at Engelmann, along with songbirds, woodpeckers, and nuthatches.

If you plan a group hike here, carpool to the trailhead. Its tiny parking area has room for only three cars. A map of the area is posted on the trailhead kiosk, with a box full of extra copies for hikers. The official distance is 1.5 miles, but by the time you backtrack the loop access spur you'll hike almost 2 miles. The route is marked with

## GPS TRAILHEAD COORDINATES (PARK ENTRANCE)

| | | |
|---|---|---|
| UTM ZONE (WGS84) | 15S | |
| | EASTING | 694010 |
| | NORTHING | 4270697 |
| LATITUDE-LONGITUDE | | |
| | NORTH | N38° 33' 48.8040'' |
| | WEST | W90° 46' 23.6210'' |

## ▶ DIRECTIONS

Drive 3 miles west on MO 100 from its intersection with MO 109. Turn right on MO T and follow it 6 miles west to Engelmann Woods. Watch for a sign and small trailhead parking area on the right as you top the long hill after St. Albans's west entrance.

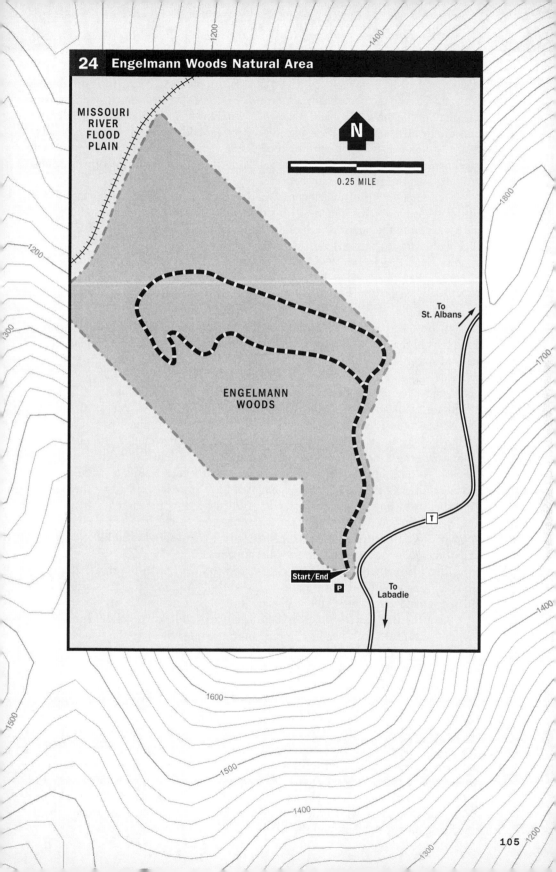

MISSOURI
RIVER
FLOOD
PLAIN

**N**

0.25 MILE

ENGELMANN
WOODS

To
St. Albans

T

Start/End

P

To
Labadie

brown wooden signs emblazoned with "TRAIL," supplemented by arrows on trailside trees and occasional signs bearing footprint outlines. Because much of the topsoil covering Engelmann's ridges and hollows is windblown silt from nearby Labadie Bottoms on the Missouri River, the trail can get pretty muddy and slippery after rain. The upside of this soil is that it sprouts nice displays of spring wildflowers to decorate Engelmann's moist, fertile landscape, including beautiful celadine poppies, whose outline graces the area brochure's cover.

Your exploration of Engelmann Woods starts at the steel gate on the eastern side of the parking area and heads north on an old road overlooking MO T, with pretty views into the hollow south of the highway. You'll traverse a little saddle on the ridge with vistas to the left and right, cross a pipeline cut, and come to a sign welcoming you to Engelmann Woods. Behind the sign are a couple of big boulders. And in winter when the trees are bare you can see all the way north to the bluffs across the Missouri River. After a little down and up to cross another saddle, you'll reach the beginning of the main loop at 0.4 miles into your hike.

If you take the right fork and hike the trail counterclockwise, you'll continue along the old road for a short way to the natural area's northeastern boundary. There the trail swings left off the old road and begins descending along a single-track path into a deep hollow. As you move away from MO T the hike gets really peaceful and wild, almost like a trail deep in the Ozarks. You'll descend for nearly a half mile, sometimes easily and sometimes steeply, paralleling the hollow bottom to your left, with several pretty rock outcroppings decorated with bright green patches of moss scattered along the way. You'll end your descent standing right in the middle of a usually dry stream near where the hollow opens into Labadie Bottoms.

This is a beautiful spot. The streambed is a slick rock trough for about 25 feet, and the trail goes right down it. You might think you're lost, standing there in the streambed with no obvious path to take. But just follow the stream's bend to the southwest, and you'll immediately see where the trail climbs from the wash on some wooden steps. Huge trees shade the hollow, and a broad-shouldered hill guards each side of the hollow's opening into the Missouri River bottomlands.

If you have energy to burn, work your way up the hill on the right side. At the top you'll find a bluff with nice vistas of the Labadie Bottoms, the Missouri River on the bottomland's northwest side, and the bluffs of St. Charles County beyond.

After the trail leaves the streambed, it curves southeast to follow another hollow for a short way, then begins climbing onto the ridge dividing the two hollows in Engelmann Woods. You'll climb for most of the next half mile, steeply at first over several switchbacks onto the spine of the ridge, then gradually along the ridge to the loop's end, 1.5 miles into your hike. There are ridgetop vistas when tree leaves are off, and you'll see the massive stacks of the Labadie Power Plant poking above the skyline to the west as you follow the ridge to close the loop.

A second trail heads northwest from the trailhead, fading out shortly after crossing the pipeline cut. It's an old trail that really goes nowhere, but does offer a short option for families and folks wanting a quick and easy taste of the outdoors. Follow this path to the pipeline cut, turn right to follow the cut's wide grassy swath to the main trail, then turn right again and return to the trailhead. It's an easy and scenic half-mile jaunt with little difficult climbing and several nice vistas from the hills along the pipeline cut and the highway.

# GRAHAM CAVE STATE PARK

Graham Cave, a deep overhang beneath a massive rock dome, sheltered prehistoric Americans who once hunted along the Loutre River valley. Visit this haunting cavern, then explore the ancients' old hunting grounds on a network of trails that meander through the park's rugged hillsides and lush bottomlands.

▶ **DESCRIPTION**

Graham Cave State Park was once owned by Daniel Morgan Boone, son of the famous frontiersman. The park is named for Robert Graham, who purchased river bottomland in the park from Boone in 1816. In 1847 he acquired the parcel of land containing the cave. The land stayed in the Graham family through four generations until Frances Graham Darnell, Robert Graham's great-granddaughter, donated it to the state park system in 1964.

D. F. Graham, Robert's son, used the cave for a pigpen, but the artifacts he found in the cave piqued his interest. In 1930, archaeologists from the university, after being shown Graham's collected artifacts by his son Benjamin, examined the cave. No excavation was done until the late 1940s, when Ward Darnell, Frances's husband, began digging into the cave to enlarge the pigpen. Hearing of this, archaeologists convinced him to let them excavate first.

The excavations uncovered artifacts dating prehistoric occupation 10,000 years into the past. Graham Cave became a National Historic Landmark in 1961, the first archaeological site in the United States to be so designated. The cave is 120 feet wide and 16 feet high at its entrance, and

▶ **DIRECTIONS**

Drive west on I-70 to Exit 170 for MO 161, Danville, Montgomery City, and MO J. Go west on MO TT, which is the north outer road. In 2 miles MO TT ends in the park.

**KEY AT-A-GLANCE INFORMATION**

**LENGTH:** 4 miles on 3 short trails

**CONFIGURATION:** Two loops, connected by a point-to-point trail

**DIFFICULTY:** Easy

**SCENERY:** Wooded hills, rocky streams with riffles and cascades, mossy outcrops, Graham Cave

**EXPOSURE:** Shady, with several exposed stretches

**TRAFFIC:** Heavy on Graham Cave Trail, light on all others

**TRAIL SURFACE:** Packed earth, many rocky sections

**HIKING TIME:** 1 hour on Loutre River and Indian Glade Trails; 1 half-hour on Graham Cave Trail

**ACCESS:** Open 7 a.m.–sunset

**MAPS:** Montgomery City USGS topo; trail map available at park office

**FACILITIES:** Water, visitor center, restrooms, camping, phone, picnic shelter

**SPECIAL COMMENTS:** Pets on 10-foot leash

**GPS TRAILHEAD COORDINATES (PARK ENTRANCE)**

| UTM ZONE (WGS84) | 15S |
|---|---|
| EASTING | 623365 |
| NORTHING | 4307513 |
| LATITUDE-LONGITUDE | |
| NORTH | N38° 54' 28.2807'' |
| WEST | W91° 34' 37.9275'' |

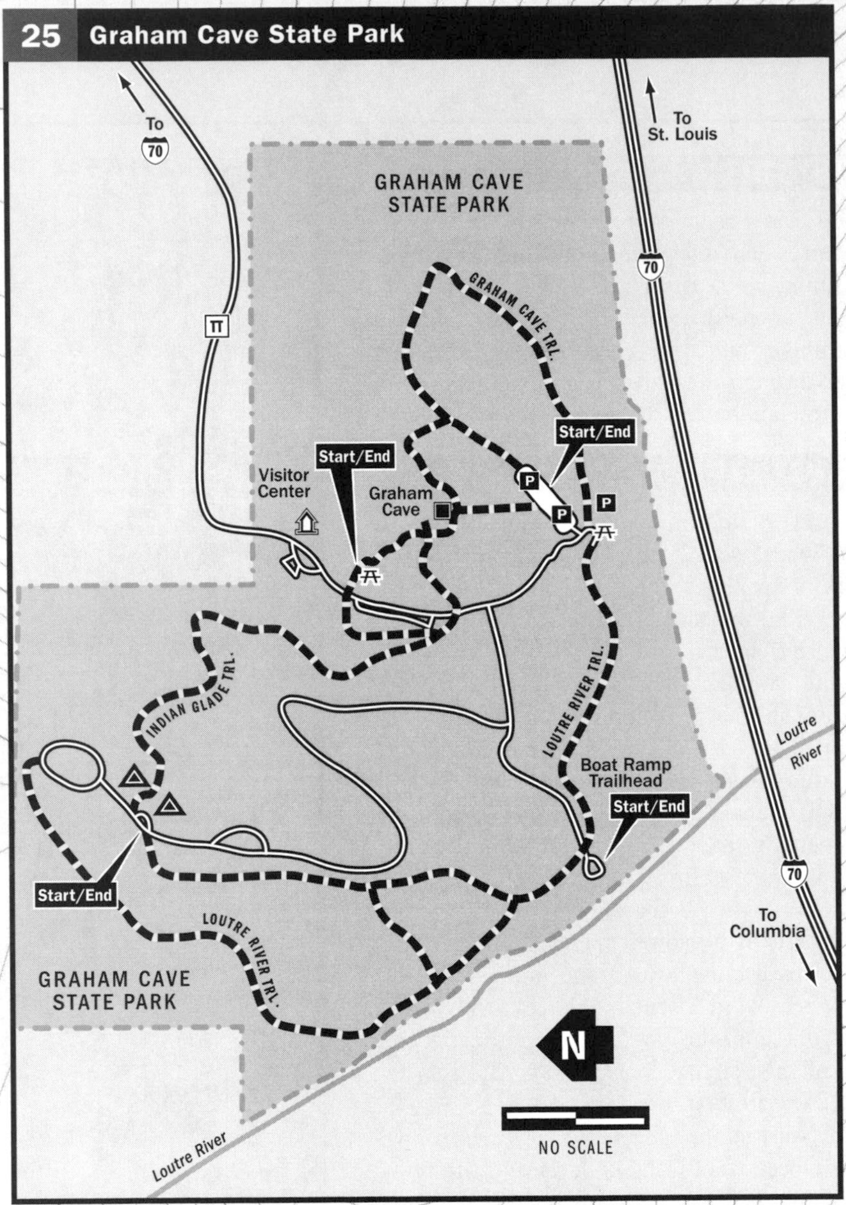

25
Graham Cave State Park
To
70
To
St. Louis
GRAHAM CAVE
STATE PARK
GRAHAM CAVE TRL.
70
TT
Start/End
Start/End
Visitor
Center
Graham
Cave
P
P
P
INDIAN GLADE TRL.
LOUTRE RIVER TRL.
Boat Ramp
Trailhead
Start/End
Loutre
River
Start/End
70
To
Columbia
LOUTRE RIVER TRL.
GRAHAM CAVE
STATE PARK
N
NO SCALE
Loutre River

extends 100 feet into the rocky hillside. Much of its deeper portion has yet to be excavated. A fence protects the unexcavated back part of the cave, but you can still enter its front areas and imagine what it was like here thousands of years ago. A paved path leads from the parking area to Graham Cave's mouth, and interpretive panels describe the cave's history. Additional interpretive displays are located at the park's visitor center.

Graham Cave State Park is more than just a cave. Three hiking trails lead away from the prehistoric shelter and wander a diverse 356-acre landscape of moist river bottom, forested hills, rocky glades, and rugged rock formations. The longest is the Loutre River Trail, a 1.5-mile loop accessed by a 0.6-mile spur. The trail heads west from the picnic shelter at the end of the parking lot, traveling gently downhill through the woods to T into the road leading to the boat launch. There you'll turn left, walk the road to the boat launch, then head northwest along the Loutre River and into the woods.

Shortly after entering the woods, the trail forks, and the 1.5-mile loop begins. Taking the right fork, you'll climb for most of the next half mile, passing a cutoff trail and hiking through a field of mossy rock outcrops before breaking into the campground behind the restrooms. Next, head uphill to the end of the camp loop, where the trail leaves it between sites 45 and 49. You'll descend for the next half mile on your way back to the Loutre River, twice crossing a little rocky-bottom stream with a couple of waterfalls. The trail hugs the Loutre River for the last quarter mile to the loop's end. Watch for herons in the river's slow, shallow waters.

The 1-mile Indian Glade Trail links the campground to the cave. This point-to-point trail can be hiked as a loop by walking from Graham Cave to the campground on the Loutre River Trail, then returning to the cave via the Indian Glade Trail. It'll be 2.25 or 2.5 miles, depending upon which side of the Loutre River Trail loop you use. The Indian Glade Trail leaves the campground near the bathhouse, heading east. It's a rugged trail for much of its length, bouncing over rock steps and past mossy outcroppings. One deep hollow hides a 20-foot-high ledge with a deep overhang. If there's been a recent rain it forms a beautiful waterfall, and you'll cross a footbridge right above its pour-off. Just after crossing the park road, you'll walk several hundred feet on a rock ledge, then break into a rocky glade next to Graham Cave.

From this glade a side trail heads uphill to the left. It goes to the upper picnic area, then loops back to the Indian Glade Trail for an optional 0.4-mile side loop. If you walk a few steps onto the solid rock in front of you, you'll be on top of Graham Cave and looking down onto the lawn in front of the ancient shelter. The Indian Glade Trail breaks to the right from this intersection and descends over several rock layers and a wooden staircase, ending in front of the cave.

The Graham Cave Trail heads into the woods from the right side of the cave. Just less than a half mile in length, it travels some rugged, beautiful country. After leaving the cave, it follows a boardwalk staircase. If there's been recent rainfall, a waterfall pours off the ledge. Beyond the boardwalk's end, a trail to the right leads 100 yards to the parking lot. But keep going—more beauty awaits. You'll make a short and steep rocky climb, then level out along a 20-foot-tall moss-covered rock face marked with fascinating striations. From there it's an easy descent to the parking lot.

The Loutre River Trail is marked inconsistently with blue arrows. Other than signs at some of the entry points, the other trails have no markings. All the trails are easy to follow, though, so you'll have no problem finding your way around Graham Cave State Park.

# HILDA YOUNG CONSERVATION AREA

## KEY AT-A-GLANCE INFORMATION

**LENGTH:** 3 miles

**CONFIGURATION:** 3 interconnected loops

**DIFFICULTY:** Very easy

**SCENERY:** Wooded hills and riverside meadows

**EXPOSURE:** Even mix of open meadow and shady forest

**TRAFFIC:** Light

**TRAIL SURFACE:** Packed earth with occasional rocky or rooty stretches

**HIKING TIME**: 1–2 hours

**ACCESS:** Open 4 a.m.–10 p.m.

**MAPS:** Department of Conservation map of area available at trailhead; Pacific USGS topo

**FACILITIES:** None

**SPECIAL COMMENTS:** Pets must be on a leash; watch for the occasional rabbit hunter during winter hikes

### GPS TRAILHEAD COORDINATES (TRAILHEAD)

| | | |
|---|---|---|
| UTM ZONE (WGS84) | 15S | |
| EASTING | 704117 | |
| NORTHING | 4258150 | |
| LATITUDE-LONGITUDE | | |
| NORTH | N38° 26' 53.9457'' | |
| WEST | W90° 39' 39.5116'' | |

## IN BRIEF

Explorations of Hilda Young Conservation Area will treat you to brushy meadows, grassy fields, breezy hilltop pine groves, and exquisite cascades and waterfalls along the tributary streams of LaBarque Creek.

## DESCRIPTION

The beautiful 970-acre Hilda Young Conservation Area was acquired by the Department of Conservation in 1986. And happily for us woodland wanderers, the masses still haven't discovered this hideaway. In Hilda Young, you'll hike past brushy meadows and open grasslands, splash across clear brooks, amble through cool forests, and meander along scenic LaBarque Creek and its side streams. On a hilltop along the south trail loop you'll circumnavigate a pine plantation, where tall evergreens sway and sigh in the breeze, and hike through a small glade. Waterfalls grace one of LaBarque Creek's tributaries. In spring, colorful wildflowers dot the grasslands, forested hills, and moist bottomlands at Hilda Young. A pretty bluff overlooks LaBarque Creek from the pine plantation; a pond offers fishing for bass, channel cat, and bluegill.

With a variety of habitats, Hilda Young is a great place for observing wildlife. Streams, moist bottomlands, dry uplands, forest, brushy meadows, and open grasslands are all found here, and the Meramec River flows by a few hundred yards northwest. The Department of Conservation adds to the mix by digging ponds, growing food plots, and building brush piles to attract lots of critters.

## DIRECTIONS

From I-44 Exit 264, Eureka–MO W–MO 109, drive 2.3 miles south to MO FF. Turn right on MO FF and follow it 2.8 miles southwest to the trailhead on the east side of the highway.

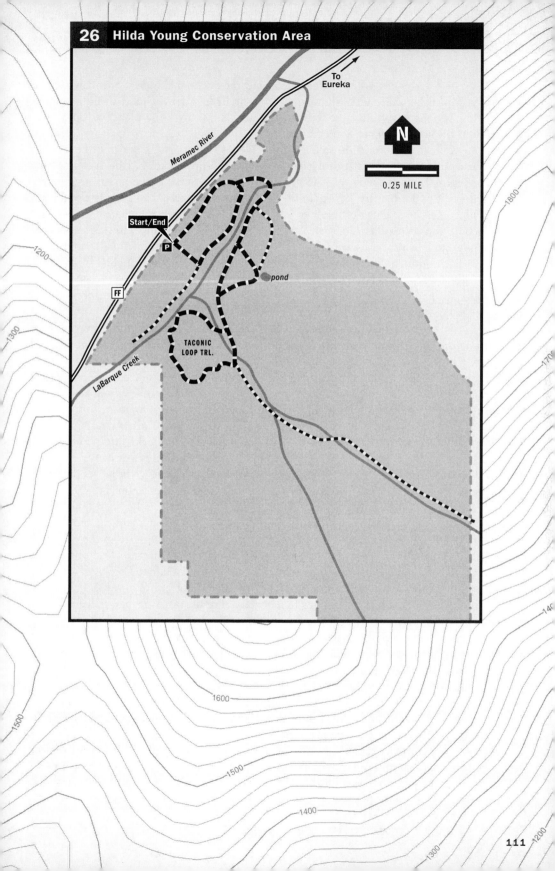

To
Eureka

Meramec River

N

0.25 MILE

Start/End

P

FF

pond

1200

1300

LaBarque Creek

TACONIC
LOOP TRL.

1800

1700

1600

1500

1500

1400

1300

1400

1200

1300

Deer, turkey, coyotes, raccoons, squirrels, and the occasional bobcat or fox live in the area. Kingfishers flit raucously up and down the creek, hawks hunt above the open fields, various songbirds dart through the woods and over the meadows, and owls haunt the area by night.

You can explore Hilda Young on the Taconic Loop Trail, a series of connected loops. Area literature calls the Taconic Loop a 2.5-mile hike, but by the time you backtrack the connecting trails to complete the loops you'll hike just over 3 miles, and you can double that by exploring side paths to waterfalls and bluffs not on the main route. Since much of the hike follows old roads with gently graded slopes, the Taconic Trail is excellent for trail running or side-by-side hiking with a companion. While most of this conservation area is forested, a big chunk of the Taconic Loop Trail goes through sunny open fields that'll warm you on winter hikes. In the cold months leafless trees open up wide views of the surrounding countryside, and frozen waterfalls and rock ledges sporting icicle mustaches decorate the landscape.

Trail intersections are marked with carsonite posts bearing arrows pointing the direction of travel, and occasional square signs emblazoned with "Trail" are scattered along the path. Begin your hike at the north end of the trailhead parking lot and follow a mown path north through a brushy field with nice views of the hills overlooking Hilda Young to the northeast. At the field's north end you'll pass a fork to the right. It finishes off the trail's northwest loop, and you'll go that way at the end of your hike. Continue straight ahead, pass through an evergreen archway formed by a couple of cedars, and make a curving descent through a belt of trees that ends heading south on a picturesque bridge over LaBarque Creek. Rock outcroppings and ledges edge the creek west of the bridge, and a wooded hillside rises to the east.

From the bridge, the trail goes south between the creek and a wildlife food plot. At the south end of the field there's a fork to the left. It's the Taconic Loop Trail's 0.15-mile east loop, a short hike that passes a fishing lake, then returns to the main trail a short distance to the south. The lake's a nice place to picnic, and if you follow the mown path up the hill (south of the lake), you'll be treated to gorgeous vistas across the Meramec Valley to the hills on the river's northern bank. Two other mown paths lead down from each end of the lake's dam to the field by the bridge over LaBarque Creek.

From the south end of the food plot, the main trail gets rocky as it enters the forested part of the hike and climbs to a bench above the creek. Several trailside ledges are nice overlooks of the stream below, and in winter you can see through the woods to the open fields near the trailhead. Several bone-white sycamores dot the bottomland before you, and cedars decorate the hillsides. Continuing south you'll hike along a hallway of cedars, descend through a power-line cut that opens up nice views to the left and right, and reach the Taconic Loop Trail's south loop about 1 mile into your hike.

I like hiking this scenic loop counterclockwise. You'll splash across a creek, then do a short stiff climb to a beautiful hilltop pine plantation and follow its perimeter for nearly a mile on a path intermittently covered with pine needles. Cross the power-line cut twice, enjoying vistas to the northeast and southwest. Pines tower to your left, and shorter cedar trees shade the right side of the trail. On the loop's western side, the path follows a low bluff over LaBarque Creek, where a bench makes the perfect rest stop on a pleasing overlook above the stream. After the second power-line crossing you'll hike through a small glade that's being restored, then descend back to the creek you crossed at the beginning of the south loop.

At the bottom of that descent, the trail hits a T-intersection with an old road. The trail goes left, crosses the stream, and closes the loop 200 yards to the north. To see some really cool waterfalls, turn right instead and follow this old road southeast. If the creek's up, you'll see six really impressive cascades and lots of ledgy, slick-rock stream bottom between the trail fork and the area's east boundary located a mile upstream from the fork. The first three cascades are ledge falls formed where the stream pours over rock layers. The fourth one, about a half mile from the trail fork, is the best. The creek filters over and through massive broken rock layers that resemble a washed-out highway. Pick out a flat rock, stretch out, and cool your feet in the pool below the falls. Above the falls, the trail begins to fade in and out. But push on another quarter mile and admire a 6-foot cascade over a miniature staircase of 20 or 30 crooked ledges in the streambed. It looks like the creek's flowing over the world's largest layer cake.

To return to your car, retrace your steps until you hit that first intersection in the field north of the trailhead, and go left to complete the northwest loop of the Taconic Loop Trail. You'll walk east to the LaBarque Creek, then hike south along the stream for a quarter mile. The path then leaves the creek, turns right, and heads gently uphill 200 yards to the trailhead. Before you finish your hike, though, take one last scenic side jaunt. Where the trail leaves LaBarque Creek for the last time, follow a mown path south past a bench and continue along the stream. A short way down this path, you'll see the start of a bluff on the opposite side of the creek. It rises higher and higher as you hike upstream, until it towers 40 feet above LaBarque Creek. The pine plantation on the south loop covers the hill above this pretty bluff, and short side trails lead from the mown path to scenic viewpoints and wading holes in the creek bed.

## ▶ NEARBY ACTIVITIES

Additional nearby hikes are at West Tyson, Lone Elk (page 55), Greensfelder (page 45), and Route 66 (page 75) parks.

# KLONDIKE PARK

## KEY AT-A-GLANCE INFORMATION

**LENGTH:** 5 miles, with longer options via the Katy Trail

**CONFIGURATION:** Loops with spurs

**DIFFICULTY:** Very easy

**SCENERY:** Rocky bluffs, expansive views of the Missouri River

**EXPOSURE:** Mostly shaded on natural-surface trails; Lewis and Clark and Lake Loop mostly open

**TRAFFIC:** Medium

**TRAIL SURFACE:** Packed earth with many rocky sections on Hogsback, Power Line, Strip Mine, and Donkey Kong trails; gravel and asphalt on Lewis and Clark Trail and Lake Loop

**HIKING TIME:** 1 half-hour–3 hours, depending on trail choices

**ACCESS:** Open 7 a.m.–10 p.m., March–November; 7 a.m.–6 p.m., December–February

**MAPS:** Available at shower house; Labadie USGS Topo

**FACILITIES:** Water, camping, cabins, conference center, picnic shelters, restrooms

**SPECIAL COMMENTS:** Pets must be on 8-foot leash. The Montelle Winery and its bluff-top views are just west of Klondike on MO 94, and Sugar Creek Winery is a few miles north. Six miles southwest on MO 94 is Augusta, with wineries, a brewery, and fascinating antique and specialty shops.

### GPS TRAILHEAD COORDINATES (PARK ENTRANCE)

| | | |
|---|---|---|
| UTM ZONE (WGS84) | 15S | |
| EASTING | 687971 | |
| NORTHING | 4272596 | |
| LATITUDE–LONGITUDE | | |
| NORTH | N38° 34' 55.0438'' | |
| WEST | W90° 50' 31.1288'' | |

## ▶ IN BRIEF

Klondike Park is a scenic jewel in St. Charles County's rapidly expanding park system. Built on the grounds of an abandoned quarry, this rugged landscape features scenic Missouri River views; paved, packed-gravel, and natural-surface hiking trails; and rugged bluffs reflected in the old quarry pool.

## ▶ DESCRIPTION

Opened in the summer of 2004, Klondike Park sits on the worked-over landscape of the old Klondike Quarry, whose most important product was silica sand for manufacturing glass. Now this rugged 250-acre chunk of St. Charles County has been transformed into the area's newest outdoor getaway. In addition to its trails, Klondike features picnic shelters, access to the Missouri River, cabins, a small conference center, and a campground that's badly needed by users of the Katy Trail. A picturesque lake left over from the quarry is stocked for catch-and-release fishing, and the pool's calm surface reflects the steep and rugged quarry walls.

In the eastern end of Klondike Park you can admire this scenery from stupendous overlooks on the 1.5-mile Hogsback Trail, with vistas of the Missouri River, its huge sandbars and wide bottomland fields. This trail is best hiked counterclockwise. That way you'll make the climb to the overlooks on a gentler grade, and you'll save the overlook views for last. Look uphill to the south before hitting the trail and note the two-tiered bluff towering over the conference center. That's where you'll admire the scenery from at the end of your hike.

## ▶ DIRECTIONS

Drive west on I-64–US 40/61 to Exit 10 for Weldon Spring, Defiance, and MO 94. Turn left on MO 94 and drive 14 miles south, through Defiance and Matson Hill, to the park entrance on the left. Klondike is 5 miles south of Defiance.

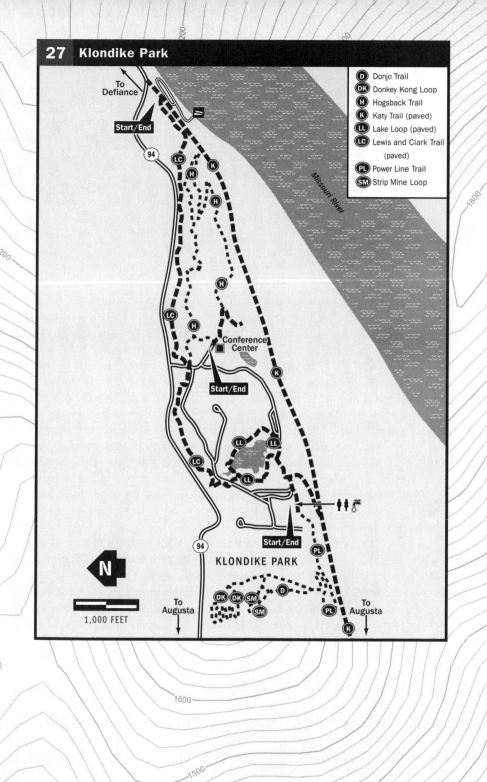

To Defiance

Start/End

94

Missouri River

D Donjo Trail
DK Donkey Kong Loop
H Hogsback Trail
K Katy Trail (paved)
LL Lake Loop (paved)
LC Lewis and Clark Trail
(paved)
PL Power Line Trail
SM Strip Mine Loop

LC
K
H
H
H
LC
H
Conference Center
Start/End
K
LL
LL
LC
LL
Start/End
PL
94
KLONDIKE PARK
N
DK DK SM D
SM
PL
1,000 FEET
To Augusta
K
To Augusta

Begin by heading north from the trailhead next to the conference center, dropping immediately into a brushy flat scattered with huge rocks left over from the park's quarry days. The trail then angles close to the highway, parallels it for a few yards, then veers away to the east-southeast and deeper into the woods. You'll cross a little hollow, and if you look uphill to the right you'll see the fence that runs along the cliff above the Missouri River.

Soon the hillside to your right steepens, and at the half-mile point you'll come alongside a mossy rock wall. The trail follows this wall for a short way, then does three quick switchbacks to climb up a bowl-like gap in the steep rock slope. After edging up the wall, the trail drops briefly, then begins angling up the steep slope to the south. It's a gentle climb for the next half mile over three long switchbacks. Bright-green moss-covered rock outcrops are scattered up and down the hill; you'll hike next to several of these. And one nifty stretch of the trail runs on top of an overhanging ledge for 20 yards. As you climb you'll have views through the trees of a big sweeping bend of the highway to the north, and at the end of the first switchback you can look straight down at a bridge on the Katy Trail.

When the climb tops out, the trail heads west next to a wooden fence along the bluff overlooking the Missouri River. An especially pretty stretch of trail begins here—cedars fringe the bluff, and you'll get glimpses of the river lazing along below the cliff. After a quarter mile along the fence the trail breaks away from the bluff's edge and heads downhill 100 yards to join a paved pathway with two forks. The right fork goes steeply downhill to the trailhead, and the left one leads to a beautiful overlook from a wide rock patio carved out during the Klondike Quarry's heyday. To the south is the Missouri River with its wide bottomlands and expansive gravel bars, and to the west you'll overlook the park's shelters and picnic areas. Directly below you'll see the white gravel path of the Katy Trail running along the base of the bluff. A few tables scattered across this rocky patio make an ideal picnic spot near the end of your hike back on the Hogsback Trail.

The west end of Klondike is explored by a tight network of rugged-but-scenic trails totaling just less than 2 miles in length. Named Power Line Trail, Strip Mine Loop, Donkey Kong Loop, and Donjo Trail, they meander among boulder piles and craggy-walled holes left from the area's quarry days. Beginning from the parking lot near the shower house and easily hiked in an hour, this network features views of the Missouri River valley, open fields, sheer bluffs, thick woods, and a couple of distant views of church steeples in the nearby village of Augusta. Both these trails and the Hogsback Trail were constructed by the Gateway Off-Road Cyclists, who did a superb job of choosing routes and constructing the treadway for these hikes.

The 1.3-mile Lewis and Clark Trail and half-mile Lake Loop are a network of walking/biking paths exploring the parks bottomlands and the area around the lake on a combination paved and gravel path. Both ends of the Lewis and Clark Trail connect to the Katy Trail, forming a 2.5-mile loop. If you're feeling ambitious, you can hike the Katy all the way to St. Charles to the northwest or halfway across the state westward to Sedalia. For more realistic hikers, it'd be an easier trek a couple of miles northeast on the Katy to the Sugar Creek Winery in Matson Hill, or 4 miles west to Augusta, where you'll find wineries, a brewery, and several restaurants for refueling yourself for the trip back to Klondike.

# LEWIS AND CLARK TRAIL

## ▶ IN BRIEF

The Lewis and Clark Trail is the favorite of many hikers in the greater St. Louis area. Though it's next to the big city, hiking here feels like being deep in the Ozarks.

## ▶ DESCRIPTION

The Lewis and Clark Trail explores part of Weldon Spring Conservation Area, a landscape rich in both natural beauty and history. This country was first settled by John Weldon in 1796 as a 425-acre Spanish Land Grant. During World War II the government took control of the area and much of the surrounding land for use as a munitions plant. For 20 years after the war, the land was owned by the University of Missouri and used as an agricultural-experiment station. The Missouri Department of Conservation acquired the property in 1978 and began restoring the area's natural beauty.

As you hike the Lewis and Clark Trail, it's hard to imagine the activity that once took place in this seemingly undisturbed wildlife area. Now it's a surprising wilderness-like landscape next to a major metropolitan area. Though it has a few challenging long grades, this trail is wonderfully designed, taking in the area's natural beauty with few steep grades and rugged sections. It's a superb place for trail running.

The varied terrain along the trail showcases everything that's great about Missouri's outdoors. You'll hike through cool woods, along breezy cedar-studded ridges, wander through deep hollows, skirt open food-plot fields for wildlife, and admire

## ❶ KEY AT-A-GLANCE INFORMATION

**LENGTH:** Choice of 5.3 or 8.2 miles

**CONFIGURATION:** Loop

**DIFFICULTY:** Moderate

**SCENERY:** Wooded ridges, deep hollows, and breathtaking overlooks from towering limestone bluffs edging the Missouri River

**EXPOSURE:** Mostly shaded except for open areas on bluff vistas

**TRAFFIC:** Light to moderate

**TRAIL SURFACE:** Mostly packed earth with a few rocky and rooty sections scattered throughout; parts of the trail get very muddy after rain

**HIKING TIME**: 4-5 hours for long loop, 2-3 hours for short loop

**ACCESS:** Open from 4 a.m.–10 p.m.

**MAPS:** Weldon Spring Conservation Area map; Weldon Spring USGS topo

**FACILITIES:** No facilities available at the trailhead; water, bathrooms, and maps available at DOC Headquarters and Visitor Center 2 miles west of MO 94 on MO D

**SPECIAL COMMENTS:** Pets must be leashed; monitor children on bluff overlooks

## ▶ DIRECTIONS

Drive west from St. Louis on I-64–US 40 to the Weldon Spring–Defiance–MO 94 exit. Turn left and drive 2.5 miles southwest to the trailhead. The trailhead will be on your left as you enter the forest just past Francis Howell High School.

### GPS TRAILHEAD COORDINATES (PARK ENTRANCE)

| | | |
|---|---|---|
| UTM ZONE (WGS84) | | 15S |
| | EASTING | 697930 |
| | NORTHING | 4285028 |
| LATITUDE-LONGITUDE | | |
| | NORTH | N38° 41' 30.2620'' |
| | WEST | W90° 43' 27.0836'' |

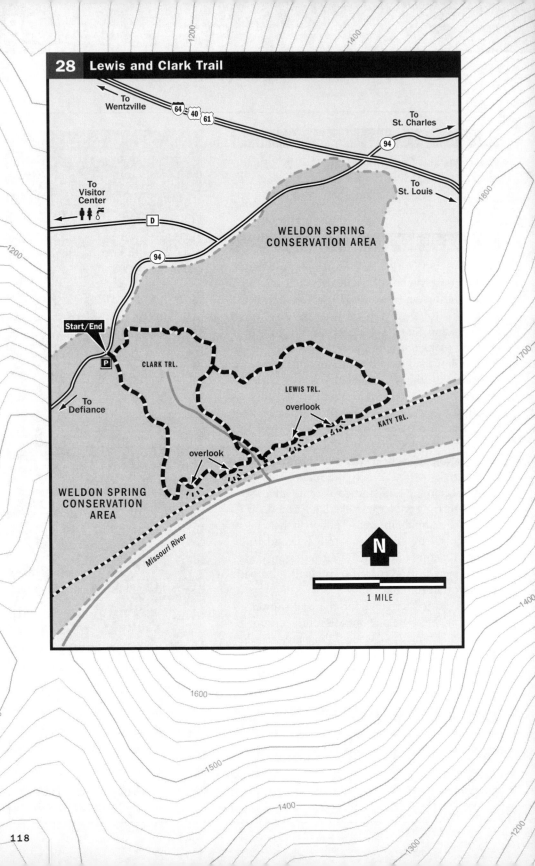

the Missouri River from the miles of bluff that parallel the river's edge. The combination of woods, hollows, and riverside habitat fosters an abundance of wildlife; the place is lousy with deer. In spring a symphony of frogs and toads sing their mating calls from the river and ponds in the area. You'll love the place if you're a birder, especially in winter, when at overlooks you can spot eagles roosting in the trees on Howell Island across the Missouri River. Turkeys roam the woods, woodpeckers and nuthatches bounce from limb to limb, and numerous songbirds make their home in this forest every spring.

I like to hike the trail clockwise, saving the overlooks for the latter stages of my hike. But since the route is marked for a counterclockwise hiker, that's how it is described here. The first mile of your hike will be fairly level, much of it following an old road that skirts hollows as it winds along a ridge toward the Missouri River. A quarter mile into the hike there's a springtime highlight—a shallow pool on the right side of the trail that's usually full of frog eggs and tadpoles. It's fascinating to stop here in mid-March when the nearly grown tadpoles are still clumped together in their jellylike egg sacks, struggling to escape into the pool and grow to adulthood before the water dries up. Raccoons get most of 'em, but a few do live to sing their song on future peaceful spring evenings.

Just after the frog pool, the trail passes through a flat area that's covered with masses of spring beauties and a scattering of other wildflowers early in the hiking season. It then meanders through a grove of pines that nicely scents the air on warm days, does a little dip across the head of a hollow descending to the left, and comes to mile marker 1. Shortly after that, you'll begin descending off the nose of the ridge. If the leaves are off you can see the Missouri River through the trees as you drop off the ridge. You'll soon come to a bench with a nice view of the river through the trees and a scenic bluff outcropping to the right. This is a good turnaround if you're looking for a short, easy hike, but I recommend continuing to the second mile marker, where you'll find the best overlook on the trail.

The trail heads north from this overlook, still descending, passing through the fascinating remains of a huge fallen oak. For years, this monster tree blocked the trail and forced a steep, slippery detour. In 2000, the Boy Scouts from O'Fallon cut and cleared it off the trail as a good-turn project. When you see the thickness of its massive trunk, you'll appreciate the Scouts' hard work clearing this behemoth from the trail.

At mile 1.5 the descent ends at the site of an old quarry. The trail turns east and south across rocky quarry debris. A short spur trail leads to a small man-made glade next to a low bluff exposed from the quarrying operation years ago. Continuing on the main trail you'll start climbing easily to the nose of a ridge, then switchback to the left for the most rugged ascent on the Lewis and Clark Trail. For 200 feet or so you'll climb steeply over exposed rock and flinty gravel to the top of the ridge. From there it's level and easy to the 2-mile marker, where a spur next to a switchback in the trail leads to a spectacular overlook.

This is most hikers' favorite overlook on the Lewis and Clark Trail and is perhaps one of the best in Missouri. Don't kick loose any rocks or debris—the Katy Trail passes by directly below this bluff-edge overlook, and you might KO a hiker or biker.

The Missouri River flows next to the Katy. Across the wide stream is Howell Island, and beyond that is the city of Chesterfield. Looking upriver you'll see the small villages of Defiance and Matson, and the monstrous Labadie power plant. This is an especially wonderful overlook in the dead of winter, when the Missouri is often choked with brilliant white ice floes from bank to bank. On a still day you can hear them bumping and grinding against each other as they drift by.

Leaving this vista, the trail skirts a hollow before reaching another overlook almost as good as the last one. Here you can stand on a pedestal rock towering over the river and admire the river valley and Katy Trail below. From here the trail descends through a series of switchbacks into a deep hollow next to the river. Be careful on the wooden steps on the third switchback—they're very slippery in cold and wet weather. At the bottom of the descent you'll hike up the hollow along an intermittent stream, cross it, and come to a fork in the trail at mile 2.9. There's a bench for resting while you decide whether to take the left fork on the Clark Trail for the 5.3-mile loop or the right fork on the Lewis Trail for an 8.2-mile hike. If you take the Clark Trail, you'll continue up the hollow for a while, then make a long gradual ascent to rejoin the Lewis Trail about a mile from the fork.

The longer Lewis Trail heads back down the hollow toward the river. Since this hollow fills with water whenever the river floods, the trail is sometimes hard to follow. Just look sharp for markings and footprints, keep heading downstream, and you'll soon pick out the route where it leaves the floodplain. The trail breaks left and heads uphill as you near the river, and a spur trail leads 100 yards east to connect with the Katy Trail. For a good look at the river, take this spur and watch the mighty Missouri roll by next to the Katy.

About a half mile after leaving the junction, you'll level out on the bluff above the river and hike next to an old fence for a while. The trail winds along the heads of shallow hollows, passing through groves of cedars that scatter their blue-bead seeds on the forest floor. Keep a sharp eye to the right—it's easy to miss my favorite overlook on the Lewis Trail. Watch for a short spur leading out to a pedestal-like rock protruding from the bluff about a mile after the junction. Extending out from the bluffline, it's an ideal spot to lie in the sun, picnic, and admire the view. The river stretches to the left and right. Downriver you can see the Interstate 64 bridge. Immediately below the overlook is the Katy Trail, and between the bluff and the river is a wilderness of huge sycamores, cottonwoods, and dead snags—a wonderful place for birders to scan with binoculars. Contrasting with the natural scene are Spirit of St. Louis Airport across the river and the skyline of Chesterfield in the distance to the east.

A quarter mile after this overlook the trail leaves the river and bluff and descends over five switchbacks to another deep hollow extending back from the river. It meanders up this hollow, crossing a dry stream several times. Judging from its cut banks and several deep, rocky bottoms, this stream must really kick up its heels during rain, but most of the time it's dry. In several places it's torn the earth from under large trees, dropping them across the stream and exposing fascinating nests of roots. After following this hollow and stream gradually uphill for a mile the trail begins to climb in earnest, topping out in one of the many groves of cedars found on ridgelines in Weldon Spring. I love how these cedars sigh on the breezy ridgetops.

For the next mile the trail climbs and descends through hollows and ridgetops until it rejoins the Clark Trail a little before mile 7. The remainder of the Lewis and Clark Trail is just your usual wonderful walk through the woods. It has one more big descent climb, more forested hollows, and a nice grove of shortleaf pines just before reaching the trailhead. You'll know you're near the end when you begin hearing traffic on MO 94.

Night hiking is a wonderful way to escape the Missouri heat and humidity, and the Lewis and Clark is a wonderful place to try out your night vision. It's close to town, and its overlooks offer wonderful views of the Chesterfield night skyline. The Missouri River is beautiful in the moonlight, and on your nocturnal ramblings you'll tramp to the songs of owls, whippoorwills, frogs, coyotes, and other wilderness critters.

## ▶ NEARBY ACTIVITIES

After your hike, head south on MO 94 to visit the wineries scattered along the Missouri River in Matson, Augusta, Dutzow, and Marthasville. Better yet, go there first and bring some wine, cheese, and crackers to enjoy at one of the overlooks. Defiance, only a few miles southwest of the trailhead, has two bars that serve excellent cold drinks, cheeseburgers, and onion rings.

Another attraction is the Busch Memorial Conservation Area Visitor Center, 2 miles west of MO 94 on MO D. It has wonderful displays on Missouri flora and fauna, information on Weldon Spring Conservation Area and many other Department of Conservation sites in the region, and a gift shop with lots of outdoor doodads for your family and friends.

# LOST VALLEY TRAIL

 **KEY AT-A-GLANCE INFORMATION**

**LENGTH:** 9 miles

**CONFIGURATION:** Loop, with spur trail access

**DIFFICULTY:** Easy–moderate

**SCENERY:** Forested ridges overlook long valleys featuring brushy meadows, wildlife food plots, and meandering streams

**EXPOSURE:** Open hiking along meadows and wildlife food plots, mixed with occasional shady forested stretches

**TRAFFIC:** Medium

**TRAIL SURFACE:** Mix of old double-track roads and winding single-track

**HIKING TIME:** 3–5 hours

**ACCESS:** Area open 4 a.m.–10 p.m.

**MAPS:** The Weldon Spring Conservation Area map shows the Lost Valley Trail; Defiance USGS topo

**FACILITIES:** None

**SPECIAL COMMENTS:** Pets on leash; watch for bicycles on this popular mountain-biking trail; avoid Lost Valley during late-fall deer-hunting season.

After your hike, head south on MO 94. It's a scenic drive made even more enjoyable by visits to the half-dozen wineries scattered along the highway in Defiance, Augusta, Dutzow, and Marthasville. History buffs should drive 5 miles west on MO F to the Daniel Boone Home and Boonesfield Village. There you can tour the famous frontiersman's Missouri home and wander through this growing historical village.

**GPS TRAILHEAD COORDINATES (TRAILHEAD)**

| | | |
|---|---|---|
| UTM ZONE (WGS84) | 15S | |
| EASTING | 695123 | |
| NORTHING | 4281575 | |
| LATITUDE–LONGITUDE | | |
| NORTH | N38° 39' 40.5897'' | |
| WEST | W90° 45' 26.6749'' | |

## IN BRIEF

Wandering through the quiet hideaway of Lost Valley, you'll follow the scenic meanders of Little Femme Osage Creek, hike past a crystal-clear spring, admire a man-made pond enlarged by beavers, and startle deer and turkeys from their haunts in this peaceful valley. Best of all, this beautiful trail is suitable for hikers of all ages and abilities.

## DESCRIPTION

Though the Lost Valley Trail isn't your traditional Ozarks single-track hike, it's still one of my favorite backcountry haunts in the St. Louis area. It follows old roads for more than half its length, but several reroutes built by the Gateway Off-Road Cyclists over the past couple of years have replaced some of the two-track with some wonderfully crooked single-track. Lost Valley is a great place for trail running; gentle grades make it an excellent hike for families and novice hikers, too. Hard-core hikers will enjoy the challenge of the entire 9-mile loop, while the young or not as fit can easily hike part or all of the first 3 miles of level trail along Little Femme Osage Creek, then turn around for an easy jaunt back to the trailhead.

When snow blankets the landscape, Lost Valley is a great place for cross-country skiing. The easy miles along Little Femme Osage Creek are great for beginners, while more-advanced skiers will enjoy the challenge of mild hills on the rest of the loop. Snow or not, winter is my favorite time to explore Lost Valley. Ice formations decorate Femme Osage Creek, reduced foliage opens up better views of the ridges towering over the trail,

## DIRECTIONS

From the Weldon Spring–Defiance exit on I-64– US 40/61, drive 7 miles southwest on MO 94. The trailhead is on the right side of the highway just before the Little Femme Osage Creek bridge.

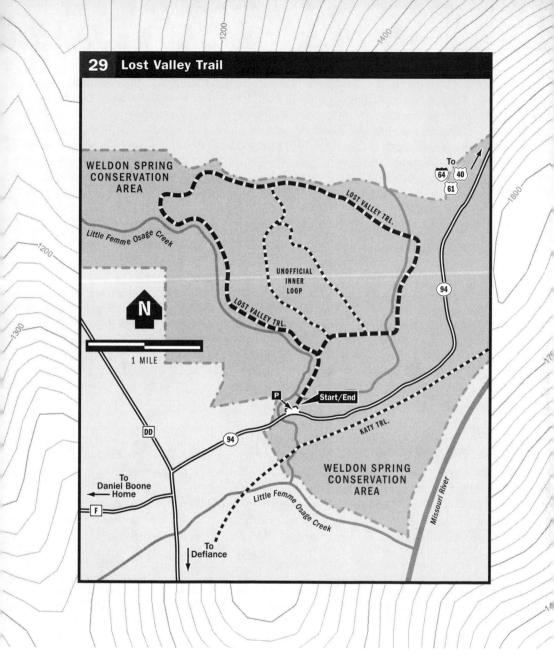

cedars and bone-white sycamore trunks stand in bright contrast with winter's gray and brown hues, and open areas along the way let bright winter sunshine warm you as you hike the frozen landscape.

The moderate temperatures of spring and fall are pretty darned good times to hike Lost Valley, too. The familiar (but always incredible and new) colors of autumn brighten the landscape in late October, and spring brings a variety of wildflowers to the hillsides and valley floors. An especially impressive scattering of redbud blooms jazzes up the spring woodlands near the end of the loop, and Missouri's signature dogwoods dot the forest throughout the area. You should definitely pack your copy of *Missouri Wildflowers* by Edgar Denison.

The spur trail to the main loop starts from the northeast corner of the parking lot and heads north on an old road. The route is well marked with signposts every few hundred yards and marker posts for each mile hiked. Except about 2 miles of single-track and a 1.5-mile stretch along a gravel service road on the north part of the loop, the trail is what you see at the trailhead—a worn two-track road through the woods.

The trail parallels Little Femme Osage Creek for its first 3 miles. It's a pretty creek with lots of meanders, eroded banks, and fallen trees, overlooked by ridges towering over each side of its bottomland. Little Femme Osage wiggles all over Lost Valley, sometimes flowing next to the trail, other times winding away to the far side of the valley floor. Just into the hike you'll walk down what I call the Sycamore Hallway. Stately trunks of these white-barked trees line both sides of the trail for a couple hundred yards, in rows so straight you'd swear these majestic pillars were intentionally planted there.

Just after the Sycamore Hallway the main loop begins. The route is signed for hiking the loop in a clockwise direction, breaking left off the old road onto a narrower two-track. In the next half mile you'll edge along a couple of fields and cross two creeks. The second creek flows from a spring just north of the trail. Push through the brush a few yards to admire this pretty little seep trickling from the roots of several sycamores at the base of the hillside.

A few hundred yards past the spring are two beautiful ponds, both man-made but enhanced by the work of some industrious beavers. The second pool is most impressive—the beavers have added sticks and mud to the top of the dam and plugged its spillway, so that when the pond is full its overflow trickles along the trail's edge. These critters' dam work is so level that the whole east end of the pond looks like a cup filled to the brim and ready to overflow. You can see the beavers' mud-and-stick lodge in the upper end of the pool, and across the lake are lots of beaver-chewed trees. Snags standing in the water are great places to spot woodpeckers, and wooden boxes placed in their boughs are nesting sites for waterfowl.

The next mile is a wonderful hike along the wide valley of Little Femme Osage Creek. Just past the beaver ponds a slope covered with yuccas looks spectacular in spring, when these spiny plants sprout tall stalks covered with soft yellow flowers. You'll swing gradually north, hiking past wildlife food plots and brushy meadows, with lots of nice views of the creek. Near the 2-mile marker you'll reach a parklike area where a tin-roofed shelter stands in a grassy spot on the forest floor. Here the hillsides close in to make this place truly feel like a lost valley. Also, don't worry about the progressively louder gunshots you're hearing—that's just the firing range on the north edge of Weldon Spring Conservation Area.

Scenery through this narrow part of Lost Valley is really beautiful. Scattered cedars add a splash of color to the forest in winter. Some 40-footers tower over the trail, and shorter ones decorate the hillsides on both sides of the valley. Little meadows are scattered along the trail, and sometimes you'll make short climbs up the hillside to stay above the creek when it squeezes you against the valley's edge. At the 2.5-mile mark you'll come to a haunting old chimney standing next to the trail in a bend of the stream, all that remains of an abandoned homesite in Lost Valley.

The valley stays narrow and crooked after the old chimney, and the two-track path becomes rough and rocky for a while. You'll climb gradually through rock layers from which seeps form curtains of icicles in cold weather, until you're 100 feet above the creek. This scenic overlook marks the 3-mile point of your hike. The trail then descends back to Little Femme Osage Creek for one last streamside hike before swinging east and leaving the creek for good.

Shortly after breaking east to climb out of the Little Femme Osage valley, you'll hit the first portion of new single-track. You'll walk through a tight grove of cedars, followed by a winding descent into a small hollow. Keep an eye peeled to the left as you near the floor of the hollow—if you spot some rusty fence, you're looking at the corner posts of a tiny graveyard. In spring you'll know you're close to the cemetery when you see jonquils along the trail. Like the old gravesite, they're left over from the area's agricultural past.

Just beyond the cemetery, the trail swings north and climbs a steep side hill with a strongly flowing spring downhill to the right. A few hundred yards beyond the spring, the trail winds through an impressive little boulder garden. And if you climb onto the suspiciously level knoll to the left, you'll realize the side hill you've been traversing is an old dam. The spring-fed lake that was once here has turned into a marsh over the years, and in April you'd be serenaded by an unbelievable chorus of frogs singing their mating calls.

From the old dam the trail climbs gradually to the east along the edge of a deep hollow, crosses the head of the hollow on a small bridge, then tops out in open fields next to the boundary fence. Next you'll hike through several fields, some edged with cedars, then T into a gravel road running north and south. While not part of the official trail, you can turn right on this road for a 2.5-mile shortcut back to the trailhead. It's the same road the trail uses at the beginning of the hike. The shortcut heads south and level for its first mile or so, passes some old building foundations, goes through a rusting metal gate, then descends gradually all the way back to the loop junction and spur to the trailhead.

The official trail jogs left a few yards, then continues east along the boundary fence. For the next 1.5 miles you'll hike on a maintained gravel road. It's closed to all but DOC vehicles, so no traffic to deal with—just an enjoyable walk through forests of hardwoods and cedar. The gravel-road stretch of your hike ends with a short descent to a creek crossing, where you'll turn right off the gravel road to follow an open valley to the south.

The trail south along the valley is an easy jaunt through meadows and food plots, with several creek crossings in an open bottomland between forested ridges. It follows a power line almost a mile before breaking west toward the woods and one last creek crossing.

After fording the creek you'll begin a second section of newly constructed single-track, a beautifully constructed stretch of trail that winds over a ridge and back into the Little Femme Osage valley. As you cross the ridge's spine, you'll see an old road going uphill to the north. This old track continues north 1 mile along the ridge to a junction with the shortcut road you saw at the midpoint of the loop, joining it next to the old building foundations. You can combine this road and the shortcut to hike an unofficial inner loop of about 3.5 miles. The official trail meanders downhill to the west and crosses a couple of usually dry streams, joins the shortcut road, turns left, and closes the loop 200 yards to the south.

# MATSON HILL PARK

 **KEY AT-A-GLANCE INFORMATION**

**LENGTH:** 2.75 miles

**CONFIGURATION:** Loop with shortcut options

**DIFFICULTY:** Easy

**SCENERY:** Wooded hills and ridges, rocky stream bottoms

**EXPOSURE:** Shaded

**TRAFFIC:** Medium

**TRAIL SURFACE:** Packed earth

**HIKING TIME:** 1–2 hours

**ACCESS:** Open 30 minutes before sunrise–30 minutes after sunset

**MAPS:** Labadie USGS topo; park maps available at trailhead

**FACILITIES:** Restrooms, picnic tables

**SPECIAL COMMENTS:** Pets must be on an 8-foot leash; no alcohol or glass containers. Sugar Creek Winery, located just south of Matson on MO 94, has delicious wines and fine views of the Missouri River Valley. Other wineries are located in nearby Augusta and Dutzow. Augusta has a microbrewery, and both bars in Defiance serve great burgers.

**GPS TRAILHEAD COORDINATES (PARK ENTRANCE)**

| | |
|---|---|
| UTM ZONE (WGS84) | 15S |
| EASTING | 690165 |
| NORTHING | 4277188 |
| LATITUDE–LONGITUDE | |
| NORTH | N38° 37' 22.2392'' |
| WEST | W90° 48' 56.0035'' |

## ▶ IN BRIEF

Built by the Gateway Off-Road Cyclists, the Matson Hill Trail was opened in June of 2002. This well-designed and superbly graded trail is open for hikers, too, and explores deep forests, shady hollows, rocky streams, and breezy ridges.

## ▶ DESCRIPTION

Though the Matson Hill Trail was built by mountain bikers for mountain bikers, it's a fine destination for hikers, too. Working with St. Charles County Parks, the Gateway Off Road Cyclists (GORC) built this wonderful 2.75-mile trail system in the spring of 2002. GORC's Web site says that once construction was approved, they built the trail in four workdays. That's impressive—a trail this well engineered couldn't have come together so quickly and so beautifully without much planning and hard work.

The Matson Hill Trail explores a 68-acre tract of wooded landscape in southern St. Charles County. Unlike nearby hikes on the Lewis and Clark Trail and Klondike Park, there's little in the way of scenic vistas in Matson Hill Park. This twisty trail is a fine hike just the same. It wiggles over the side hollows of a small creek drainage like a snake on a roller coaster, following a smooth packed-earth path with only a few rough sections and steep grades. It's an excellent trail-running destination. In fact, one leg of the county

## ▶ DIRECTIONS

Drive west on I-64–US 40/61 to Exit 10 for Defiance, Weldon Spring, and MO 94. Turn left and drive 11 miles southwest on MO 94 to Matson Hill. Turn right on Matson Hill Road, which becomes gravel as you leave town. Go 1.25 miles to a T intersection with a paved road. Turn right to continue on Matson Hill Road, and drive a half mile to Matson Hill Park.

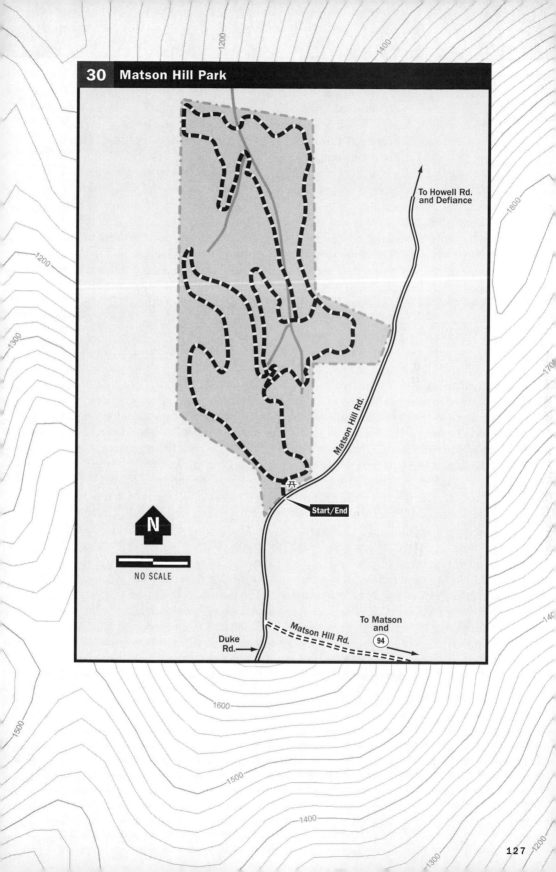

To Howell Rd.
and Defiance

Matson Hill Rd.

Start/End

N

NO SCALE

Duke
Rd.

Matson Hill Rd.

To Matson
and
94

park department's Wild in the Woods Trail Run Series is held at Matson Hill. For those less energetic outdoor lovers (like me) it's a great place to do a quick hike before visiting one of the wineries scattered up and down MO 94 near the park.

Matson Hill Park has a nice wild feel for such a small tract of land. Mature forest covers the entire park, complete with lots of fallen timber and fantastic upended root wads. Located far from major highways or towns of any size, it's peaceful and secluded in this forested enclave. Its moist hollows grow colorful wildflowers, and its rocky streams come to life in spring or after rainfall. Sheltered by a thick forest canopy, the park is shady and cool even on hot summer days.

You can hike the entire loop for a 2.6-mile trek or use two shortcut trails for shorter options. Hiking the loop closest to the trailhead results in a 1.1-mile walk, and combining the first and second loops results in a hike of 1.6 miles. The trail is marked with orange metal discs nailed to trailside trees, supplemented at intersections with white carsonite posts with arrows and hiker silhouettes. Markings are a little sparse on the far reaches of the third loop, but the trail is so easy to follow that you wouldn't get lost even if there were no markers.

Hiking the loop counterclockwise, you'll head downhill and eastward from the trailhead, then switchback to the left and pass a sinkhole. About a quarter mile into the hike you'll veer north and come to the first connector trail. Going left on the connector, it's 100 yards or so to the other side of the loop, where you could continue back to the trailhead on the 1.1-mile option. The main loop veers southeast to work its way around the head of a hollow, then winds and rolls along the hillside to the second connector 0.75 miles into the hike. You'll be near the main stem of the creek that drains the park and will see the other side of the loop across the creek.

After the intersection, you'll hike gently up for the next quarter mile, going through rocky stretches and angling uphill above the drainage. As you near the park's north end you'll veer west along the boundary and descend quickly to the bottomland, crossing the usually dry creek on a rock ledge spanning the streambed—a scenic little spot indeed. A few yards down the trail you'll cross a rocky-bottom tributary whose streambed resembles a rock staircase. For the next half mile you'll angle south to another side hollow, break north to follow it back to the creek, then switchback south to follow the park's main hollow to the northern cutoff trail.

From this trail junction you'll make a sweeping quarter-mile arc to the southern cutoff trail 0.75 miles from the trailhead. This last stretch to close the loop is a nice hike—more sweeping turns, a long stretch of bench-cut trail in a steep hillside, and deeper, darker hollows than anywhere else in the park. You'll leave those hollows on an ascending ridge spine, leveling out and finishing off the loop on a hogback ridge with steep descents on both sides of the trail.

# QUAIL RIDGE COUNTY PARK

## ▶ IN BRIEF

Quail Ridge has paved trails in open grasslands, natural-surface trails on wooded hillsides, and, for those who demand a little more from their hiking experience, an 18-hole disc golf course.

## ▶ DESCRIPTION

Nestled in a bend of Peruque Creek, Quail Ridge County Park is one of several new outdoor gems in the St. Charles County Department of Parks. Quail Ridge Park has 3 miles of paved path and about 3 miles of natural-surface trail, with plans to expand in future years. In addition to the trails already in Quail Ridge, the park has several shelters, a playground, a conference center, and an 18-hole disc golf course.

Before it became a park, Quail Ridge's 250 acres were used as an equestrian farm. Horses were stabled, hayrides and trail rides were organized, and horse paths wound all over the hills and creek bottoms. The park's open prairie spaces were once grazing lands for the horses. Two pastures along Peruque Creek in the south end of the park are being turned into wetlands. One will be a typical marsh, with cattails, pools, and all the things you expect of a wetland. The other will be a wet-mesic prairie, with lush grasses growing six feet high. An old watering hole has become Henry's pond, and a bigger lake has been built along Peruque Creek in the park's western side.

The parks department laid out its network of hikes on the old horse trails lacing the area, choosing to keep some trails while letting others

### ⓘ KEY AT-A-GLANCE INFORMATION

**LENGTH:** 6 miles

**CONFIGURATION:** Several loops joined by connector trails

**DIFFICULTY:** Very easy

**SCENERY:** Prairies, wooded hillsides, creek bottoms, and 2 lakes

**EXPOSURE:** Mix of sunny and shaded

**TRAFFIC:** Medium

**TRAIL SURFACE:** Packed earth, gravel, and paved

**HIKING TIME:** 2–3 hours

**ACCESS:** Open 7 a.m.–10 p.m., March–November; 7 a.m.–6 p.m., December–February

**MAPS:** Wentzville USGS topo; park map available from St. Charles County Parks

**FACILITIES:** Water, restrooms, picnic shelters, disc golf course, stables

**SPECIAL COMMENTS:** Pets on 8-foot leash

## ▶ DIRECTIONS

From the intersection of I-70 and US 40/61 in Wentzville, drive 1 mile south to Callahan Road. Turn right onto Callahan, then immediately right again onto Quail Ridge Parkway. Follow Quail Ridge Parkway 1 mile to the park.

### GPS TRAILHEAD COORDINATES (PARK ENTRANCE)

| | | |
|---|---|---|
| UTM ZONE (WGS84) | 15S | |
| EASTING | 687493 | |
| NORTHING | 4297333 | |
| LATITUDE-LONGITUDE | | |
| NORTH | N38° 48' 17.3763'' | |
| WEST | W90° 50' 26.8111'' | |

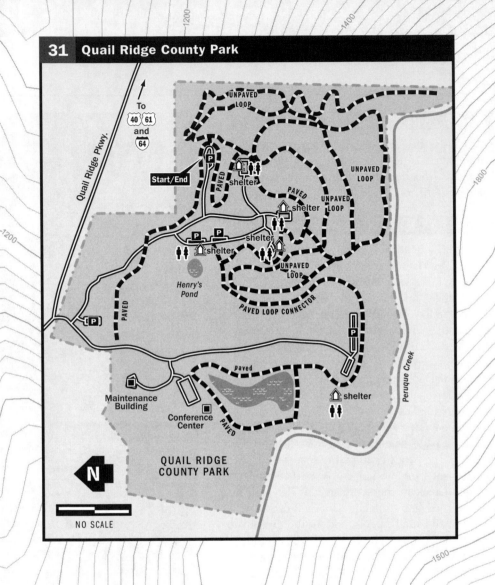

To
40 61
and
64

Quail Ridge Pkwy.

Start/End

P

shelter

PAVED

UNPAVED LOOP

UNPAVED LOOP

PAVED

shelter

UNPAVED LOOP

shelter

P P

shelter

Henry's Pond

PAVED

UNPAVED LOOP

PAVED LOOP CONNECTOR

P

P

paved

PAVED

Peruque Creek

shelter

Maintenance Building

Conference Center

QUAIL RIDGE COUNTY PARK

1200

1400

1800

1200

1300

1700

1500

1400

N

NO SCALE

grow over. Some markings were already in place—while hiking Quail Ridge Park, you'll find your way with metal discs on trailside trees and carsonite posts with directional arrows at intersections. Also along the trail are weathered wooden signs identifying some of the park's trees, left over from the equestrian farm's trail-ride routes.

To reach the hiking trailhead, take the first left off the east park road, just past Henry's Pond. Even with incomplete markings, it's easy to find your way along trails in this relatively small park with lots of open space. The only place that's confusing is where the trail shares the path with the disc golf course.

Playground Sculpture, Quail Ridge Park

That will improve as this still-developing park takes shape. For now, just bring along a Frisbee and turn your confusion into a couple of enjoyable holes of disc golf—unless you agree with native son Mark Twain, and think that would be a Frisbee version of "a good walk spoiled."

When the wetlands along Peruque Creek are fully developed and attracting their full complement of wildlife, that area might be the best hiking area in the park. For now, the best trails are in Quail Ridge's eastern end. A 0.75-mile loop just east of the trailhead is a nice hike. It bounces over several tiny hollows, then follows a side hill above a hollow off Peruque Creek. At its southern end, a 0.4-mile spur follows a ridge toward the creek, with views west across the park. There's a nice 0.6-mile loop in the bottomland, worth the walk just to see beaver sign on Peruque Creek. As you walk the stream bank, look for pointy beaver-chewed sapling stumps at the water's edge.

The hiking trailhead also serves as tee-off for the disc golf course. Pencils and scorecards with maps of the course are found there, along with an invitation to show up any Sunday morning, rain or shine, for doubles disc golf.

## ▶ NEARBY ACTIVITIES

For wilder, more challenging hikes, visit the Lewis and Clark Trail (page 117) in Weldon Spring Conservation Area.

# Hikes in the
## SOUTHWEST
### of the
## ST. LOUIS AREA

# BELL MOUNTAIN
# WILDERNESS AREA

## IN BRIEF

The top of Bell Mountain, one of Missouri's highest peaks, is in Missouri's third largest wilderness area. There are incredible vistas from an expansive glade on Bell's summit. And in this rugged, seldom-visited wildland, you'll likely have the whole mountain to yourself.

## DESCRIPTION

At 1,702 feet above sea level, Bell Mountain is nearly as tall as Taum Sauk Mountain, the state's highest peak—but it's number one with me. Unlike Taum Sauk, Bell is smack-dab in the middle of 9,027 acres of Ozark wilderness.

When you top out on Bell Mountain and walk into the open rocky glade on the summit, you'll likely have all the views to yourself. The 5-mile hike to this wild mountaintop shakes out the less energetic.

Bell Mountain is named for the family that, believe it or not, once farmed this rocky highland. On the way up it looks far too rugged to support a farm, but once on the mountain you'll find level areas that by farming standards of the past would have served as decent fields and pastures. One of these flats is just east of the southern loop junction, where a small pond might have been used to water livestock. Now the mountaintop is home only to granite glades, hardwood forests with scattered groves of cedar and pine, wildlife, and a few wandering hikers.

The trail on Bell Mountain is a 6-mile loop along Bell's long ridge on its eastern side and the

## DIRECTIONS

From Caledonia, MO, drive 5 miles south on MO 21 to MO 32. Go 7 miles west on MO 32 to MO A, and go south. The southern trailhead is 5.5 miles south on the west side of MO A. The northern trailhead is a half mile south on MO A, then 1.5 miles east on FS 2228.

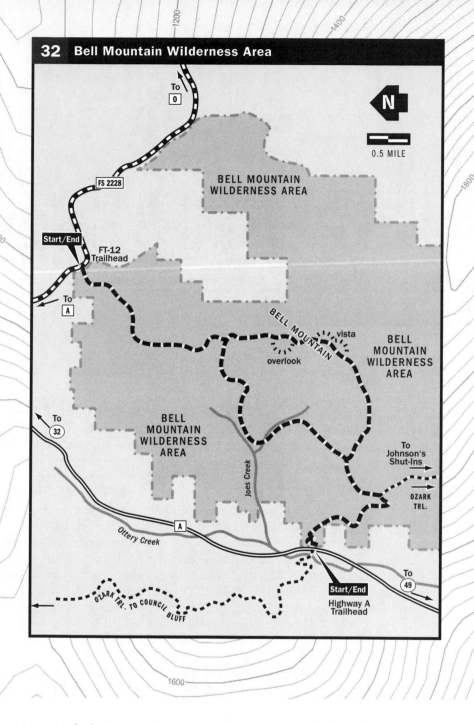

Joes Creek drainage on its western side. Access to the loop is via two spur trails, a 3.25-mile hike from the Bell Mountain trailhead on MO A or a 2.5-mile trek from the FT-12 trailhead north of the mountain on FS 2228. Elevation change on the loop is significant—at 970 feet, Joes Creek is more than 700 feet below the peak—but the steady grades along the trail aren't terribly

Panoramic vista from the summit
of Bell Mountain

steep. Except for the single-track spur from MO A to the loop, all trails on Bell Mountain follow abandoned roads.

There are five ways to hike Bell Mountain. The easiest hike is from the FT-12 trailhead to the peak and back. This 8-mile option is the shortest and, with 1,500 feet elevation at the trailhead, involves the smallest elevation gain. Another plan is to hike in
from FT-12, go around the loop, and return to FT-12 on an 11-mile trek. A third option
is hiking from the Bell Mountain trailhead on MO A to the summit and back for a
10-mile jaunt, and a fourth is the 12.5-mile hike from MO A to the loop, around the
loop, and back. If you have a group and more than one car, there's a fifth option: Split
your group, spot a car at each trailhead, then hike from one trailhead to the other in
separate groups going opposite directions. Both groups would through-hike the wilderness on a 9-mile trek over the mountain and could meet at the summit for a picnic.

Most folks skip the loop and hike from one of the trailheads to the summit and
back. Since it involves the smallest elevation gain and is quite a bit shorter, lots of
folks prefer starting from the FT-12 trailhead. Others, myself included, would rather
start from the Bell Mountain trailhead on MO A. Though it's longer and involves a lot
more climbing, its payback is pretty scenery. The hike from the FT-12 trailhead is easy,
but just your basic walk in the woods until you reach the summit. On the climb from
the Bell Mountain trailhead you'll huff and puff a bit, but there'll be lots of views from
the western side of Bell Mountain. On one mile-long stretch you'll ramble along a rock
layer, popping in and out of little glades with nice vistas to the southwest.

Signs at the trailhead say the route isn't well marked, but that wasn't the case
when I visited. The trail was marked with white-and-gray plastic diamonds; at intersections, notations on the diamonds told what lay in each direction. The first 2 miles from
the trailhead on MO A are shared with the Ozark Trail, and are marked with its distinctive placards. With these markings, a compass, and the forest service's excellent map of
the wilderness area, you should have no problem finding your way to the mountaintop.
In fact, the more-popular southeast half of the loop that travels over the summit has the

fewest markings, but the path is clearly defined and easy to follow. The less-traveled northwest part of the loop in Joes Creek is often somewhat overgrown in summer, but frequent markings in this lush bottomland make it easy to stay on track.

For a wild, primitive area with more than 700 feet of topographic relief, Bell Mountain is a relatively easy hike. If you go to the peak and back from the FT-12 trailhead, there's hardly any climbing at all. You'll start at 1,530 feet, descend to 1,400, then climb up to 1,700 at the summit. Starting from the Bell Mountain trailhead on MO A you'll have only one long climb, getting the hardest part out of the way early in the hike when you're raring to go. If you hike the loop and descend to Joes Creek, you'll face a second, long, but not-too-difficult climb from the creek back to the mountaintop.

Here's how your hike will go starting from the Bell Mountain trailhead on MO A, hiking the more scenic approach spur, then trekking around the loop.

The trail heads north from the parking lot, breaks right to cross MO A, then the climbing begins. It'll be serious uphill for a half mile to the first glade overlook. Then it gets easy for a mile, doing little rollers along a rock layer through numerous rugged glades with views over the Ottery Creek valley. Most of the glades are tiny, but one huge one—as big as several tennis courts—has expansive views to the southwest. After that easy run you'll face another climb that ends at a trail fork. The Ozark Trail goes right, and your path onto Bell Mountain goes left.

From this junction you'll head northeast, climbing gently, until you hit the southern end of the wilderness loop 3.25 miles into your hike. The left fork leads to Joes Creek, and the right leads to Bell Mountain's summit. If I'm hiking the loop, I prefer turning left, hiking the less-spectacular Joes Creek first and enjoying the summit view in the later part of my hike. From the intersection the left fork descends for the next 0.75 miles, steadily steepening until you level out in a hollow that's a side stream off Joes Creek. A half mile into this hollow you'll join the main stem of Joes Creek, turn right, walk up Joes hollow for another half mile, then leave the bottomland to climb 0.75 miles to Bell Mountain's ridge. After striking the ridge you'll soon reach the north trail junction and the spur to the FT-12 trailhead.

From here you'll hike steadily up until you reach the summit, about 1.25 miles south of the intersection. The path gets really rocky the last few hundred yards, with several great views to the northwest. Keep an eye peeled to the left as you near the summit, watching for side trails running to an open, rocky flat 50 yards to the east. Follow the side trails and you'll stroll out of the brush onto a rock patio with sweeping views north, east, and west of Bell Mountain—the best vistas in the whole wilderness area. Save your trail snacks for a picnic on this awesome overlook. It's a wonderful spot to relax and savor the view, especially on late fall and winter days when the sun warms this granite expanse.

A short way south of this overlook is the summit. You're on the mountaintop when you see an old foundation just east of the trail. From the peak it's 1.75 miles to the southern end of the loop, downhill for the first half mile, then level the rest of the way to the intersection. In the last half mile of this stretch you'll wander through a nice pine and cedar grove, and just before reaching the junction you'll pass the old farm pond. From the junction you'll backtrack the 3.25-mile spur to the trailhead, enjoying its superb views one more time—perhaps looking even more spectacular in the rich late-afternoon sunlight at the end of a rewarding day on Bell Mountain.

# BERRYMAN TRAIL

## KEY AT-A-GLANCE INFORMATION

**LENGTH:** 24 miles

**CONFIGURATION:** Loop

**DIFFICULTY:** Very, very hard (due to its long distance)

**SCENERY:** Hills and hollows forested with deciduous trees and beautiful plantations of majestic pines

**EXPOSURE:** Shaded throughout

**TRAFFIC:** Light hiking traffic; medium trail use by mountain bikers and equestrians

**TRAIL SURFACE:** Packed earth, with many rocky and rugged sections

**HIKING TIME:** 12 hours–2 days for entire trail

**ACCESS:** No fees, permits, or closing times

**MAPS:** Berryman and Anthonies Mill USGS topos; trail map available from Mark Twain National Forest

**FACILITIES:** Campgrounds at Brazil Creek and Berryman; no potable water available

**SPECIAL COMMENTS:** The Berryman's length makes its difficulty rating very, very hard, but the trail is only moderately difficult based upon ruggedness and topography.

Another nearby hike is on the Courtois Section of the Ozark Trail. It takes off from the Berryman just west of the Berryman Campground. Excellent canoeing is available on the nearby Meramec River, and on Huzzah and Courtois Creeks.

### GPS TRAILHEAD COORDINATES (BERRYMAN CAMP)

| | | |
|---|---|---|
| UTM ZONE (WGS84) | 15S | |
| | EASTING | 670080 |
| | NORTHING | 4199848 |
| LATITUDE-LONGITUDE | | |
| | NORTH | N37° 55' 49.0723'' |
| | WEST | W91° 3' 53.0320'' |

## IN BRIEF

The Berryman, a National Recreation Trail, follows breezy ridges, wanders through deep, cool hollows strewn with wildflowers, and splashes across intermittent streams. With campgrounds and a couple of springs that make ideal backcountry camps, this long path is a great two-to-four-day backpack route. Numerous forest road crossings let you break it into shorter chunks for excellent day hiking.

## DESCRIPTION

The Berryman Trail is a nice hike meandering through deep Ozark woods. Originally designed for equestrian use, its treadway uses countless switchbacks to gently grade numerous climbs and descents. Truly steep sections are rare. Even the most rugged, rocky, and rooty stretches are easily negotiated. It's always a shady hike, too. Heavy concentrations of oak, hickory, dogwood, and other deciduous trees cover the hillsides and hollows along the Berryman, and forests of stately shortleaf pine, planted by Civilian Conservation Corps men in the 1930s, shade many of the ridges.

The only drawback to all that shade is that it allows few scenic vistas along the Berryman. You'll have hints of distant panoramas in winter, when leaves are crunching under your feet instead of blocking your view, but scenes from the hills explored by this trail are usually obscured. It's

## DIRECTIONS

Trailheads are at Brazil Creek and Berryman campgrounds. Berryman Campground is 17 miles west of Potosi on MO 8, then 1 mile north on FS 2266. Watch closely for the turnoff, because it's easy to miss the small sign pointing to Berryman Campground. To reach Brazil Creek, drive 17 miles southeast from Sullivan on MO 185, then 8 miles west on MO N, then 9 miles south on MO W.

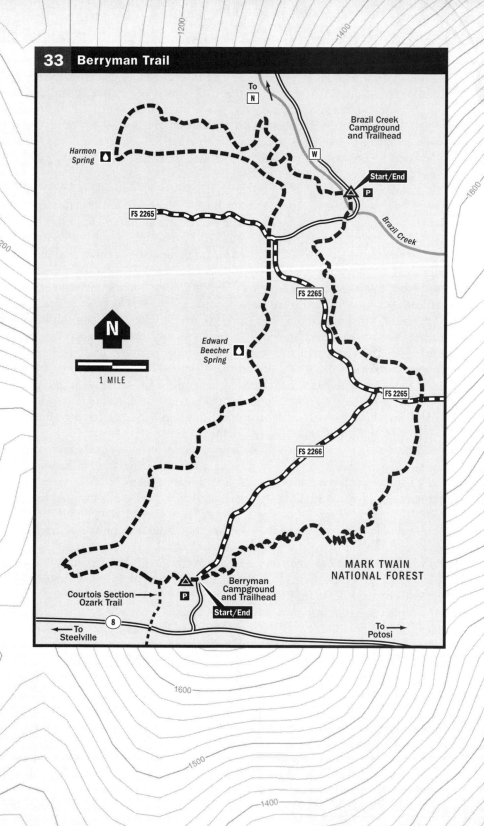

To
N

Brazil Creek
Campground
and Trailhead

W

Harmon
Spring

Start/End
P

FS 2265

Brazil Creek

N

1 MILE

FS 2265

Edward
Beecher
Spring

FS 2265

FS 2266

MARK TWAIN
NATIONAL FOREST

Courtois Section
Ozark Trail

Berryman
Campground
and Trailhead

Start/End

P

8

To
Steelville

To
Potosi

still a wonderful hike on an exceptionally well-designed and graded path through a beautiful landscape. In many places the trail's tread is cut into steep side hills, swooping around heads of hollows with sharp drops tailing into the deep hollows below. The thick forest is excellent for wildlife observation. You'll often see deer, turkey, hundreds of songbirds, and maybe a secretive bobcat. One spring, I startled a turkey and its brood from the side of the trail, and listened while she called her chicks back to her side in the brush.

Its superb design, almost exclusively single-track, makes the Berryman very popular with equestrians and mountain bikers. Trail runners love this trail, too, though its distance keeps many away. The Berryman still doesn't feel crowded: on a nice fall or spring day, you probably won't see 25 other trail users, unless there's an organized bike race or trail ride. Located far from population centers and main thoroughfares, the Berryman has a wonderful, isolated feel. The forests it traverses are only a step or two short of wilderness. The trail often follows intermittent streams and leads you past two springs at Harmon and Edward Beecher trail camps.

Though streams, springs, and stock ponds are scattered along the Berryman, none are potable—not even the limpid artesian flow at Edward Beecher Spring—nor is there water at either trailhead, other than the nonpotable stream at Brazil Creek Campground. Bring plenty of water on this long trail, or pack a filter or tablets for purification. In periods of prolonged drought, none of the streams except Brazil Creek will be running. In normal seasons, the longest stretch without access to water for filtration is the 10-mile reach from Brazil Creek to Berryman Campground on the loop's east side, where you'll pass only an unattractive stock pond.

Though the Berryman's 24-mile length seems to limit it to overnight hikers, that's not necessarily the case. With friends, you can arrange shuttles between Brazil Creek and Berryman campgrounds for point-to-point hikes of 10 to 14 miles. Furthermore, forest roads winding through the area let you carve the trail into short loops. The best of these short loops begins at Brazil Creek Campground. Hike along MO W until it turns to gravel about a mile from camp. Continue 100 feet west on gravel to the trail crossing and turn right onto the trail. Follow the trail back to camp and you'll enjoy an 8-mile loop on the northern reaches of the Berryman. Use a topo, the trail map, or a travel map of the Potosi-Salem district of the Mark Twain National Forest to choose other loops.

Hikes can begin at either Berryman or Brazil Creek campgrounds. The more-developed Berryman Campground has plenty of parking, nice picnic sites, and a picnic shelter dedicated to CCC Company 3733, whose camp was located on this spot. They planted many of the majestic pine groves you'll hike through on the Berryman. Wander around the woods a bit and you'll find foundations from the camp's structures.

I prefer to start from Brazil Creek, a grassy campground shaded by tall pines, where there's a nice stream for a posthike dip. Unless erosion has changed things, there's a good swimming hole under the nearby bridge on MO W. Hikes from Brazil begin with a long climb but end with a 1-mile descent. Drawbacks to Brazil Creek are limited parking and heavy use by equestrian campers, making it a bit ripe at times.

Carry the forest service's excellent map of the Berryman the first few times you hike here. It's superimposed over topographic features, with mile markers starting from 0 at the Berryman Campground and traveling the loop clockwise. You'll occasionally find weathered mile markers along the path, but many of these wooden posts have rotted away. The trail is blazed with white plastic diamonds nailed to trees along the path. On the loop's western side it shares the path with the Ozark Trail and has the distinctive OT diamond blazes on the trees, too. It's hard to get lost on the well-traveled Berryman, but the map is perfect for keeping track of your progress.

Leaving from Berryman and traveling west, you'll join the Ozark Trail 0.3 miles from camp. After the junction, the trail heads west to mile 2 then swings north-northeast, crossing several hollows and ridges on long climbs and descents. In the hollows you'll follow intermittent streams, and on the ridge stretches amble through shady pine groves. Several ATV roads cross the trail, offering opportunities to shorten the loop by turning right, following one to FS 2266, and turning right to go back to the trailhead. You'll reach Edward Beecher Spring at 5.5 miles into the hike, where cool artesian well water gurgles through a pipe into a ground-level concrete tank.

After Beecher Spring you'll climb 0.75 miles onto a ridge, then at the 7.5-mile mark sidle around deep hollows to the road crossing. Just to the right is the end of MO W, marking the beginning of the 8-mile short loop from Brazil Creek. From this crossing you'll go predominantly downhill for 2.5 miles, slowly curving to the west. You'll pass a stock pond in a pine grove, follow a gently descending hollow for nearly a mile, and level out in a small glade. After the glade, the trail crosses an ATV road, then parallels a stream to the big open meadow where you'll find Harmon Spring.

The trail breaks north from Harmon Spring. At 0.1 mile past the spring, the Berryman breaks east and the Ozark Trail continues north. The OT is a forlorn-looking path here—it goes nowhere and is barely noticeable in the overgrowth. Someday it'll extend to the Huzzah State Forest. The Berryman descends quickly to a stream crossing, climbs onto a fascinating rock outcropping, and begins a 0.5-mile climb.

This northern reach of the Berryman is very nice. After reaching the top of the climb, the path swoops around several wild, isolated hollows shaded by towering woods. Near Brazil Creek you'll get an obscured view of a farm in the valley below. The last stretch to the camp is a long, easy descent finishing with five steep and rugged switchbacks. Part of the downhill to Brazil Creek is really flinty, as I discovered on a night hike on the Berryman. Every time I scuffed my boots on the trail, I saw tiny sparks in the darkness.

From Brazil Creek, mile 14.5 on the trail, the path turns south. You'll make several climbs and descents over the next 5 miles, rounding pretty hollows on a hillside trail with steep drops to the valleys below. At mile 19 you'll drop into Smith Mill Hollow, where you'll enjoy a gentle half-mile downhill on a forest floor carpeted with wildflowers. The trail turns west at mile 20, leaves this lush bottomland, and begins the first of four climbs and descents on the most crooked and twisty stretch of the Berryman. For 3 miles it's up and down and switchback after switchback as you work your way over four hollows and ridges in rapid succession. It's a surprisingly fun part of the trail, with well-graded climbs to windy, pine-studded ridgetops.

The last mile of the Berryman is a delight, twisting and turning to skirt hollows along a ridgeline near the trailhead. You'll finish your hike in a breezy pine grove, winding among majestic trees, old needles softening your weary footfalls, and live ones sweetly scenting the air—the legacy of the men who once worked the forest around the Berryman CCC Camp.

# COUNCIL BLUFF LAKE

 **KEY AT-A-GLANCE INFORMATION**

**LENGTH:** 12 miles

**CONFIGURATION:** Loop

**DIFFICULTY:** Moderate–difficult

**SCENERY:** Open lakeside vistas overlooked by forested mountains

**EXPOSURE:** Shady, with occasional open stretches on shorelines

**TRAFFIC:** Light

**TRAIL SURFACE:** Packed-earth and gravel trail with many rugged, rocky stretches

**HIKING TIME:** 4–6 hours

**ACCESS:** $3 per car day-use fee

**MAPS:** Johnson Mountain USGS topo; Council Bluff Lake Recreation Area map available from the Forest Service shows the Lakeshore Trail

**FACILITIES:** Water, toilets, swimming beach, campground, boat launch, picnic sites

**SPECIAL COMMENTS:** No water available during cold months; swimming area closed September–May; campground closed mid-October–April; Wild Boar Hollow Boat launch and picnic area, trailhead, and Lakeshore Trail are open year-round

**GPS TRAILHEAD COORDINATES (TRAILHEAD)**

| | |
|---|---|
| UTM ZONE (WGS84) | 15S |
| EASTING | 682583 |
| NORTHING | 4177747 |
| LATITUDE-LONGITUDE | |
| NORTH | N37° 43' 43.7171" |
| WEST | W90° 55' 41.2685" |

## ▶ IN BRIEF

The Lakeshore Trail in Council Bluff Recreation Area is an enthralling ramble along the wooded shores of a deep, blue Ozark lake. Though rugged in places, this trail's gentle grade makes it a surprisingly easy long hike. And countless relaxing vistas of the lake's inviting waters bring pleasure with every step.

## ▶ DESCRIPTION

Scenic vistas are par for the course at Council Bluff Recreation Area. Johnson Mountain towers to the east, and the lake's calm surface reflects the forested hills as you wander through this enchanting landscape. Completed in 1997, the Lakeshore Trail hugs the water's edge for much of its length. It's rocky and rugged in many places, so it's no cakewalk. But short climbs and few steep grades make it a surprisingly easy long hike, letting you admire the surrounding beauty as you work your way around the lake.

You may want to bring your rod and reel on this trail. Since it was built in the mid-1980s, Council Bluff Lake has been stocked with catfish, bass, crappie, bluegill, and sunfish. You may see beaver in the lake, and the old snags standing in the water attract kingfishers, woodpeckers, hawks, and the occasional osprey or eagle. Herons work the shallow coves, dining on fish and frogs that overload the spring evenings with their mating serenades. Council Bluff is an excellent place to combine birding with hiking.

The trailhead is at the Wild Boar Hollow boat launch on the tip of the lake's western arm.

## ▶ DIRECTIONS

From Potosi, drive 13 miles south on MO P to MO C. Drive a quarter mile west on MO C to MO DD. Take MO DD 7 miles south to the Council Bluff Recreation Area entrance and follow signs to Wild Boar Hollow boat launch and picnic area.

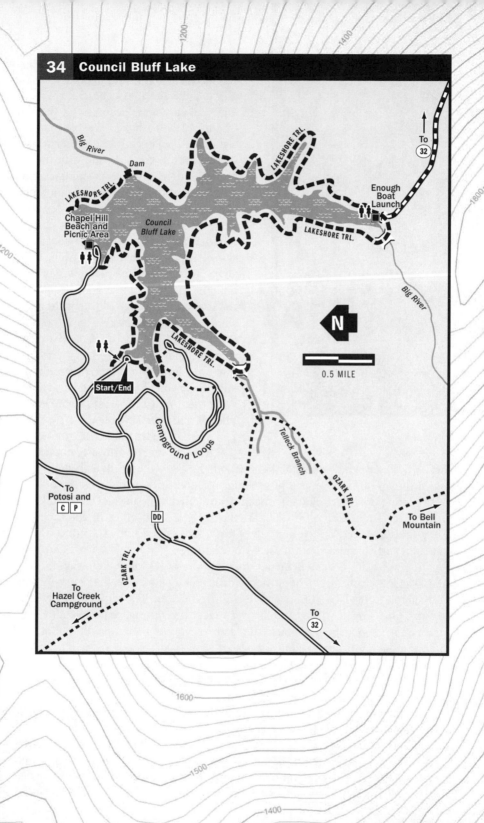

Big River

Dam

LAKESHORE TRL.

LAKESHORE TRL.

LAKESHORE TRL.

To
32

Enough Boat
Launch

Chapel Hill
Beach and
Picnic Area

Council
Bluff Lake

LAKESHORE TRL.

Big River

N

0.5 MILE

LAKESHORE TRL.

Start/End

Campground Loops

Telleck Branch

OZARK TRL.

To Bell
Mountain

To
Potosi and
C P

DD

OZARK TRL.

To
Hazel Creek
Campground

To
32

A beautiful winter hike on the Lakeshore Trail at Council Bluff Lake

There are nice picnic sites in this quiet cove, and a dock for fishing and hanging out. I like to hike the trail counterclockwise, saving the easy and scenic stretch between Chapel Hill Beach and the boat launch for last. That way I can take a dip or wiggle my sweaty toes in the wet sand near the end of my hike, then enjoy a relaxing picnic at the swimming beach before finishing off the final 2 miles of the loop.

The trail, marked with gray plastic diamonds, heads south from the boat launch a short way, then breaks east on a bench above the lake. At the half-mile point you'll hit the first of two spur trails leading up to the campground on Wild Boar Ridge. For a shorter hike, head up this spur 0.6 miles to the campground. Turn left and follow the campground road to its end, where the second spur leads from the campground to the lake. Following it back to the Lakeshore Trail and returning to the boat ramp gives you a hike of just over 1.5 miles.

Hiking past the campground spurs, you'll soon veer southwest around a long cove, winding around little side hollows off the lake. Telleck Branch flows into the lake at the tip of the cove, and just before the footbridge over the creek you'll spot a sign pointing up Telleck Branch, directing you a half mile to the Ozark Trail. It leads to the Trace Creek Section of the OT, and to miles and miles of additional scenic Ozark hiking. From Council Bluff, the Ozark Trail goes 25 miles north to the Berryman Trail and 11 miles south to Bell Mountain.

After crossing Telleck Branch, the Lakeshore Trail swings east again for nearly a mile, wiggling through a tight grove of cedars for a short way, then curves south for a 3-mile run to the lake's upper end. It's a nice piece of trail with lots of views across the lake. One stretch follows an old road that dives into the water just after the trail angles off it, then reappears a half mile later to carry you around a thumb of the lake and on to the Enough boat launch. Located at the lake's southern tip, Enough is just past the halfway mark of the Lakeshore Trail. A footbridge crosses the Big River just before you reach the boat launch, where you'll find toilets and a nice grassy area for a midhike break.

From Enough, it's a 4-mile hike along the lake's east side to the dam. This is the most remote stretch of hiking at Council Bluff, and the toughest. The trail winds around four thumbs of the lake, sometimes climbing the hillsides above the coves on short, steep stretches. In spring or rainy times you'll ford small creeks trickling into the apex of each cove. The lake will often be out of view as you circumnavigate its coves. The last half mile before the dam is the rockiest section of the Lakeshore Trail—but it's a very scenic half mile. You'll be back on the lakeshore, treading carefully over rugged terrain decorating the water's edge, admiring fine vistas across the water.

More pleasing views await on the level ramble across the dam. To the west you'll look far up the lake's western arm. To the northeast the Big River valley stretches into the distance, and across the lake northwest is Chapel Hill Beach, 1 easy mile away via the trail. Chapel Hill is the perfect spot to hang out awhile—its sandy beach is an ideal place to dive into the sparkling blue lake that's been beckoning you for the last 10 miles. Technically, the beach only opens in summer, but the trail goes right through it. And if you're hiking through on a warm late-September day, who's to stop you from a refreshing, well-deserved dip? Plan a snack stop, too—Chapel Hill has picnic tables and shelters perfect for lunch with a blue-water view.

The last 2 miles to Wild Boar Hollow are a delight. After your cooling dip at the beach, you won't even break a sweat on the few short and gently graded climbs, and the trail hugs the shoreline almost all the way back to the trailhead. The path twists and turns around a half-dozen pretty little coves on its stretch run, with plenty of final breathtaking vistas of Council Bluff Lake. It ends with a short paved section through Wild Boar Hollow picnic area, another nice place to snack, nap, or admire the lake and wooded hills.

Council Bluff Recreation Area is the perfect destination for a weekend getaway. If you enjoy two-wheeled fun, the Lakeshore Trail is also open to mountain bikes. You're close to Bell Mountain Wilderness Area, where a 5-mile hike leads to one of Missouri's finest mountaintop vistas. The fishing's great here, and the lake is a wonderful place to paddle around in your canoe. Council Bluff's campground is a nice base for your getaway. It features well-spaced, shady sites scattered along the spine of Wild Boar Ridge.

### ▶ NEARBY ACTIVITIES

Nearby hiking opportunities are Bell Mountain Wilderness Area (page 134) just south of Council Bluff, the Trace Creek Section of the Ozark Trail, and the Berryman Trail (page 138) west of Potosi. Thirty miles east are the fascinating pink-granite scenes of Elephant Rocks State Park (**www.mostateparks.com**).

# GREEN'S CAVE BUSHWHACK: HAMILTON HOLLOW ROUTE

## KEY AT-A-GLANCE INFORMATION

**LENGTH:** 5.5 miles round-trip

**CONFIGURATION:** Out-and-back

**DIFFICULTY:** Easy

**SCENERY:** Springs, bluffs, old farmsteads, and caves

**EXPOSURE:** Mix of shaded and exposed

**TRAFFIC:** Light

**TRAIL SURFACE:** Dirt, gravel, a few rugged stretches

**HIKING TIME:** 2–4 hours

**ACCESS:** Always open

**MAPS:** Meramec State Park USGS topo; Meramec State Park Trail and Natural Area Guide

**FACILITIES:** None

**SPECIAL COMMENTS:** Pets on 10-foot leash; bring topo map, park trail map, and compass to this wild and undeveloped area. Due to overgrowth and ticks, this hike is best done between late October and March.

## GPS TRAILHEAD COORDINATES (TRAILHEAD)

| | | |
|---|---|---|
| UTM ZONE (WGS84) | 15S | |
| EASTING | 669286 | |
| NORTHING | 4226341 | |
| LATITUDE-LONGITUDE | | |
| NORTH | N38° 10' 8.7224'' | |
| WEST | W91° 4' 2.9772'' | |

## IN BRIEF

If the beautiful mural of Green's Cave and Bluff at Meramec State Park's visitor center lights your fire, here's the first of two unmarked "bushwhack" routes to see it firsthand. Along the way you'll see a cave, springs, and an abandoned iron smelter. Bring your topo map and compass—and your camera—on this wild hike.

## DESCRIPTION

Of the two bushwhacks to Green's Cave and Bluff—one of the most captivating scenes in all of Missouri—this is my favorite. On this 5.5-mile trek along Hamilton Creek and the Meramec River, you'll hike past an old iron smelter, Hamilton Cave, two springs, and an abandoned homestead. The approach to the cave is especially beautiful. On the Sleepy Hollow Bushwhack, you don't see the cave and cliff until you're standing on top of them. But from Hamilton Hollow you approach the huge bluff from upriver, picking your way along its rocky base for the last half mile.

Green's Cave and the Hamilton Creek valley are beautiful places, but if you're only comfortable on blazed trails with marked intersections you shouldn't do this hike. It's not an official trail, and there are no markings whatsoever. Definitely bring photocopies of this chapter, a compass, and both the park trail map and the topo map on this hike. The Meramec State Park topo is usually available at the visitor center for a fee, and the park map is free. Only do this hike between late fall and early spring—in warm months overgrowth in the creek

## DIRECTIONS

From Meramec State Park's entrance, drive east across the river and turn right onto Sleepy Hollow Road. Drive 1.6 miles to an unmarked fork. Turn right and drive 2.6 miles to the trailhead, just past the slab bridge over Hamilton Creek.

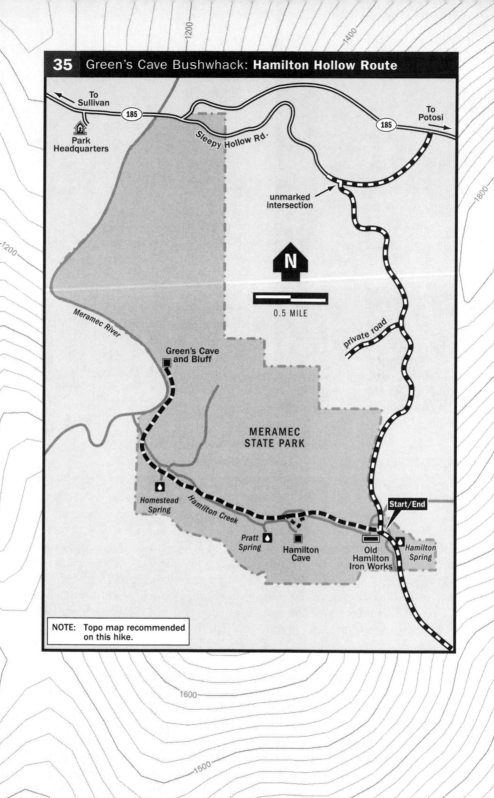

**35** Green's Cave Bushwhack: **Hamilton Hollow Route**

To Sullivan

185

Park Headquarters

Sleepy Hollow Rd.

To Potosi

185

unmarked intersection

N

0.5 MILE

Meramec River

private road

Green's Cave and Bluff

MERAMEC STATE PARK

Homestead Spring

Hamilton Creek

Pratt Spring

Hamilton Cave

Start/End

Old Hamilton Iron Works

Hamilton Spring

NOTE: Topo map recommended on this hike.

Old cooling house at Homestead Springs

and river bottoms gets dense, and the ticks are often nightmarish. While this is the easiest of the two bushwhacks to follow—you simply walk along Hamilton Creek to the Meramec, then follow the river to the cave—you'll have to pick your way through the brush once you get past Homestead Spring.

The trailhead for this hike is an interpretive site for the old Hamilton Iron Works, remnants of which you'll see around the parking area. A short 0.3-mile trail goes around the furnace itself describing the different functions. It's kind of a neglected place, but still fascinating. The massive stone smelter looms against the hillside near the trailhead, and several other foundations mark the old works—reminders of busier days in this quiet hollow. This hike goes west from the old iron works, following Hamilton Creek on an abandoned road that's occasionally used by four-wheelers. (Use of four-wheelers is illegal. No ATVs or horses are allowed in the park.) You'll see lots of tumbledown fence on the 2-mile stretch between the Iron Works and the Meramec River. Though this is the easier to follow of the two bushwhacks to Green's Cave, it'll involve more creek crossings than the Sleepy Hollow route. Be prepared to get your feet wet a time or two, especially in spring. If the Meramec is in flood, don't go at all: the flats at the mouth of Hamilton Hollow may be under water.

Heading west from the abandoned Iron Works, the old road follows Hamilton Creek. It crosses the stream several times in its first mile. An old pasture on the north side of the path, overgrown with cedars and saplings, is a great place to spot birds. After the second creek crossing, you'll see a faint road to the left. Take this side path—it leads past an old stone wall, climbs over a little knoll, and ends at the mouth of Hamilton Cave. The cave is gated to protect the bat population inside. A stream gushes from the cave and flows 200 yards over to Hamilton Creek. A second two-track road parallels this stream, leading you back to the old road down Hamilton Hollow.

Once back on the old road you'll cross Hamilton Creek for the third time, landing on its north side. Keep an eye to the left as you hike downstream: a few hundred yards down-hollow from Hamilton Cave, Pratt Spring flows from a low cave in the hillside into a clear, deep pool. Beavers often dam the pool's narrow outlet, making it even bigger. A half mile south of Pratt Spring the old road crosses to Hamilton Creek's south side, at a place where it's easy to lose the path. It's a really washed area, where the creek splits to go around a long island. At the head of the island, cross to the south side and pick up the old road on the other side. If you do somehow lose the way here, just continue downstream to the Meramec. Try not to miss this crossing, though. It leads to Homestead Spring, a haunting and beautiful abandoned farmstead in the woods next to Hamilton Creek. It might be muddy near the spring; when I was last there, beavers had built a long, curving dam on the spring stream, forming an expansive marsh pond. However you do it, work your way into the woods and find this cold, clear spring—it's a truly captivating spot. A weathered corral fence stands sentinel over the spring pool, which wells out of the ground and flows down an old driveway toward the beaver pond. This old drive, filled from shoulder to shoulder with Homestead Spring's outflow, is a carpet of bright green watercress stretching 200 feet downstream toward the beaver pond. In the spring's shallow pool stand a set of concrete walls, all that's left of a cooling house built by the farmer to serve as a natural refrigerator. Watercress grows all around this crumbling old icebox, too, almost luminescent in the deep woods.

From Homestead Spring it's a little more than a quarter mile to the Meramec River. The old road fades out after the homestead, so just pick your way along the creek. To stay on park property, you'll have to cross to the creek's south side just before reaching the river. Where Hamilton Creek pours into the Meramec, a grove of trees shades a grassy flat, and you can see Green's Cave Bluff downriver to the northeast. From here it's an easy walk downriver to the cave, picking your way among fallen rocks along the cliff's base for the last half mile.

You'll hear the gentle rush of the cascade tumbling from Green's Cave echoing off the bluff well before you reach the entrance. Once there, you'll find a stone bench under the overhanging bluff, with a pretty view over the cascade to the Meramec River. Check out the fascinating grottos in the cave wall above the bench—pigeons might bolt from these, scaring the bejeebers out of you while you relax in this idyllic spot. They scared the heck out of me! To get on the bluff above the cave, hike a short way downriver. At a gap in the bluff, a short trail leads up onto the cliff. You'll be 110 feet above the cave's mouth and 140 feet above the river, with beautiful views up and down the Meramec.

## ▶ NEARBY ACTIVITIES

Additional hiking trails are across the river at Meramec Conservation Area (page 165). Onondaga Cave State Park (page 177), a few miles upriver, offers still more hiking and cave tours.

# GREEN'S CAVE BUSHWHACK: SLEEPY HOLLOW ROUTE

 **KEY AT-A-GLANCE INFORMATION**

**LENGTH:** 5.5 miles round-trip

**CONFIGURATION:** Out-and-back

**DIFFICULTY:** Easy–moderate

**SCENERY:** Springs, bluffs, old farmsteads, and caves

**EXPOSURE:** Mostly open; some shaded stretches

**TRAFFIC:** Light

**TRAIL SURFACE:** Dirt, gravel, a few rugged stretches

**HIKING TIME:** 2–4 hours

**ACCESS:** This wild area is always open.

**MAPS:** Meramec State Park USGS topo; Meramec State Park Trail and Natural Area Guide

**FACILITIES:** None

**SPECIAL COMMENTS:** Pets on 10-foot leash; bring topo map, park trail map, and compass to this wild and undeveloped area. Due to overgrowth and ticks, this hike is best done between late October and March.

**GPS TRAILHEAD COORDINATES (PARKING AREA)**

| | |
|---|---|
| UTM ZONE (WGS84) | 15S |
| EASTING | 667405 |
| NORTHING | 4230376 |
| LATITUDE–LONGITUDE | |
| NORTH | N38° 12' 20.8351'' |
| WEST | W91° 5' 16.8148'' |

## IN BRIEF

At Meramec State Park's visitor center, a beautiful mural depicts a majestic bluff towering above the river, with an exquisite cascade gushing from a cave in its face. Here's the second of two unmarked "bushwhack" routes to the scenic natural wonder that is Green's Cave. Bring your topo map and compass—and your camera—on this wild hike.

## DESCRIPTION

Green's Cave is one of the most beautiful places in the Ozarks. It's worth the hike to get there, even if you get lost a time or two along the way. This route is unmarked but follows old roads that, with a map and compass and a little route finding, will take you right to the prettiest spot on the Meramec River. Some of the route uses construction roads left from the abandoned Corps of Engineers dam project that would've forever buried Green's Cave under tons of water. On this bushwhack to the cave you'll walk past the slowly healing scars of the aborted dam, wander through an old homestead, and, with a short side hike, take a cooling dip in a Meramec River swimming hole.

If you're only comfortable on blazed trails with marked intersections, don't do this hike. It's not an official trail, there are no markings whatsoever, and you'll need to find your way by following landscape features and old roads. Definitely bring along photocopies of this hike profile, a compass,

## DIRECTIONS

From the entrance to Meramec State Park, drive east across the river. Immediately after the bridge, turn right onto Sleepy Hollow Road. A quarter mile down the road, just past an old silo, there's a small parking area on the right, next to a rocky berm. Park there, and head down the old road beyond the berm.

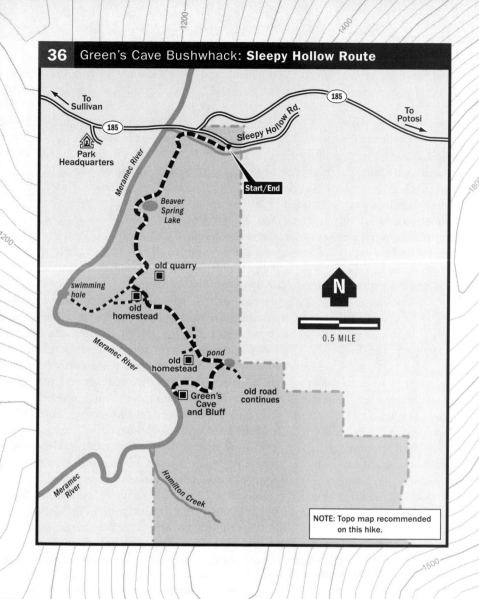

To
Sullivan

185

Park
Headquarters

Sleepy Hollow Rd.

185

To
Potosi

Meramec River

Start/End

Beaver
Spring
Lake

old quarry

swimming
hole

old
homestead

Meramec River

old
homestead

pond

Green's
Cave
and Bluff

old road
continues

Meramec
River

Hamilton Creek

N

0.5 MILE

NOTE: Topo map recommended
on this hike.

and both the park trail map and the topo map. The Meramec State Park topo is usually available at the visitor center for a fee, and the park map is free. Only do this hike between late fall and early spring—in the warm months overgrowth takes over the old roads, and ticks are often nightmarish. Of the two bushwhacks to Green's Cave, this one is the tougher to follow. But if you know how to read topo maps, you'll have little trouble finding your way to the cave and bluff.

The trailhead for this hike isn't an official one. A road used to go down Sleepy Hollow toward the river, and a dirt berm was pushed up to block it. The space in front of the berm is the trailhead, and there's room enough for about three cars. Step over the berm, get on the old road, and you're on your way. For a quarter mile you'll head west toward the Meramec, paralleling a small creek. If you hike this path in spring, Miami mist blossoms will be thick in this little bottomland. Next, hit the river valley and turn south. The old road gets really wide after the turn and parallels a 30-foot-high bluff for the next half mile. Marshes dot the western side of the old road in spring, so frogs really make some noise here in March and April.

At 0.75 miles into the hike you'll arrive at Beaver Spring Lake, a clear blue pool nestled against a cedar-studded bluff. This man-made lake was to be the footing for the eastern end of the Meramec Dam. Work on the reservoir had already begun when the project was deauthorized, leaving a rocky hole in the ground. Workers struck a spring while digging the footing, so after construction ceased the abandoned hole slowly filled to create this pretty lake. Climb up the roadside berm west of the lake, and you'll see the Meramec rolling by to the right of the trail.

From Beaver Spring Lake, the old road slowly curves southeast and heads up Miller Hollow. Just after the curve straightens, turn right onto a grassy double-track going southwest toward a creek. If you miss this turn, you'll soon dead-end in an old quarry, and can backtrack. The two-track goes straight across the creek, climbs out the other side, and soon comes to a fork. While the left fork is the correct path, the right one is an interesting side trip. It leads a half mile to the Meramec River, ending across from a low bluff where there's a nice swimming hole. Along the way you'll cross an old culvert, and next to it there's an abandoned 1940s-vintage dump truck. Don't bring your gun, though—it's been shot up enough already.

Back on the left fork, the path to the cave angles southeast and follows another grassy two-track gently uphill, soon entering a grassy meadow. You're near an old homestead here, and will see vestiges of pasture and corral fences. As you near a grove of cedars at the upper end of the meadow, you'll see old concrete foundations on the right side of the old road. Look behind you as you climb through this homestead— you'll see pretty vistas of the hills across the river, and will see why the farmer picked this spot for his home. Behind the cedars is an old pond, and then another fork in the trail. Once again, take the left fork. The right one leads west to join the previously described side trail to the river.

The left fork climbs a quarter mile after the old homestead, then follows the northeast side of the ridge above Miller Hollow. About a half mile after the old homestead you'll see other old roads going right and left. The path to Green's Cave continues straight, but a short side trip to the right leads to another old homesite. The main route continues along the northeast side of the ridge and curves east to round the head of Miller Hollow, then swings back southeast and climbs a bit. At the top of the climb, about a quarter mile from the last intersection, you'll see a pond on the left and an old road to the right. At this point you're just 0.4 miles from Green's Cave.

Bear right at this fork and follow this faint old road. While most of the roads you've been on to this point will have had some four-wheeler traffic (Use of four-wheelers is illegal here.) this one probably won't have, so it might be a bit overgrown. You'll start out level, heading south on a ridge spine, then make a sweeping turn to the north, descending into a hollow on a rocky, washed-out path. You'll soon veer back west, continue descending, and then find yourself on a low bluff right above the Meramec, with two trails going left. The uphill path leads onto the 110-foot bluff above Green's Cave, and the second goes down to the river and the cavern's entrance.

Both paths lead to places of great beauty. From up on the bluff you'll look several miles up and down the Meramec Valley. Across the river there's a pastoral farm valley, and looking straight down you'll see the stream from Green's Cave cascading into the river. Walk as far upriver on the bluff as you can—the cliff extends for another 100 yards or so. After enjoying the view from on high, head down to the mouth of Green's Cave, and look up to where you just were. A tremendous overhang protects Green's Cave, and a stream cascades noisily from the cavern's mouth. Only a few feet away the Meramec rolls serenely by, and a stone bench under the overhang is the perfect spot to relax after your bushwhack from Sleepy Hollow.

## ▶ NEARBY ACTIVITIES

Additional hiking trails are across the river at Meramec Conservation Area (page 165). Onondaga Cave State Park, a few miles upriver, offers still more hiking and cave tours (page 177).

# HUGHES MOUNTAIN NATURAL AREA

*Dry*

## KEY AT-A-GLANCE INFORMATION

**LENGTH:** 1.5 miles

**CONFIGURATION:** Loop with spur

**DIFFICULTY:** Very easy

**SCENERY:** Expansive, otherworldly rock dome on a forested Ozark hillside

**EXPOSURE:** Open

**TRAFFIC:** Medium

**TRAIL SURFACE:** Solid rock on the rock dome; packed earth or gravel on approach trail

**HIKING TIME:** 1–2 hours

**ACCESS:** Open 4 a.m.–10 p.m.

**MAPS:** Irondale USGS topo; map available from Department of Conservation

**FACILITIES:** Trailhead parking

**SPECIAL COMMENTS:** Pets must be leashed; watch children closely on steep cliffs

## GPS TRAILHEAD COORDINATES (TRAILHEAD)

| | |
|---|---|
| UTM ZONE (WGS84) | 15S |
| EASTING | 700788 |
| NORTHING | 4186809 |
| LATITUDE–LONGITUDE | |
| NORTH | N37° 48' 23.8123'' |
| WEST | W90° 43' 9.0432'' |

## IN BRIEF

The Devil's Honeycomb Trail explores a vast glade on the huge domelike outcropping of pre-Cambrian rock that caps Hughes Mountain. The pinkish, multisided rhyolite columns for which the trail is named formed when ancient lava flows cooled and contracted. Pleasant mountain breezes sweep the rocky expanse and panoramic vistas stretch away in three directions, making Hughes Mountain an ideal place to admire the sunset.

## DESCRIPTION

This fantastic rock landscape is named for John Hughes, whose family owned the mountain from the early 1800s until the Department of Conservation bought it in 1985. To protect this unique landscape, the 430 acres on and around Hughes Mountain are a designated Missouri Natural Area. A wide expanse of rock covers about 150 acres on the mountain's upper reaches. Unique pre-Cambrian rhyolite formations more than a billion years old are scattered around the summit. The 1.5-mile path exploring Hughes Mountain, the Devil's Honeycomb Trail, is named for these ancient rhyolite formations. When you see them, you'll know why. Small columns of rock nested together in tight beds, they look exactly like vertical honeycombs.

The Devil's Honeycomb Trail isn't very long, but it's a fascinating and beautiful hike. Driving toward Hughes Mountain on MO M you'll see the open space on the hillside, but you won't appreciate how big it is until you climb onto its slopes. The trail up to the glade, marked by white placards

## DIRECTIONS

Drive 10 miles south of Potosi on MO 21 to MO M. Drive 3.5 miles east on MO M to CR 541, where you'll see a sign for Hughes Mountain. Go 0.3 miles south on CR 541 to the trailhead on the left side of the road.

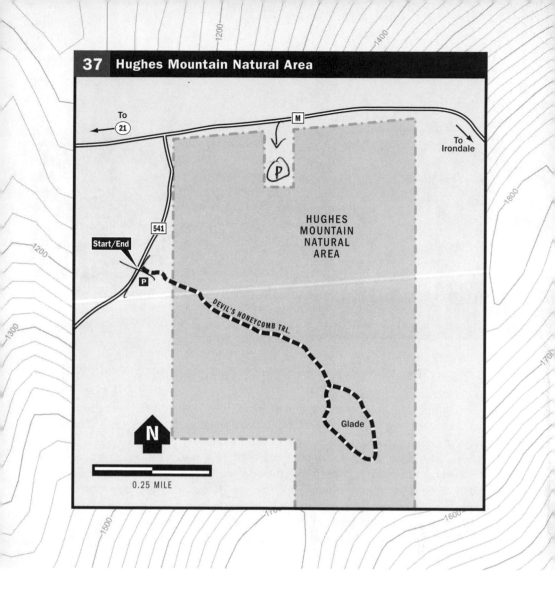

To
21

M

To
Irondale

P

541

Start/End

P

HUGHES
MOUNTAIN
NATURAL
AREA

DEVIL'S HONEYCOMB TRL.

Glade

N

0.25 MILE

with hiker silhouettes, is a nice one. It wanders through a forest, skirting a couple of small glades. Half-buried boulders splashed with bright-green mosses and lichens litter the hillside. The trail climbs gently over a half mile on its way to the summit, with occasional views across the valley west of the mountain, and then opens dramatically into the monstrous rocky glade.

Breaking into the glade is like stepping onto the moon or the remnants of an ancient volcano. Rock slopes rise endlessly ahead of you, to your right and to your left. Scattered patches of grass, wildflowers, and shrubs add a bit of life to the landscape. The trail to the summit is marked with green arrows painted on the rock surfaces, but they're pretty hard to find. Just head toward the high point, and you'll be on the route. Off to your right you'll see the return trail marked with placards on posts. You won't really need markings up

Vistas from the lunar landscape
on top of Hughes Mountain

here, anyway. It's hard to get lost in the open expanses of rock on Hughes Mountain, so explore freely.

As you work your way up the rock dome, keep looking over your shoulder. The view keeps getting better and better until you reach the summit, with its dramatic sweeping panoramas of the St. Francois Mountains and the farms tucked into their valleys. It's pleasant here in summer, when breezes sweep this open mountainside. It's a wonderful place in winter, too; the sun warms the rock, and white snowfields gently contrast with the salmon-pink rhyolite. Rainstorms are fascinating on this rocky hillside—dormant streams come to life, gurgling noisily over the massive stone surfaces. When the sun breaks through the clouds, leftover pools reflect bright blue sky. Sunsets on Hughes Mountain are magnificent, the pinkish rhyolite glowing softly in the evening sunlight.

The rhyolite formations thicken as you go higher, until its thousands of vertical columns unevenly cover every spot at the summit. They look exactly like a devil's honeycomb—a bunch of otherworldly little creatures jammed together on a forbidding mountaintop. I think the only thing evil about them is they're hard to sit on. I like to relax in high places, have a snack, and admire the view. But I get cheated out of that small pleasure on the summit of Hughes Mountain, where it's hard to find a smooth place to rest my derriere on the uneven rhyolite.

From the summit it's difficult to find markings to continue the loop, but it's obvious where you should go. Work your way off the summit and into the woods to the west, where you'll hit an old road. If you turn left on this old road, you can explore the forest south of the summit and, with a little exploration, will find another, less spectacular glade on the southern boundary of the property. To stick to the trail, turn right, follow the old road north, and you'll soon break into the glade. There you'll spot trail signs on posts leading across the glade to the access trail, then on to the trailhead.

# JOHNSON'S SHUT-INS STATE PARK

## ▶ IN BRIEF

*Shut-ins* is an Ozark term referring to water-sculpted formations in deep, narrow gorges where rivers are "shut in." Johnson's Shut-Ins are the most spectacular in Missouri. You can clamber over them, bathe in their chutes and potholes, and swim in the deep pools below these other-worldly volcanic-rock formations.

## ▶ DESCRIPTION

Johnson's Shut-Ins is one of Missouri's most popular state parks. Folks come from all over the state to camp, hike, fish, and splash in the rocky wonderland on the east fork of the Black River. This 8,670-acre scenic landscape includes three designated Missouri Natural Areas—the 180-acre Johnson's Shut-Ins Natural Area, the 1,110-acre East Fork Wild Area, and the 4,814-acre Goggins Mountain Wild Area. Nine hundred kinds of plants have been catalogued in the park, and its bird checklist tallies more than 200 species.

Until 2005, the park's main draw was the geological wonder of the shut-ins. They're the remnants of igneous rock formed more than a billion years ago, when volcanic material cooled to become the blue-gray rhyolite you see in the shut-ins today. In late 2005, a man-made disaster added another geologic wonder to the park—a huge scar from a devastating flood. The Upper Reservoir on Ameren UE's Taum Sauk Hydroelectric Plant burst, sending a massive flood through the heart of the park. It stripped away acres of

## ℹ KEY AT-A-GLANCE INFORMATION

**LENGTH:** 2.5 miles on Shut-Ins Trail; 10 miles on Goggins Mountain Trail

**CONFIGURATION:** Two separate loops

**DIFFICULTY:** Easy on Shut-Ins Trail; moderate on Goggins Mountain Trail

**SCENERY:** Scenic overlooks from rugged mountainsides, fantastic water-carved rock sculptures in the Shut-Ins, deep, green pools in the Black River, and unbelievable scarring from the 2005 Upper Reservoir flood

**EXPOSURE:** Mostly shaded, with exposed areas along the shut-ins and in glades along the trails

**TRAFFIC:** Heavy on Shut-Ins Trail; light on Goggins Mountain Trail

**TRAIL SURFACE:** Packed earth, gravel, many rugged sections

**HIKING TIME:** 2 hours for Shut-Ins Trail; 5–7 hours for Goggins Mountain Trail

**ACCESS:** Open sunrise–sunset

**MAPS:** Johnson's Shut-Ins USGS topo; trail maps available at office

**FACILITIES:** Water, restrooms, campground, picnic areas, phone, store (in season), swimming; some facilities unavailable until 2005 flood devastation is repaired

**SPECIAL COMMENTS:** Pets not allowed in shut-in area, other areas on 10-foot leash; climbing by permit only; no food or drink on Shut-Ins Trail. Due to ongoing flood-devastation repairs at time of publication, expect some discrepancies in this chapter; for updates check the park's Web site, **www.mostateparks.com/jshutins.htm.**

## ▶ DIRECTIONS

Following Interstate 55 and US 67, drive south to Farmington. Turn right at the second Farmington exit for Doe Run and MO W, and follow MO W 17 miles southwest to MO 21. Go right a half mile on MO 21 to MO N. Turn left on MO N and drive 13 miles southwest to the park.

## GPS TRAILHEAD COORDINATES (PARK ENTRANCE)

| UTM ZONE (WGS84) | 15S |
| --- | --- |
| EASTING | 690051 |
| NORTHING | 4157959 |
| LATITUDE-LONGITUDE | |
| NORTH | N37° 32' 56.5945'' |
| WEST | W90° 50' 54.9193'' |

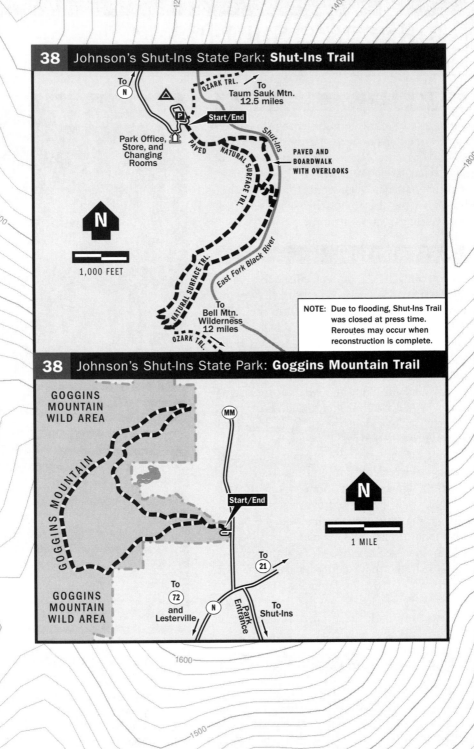

# 38 Johnson's Shut-Ins State Park: **Shut-Ins Trail**

To
N

OZARK TRL.
→ To
Taum Sauk Mtn.
12.5 miles

P
Start/End

Shut-Ins

Park Office,
Store, and
Changing
Rooms

PAVED

NATURAL SURFACE TRL.

PAVED AND
BOARDWALK
WITH OVERLOOKS

N

1,000 FEET

NATURAL SURFACE TRL.

East Fork Black River

To
Bell Mtn.
Wilderness
12 miles

OZARK TRL.

NOTE: Due to flooding, Shut-Ins Trail
was closed at press time.
Reroutes may occur when
reconstruction is complete.

# 38 Johnson's Shut-Ins State Park: **Goggins Mountain Trail**

GOGGINS
MOUNTAIN
WILD AREA

MM

GOGGINS MOUNTAIN

N

Start/End

1 MILE

GOGGINS
MOUNTAIN
WILD AREA

To
21

To
72
and
Lesterville

N

Park Entrance

To
Shut-Ins

mountainside and deposited countless tons of silt, boulders, and broken trees in the valley of the East Fork of the Black River. Thanks to a massive cleanup effort, the park had just been reopened on a limited basis at the time of this writing; full restoration won't be completed for another year or more. The Goggins Mountain Trail wasn't affected, but only part of the Shut-Ins Trail was usable when the park reopened on Memorial Day weekend 2006. A temporary half-mile interpretive trail through a boulder field deposited by the flood was open at that time, explaining the flood and its effects on the park. Check the park's Web site (see Special Comments section) for updates before heading to Johnson's Shut-Ins.

Though heavily damaged, Johnson's Shut-Ins is still one of the most beautiful places in the Ozarks. The Black River flows noisily over the blue-gray rhyolite for several hundred yards, forming pools, chutes, potholes, waterfalls, and cascades. Below the shut-ins, the Black River pauses for a while in deep, green pools, where expansive rock patios slope gently into the suddenly calm stream. Steep rock walls overlook the scene, topped with platform overlooks with views across the shut-ins and down into the pools.

With a permit from the park office, you can climb these rock walls, but most park visitors come here to swim (The Shut-Ins were closed to swimming after the flood, but will be reopened when restoration and cleanup is finished). It's a joy to climb over the rocks clad only in swimsuit and sandals, sliding in the chutes, showering under the waterfalls, or swimming in the deep pools below the shut-ins. This place gets crowded on summer weekends, so come early if you plan to swim or to hike on the Shut-Ins Trail. There's only room for 100 cars in the day-use area. Park personnel monitor the lot, letting in only as many cars as the park can hold.

Other than coming to the park during the week (an option not open to many folks), there are two ways to avoid the crush. My favorite is visiting Johnson's Shut-Ins in the off-season. Fall colors light up the park in October, and during winter the ice formations in the rugged riverbed are incredible. It's as if the stream is trying to look even more captivating than the shut-ins, showing off its own talent for fantastic sculpture. You'll have the park almost to yourself on cold days, and with no swimmers clouding the water, you'll see all the way to the bottom of the pools below the shut-ins.

The other way to avoid the crush is to hike the Goggins Mountain Trail. Located in a separate area of the park, this lightly traveled 10-mile loop is a beautiful hike through the Goggins Mountain Wild Area. Its trailhead is a few hundred yards beyond the main entrance to Johnson's Shut-Ins, then 0.75 miles north on MO MM. It's a rustic trailhead—parking spaces, hitching posts for equestrians, and that's it.

Carsonite posts with yellow arrows mark the route, supplemented with yellow plastic rectangles nailed to trees. From the trailhead you'll hike a 0.4-mile spur to the loop. The loop is a fine hike either way, but hiking clockwise results in an easier climb onto Goggins Mountain and saves the nice views for the latter part of your hike. The first mile is a gentle ascent along old roads, winding through abandoned fields now overgrown with pretty cedar groves. Upon leaving the fields you'll follow an ascending ridge 1 mile, topping out on the long spine of Goggins Mountain.

Once on Goggins Mountain's ridge you'll break north and follow its spine for 3.5 miles. It's a fun jaunt along a breezy highland through rock fields and scattered monster boulders, but trees obscure most of the vistas. The highlight of this ridgetop run is an igneous dome protruding like a dinosaur's back from a rugged glade next to the trail. This lumpy boulder field covers an area 150 feet long.

You'll follow old roads all along the ridge, slowly curving northeast. At 5.8 miles into your hike, you'll break south off the ridge on a single-track path. The trail is rugged for the next 2.5 miles, following the eastern slope of Goggins Mountain. You'll make numerous short but steep ups and downs, but the payback is several panoramic vistas from rock ledges on the mountainside. (Note also the odd-looking flat-topped mountain in the distance. It's what's left of the reservoir that blew out and flooded the park in 2005, temporarily shutting it down and changing the landscape so drastically.) The rugged stretch of the trail ends when you swing east onto a ridge, hook up with an old road, and begin descending. The road runs downhill for most of the last mile to the loop junction, where you'll hike the spur back to the trailhead.

The Goggins Mountain Trail is a nice one, but the jewel of the park is the 2.5-mile Shut-Ins Trail. (The Shut-Ins Trail was temporarily closed due to flood damage at the time of publication, but DNR plans to reopen it as quickly as possible.) It explores the Johnson's Shut-Ins Natural Area and the East Fork Wild Area. This hike starts from the day-use parking area, where an interpretive display tells how the shut-ins were formed, describes how the park came into being, and tells of the 2005 flood damage. The first half mile through the shut-ins is heavily developed, sporting paved paths, boardwalks, and long staircases. Platforms overlook the shut-ins in several places, but the one where the boardwalk ends is my favorite. It looks down a sheer cliff into the deep green pools below the shut-ins.

From the last platform the trail gets rugged and wild. You'll angle up the cliff edge to a connector trail. Marked with red arrows, it cuts across the loop to give you a 1-mile option. The rest of the loop, marked with blue arrows, heads south along the river. You'll descend a couple of quick switchbacks to river level, then follow the Black for almost a half mile. A spur trail leads back to the pool below the overlook, and several side trails lead to rock ledges and gravel bars on the river below the shut-ins.

Upon leaving the river you'll angle up the hillside and swing north, working your way up a beautiful rocky hollow with a tiny waterfall trickling over a rock-layer staircase. The trail crosses this little creek, climbs a couple of steep switchbacks next to the waterfall, then tops out with spectacular views southeast down the Black River's valley. From here it's an easy hike back to the day-use parking lot. You'll enjoy several more vistas of the river valley along the way, and the rumble of the shut-ins will steadily increase as you head north to the trailhead.

# LOWER ROCK CREEK

## ▶ IN BRIEF

Lower Rock Creek is a truly wild place. No marked trails or groomed pathways here—just lots of pine-studded hills and cliffs towering over rock-ledge waterfalls and noisy cascades in a boulder-strewn stream. Bring your camera to this tantalizing canyon, and allow plenty of time to revel in its beauty.

## ▶ DESCRIPTION

Though it's not designated as such, Lower Rock Creek feels like true wilderness. There's not a marked path and no signed trailhead, and its rugged character keeps the four-wheelers away. It's truly unspoiled, and must look much as it has for thousands of years. Some know this hideaway as Cathedral Canyon, named for the 400-foot rock walls in its upper reaches. Others call it Dark Hollow, and on cloudy days or late afternoon hikes you'll know why. Of its three names, I chose Lower Rock Creek because the stream is the beating heart of this beautiful natural wonder.

You'll enjoy visiting Lower Rock Creek in any season, but I think it's best in spring and winter. During winter the creek builds intriguing ice sculptures; you can better admire the rock walls when the trees are bare, and the canyon's pines and

## ▶ DIRECTIONS

Take US 67 south 3 miles past Fredericktown. Turn west on MO E and drive 9 miles to Madison County Road 511. It's just past the bridge over the St. Francis River. Turn north and follow CR 511 for 0.4 miles to a concrete stream ford. Turn left on the primitive road just past the ford, and follow it another 0.4 miles to the trailhead next to a locked gate. The farther you go, the rougher the road will be. If you're driving a low-clearance vehicle, park in one of the pullouts scattered along the first part of the road.

## ⓘ KEY AT-A-GLANCE INFORMATION

**LENGTH:** 4–8 miles, depending upon how far you explore in the canyon

**CONFIGURATION:** Point-to-point

**DIFFICULTY:** Moderate

**SCENERY:** Steep forested hills, towering rock walls, boulder-strewn stream with small waterfalls, cascades, and calm pools

**EXPOSURE:** Shady along the trail leading to Lower Creek; exposed in many parts of the canyon

**TRAFFIC:** Light

**TRAIL SURFACE:** Packed earth and gravel on access trail; incredibly rocky in canyon of Lower Rock Creek

**HIKING TIME:** 3–5 hours

**ACCESS:** No permits or fees

**MAPS:** Lake Killarney, Rhodes Mountain, Rock Pile Mountain USGS topos; no official forest service map available for Lower Rock Creek

**FACILITIES:** None

**SPECIAL COMMENTS:** Lower Rock Creek is beautiful, but it's an incredibly rugged place. It's a place for decent boots, and trekking poles if you've got them.

**GPS TRAILHEAD COORDINATES (TRAILHEAD)**

| UTM ZONE (WGS84) | 15S |
| --- | --- |
| EASTING | 723800 |
| NORTHING | 4154287 |

LATITUDE–LONGITUDE

| NORTH | N37° 30' 30.3068'' |
| --- | --- |
| WEST | W90° 28' 4.7195'' |

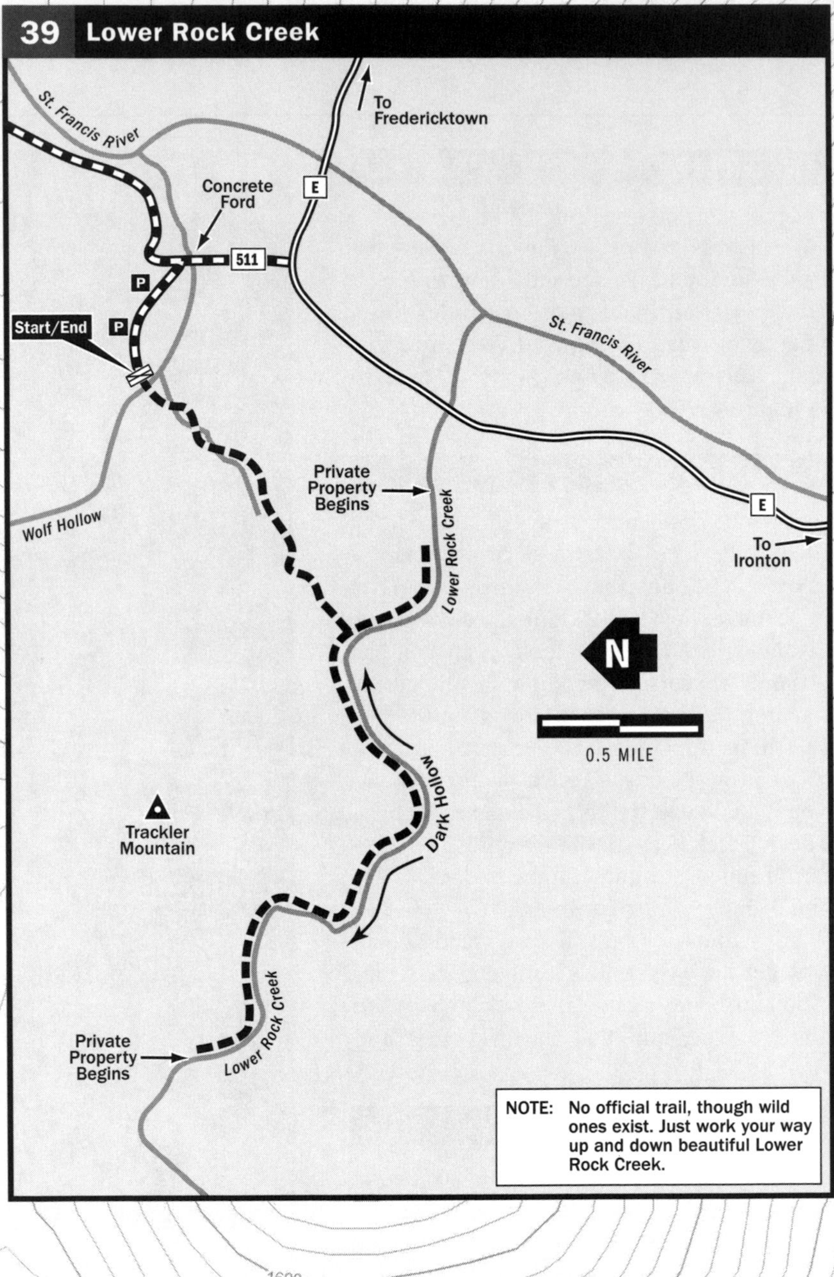

## 39 Lower Rock Creek

St. Francis River

To Fredericktown

Concrete Ford

E

511

P

P

Start/End

St. Francis River

Wolf Hollow

Private Property Begins

Lower Rock Creek

E

To Ironton

N

0.5 MILE

Dark Hollow

Trackler Mountain

Private Property Begins

Lower Rock Creek

NOTE: No official trail, though wild ones exist. Just work your way up and down beautiful Lower Rock Creek.

1200

1400

1800

1200

1300

1700

1400

1500

1500

1600

1400

1300

1200

cedars brighten the place with splashes of green. You can still enjoy those views in early spring before the trees leaf out. The waterfalls and cascades really make some noise when the seasonal rains are running off. Wildflowers color the benches and hillsides next to the creek as the weather warms. One flower or another is in bloom all the way through summer and into fall, when autumn's splashy colors contrast with the gray canyon walls. Hiking Lower Rock Creek in Missouri's hot, humid summer becomes bearable—even enjoyable— with cooling dips in the several deep pools that grace this year-round stream.

The larger pools are home to small fish and crawdads. It's fun to watch them as they dart through the water, seeming to race their shadows across the rocky bottom. Watch for blue and green herons standing silently in the pools, hoping a fish or a crawdad will come close enough to become lunch. Kingfishers flit up and down the canyon, breaking the silence with their clattering song. I once startled a bunch of wood ducks off a pool in the upper end of the creek, where

Lower Rock Creek

the canyon walls are lower and the pools bigger. If you're a reptile lover, watch for snakes and lizards sliding and skittering among the rock-strewn streambed.

Mileage on this hike depends upon how far you explore up and down Lower Rock Creek. Unless you bushwhack back to the trailhead, you'll have to turn around and retrace your steps back to the car on an out-and-back trek. The spur from the trailhead into the canyon is an easy 1.25-mile hike. Step around the gate at the trailhead and head southwest on an old road a few hundred yards until you reach a fork. Bear left, and after a fairly easy hike over a low divide you'll break into Lower Rock Creek.

Even though the canyon walls aren't so tall here, I think this is the most beautiful part of Lower Rock Creek, worth the hike all by itself. A few samples of pink granite, like that found at Elephant Rocks State Park, contrasts with the predominant gray stone found in the canyon. Downstream, a 25-foot wall rises above a huge slab that slopes gently into a deep pool, the perfect place to be on a hot summer day. Around the bend and downstream, more pools scattered among upended rock layers are being worn away by the creek. For several hundred yards upstream from the trail junction, moss- and lichen-encrusted rocks rise in steps above the creek, overlooking a rocky bottom of fractured layers forming cascades, riffles, and pools. One of the pools has a three-foot square hole in the bottom—perfect for soaking tired feet after a tough hike. Cedars overlook it all, contrasting brightly with the gray rock walls and streambed.

If you continue upstream, you might need to soak your feet on the return trip. Though the terrain is level, the stream bottom is full of boulders all the way past the high walls 1.5 miles upstream, making for a challenging hike and sore feet. There is a faint trail most of the way up the canyon. It comes and goes, but will keep you up out of the rocky streambed if you can find and follow it. Walking the rugged streambed is worth the effort, though: you'll get better views, the boulders are impressive, and you'll be right on top of Rock Creek's cascades and waterfalls. They're most impressive after rainstorms, which unfortunately means slippery rocks and possibly a boot full of water, but I still think it's fun to work your way up the rushing stream. Good boots are a must, and trekking poles would be a great help in pushing your way up the hollow. Bring some spare socks, too, just in case you misjudge a step or two.

I like to wear myself out hiking slowly up the canyon in the streambed to the high walls, then return on the rudimentary trail. This hard-to-find footpath is usually on the right side of Lower Rock Creek when you're heading upstream. To find the trail, locate one of the several backpack campsites on streamside benches below the wall, and look for the trail heading along the creek. I guarantee you'll lose it several times, but it'll be a fun exercise in route finding. You can't get lost in the canyon, so it's the perfect place to hone your trail-finding skills.

An enjoyable trek into Lower Rock Creek requires a different mind-set from most hikes in this book. Don't come here expecting to get in a rhythm and hammer out the miles—the rugged character of this hideaway dictates slower, more deliberate travel. Moving slowly and carefully over Lower Rock Creek's rugged terrain offers a chance to understand a piece of the outdoors in a more intimate way, fully absorbing the beauty and "lost canyon" atmosphere of this hidden valley.

## ▶ NEARBY ACTIVITIES

Just west of Fredericktown, you'll find more awesome rock formations and waterfalls at Millstream Gardens, and a deep swimming hole in the St. Francis River awaits you at Silver Mines Recreation Area (page 227).

# MERAMEC CONSERVATION AREA

## ▶ IN BRIEF

In these forested hills and hollows, trails of varying lengths wind along the Meramec River, climb to a panoramic overlook of a horseshoe bend, meander along intermittent streams, visit an abandoned fire lookout, and wander past springs and caves. With the 1.3-mile paved Woodland Trail, the 6-mile Old Reedville School Trail, and the 10-mile J. Avery Ruble Bridle Trail, there's a hike for every level of backcountry wander at Meramec Conservation Area.

## ▶ DESCRIPTION

The 4,045-acre Meramec Conservation Area is a wonderful place to sample Missouri's natural wonders and historical past. On its 18-mile trail system you'll roam along the Meramec River, wander past caves, admire springs gurgling from rock faces, and travel along intermittent streams. You'll visit the site of the Old Reedville School, now only a stone marker in the woods, and climb Lone Hill, where you'll picnic at an old fire tower site. A Civilian Conservation Corps camp was here in the 1930s, housing workers who built nearby Meramec State Park.

Meramec Conservation Area and Meramec State Park comprise an 11,000-acre block of public land straddling the Meramec River. This large semiwild area's varied habitats make it an ideal

## ▶ DIRECTIONS

Drive southwest on I-44 to Exit 226 for Sullivan, Meramec State Park, and MO 185. Drive 5 miles southeast on MO 185 to Meramec Conservation Area. Turn left on the gravel entrance road and follow it 1.5 miles to the trailhead. A secondary trailhead is on the eastern side of the conservation area. To reach it, drive 1 mile farther on MO 185 to MO K. Turn left 1.5 miles on MO K to Spanish Claim Road. Follow this gravel road 2.2 miles north to the trailhead on the left.

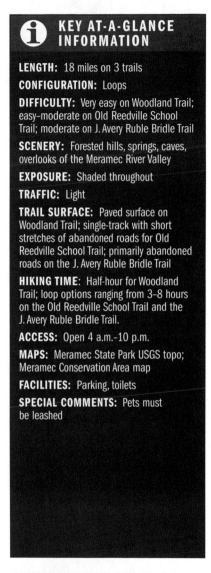

### ℹ KEY AT-A-GLANCE INFORMATION

**LENGTH:** 18 miles on 3 trails

**CONFIGURATION:** Loops

**DIFFICULTY:** Very easy on Woodland Trail; easy–moderate on Old Reedville School Trail; moderate on J. Avery Ruble Bridle Trail

**SCENERY:** Forested hills, springs, caves, overlooks of the Meramec River Valley

**EXPOSURE:** Shaded throughout

**TRAFFIC:** Light

**TRAIL SURFACE:** Paved surface on Woodland Trail; single-track with short stretches of abandoned roads for Old Reedville School Trail; primarily abandoned roads on the J. Avery Ruble Bridle Trail

**HIKING TIME:** Half-hour for Woodland Trail; loop options ranging from 3–8 hours on the Old Reedville School Trail and the J. Avery Ruble Bridle Trail.

**ACCESS:** Open 4 a.m.–10 p.m.

**MAPS:** Meramec State Park USGS topo; Meramec Conservation Area map

**FACILITIES:** Parking, toilets

**SPECIAL COMMENTS:** Pets must be leashed

### GPS TRAILHEAD COORDINATES (TRAILHEAD)

| | |
|---|---|
| UTM ZONE (WGS84) | 15S |
| EASTING | 667877 |
| NORTHING | 4231845 |
| LATITUDE-LONGITUDE | |
| NORTH | N38° 13' 8.1686'' |
| WEST | W91° 4' 56.1699'' |

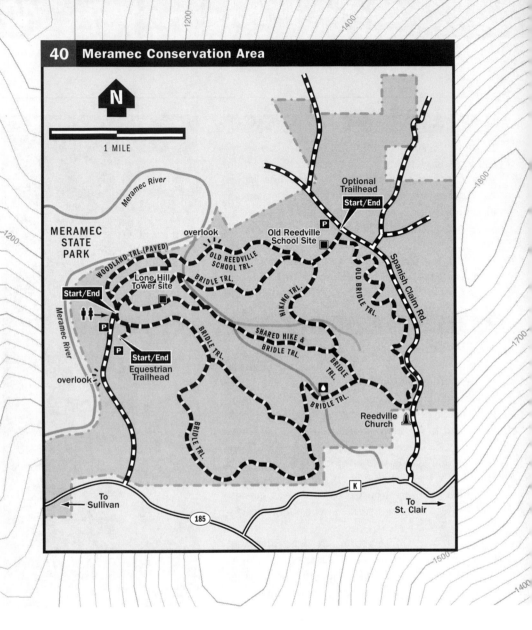

place for wildlife watching. Black bears, gradually moving back to Missouri from Arkansas, have been sighted here. Turtles sun themselves on snags in the Meramec, and otters and muskrats swim just under the surface. Blue and green herons feed stealthily in the river, and a wide variety of songbirds inhabits the riverside woods. Ospreys are occasionally spotted fishing in the Meramec. Bats from the area's caves flit through the woods at dusk. And if you're secretive enough you might surprise a bobcat, fox, or coyote.

Spring is the best time here, particularly during or after rainstorms. Rainfall brings the intermittent streams to life with cascades and waterfalls. Runoff percolates through rock layers and wells up in springs, and a stream gushes from Lone Hill Onyx Cave. Wildflowers are everywhere, especially in the moist bottomland of Silver Hollow on the bridle trail. It turns a delicate white with a spring carpet of Miami Mist. Fall and winter are good times to visit, but the streams and springs are often dry.

The easiest hike in Meramec Conservation area is the 1.3-mile Woodland Trail. This paved, accessible trail has benches every 100 yards. Several are right on the river, with wonderful views of the Meramec. Another sits near bird feeders in an open space next to a creek. This scenic trail explores groves of pine, cedar, and hardwoods. Several huge sycamores lean out over the Meramec. The Woodland Trail's highlight is Lone Hill Onyx Cave, a cavern in the base of a mossy bluff. A viewing platform overlooks the cave, and in rainy times a stream rushes from the cavern.

The area's best hike is the 6-mile Old Reedville School Trail. It breaks off from the far end of the Woodland Trail and follows the riverbank. It's poorly marked—only a couple of yellow carsonite posts with hiker symbols mark its departure from the Woodland Trail, with nothing to indicate which trail you're taking. Additional yellow posts, supplemented with hiker-silhouette placards, are inconsistently scattered along the trail, and intersections are poorly marked. Still, the trail isn't difficult to follow. Just bring a map, consult it often, and backtrack when in doubt.

After breaking off the Woodland Trail, the Old Reedville School Trail follows the river for a quarter mile, then goes south into the woods. You'll soon come to a low bluff with a cave in its face, where the trail seems to disappear. Walk around the right side of the bluff, and you'll see an old road heading up the hill along the bluff edge. This is the trail, and it climbs steadily along the bluff for a quarter mile. It tops out at an overlook platform with benches, perfect for admiring the view of a horseshoe bend in the Meramec River.

After the overlook, you'll leave the river and travel level on a ridge. A quarter mile after leaving the overlook, the trail joins a narrow logging road. This narrow track soon strikes a wider road and turns left to follow it east. This is also the north loop of the bridle trail. A right turn would take you west to the trailhead. The Old Reedville School Trail goes east on this road for 200 yards, then breaks off it to go south.

To see the trail's namesake school site, bypass the turn for now and continue another 300 yards east. You'll find a marker stating "Reedville Log School 1859–1890" and one remnant log from the old structure. Nearby there's a stone tablet carved with teachers' names and their years of service at the old school. A hundred yards east of the school site is the east trailhead for the conservation area.

After backtracking to the main trail, you'll follow it south for a half mile, descend into Wet Hollow, cross a creek, and climb steeply onto the ridge south of the hollow. There you'll strike another trail. This is a shared section of trail open to both horses and hikers, and a left turn would take you a quarter mile to the bridle trail. The Old Reedville School Trail turns right on the ridge and follows its descending spine on a half-mile descent back into Wet Hollow. If the streams are flowing, Wet Hollow is a magical place. When you hit the hollow bottom there'll be a series of waterfalls pouring over mossy rocks on your left. You'll follow the creek downstream, crossing it three times within a half mile.

After the third crossing, the hiking trail breaks left from the horse trail and climbs onto Lone Hill. It's a half-mile climb with switchbacks to the summit, where there's a wonderful place for a break. In a grassy meadow you'll see footings of the old lookout tower, along with the stone chimney from the tower keeper's house. Built against the chimney is a picnic shelter and a table. If there's any breeze on a hot day, you'll feel it on Lone Hill's summit. From Lone Hill it's mostly downhill 0.9 miles to the trailhead. Along the way you'll notice odd depressions on the hillside—leftover test pits from mineral prospectors in the early 1900s.

The 12-mile J. Avery Ruble Bridle Trail is also open to hikers. It's divided into a 7-mile north loop and 5-mile south loop. Hiking the perimeter is a 10-mile trek. Because of recent logging activity, the north loop is rerouted along part of the hiking trail, shortening it by 3 miles. The old trail is still open and easy to follow. Placards with equestrian silhouettes mark the loop. Following old roads for most of its length, the bridle trail is good for trail running or side-by-side hiking.

The bridle path heads east from the trailhead, following an old mining road up Silver Hollow. One mile in you'll hit the shortcut trail dividing the two loops. The shortcut trail goes 1 mile gradually uphill to the loop's eastern side. The south loop is to the right. It has no spectacular features, but it's a nice walk in the woods. It makes two long climbs and one long descent before rejoining the shortcut trail 2.4 miles later.

From the shortcut trail's eastern end, the north loop descends a half mile to the upper reaches of Wet Hollow, then turns upstream. This is a neat place when the water's flowing. Two streams braid their way along the hollow floor, and a spring flows from the base of a low bluff. Just beyond the spring the trail starts a quarter-mile climb. At the top of the climb, signs direct you left on an old road. This is the logging reroute that cuts 3 miles off the north loop. You'll have already seen most of this reroute if you've hiked the Old Reedville School Trail. It travels level or gradually downhill for 1.8 miles, rejoining the old bridle route in Wet Hollow.

To continue the old route, ignore the turn and keep going north. Markers are still in place, and their guidance and an eye on the map will steer you right. You'll cross occasional logging cuts, but equestrians still use the old route frequently, keeping the trail well worn and easy to follow. You'll pass behind Reedville Church, then travel north 3 miles to the east trailhead and the Reedville Log School site. From there it's an easy 2.2-mile hike west to the trailhead.

# MERAMEC STATE PARK'S SHORT TRAILS

## ▶ IN BRIEF

Meramec State Park's five short trails, ranging in length from 0.5 to 1.8 miles, explore deep hollows, steep cliffs, cave entrances, riverside forests, and climb to several panoramic overlooks of the Meramec River. When you tire of the park's outdoor scenery, you can descend into its underground wilderness with a guided tour of Fisher Cave.

## ▶ DESCRIPTION

Meramec State Park's beauty is both above and below the ground. Trails lace the pretty hills next to the Meramec River, and more than 40 caves wind through the limestone and dolomite layers underneath the park. You'll go by several caves as you wander the park's trails, and feel the earth's cool breath as you pass their entrances. With a tour of Fisher Cave you can do a little underground trekking, too—the perfect hike on a hot summer day.

The state bought the first of Meramec State Park's 6,986 acres in 1926. Development took off in the 1930s, when the Civilian Conservation Corps sited two camps in the area and began building trails. Many of the structures you'll see on your hikes were built by the CCC. In addition to trails and a campground, the park offers rustic cabins, a dining hall with a wonderful view of the river valley, and a superb visitor center.

Start your first trip to the park at the visitor center. I like to stop in whenever it's open and admire its fine exhibits. You can get maps there, along with a preview of the landscape you're about

## ▶ DIRECTIONS

Drive southwest on I-44 to Exit 226, Sullivan–MO 185. Turn left and drive 3 miles southeast on MO 185 to the park. Maps are available at the visitor center. See text for trailheads for each hike.

### KEY AT-A-GLANCE INFORMATION

**LENGTH:** 6 miles on 5 trails

**CONFIGURATION:** Natural Wonders, Walking Fern, Bluff View, and River trails are loops; Deer Hollow Trail is a point-to-point hike.

**DIFFICULTY:** Very easy

**SCENERY:** Forested hills, bluff overlooks of the Meramec River, marshy stream banks, caves, and springs

**EXPOSURE:** Shady with short exposed stretches

**TRAFFIC:** Moderate

**TRAIL SURFACE:** Rocky or packed gravel on hillsides; packed earth on hollow bottoms and riverside trails

**HIKING TIME:** 1 hour or less on each trail

**ACCESS:** Park open 7 a.m.–9 p.m., November–March; 7 a.m.–10 p.m., April–October

**MAPS:** Available at visitor center; Meramec State Park USGS topo

**FACILITIES:** Visitor center, dining lodge, campground, cabins, playground, showers, water, store, canoe rental, conference center

**SPECIAL COMMENTS:** Pets must be leashed; supervise children on cliff overlooks; some caves require permit for exploration

### GPS TRAILHEAD COORDINATES (VISITOR CENTER)

| | | |
|---|---|---|
| **UTM ZONE (WGS84)** | | 15S |
| | **EASTING** | 665947 |
| | **NORTHING** | 4230581 |
| **LATITUDE-LONGITUDE** | | |
| | **NORTH** | N38° 12' 28.4633'' |
| | **WEST** | W91° 6' 16.5770'' |

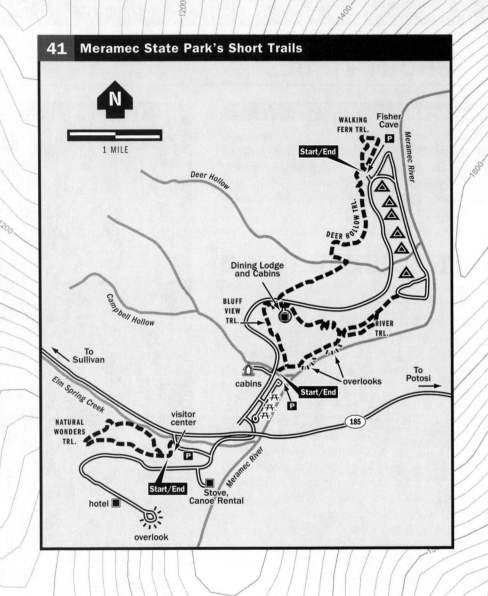

N

1 MILE

WALKING
FERN TRL.

Fisher
Cave

Start/End

Meramec River

Deer Hollow

DEER HOLLOW TRL.

Dining Lodge
and Cabins

BLUFF
VIEW
TRL.

Campbell Hollow

RIVER
TRL.

To
Sullivan

To
Potosi

cabins

overlooks

Start/End

Elm Spring Creek

185

NATURAL
WONDERS
TRL.

visitor
center

Meramec River

Start/End

Stove,
Canoe Rental

hotel

overlook

to explore. An excellent slide show describes the land's features and what critters and wildflowers you're likely to see. A 3,500-gallon aquarium houses fish and amphibians from the river, and a diorama called "Life on the Bank" shows the plants and animals you might see next to the Meramec. Be sure your kids press the button that makes the mink pop up with a frog in its mouth.

The visitor center has fine displays on the park's human history, too. One features prehistoric people, with drawings, projectile points, and pottery used by Native Americans who once lived in the river valley. A second describes the valley's hard-rock mining days. And a third shows a typical

Ozark pioneer farm. The last exhibit is a photo display documenting initial construction of the Meramec dam, which, if completed, would have flooded more than 40 miles of the Meramec. In 1978, voters turned thumbs down in a referendum on the dam. Work on the project was stopped, and all that remains are two ponds originally excavated for the dam's footings.

The 1.3-mile Natural Wonders Trail starts from the visitor center parking lot. Traveling counterclockwise, you'll first cut through a nice grove of pines, level out beside Elm Spring Creek, and follow it for several hundred yards. Bright green patches of watercress in the stream indicate it's spring-fed. You'll break away from the creek on a little side stream and find a spring trickling from a cave in a low bluff. The trail climbs onto the rock layer overlooking the cave, then traverses the downhill edge of a rocky glade.

From the glade, the trail climbs gradually for several hundred yards, then crosses a hollow on a raised berm under which there's another cave. If there's been rain, this one will have a stream trickling into it. The trail switchbacks around to head down the hollow for a while, then climbs high up its side onto a rock layer. Walking on the rock layer for a short way, you'll come around a curve and pass a third cave in the mossy rock face by the trail. A little stream dribbles from it, and icicles festoon the entrance in winter. From this pretty spot it's a gentle descent back to the trailhead.

You can combine the 1.5-mile Bluff View Trail and 0.8-mile River Trail to form a 2.7-mile figure-eight loop. The Bluff View Trail starts at the north end of the picnic area, behind shelter number 3. First you'll climb a spur to a CCC-constructed overlook shelter, and admire views up and down the Meramec. The loop begins next to the shelter, so you'll enjoy vistas at both the start and finish of your hike. Traveling clockwise on the loop, you'll leave the bluff edge and travel predominantly uphill for a half mile, topping out at the dining lodge and crossing the parking lot.

It's easy to miss the trail when it leaves the dining lodge. An old road looks like the way to go, but it's not. Bear right along a hollow that runs downhill behind the lodge and cabins, and you'll see the trail. For the next half mile you'll descend, winding around the head of a rugged little hollow and leveling out at a trail shelter near the river. This is the intersection of the figure-eight loop, and on the other side of the shelter is the River Trail. It explores a wooded bench next to the Meramec, running next to the river for part of its length, then looping back through the forest on an old road back to the shelter. It's level throughout its length. From its northeast end a spur leads to the group campground.

From the shelter, the next quarter mile of the Bluff View Trail climbs steeply along a cliff above the river with excellent views of the Meramec. Next, descend from the bluff to a moist hollow on the river, where there's a nice overhanging cliff arching over a stream, then climb steeply to another beautiful stretch of bluff-edge trail that'll lead you back to the overlook shelter, closing the loop.

The half-mile Walking Fern Trail and 1.8-mile Deer Hollow Trail start from the mouth of Fisher Cave. Walking Fern packs a lot of punch in a short hike. Traveling counterclockwise, it's level at first. Steep bluffs tower to one side; marshes are on the other. Several hundred yards down the trail a staircase up the bluff leads to Indian Cave. Prehistoric artifacts were found in this dry, shallow cave. It goes 20 or 30 yards

Bluff View Trail, Meramec State Park

back into the cliff, and is a neat exploration for kids. Just beyond Indian Cave the trail climbs steeply up a tight, rugged hollow onto the top of the bluff, then follows the highlands back to the cave. You'll see lots of mossy outcroppings and several vistas of the campground and river before descending to the amphitheater behind Fisher Cave.

The Deer Hollow Trail is a point-to-point hike running from Fisher Cave to the dining lodge. It climbs for the first quarter mile, slowly veering south and west, into Deer Hollow. You probably will see deer there, too. After 0.75 miles you'll descend into the hollow, then swing east to follow it toward the river for several hundred yards. You'll then veer back west, and climb the last half mile to the dining lodge. There's nothing superspecial about this hike—it's just a nice walk in the woods, with deer and wildflowers in the hollow.

You can hike the Deer Hollow Trail as a wonderfully decadent dinner loop, too. Follow Deer Hollow from Fisher Cave to the rustic CCC dining lodge, and load up with one of their great meals. A huge fireplace graces the dining room, and views from the patio are stupendous. Work off your belly full of grub by hiking the Bluff View Trail down to the River Trail, following the River Trail back to the campground and walking campground roads back to the trailhead. It's a 4-mile loop, showcasing much of Meramec State Park's beauty.

▶ **NEARBY ACTIVITIES**

Additional hiking trails are across the river at Meramec Conservation Area (page 165). Onondaga Cave State Park, a few miles upriver, offers still more hiking and cave tours (page 177).

# MERAMEC STATE PARK: THE WILDERNESS TRAIL

## ▶ IN BRIEF

The Wilderness Trail, Meramec State Park's longest hike, is beautiful and remote. You'll enjoy splendid solitude as you wander past caves, springs, bluffs, glades, and hundreds of rock outcroppings and ledges. With ten backpack camps scattered along its length, the Wilderness Trail is an excellent trek for day hikers and backpackers alike.

## ▶ DESCRIPTION

Meramec State Park's short trails (see previous profile) are nice, but for my money, the Wilderness Trail is the place to go. This isolated path covers the most remote terrain in the park. In its northern reaches you'll hike through the Meramec Upland Forest Natural Area, where Copper Hollow Spring pours from a cave opening on a mossy bluff. Black bears, slowly moving back to Missouri from Arkansas, have occasionally been spotted in the Meramec State Park area. The lonesome territory on the Wilderness Trail's north loop seems like the perfect place to see one.

A shortcut path divides the Wilderness Trail into a 6-mile south loop and a 4-mile north loop. Unless you're willing to park at one of the trail crossings on the MO 185 Spur to hike the north loop, you'll have to hike the south loop to reach the north one—thus limiting your distance choices to 10 or 6 miles. This well-designed trail's many long, level stretches and nicely graded inclines make the 10-mile loop an easy four- to five-hour hike, leaving plenty of time to check out Copper Hollow Spring and other scenic spots along the way.

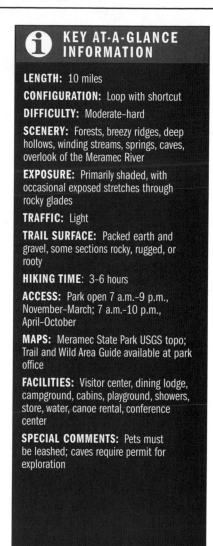

## ⓘ KEY AT-A-GLANCE INFORMATION

**LENGTH:** 10 miles

**CONFIGURATION:** Loop with shortcut

**DIFFICULTY:** Moderate–hard

**SCENERY:** Forests, breezy ridges, deep hollows, winding streams, springs, caves, overlook of the Meramec River

**EXPOSURE:** Primarily shaded, with occasional exposed stretches through rocky glades

**TRAFFIC:** Light

**TRAIL SURFACE:** Packed earth and gravel, some sections rocky, rugged, or rooty

**HIKING TIME:** 3-6 hours

**ACCESS:** Park open 7 a.m.–9 p.m., November–March; 7 a.m.–10 p.m., April–October

**MAPS:** Meramec State Park USGS topo; Trail and Wild Area Guide available at park office

**FACILITIES:** Visitor center, dining lodge, campground, cabins, playground, showers, store, water, canoe rental, conference center

**SPECIAL COMMENTS:** Pets must be leashed; caves require permit for exploration

## ▶ DIRECTIONS

Drive southwest on I-44 to Exit 226, Sullivan–MO 185. Turn left and drive 3 miles southeast on MO 185 to the park. Turn right, pass the visitor center, and turn left at the T intersection. The trailhead is 0.7 miles to the left, near the cabins across the road from the picnic area.

### GPS TRAILHEAD COORDINATES (TRAILHEAD)

| | | |
|---|---|---|
| UTM ZONE (WGS84) | 15S | |
| EASTING | 666864 | |
| NORTHING | 4230987 | |
| LATITUDE-LONGITUDE | | |
| NORTH | N38° 12' 41.0161'' | |
| WEST | W91° 5' 38.5308'' | |

# 42 Meramec State Park: **The Wilderness Trail**

N
0.5 MILE
Copper Hollow Spring
Meramec River
Cane Hollow
MO 185 spur
Fisher Cave
MERAMEC STATE PARK
Deer Hollow
Campbell Hollow
Dining Lodge and Cabins
Meramec River
To Sullivan
Cabins
Start/End
P
185
185
To Potosi
Visitors Center
Store
To Overlook and Hotel

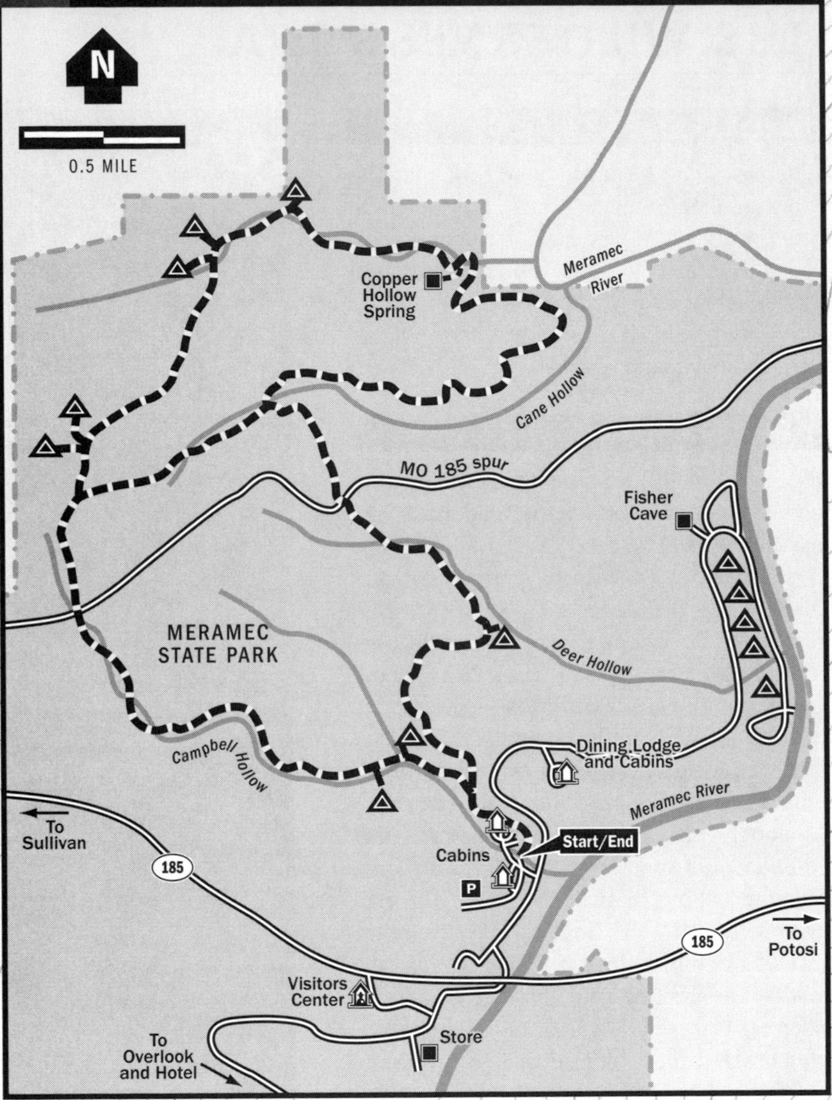

Ten backcountry camps scattered along the route make the Wilderness Trail perfect for first-time backpackers. The trail is challenging but not difficult, and the map is easy to follow. With the MO 185 Spur cutting across the loop, you're always less than 3 miles from an escape point. Most campsites are near a spring or stream, though in summer the creeks may be dry. For those who like to pick their own spot, excellent "wild" campsites are everywhere.

The Wilderness Trail is marked for clockwise travel, but I prefer to hike it counter-clockwise. That way I get the hilly portions out of the way first, and end my hike with a 2-mile gradual descent along Campbell Hollow. Markings are pretty sparse—intersections are well marked and clear, but there aren't any blazes on the trail. The well-worn path is almost impossible to lose; the park's trail map is an excellent one; and at each back-country camp there's a small guide map showing where you are. No matter which direction you choose, it's tough to get lost on this hike.

From the trailhead, the spur to the main loop goes behind some cabins, past a registration box, through several small glades, and reaches the fork 0.4 miles from the start. For much of the next half mile it's uphill, topping out on an old ridgetop road. Next the trail descends into Deer Hollow, leveling out near backcountry camp H. If you turned right here and bushwhacked a half mile downstream you'd intersect the Deer Hollow Trail, one of the park's short trails.

The Wilderness Trail turns left, then goes predominantly uphill northwest for 0.75 miles, crosses MO 185 Spur, and levels out in a grove of huge pines. By Missouri standards, these are monsters—some of them are two feet thick at the base. The trail winds through them for 200 yards, the masses of pine needles soft and quiet under-foot. Leaving the pine grove you'll travel level for a short way, do a quarter-mile descent into Cane Hollow, then hit the shortcut trail. The descent switchbacks and crosses some nice moss-covered rock outcroppings. Look left just before the shortcut trail, and you'll realize that on one switchback you walked over a cave entrance.

Turn left at this intersection for the 6-mile hike. It's a well-marked intersection, complete with arrows and distance notations on carsonite posts. The shortcut trail goes steadily up Cane Hollow for most of its length, passing a couple of streambed ledges that make nice waterfalls during rainy times. After a half mile, the shortcut trail tops out in a sweet-smelling pine plantation, then joins the loop's western side a few hundred yards later.

Continuing on the long loop, you'll climb quickly up the far slope of Cane Hollow, then parallel the hollow on a side-hill trail for the next 1.5 miles. This is a nice stretch of trail—easy grades, quick little switchbacks to circumnavigate side hollows, and lots of cool rock outcroppings. In some places you'll clamber through rock layers and walk along their ledges, sometimes with boulders broken off the layers scattered on the slope below. You'll pass through five glades, two of them wide and grassy, with rugged rock layers poking up through the thin soil. These south-facing glades are sunny and warm on chilly winter hikes.

When this pleasant run above Cane Hollow ends you'll veer north, strike an old road, and follow it left. It'll continue curving until you're pointed west. Keep an eye peeled to your right while making the curve: the trail comes close to a bend in the Meramec here, and you can glimpse the river through the trees. Push 100 yards down through the brush and admire a view of the river undercutting a cedar-topped bluff.

When its flow is strong, the river makes slurping noises as it nibbles away at the cliff. You'll be next to the river only for a short time—the trail soon heads west in the woods, crosses a few intermittent streams, then passes an interesting box canyon with bluff outcroppings on its rim.

Shortly past the box canyon the trail makes a hard left, crosses a stream, and reaches the prettiest spot on the hike: Copper Hollow Spring and Cave. Situated near the loop's halfway mark, this enchanting natural wonder is the perfect rest stop. A 50-foot-tall, 150-foot-long overhanging bluff protects the cave and spring. The strong outflow gushes from the cave, bounces over several rock layers, under a couple of mossy fallen trees, and into a pool filled with delicate, bright-green watercress. The watercress stretches 50 feet downstream. This is an incredible spot in winter—the watercress is a verdant slash of green across the brown-and-white landscape, the cave's breath feels warm during January cold snaps, and the overhanging bluff protects you from snow and sleet.

Leaving the cave and spring, you'll start a gradual uphill in Copper Hollow that lasts almost 2 miles. Along the way you'll pass more backpack camps, splash through several intermittent streams, and admire a bunch of rock outcroppings and low cliffs. The last half mile of the ascent is really fascinating. The hollow squeezes tighter and tighter as you climb, and if the stream's flowing there'll be a ton of small waterfalls tumbling over the rocky ledges in the streambed. The climb tops out just before you reach the western end of the shortcut trail at the 7-mile point of your hike.

After the shortcut trail, you'll enjoy a fairly easy jaunt along Campbell Hollow to the trailhead. You'll cross MO 185 Spur at mile 8, then hike a short way down a wide, level bottomland. The trail soon gets rocky again, spending much of the last 1.5 miles climbing over ledgy outcroppings, across intermittent streams, and past low bluffs with miniature cave grottoes. It's a wild stretch of trail, but not too difficult— a pleasant way to end your 10-mile ramble on the Wilderness Trail.

## ▶ NEARBY ACTIVITIES

Additional hiking trails are across the river at Meramec Conservation Area (page 165). Onondaga Cave State Park, a few miles upriver, offers still more hiking and cave tours (page 177).

# ONONDAGA CAVE STATE PARK

## ▶ IN BRIEF

During fine weather at Onondaga Cave State Park, you'll wander through deep forests, tramp across scenic glades, and tiptoe along sheer bluffs over the Meramec River. When summer's heat and humidity make surface hiking a miserable trudge, you can escape to underground beauty on guided walking tours of Onondaga and Cathedral caves.

## ▶ DESCRIPTION

With more than 5,000 caves, Missouri offers more subterranean beauty than any other state. And Onondaga Cave State Park, a National Natural Landmark, showcases one of its most beautiful caverns. Considered one of America's most spectacular caves because of the quality of its formations, Onondaga Cave features stalactites, stalagmites, columns, flowstones, draperies, soda straws, cave coral, rimstone dams, and underground lakes. A stream flows through Onondaga Cave, and the Lily Pad Room, an underground pool where stalagmites and stalactites grow near circular underwater formations, is a highlight of the cave's 0.9-mile guided walking tour. More-adventurous explorers of the underworld can schedule tours of the park's less-developed Cathedral Cave and probe its coal-black darkness with only handheld lanterns for viewing Cathedral's wonders.

Onondaga came close to being destroyed by businessmen hoping to make a killing on its onyx deposits, but luckily for us the cave's small entrance, the unsuitable quality of its onyx, and low market prices discouraged the miners. Instead, tourism became the cave's main use from its discovery near the

## ▶ DIRECTIONS

From I-44, take Exit 214 for Leasburg–MO H. Drive 7 miles south on MO H to Onondaga Cave State Park. Hikes can start at the visitor center or from the trailhead in the campground near the restroom and shower house.

## ⓘ KEY AT-A-GLANCE INFORMATION

**LENGTH:** 6.5 miles on 3 trails

**CONFIGURATION:** 2 loop trails, 1 point-to-point

**DIFFICULTY:** Moderate–hard

**SCENERY:** Wooded hills, long views from a couple of glades, beautiful overlooks of the Meramec River

**EXPOSURE:** Forested and shady, with several open areas in glades and bluffs

**TRAFFIC:** Medium

**TRAIL SURFACE:** Mixture of gravel and packed earth; many short rocky and rooty sections

**HIKING TIME:** 15–30 minutes for Blue Heron Trail; 1–2 hours each for Deer Run and Oak Ridge Trails

**ACCESS:** Park open 7:00 a.m.–11 p.m.

**MAPS:** Trail maps are available at the visitor center; Onondaga Cave USGS topo

**FACILITIES:** Water, restrooms, picnic areas, campground, visitor center, cave tours, canoe launch, boat ramp

**SPECIAL COMMENTS:** Pets must be leashed.
Still more hiking awaits you in nearby Meramec Conservation Area (page 165) and Meramec State Park (see pages 146, 150, 169 and 173). Additional cave tours are available at Meramec State Park and Meramec Caverns.

### GPS TRAILHEAD COORDINATES (VISITOR CENTER)

| UTM ZONE (WGS84) | 15S |
| EASTING | 655398 |
| NORTHING | 4214285 |
| LATITUDE-LONGITUDE | |
| NORTH | N38° 3' 46.7715'' |
| WEST | W91° 13' 42.9313'' |

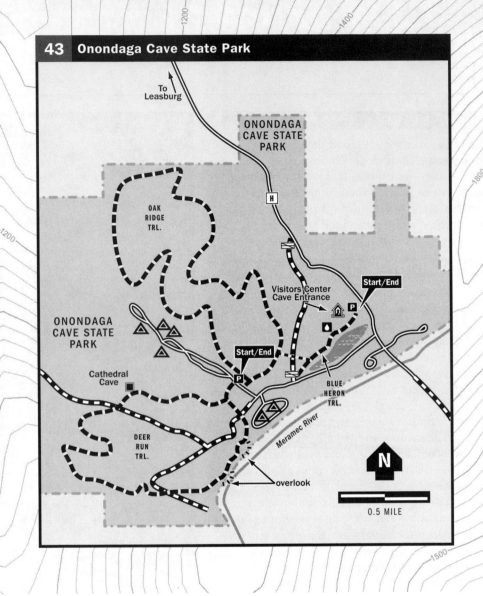

end of the 19th century. A mill was built on the spring branch flowing from
Onondaga. Believing a larger cave lay behind the spring's outlet, two locals sank a
johnboat in the spring pool above the mill, worked it under the bluff, and paddled
around admiring the caverns' wonders. Soon tourists were exploring the beauty of
Onondaga Cave on private tours operated by its first explorers.

Private ownership of the cave culminated with Lester Dill, who owned
Onondaga from the early 1950s through 1980. Dill ran cave tours with an eye
toward preservation of Onondaga's natural beauty and hoped in his later years
that it would eventually become a state park. Dill's wish came true shortly
after his death in 1980, when The Nature Conservancy bought the land from
his heirs and transferred it to the state.

Though the cave's operation was smooth and well organized from Dill's time to the present, property disputes colored Onondaga's earlier tourism history. The strangest disagreement occurred in the 1930s, when the owner of the entrance, who believed he owned all of Onondaga, operated tours of the entire cave. An adjacent landowner, upon learning that half of the cave lay under his property, dug a separate entrance, built a barbed-wire fence along the supposed property line in the cave's Big Room, told the first operator to stay off his half of Onondaga, and ran tours in his side of the cave! The story of this and other disputes is crazy, confusing, and fascinating. To learn more about Onondaga's convoluted and interesting history, check out the park's page on the Missouri State Parks Web site (**www.mostateparks.com/onondaga.htm**). There you'll find a detailed history of both the human and geologic history of Onondaga Cave State Park, along with detailed descriptions of both Onondaga and Cathedral caves.

With its amazing caverns being the featured attraction at Onondaga, most visitors don't give a thought to the rest of the park. Well, you shouldn't miss touring the awesome beauty of both caves, but the park's aboveground scenery is excellent, and you can admire it from three trails that meander for 6.5 miles over the park's hills, hollows, and bluffs. I like to cover them in one long hike, starting with the point-to-point Blue Heron Trail, then connecting to the Oak Ridge Trail, and finishing with the Deer Run Trail.

I like to make a quick stop in the center before my hike. It features displays of Missouri flora and fauna, a topographic model of the park showing the trails you're going to hike, a gift shop, and an active seismograph showing recent earth tremors. There's also a set of bird feeders at the center, with picnic tables perfect for watching the impressive variety of birds attracted from the riverside environment at Onondaga Cave State Park.

The Blue Heron Trail starts from the southeast corner of the parking lot and runs an easy and level half mile west to the campground. Marked with blue arrows along a wide gravel path, it's a novice hike, but a beautiful one, passing along the north side of an oxbow lake formed from a left-behind meander of the Meramec River. Along much of the Blue Heron, bluffs rise steeply to the north and blue waters of the oxbow lake ripple to the south. Halfway to the campground you'll veer into an alcove where Onondaga Spring exits the cave and forms a deep, clear pool. This is the site of the mill that once operated on the spring's outflow, and it's the natural entrance to Onondaga Cave. Benches are scattered around the water's edge, and the trail crosses the spring branch on the old mill dam and raceway.

Near the campground end of the Blue Heron Trail you'll see the connector leading north to the 3.25-mile Oak Ridge Trail. You can also access the Oak Ridge Trail from the trailhead in the campground. It's across from the host campsite near the bathhouse. Both the connector and the Oak Ridge Trail itself are marked with red blazes and ribbons. Blazes are sparse on the Oak Ridge, but there are plenty of ribbons and a clear enough path to keep you on track. It's a tougher trail than the Blue Heron, with some rough and rocky sections that give it a nice wild feel, but still a great hike for novices fit enough for its distance.

A short spur leads from the campground trailhead to the main Oak Ridge loop. Hiking counterclockwise, you'll start off with a quick little up and down, then follow a dry wash gently uphill to the north. The climb gets steeper and the trail swings west up the side of a ridge, then travels along a beautiful rock ledge for a short way. Just past the ledge the climb tops out on the ridge spine, then breaks into an open glade with beautiful views of a valley and distant ridges. The glade is my favorite part of the trail, especially in winter, when the sun makes it a warm, sunny break in the woods. It's the perfect place for a midhike picnic. You'll meander through this rocky glade and admire the open views for the next quarter mile, then reenter the forest at about the 1-mile mark of the Oak Ridge Trail.

After leaving the glade you'll bear north to follow the ridge on an old road. You'll come to a bench, then break west off the old road and descend for the next 0.4 miles and pass some nice rock outcroppings before bottoming out in a deep hollow. The rest of the hike is level in this deep hollow. The next quarter mile is pretty during or after rainfall—you'll follow an intermittent watercourse with lots of slick-rock cascades and overhanging ledge waterfalls in its streambed. The trail bends gradually to head southeast, until at the 2-mile mark you begin paralleling the campground loop that's a couple hundred yards to the right. Except for one eastward bend to explore a side hollow, you'll be near the campground for the remainder of the hike. Several side trails head west to the campground loop.

The 2.75-mile Deer Run Trail, my favorite hike at Onondaga, starts across the road from the Oak Ridge. To find it, walk the path from the bathhouse to the amphitheater. Take the spur trail breaking southwest into the woods and follow it a short way to the beginning of the loop. The Deer Run Trail is marked with green arrows and ribbons for counterclockwise travel. Most of the first half mile is an easy climb to the west, topping out at a gravel road crossing and bench. On this climb you'll pass the entrance to Cathedral Cave. After the road the trail descends for a while, leveling out near the 1-mile mark at the second most beautiful spot on this trail—a long, narrow, secluded glade in a pretty cedar grove, with rock-ledge terraces running through it. You'll hike right through this peaceful little spot for a couple hundred yards, follow one of the ledges for a while, then drop through a gap in the rock layer to hike along its base for a short way, then begin a winding descent into a deep hollow.

You'll follow the hollow for a half mile or so, then cross a gravel road. A few hundred yards down this road is Onondaga's Scout camp, where you'll find picnic tables, toilets, and spur trails leading to the Meramec River. It's the perfect spot for a dip or to soak your feet, and looking downstream you'll see tall bluffs towering over the river. After the road crossing, the trail climbs through beautiful rock outcroppings and onto the bluff, with spectacular views up and down the river. The Meramec flows from the south and makes a hard turn east at the bluff's base.

The next quarter mile is the prettiest stretch of trail in Onondaga. You'll follow the bluff edge for a short way, with side trails leading to overlooks. The trail then takes you away from the river and around the upper edge of a beautiful steep-walled amphitheater opening onto the river, with imposing rock walls guarding its mouth. After rounding the amphitheater, follow the edge of a second bluff with still more overlooks, then veer away from the river for good. The trail swings north and winds past a couple of rock-wall outcroppings before the loop ends back at the amphitheater.

Hiking, cave touring, fishing, canoeing, and swimming in the Meramec—there's a lot to do at Onondaga. On seasonally busy weekends there are interpretive talks at the amphitheater, and park naturalists offer morning nature walks on various subjects, including possible summer weekends those walks might be "nature wades" in the Meramec River.

# OZARK TRAIL: COURTOIS SECTION

## ▶ IN BRIEF

On this little-traveled section of the Ozark Trail you'll edge along riverside bluffs, meander along breezy highlands, and visit The Narrows, a skinny ridge dividing the Huzzah and Courtois valleys.

## ▶ DESCRIPTION

This 9-mile stretch of the Courtois Section of the Ozark Trail has a little of everything—single-track trail, some old roads, stream crossings, vistas from breezy ridgetops, bluffs, caves, and mixed pine and deciduous forests. For overnighters there are campgrounds at Onondaga Cave State Park, Ozark Outdoors, and at the south trailhead in Huzzah Conservation Area. If you prefer roughing it smoothly, Ozark Outdoors, located next to the north trailhead, offers cabin rentals and shuttles. If you burn out on hiking, you can rent canoes and tubes and float the wide and lazy Meramec River or the more intimate and challenging Huzzah and Courtois creeks.

Courtois Creek is the centerpiece for this trek on the Ozark Trail, and the best hiking on this stretch is near the campground in the Huzzah Conservation Area. If your time is limited, the preferred hike is a quick out-and-back from the campground to The Narrows, an easy and scenic

## ▶ DIRECTIONS

From I-44 take Exit 214 for Leasburg–MO H. Drive 7.5 miles south on MO H past Onondaga Cave State Park and cross the Meramec River. Pavement ends, and road becomes Cave Road. The northern trailhead is a small parking lot on the left just past the bridge. To reach the Huzzah Conservation Area trailhead continue another 2.7 miles on Cave Road and turn left (south) on another road marked "Shooting Range." Follow it 0.5 miles south to a trailhead in Huzzah Campground's east end.

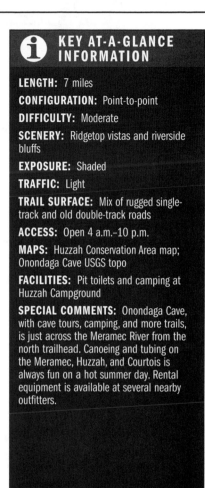

### ⓘ KEY AT-A-GLANCE INFORMATION

**LENGTH:** 7 miles

**CONFIGURATION:** Point-to-point

**DIFFICULTY:** Moderate

**SCENERY:** Ridgetop vistas and riverside bluffs

**EXPOSURE:** Shaded

**TRAFFIC:** Light

**TRAIL SURFACE:** Mix of rugged single-track and old double-track roads

**ACCESS:** Open 4 a.m.–10 p.m.

**MAPS:** Huzzah Conservation Area map; Onondaga Cave USGS topo

**FACILITIES:** Pit toilets and camping at Huzzah Campground

**SPECIAL COMMENTS:** Onondaga Cave, with cave tours, camping, and more trails, is just across the Meramec River from the north trailhead. Canoeing and tubing on the Meramec, Huzzah, and Courtois is always fun on a hot summer day. Rental equipment is available at several nearby outfitters.

### GPS TRAILHEAD COORDINATES (TRAILHEAD)

| | | |
|---|---|---|
| UTM ZONE (WGS84) | 15S | |
| EASTING | 655905 | |
| NORTHING | 4213752 | |
| LATITUDE-LONGITUDE | | |
| NORTH | N38° 3' 29.1591" | |
| WEST | W91° 13' 22.5418" | |

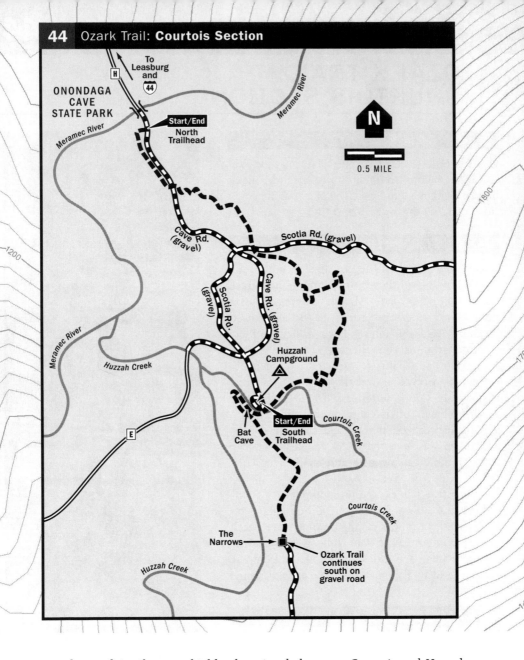

ONONDAGA
CAVE
STATE PARK

To Leasburg
and
44

Start/End
North
Trailhead

Meramec River

Meramec River

N

0.5 MILE

Cave Rd.
(gravel)

Scotia Rd. (gravel)

Scotia Rd.
(gravel)

Cave Rd.
(gravel)

Huzzah
Campground

Huzzah Creek

Bat
Cave

Start/End
South
Trailhead

Courtois Creek

E

Courtois Creek

The
Narrows

Ozark Trail
continues
south on
gravel road

Huzzah Creek

1800

1200

500

1700

1400

round trip of 4 miles on a highland peninsula between Courtois and Huzzah
creeks. Your first challenge on this hike will be an immediate crossing of the
Courtois. It'll be a wet ford on sharp rocks, so if you're a tenderfoot like me
you'll need some sandals or an extra pair of socks for the crossing.

Once across the creek you'll head downstream along the bluff across the
stream from the campground. Bat Cave is the first attraction you'll see, a deep cavern gated for protection of bat populations living in its depths. You'll follow the foot
of the bluff a quarter mile downstream, then switchback to the south and climb onto
the ridge above camp. When the climb tops out you'll be directly above the cave, and
a short bushwhack to the left leads to a nice overlook of the creek and campground.

For the next mile you'll do gentle ups and downs along a ridge heading southeast along an abandoned road. When the old road intersects with a two-track road that shows some use, the vistas begin. You'll break southwest and follow a bluffline for the next half mile, with nice views of pastures and farms down in the valley of Courtois Creek. At the end of that half mile you'll hit another intersection where lots of blue paint on the trees marks the corner of Huzzah Conservation Area. Another couple hundred yards down this road is the skinniest point of The Narrows, a knifelike ridge between the Huzzah and Courtois valleys, with pretty views in both directions. Since at this time the north part of the Courtois Section of the Ozark Trail ends here at The Narrows, it's the turnaround point for this hike. The 8-mile gap between this trail and the southern part of the Courtois Section of the OT will one day be bridged with a new route, but for now hikers wishing to continue can cross the gap via gravel roads.

One of several streamside grottoes along Courtois Creek

Hiking from the Huzzah Campground north, the most spectacular part of your trek hits you in the first quarter mile. Immediately east of the trailhead you'll walk an enchanting stretch of trail on a narrow ledge between the Courtois and the bluff towering above the stream. This impressive stone wall has numerous grottos and shallow caves, including one long overhanging shelter cave. In one narrow spot you'll squeeze between the cliff and a tall breakaway slab leaning against the bluff, and a deep cove in the cliff looks like the remains of a collapsed cavern. At the end of the bluff where the creek breaks south, the trail breaks north and climbs into the highlands above the stream. It's a stiff half-mile climb, but a well-crafted trail; impressive rock layers and several views of the Courtois through the trees make it a relatively enjoyable ascent. At the summit, a bench with forest-obscured distant views is a nice place to rest up from the climb.

The summit bench is a logical turnaround point for those not wishing to hike all the way to Onondaga Cave. If you arrange a shuttle or have the energy to hike both ways, the northern reaches of the trail, while not as impressive as the south segment, are well worth exploring. The next mile north from the summit consists of gentle ups and downs along a ridge with occasional vistas through the trees. Just before breaking left off the old road you'll hike through a quiet pine plantation, enjoying a soft cushion of pine needles under your boots. After the pines you'll break to the west on a single-track path and descend a half mile to an abandoned, overgrown quarry that makes for some interesting scenery. If you're overnighting on the trail, there are several good campsites near the quarry.

After leaving the quarry, the trail makes a short, steep climb, runs level through the woods for a while, then crosses Scotia Road. It then stays level along gravel roads through an experimental forest for 0.75 miles, then turns off onto single-track and begins the gradual mile-long descent to the Meramec River valley to end at the small trailhead just across the river from Onondaga Cave State Park.

If you prefer not paying shuttle fees but want a shorter hike back to the Huzzah Campground trailhead, just head back on Cave Road. Instead of 5 miles by trail you'll walk an easier and more direct 3.25 miles on this gravel road. With a little luck you might hook a ride from a passerby.

# SHAW NATURE RESERVE

## ▶ IN BRIEF

If you love wildflowers, Shaw Nature Reserve is the place to go. Its landscape blooms from spring to fall, showcasing its blossoms in a wide variety of habitats. A prehike walk through the Whitmire Wildflower Garden, where hundreds of flowers are identified in a condensed area, is a perfect way to learn what you'll see while hiking Shaw's wilder spaces.

## ▶ DESCRIPTION

Shaw Nature Reserve is the most spectacular place to view wildflowers in all of Missouri, if not the whole Midwest. The place is absolutely incredible in late spring, when the early-blooming woodland flowers overlap with the slow-to-bloom grassland varieties. Shaw isn't just about flowers, though—its landscape includes savanna, forests, glades, river floodplains, a 20-acre marsh wetland, and more than 100 acres of tall-grass prairie. With all these habitats and plenty of open space, it's a superb place for birding.

This beautiful reserve is owned by the world-renowned Missouri Botanical Garden in St. Louis. The garden bought land here in 1925 as a place to protect its living plant collections from the city's coal smoke. Its 2,400 acres include 550 acres on the south side of the Meramec, putting 3 miles of the river on the reserve. Shaw is a fascinating blend of natural and managed landscapes. While here you'll see lots of wild country, but might also witness human interventions such as controlled prairie burns and tree cutting for glade restoration.

## ▶ DIRECTIONS

Drive west on I-44 to Exit 253 for Gray Summit. Turn south, cross I-44, turn right on South Outer Road, then immediately turn left into Shaw Nature Reserve. Plenty of signs show you the way.

## ⓘ KEY AT-A-GLANCE INFORMATION

**LENGTH:** 14 miles on 10 short trails

**CONFIGURATION:** Network of inter-connecting point-to-point trails

**DIFFICULTY:** Easy

**SCENERY:** Forest, river bottoms, prairies, bluffs, wildflower gardens

**EXPOSURE:** Mix of shady and open

**TRAFFIC:** Heavy

**TRAIL SURFACE:** Mostly packed earth and gravel; mix of single-track, old roads, and gravel road

**HIKING TIME:** Less than 1 hour on each trail; longer hikes possible if several trail segments are combined

**ACCESS:** Open 7 a.m.–sunset; entry fee $3 for adults, $2 for seniors; children and members free

**MAPS:** Gray Summit USGS topo; trail map available at visitor center

**FACILITIES:** Water, restrooms, picnic areas, visitor center

**SPECIAL COMMENTS:** No pets; no collecting of wildflowers or natural material of any kind; no smoking or alcoholic beverages

**GPS TRAILHEAD COORDINATES (VISITOR CENTER)**

| | | |
|---|---|---|
| UTM ZONE (WGS84) | 15S | |
| EASTING | 689808 | |
| NORTHING | 4261560 | |
| LATITUDE-LONGITUDE | | |
| NORTH | N38° 28' 55.8519" | |
| WEST | W90° 49' 26.0575" | |

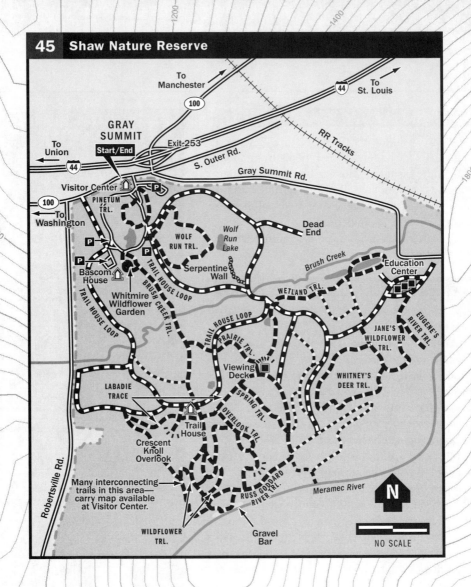

GRAY SUMMIT

To Manchester

To St. Louis

Start/End

Exit 253

S. Outer Rd.

To Union

Gray Summit Rd.

RR Tracks

Visitor Center

To Washington

PINETUM TRL.

WOLF RUN TRL.

Wolf Run Lake

Dead End

Brush Creek

Education Center

Bascom House

Serpentine Wall

WETLAND TRL.

EUGENE'S RIVER TRL.

Whitmire Wildflower Garden

TRAIL HOUSE LOOP

BRUSH CREEK TRL.

TRAIL HOUSE LOOP

PRAIRIE TRL.

JANE'S WILDFLOWER TRL.

Viewing Deck

WHITNEY'S DEER TRL.

LABADIE TRACE

SPRING TRL.

OVERLOOK TRL.

Trail House

Crescent Knoll Overlook

Many interconnecting trails in this area— carry map available at Visitor Center.

RUSS GODDARD RIVER TRL.

Meramec River

Robertsville Rd.

WILDFLOWER TRL.

Gravel Bar

**N**

NO SCALE

Shaw is an ideal nature-study laboratory. It's one of those places where, with interpretive signs and guides from the visitor center, you can develop an understanding of the natural world that'll enhance all your hikes around St. Louis. Every trip to Shaw begins at the visitor center, where you'll find detailed hiking guides for $1 each. "The Prairie Trail Guide" and "Trail Guide to the Wildflower, Overlook, and River Trails" match interpretive information to numbered stations along those trails, and the "Brush Creek Trail Native Tree Guide" introduces you to marked trees along the Brush Creek Trail. The visitor center also has every field guide imaginable. Plants, bugs, birds, reptiles, any category of mammals—you name it, and they'll have a book on it.

The Bascom House is another must-see before hitting the trail. A restored 1879 two-story brick home, the ground floor showcases an exhibit called "People on the Land." It describes human history on the reserve, including Native Americans who wandered here, the farming families that worked the land, and the current activities of the botanical garden. Next to the Bascom House is the Whitmire Wildflower Garden. Hundreds of colorful blooms grow in this five-acre garden, grouped by habitat. There's even a section on home gardening, with hints on growing wildflowers in your own backyard. Bring your field guide, do some study here, and when you head down the reserve's trails you'll know exactly which blossoms you're admiring.

When you pull into Shaw, the first thing you'll see is the Pinetum. This 55-acre wonderland contains conifers from all over the world, flowering trees like dogwood, redbud, and magnolia, and grassy hillsides that sprout thousands of daffodils in spring. The 0.3-mile Pinetum Trail explores the east part of this pretty landscape, and a paved loop drive with scattered parking areas goes around it. Most hikes on the reserve start from Pinetum's loop drive. More than 14 miles of hiking trails are here, much of it on single-track or old woods roads. The remaining miles follow service roads and the gravel Trail House Loop.

The Trail House Loop is a 3-mile road through the central part of Shaw Nature Reserve. From April through November, the loop is open to vehicles from 8 a.m. to 4 p.m., Monday through Thursday. The rest of the time it's pedestrian and bike traffic only. It connects to many of the reserve's other trails on its winding route. On busy weekend days the "Wilderness Wagon" shuttle travels around the Trail House Loop, letting you hop from trail to trail.

The 1-mile Wolf Run Trail leaves the Pinetum and goes east. It's a nice walk in pine and hardwood forests, with Wolf Run Lake at its midpoint. Picnic tables and little piers make the lake a nice place to rest. If you cross the dam and look south, you'll see the serpentine wall, built years ago as a garden windbreak; 649 feet long and 5 feet high, it was modeled on a similar wall designed for the University of Virginia by Thomas Jefferson.

The Brush Creek Trail heads south from the Pinetum and goes 0.75 miles to the Trail House. Like the Trail House Loop, it connects to several other trails on the reserve. In its first few feet you'll pass side trails into the Whitmire Wildflower Garden. South of the garden you'll go by several frog ponds and see numerous trees identified to match the trail's guidebook. Shortly after breaking into the grasslands, the Brush Creek Trail passes the western end of the Prairie Trail, then continues south to the Trail House.

The Trail House is a massive stone structure with modern restrooms, fountains, and a covered patio with picnic tables. The patio's textured floor resembles a rock layer, and tracks of deer, turkeys, and raccoons are imprinted in it. Just west of the Trail House is the Crescent Knoll Overlook. It's set in a glade with panoramic views across the Meramec River valley; binoculars swiveling on a permanent tripod help you enjoy the view. Labadie Trace, a path leading east and west from the Trail House, was once a Native American trail.

Boardwalk on the Wetland Trail,
Shaw Nature Reserve

From the Trail House, several paths explore the hollows descending toward the Meramec River. The most popular are the 2-mile Russ Goddard River Trail, the 0.75-mile Overlook Trail, and the 0.75-mile Wildflower Trail. On the River Trail you'll see a 250-year-old sycamore, wander along a gravel bar in the Meramec, and walk below rocky bluffs. On the Wildflower Trail you'll hike a ledge on that bluff face, and on the Overlook Trail you'll stand on top of the bluff and stare across the Meramec River valley. Other trails winding across this landscape give you numerous hiking options. The reserve map shows all these trails very accurately, and many intersections have plastic-covered maps on posts with "You Are Here" markings. These are a nice touch, as are benches scattered throughout the area. Made from trees cut during glade restoration, each bench has a quote from Aldo Leopold's *Sand County Almanac* on its backrest.

Many folks skip the Trail House hikes, preferring the gentle openness of the Prairie Trail. The prairie's hardy grasses grow five to ten feet tall, and 70 varieties of wildflowers can be found along the trail. The Prairie Trail goes uphill from its junction with the Brush Creek Trail, topping out at an overlook platform with panoramic views of Shaw Nature Reserve's north half. From the platform, a connector trail goes 0.1 mile south to Labadie Trace and the Trail House hikes. The Prairie Trail angles northeast from the platform to the Trail House Loop road, joining it near the trail-head for the Wetland Trail.

The Wetland Trail is a 0.75-mile path through a 20-acre landscape of marshes and pools. On the spur trail to loop around the pools, there's an observation blind with bird-identification cards and permanently mounted binoculars to help spot them. In the marsh and pools you might see herons, geese, ducks, red-winged blackbirds, sandpipers, and eastern bluebirds. When you reach the loop, you'll hike around a pond, including a walk along a boardwalk over the water for 300 feet. The boardwalk—plastic planks made from recycled detergent bottles—has several benches for relaxed observation of the wetland.

Two trails lead south from the Wetland Trail. These go to the reserve's education centers. There you'll find trails that aren't on the reserve map. It's a small system consisting of Jane's Wildflower Trail, Whitney's Deer Trail, and Eugene's River Trail. Jane's Trail makes a wide arc from the education center to the small parking area to its west. Whitney's Trail is a loop off of Jane's. It explores a glade, a deep hollow, and river-bottom forest. Eugene's River Trail goes from the education center to the Meramec River. All are less than a mile long.

All of the trails at Shaw Nature Reserve are great trail-running routes, and many are superb for cross-country skiing. Shaw Nature Reserve is really busy on pleasant spring and fall weekends. For solitude, visit on weekday evenings or in the off-season. The flowers aren't blooming then, but the prairie grasses turn a beautiful red-brown, and the pines and cedars are green splashes against the otherwise gray forest. Take a look at Shaw Nature Reserve's Web site. It describes the various plant communities on the reserve, and has a "Natural History Highlights" that lists monthly nature events (**www.shawnature.org**).

# TAUM SAUK MOUNTAIN STATE PARK

## KEY AT-A-GLANCE INFORMATION

**LENGTH:** 3 miles; optional 12 miles on Ozark Trail

**CONFIGURATION:** Loop

**DIFFICULTY:** Easy

**SCENERY:** Spectacular panoramic views, tallest waterfall in Missouri, expansive rock glades

**EXPOSURE:** Mix of shady and exposed

**TRAFFIC:** Medium

**TRAIL SURFACE:** Rock, gravel, packed earth

**HIKING TIME**: 1–2 hours

**ACCESS:** Open sunrise–sunset

**MAPS:** Ironton and Johnson's Shut-Ins USGS topos; Taum Sauk map available at trailhead

**FACILITIES:** Water, toilets, camping, picnic shelter

**SPECIAL COMMENTS:** Pets must be on a 10-foot leash. **Until flood damage near Johnson's Shut-Ins State Park is repaired, the Ozark Trail is closed beyond Devil's Tollgate.**

### GPS TRAILHEAD COORDINATES (PARK ENTRANCE)

| | | |
|---|---|---|
| UTM ZONE (WGS84) | 15S | |
| EASTING | 701283 | |
| NORTHING | 4160609 | |
| LATITUDE–LONGITUDE | | |
| NORTH | N37° 34' 13.9387'' | |
| WEST | W90° 43' 14.8780'' | |

## IN BRIEF

At Taum Sauk Mountain State Park you'll visit Missouri's tallest peak, then hike to its longest waterfall, with rocky glades and panoramic vistas galore—all in a 3-mile hike in the St. Francois Mountains. Still more attractive landscapes await you on the Taum Sauk Section of the Ozark Trail.

## DESCRIPTION

Taum Sauk Mountain, 1,772 feet above sea level, is the highest point in Missouri. Taum Sauk Mountain State Park's 7,448 acres are part of the St. Francois Mountains Natural Area, a beautiful and little-developed landscape in a mountain range nearly 1.5 billion years old. The 3-mile Mina Sauk Falls Trail leads from the state's highest peak to its longest waterfall, a 132-foot cascade over rugged volcanic rock ledges. The Taum Sauk Section of the Ozark Trail, perhaps the most scenic segment of that trans-Ozark pathway, leads 12 miles west from Mina Sauk Falls to beautiful Johnson's Shut-Ins State Park.

So, with all that hype, isn't it amazing that views from the official high point offer nothing but trees? It's just a monument in the forest on the plateaulike top of Taum Sauk Mountain. Luckily, in the glades along the trail to Mina Sauk Falls, the views really open up. Before you hit the trail, visit the Taum Sauk Mountain Lookout Tower. It's in the Department of Conservation site near the park entrance. The platform on top is usually closed, but you can climb the stairs almost to the top, and from there enjoy a 360-degree view of the St. Francois Mountains. It's a great place to survey the territory you're going to hike, and a wonderful place to watch the sunrise and sunset.

## DIRECTIONS

From Ironton, drive 5 miles south on MO 21/72 to MO CC. Turn right on MO CC, and follow it 4 miles. The highway ends in the park.

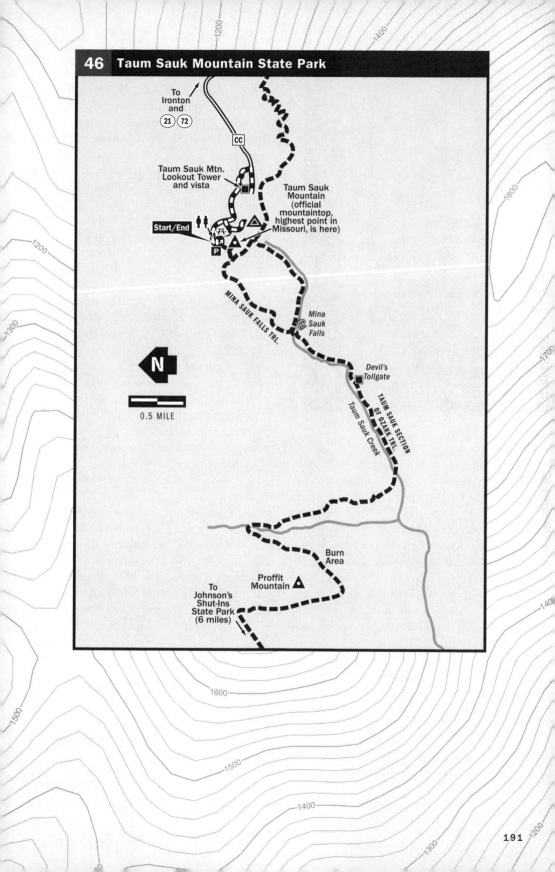

To
Ironton
and
(21) (72)

CC

Taum Sauk Mtn.
Lookout Tower
and vista

Taum Sauk
Mountain
(official
mountaintop,
highest point in
Missouri, is here)

Start/End

P

MINA SAUK FALLS TRL.

Mina
Sauk
Falls

Devil's
Tollgate

N

0.5 MILE

Taum Sauk Creek

TAUM SAUK SECTION
OF OZARK TRL.

Burn
Area

Proffit
Mountain

To
Johnson's
Shut-Ins
State Park
(6 miles)

1200

1400

1800

1200

1300

1700

1400

1600

1500

1500

1400

1300

1200

View from the Lip of Mina Sauk Falls, Taum Sauk Trail

That flat-topped mountain to the west was once the reservoir for Ameren-UE's Taum Sauk Hydroelectric plant—a 55-acre, 1.5-billion-gallon mountaintop lake. In 2005 the reservoir wall burst, loosing a catastrophic flood that roared down the mountain and devastated Johnson's Shut-Ins State Park. It also washed out the last 1.5 miles of the Ozark Trail between Taum Sauk and Johnson's Shut-Ins. Until that section of trail is rerouted and rebuilt, hopefully sometime in 2007, the Ozark Trail will be closed at the Devil's Tollgate, 1 mile beyond Mina Sauk Falls.

The Mina Sauk Falls Trail starts from the parking lot at the High Point. Interesting signboards there relate the legends behind the Taum Sauk and Mina Sauk names. The trail is marked with red arrows and blazes, with occasional rock cairns marking the way across glades. All intersections are marked with arrows and signs with mileages to the next feature or trail junction. Maps are usually available in racks next to the restrooms at the High Point parking area. The trail follows the sidewalk to the High Point, then heads west in the woods to a T intersection. The left fork leads to the Ozark Trail and will be your return route if you hike the trail as a loop. Going right leads to the falls.

Taking the right fork, you'll begin descending almost immediately, going downhill the next 1.25 miles to the falls. The scenery you expected at the High Point shows up as soon as you cross the first of four rugged glades between the peak and the falls. The views to the west are stupendous in these glades. One and a half miles from the trailhead you'll go through an especially rugged stretch of trail, curve left to avoid a couple of monstrous boulders, and step onto the wide rock ledge next to Mina Sauk Falls.

This is one of the coolest places in Missouri. Bring your camera and binoculars—Mina Sauk Falls and the cascades above it beg to be photographed, and the views west from the lip of the falls are incredible. Gray, lichen-encrusted rocks contrast beautifully with the bright-green pines that shade the falls, and incredible rock formations are everywhere. Before it crashes over the falls, Taum Sauk Creek meanders over a 100-yard-long expanse of rugged rock patios and boulders. It's a beautiful area to wander across, and numerous rock layers and steps are great seats for admiring the place. There's almost always a little water flowing over the falls, but spring is when they really go to town. Winter is a close second—cold snaps form spectacular ice sculptures on the rocky falls and cascades.

The Mina Sauk Falls hike uses the Ozark Trail to close the loop, returning to the trailhead on a steady climb next to Taum Sauk Creek. Many folks prefer hiking back the way they came instead, enjoying the glade views all over again. Don't head back yet, though: go west on the Ozark Trail for more of Taum Sauk's beauty. You'll descend an incredibly rocky slope, looking up at Mina Sauk Falls as you go. Once away from the falls, it's a gentle but rocky downhill along Taum Sauk Creek and its noisy cascades. A mile from the falls, you'll walk through the Devil's Tollgate, yet another of Taum Sauk State Park's natural wonders. It's a 50-foot passage through an 8-foot-wide gap in a 30-foot-tall volcanic rock. Legend says this route was once a military road. The only way to get wagons through this gap was to unload, haul the wagons through on edge, and reload them on the other side. It was such a hassle that they named the place the Devil's Tollgate.

Until the flood damage at Johnson's Shut-Ins is repaired and that part of the Ozark Trail is rebuilt, the trail is closed beyond the Devil's Tollgate. Once it's reopened, those who like rugged trails and spectacular vistas should continue west on the Taum Sauk Section of the Ozark Trail. The next 11 miles to Johnson's Shut-Ins State Park may be the prettiest on the entire OT. They're also the most rugged, but the payback is beautiful scenery from mountainside glades. Whether you go all the way or make an out-and-back hike from Taum Sauk, you'll know exactly how far you have to go—the trail has mile markers all the way from Mina Sauk Falls to Johnson's Shut-Ins.

Continuing west on the Ozark Trail, the next 1.5 miles are gently down or level. You'll follow Taum Sauk Creek for a while, then head north up a side hollow. The trail gets rugged in this hollow, and travels along a mountainside for 1.3 miles. It then drops into a hollow, crosses a creek, swings south, and begins to climb. You'll ascend for the next mile in an old forest burn, with wonderful vistas to make you forget how hard you're working. You'll top out on Proffit Mountain, in a glade with incredible views to the south. From here, it would be 6.5 miles back to Taum Sauk Mountain or 7 miles ahead to Johnson's Shut-Ins.

If you continue to Johnson's Shut-Ins, for the next several miles travel in and out of rugged glades along the long spine of Proffit Mountain with numerous vistas of the surrounding hills. Three miles from Johnson's Shut-Ins you'll pass the now-closed spur trail to what's left of the Taum Sauk Hydroelectric Plant's mountaintop reservoir. The last 1.5 miles of trail before Johnson's Shut-Ins was blasted completely away by the flood, and hadn't been rebuilt at the time of this writing; the new route had not been determined, either. But whatever option is chosen will still take you to Johnson's Shut-Ins State Park, where you'll be able to cool your feet in the Black River, and read interpretive displays about the flood's awesome power and its effect on this still-beautiful state park.

Once it's reopened, the Ozark Trail from Taum Sauk Mountain to Johnson's Shut-Ins is a wonderful hike that shouldn't be missed. Bring a friend and arrange a shuttle, or do out-and-back hikes from both ends so you can see this excellent stretch of trail. If you take a weekend to do it, spend your evenings at Taum Sauk State Park's mountaintop campground.

# Hikes in the
# SOUTH
## of the
# ST. LOUIS AREA

# AMIDON MEMORIAL CONSERVATION AREA

## KEY AT-A-GLANCE INFORMATION

**LENGTH:** 2 miles

**CONFIGURATION:** Loop with spur

**DIFFICULTY:** Easy

**SCENERY:** Granite canyons and boulders in a rushing stream, beneath stately pines

**EXPOSURE:** Shady, with open spaces along river and shut-ins

**TRAFFIC:** Heavy on hot summer days; medium or light the remainder of the year

**TRAIL SURFACE:** Packed earth in most areas; extremely rocky along the river

**HIKING TIME:** 1–2 hours

**ACCESS:** Open 4 a.m.–10 p.m.

**MAPS:** Higdon USGS topo; map of the conservation area available on entrance signboard at intersection of CR 208 and CR 253

**FACILITIES:** Trailhead parking

**SPECIAL COMMENTS:** Pets must be leashed; possession of glass containers is prohibited

### GPS TRAILHEAD COORDINATES (TRAILHEAD)

| | |
|---|---|
| UTM ZONE (WGS84) | 15S |
| EASTING | 751294 |
| NORTHING | 4161785 |
| LATITUDE–LONGITUDE | |
| NORTH | N37° 34' 7.8361'' |
| WEST | W90° 9' 16.8523'' |

## IN BRIEF

Amidon Memorial Conservation Area's Cedar Glade Trail takes you to the only pink-granite shut-ins in Missouri, then crosses glade restorations with expansive views.

## DESCRIPTION

The Cedar Glade Trail at Amidon Memorial Conservation Area is a short one, but what it lacks in distance it more than makes up for in scenic beauty and historical interest. The incredible boulders of pink granite in the Castor River Shut-Ins will bowl you over, and along the way you can check out two abandoned mill sites. You'll also hike through glade-restoration projects that offer views of the Castor River Valley and are speckled with wildflowers in spring.

The conservation area is named for Ellsworth and Evelyn Amidon, who donated part of their 1,630 acres to the Department of Conservation in the 1980s. Amidon's northern 209 acres are designated as the Castor River Shut-Ins Natural Area, ensuring protection of this awe-inspiring place for future generations. The 1-mile Cedar Glade Trail explores the natural area, and an optional bushwhack on unmaintained paths wanders downriver to the abandoned and overgrown site of Hahn's Mill. Another mill once operated on the north end of the natural area. All that remains of it are a few holes drilled in the rock walls of the shut-ins' northern end.

## DIRECTIONS

From Fredericktown, drive 3 miles east on MO 72 to MO J. Turn left onto MO J, drive 4.5 miles to MO W. Turn right and follow MO W until the pavement ends at County Road 208. Follow CR 208 for 1 mile to its intersection with CR 253, to the conservation area entrance. Turn left and drive 1 mile to the trailhead.

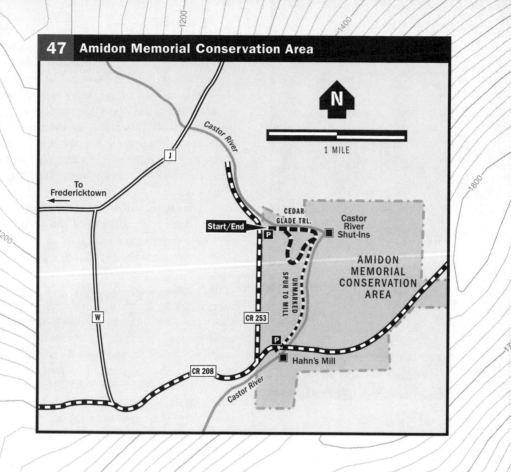

On your way to the trailhead, you'll see a vestige of Hahn's Mill—a worn millstone resting in the grass beneath the entrance sign at the intersection of County Roads 208 and 253. There's also a map box on the signboard, so stop to check out the old millstone and pick up a map of the area. Though it's beautiful here any time of the year, it's best to come to Amidon during cold weather if you want to avoid crowds. In summer the shut-ins are full of kids, young and old, wading and splashing in the rapids.

Marked with white placards emblazoned with hiker silhouettes, the trail heads east from the parking lot and travels 0.1 mile to the beginning of the loop. To see the Castor River Shut-Ins first, take the left fork. You'll hear the roar of the river pushing its way over the rocks long before you see the shut-ins. At a quarter mile from the trailhead, squeeze between a creek and low bluff, step over a little rise, and burst upon one of the most scenic spots in Missouri.

Pink canyon walls overlook the river. Boulders the size of houses lie in the stream and on its banks. Water splashing over the pink-granite shut-ins is a frothy green, and tall pines stand like sentinels. For 200 yards the stream

Castor River Shut-Ins in Amidon
Memorial Conservation Area

roils over the stones and through narrow gaps in this rock garden, forming pools and chutes for wading, swimming, or soaking your feet. The flat-topped canyon walls and boulders are ideal spots for photographing the scenery, or just lazing in the sun with the river as background noise. On winter visits to the shut-ins, glittering ice formations decorate the pink granite. It's truly a magical place.

The trail follows the river for 100 yards, then breaks away from the stream to explore a series of glades. To see more of the river and get in another 2 miles of hiking, stick with the river and follow the unmaintained path along the bank. It's a rocky, rugged track across a boulder field for a short way, but soon settles down to an easy walk through riverside trees. You'll have to pick your way now and then where flooding has obscured this abandoned trail, but it's an easy hike. The river calms beyond the shut-ins, making this a great place to fish for the Castor's several varieties of bass and sunfish. Several big, flat rocks in the middle of the stream invite you to wade out and lie in the sun for a while.

About 0.75 miles below the shut-ins, the trail becomes an ATV path, and in another 200 yards you'll hit CR 208. Don't turn around yet, though—turn right and hike the road until you cross a culvert and approach a little hill to climb up the riverbank. Before making the climb, break left into the woods along the bank, and about 75 feet into the brush you'll find the crumbling stone foundations of Hahn's Mill tucked against the earth of the riverbank—haunting reminders of the 1800s on the Castor River.

Now, turn around and hike back to the shut-ins, where you can enjoy soaking your feet in the rapids after bushwhacking down to the mill. Rejoin the Cedar Glade Trail, then immediately climb into a set of beautiful glades. Felled cedars and forest burns, signs of glade restoration, are evident as you climb through an incredible rock garden for the next quarter mile. The trail leads you along the back edge of the glades, and opens up spectacular vistas across the Castor River Valley. Hummocks of pink granite decorate the hillside across the river, and you can just see the lower end of the shut-ins.

After the trail leaves the glades and rock garden and ducks back into the forest, the remaining 0.4 miles is a pleasant walk in the woods back to the trailhead. If you skipped the bushwhack, hike downriver to the mill, it's easy to drive there after finishing the 1-mile loop. Just follow CR 253 back to CR 208, turn left, drive to the riverbank, and scout out the mill foundations in the brush south of the road.

# JOHN J. AUDUBON TRAIL

## ▶ IN BRIEF

The John J. Audubon Trail, built and maintained by the St. Louis Area Council of the Boy Scouts of America, is a memorial to the naturalist and artist who lived in nearby Ste. Genevieve in the early 1800s. His namesake trail follows piney ridges, winds through quiet hollows, and wanders along clear Ozark streams.

## ▶ DESCRIPTION

Designed and maintained by the St. Louis Area Council of the Boy Scouts, the John J. Audubon Trail is a wonderful hike along Ozark ridges and streams. Located in a rugged area of the Mark Twain National Forest, the Audubon Trail loops 12 miles through hills and hollows drained by Bidwell and Coldwater creeks. Groves of stately pines dominate the ridges, and the two creeks and their tributaries trickle over rocky-bottom streambeds with exquisite waterfalls, pools, and cascades.

Winter is the perfect time to hike the Audubon. The trail travels for miles along ridges, and when the leaves are gone you can admire views of distant hills marching away to the horizon. The pine groves color the hills, and ice formations in the creeks are fascinating. Other folks like summer on the Audubon, offsetting the heat with cooling splashes at the many creek crossings

## ▶ DIRECTIONS

Follow US 67 south to the Farmington–MO 32 East exit. Drive 3 miles east on MO 32 to MO OO. Drive 9 miles south on MO OO to MO T. Drive 5 miles east on MO T to Bidwell Creek Road–FS 2199. This easy-to-miss turn is just past the St. Francois–Ste. Genevieve county line. Turn north and then follow Bidwell Creek Road 4.5 miles to the Bidwell Creek Ford. There is no official trailhead—just park in one of the open areas next to the ford.

### ⓘ KEY AT-A-GLANCE INFORMATION

**LENGTH:** 12 miles

**CONFIGURATION:** Loop with cutoff option

**DIFFICULTY:** Difficult

**SCENERY:** Wooded hills, breezy ridgetops, deep hollows with rocky streams; may be muddy in bottomlands

**EXPOSURE:** Shaded throughout

**TRAFFIC:** Light

**TRAIL SURFACE:** Packed earth and gravel with numerous rocky, rugged stretches

**HIKING TIME:** 5–7 hours

**ACCESS:** Open 24 hours; no fees or permits required

**MAPS:** Womack USGS topo; trail map from Boys Scouts of America–St. Louis Area Council

**FACILITIES:** None

**SPECIAL COMMENTS:** Don't drive across Bidwell Creek Ford (at trailhead) during high water

### GPS TRAILHEAD COORDINATES (BIDWELL CREEK FORD)

| UTM ZONE (WGS84) | 15S |
|---|---|
| EASTING | 748963 |
| NORTHING | 4178631 |
| LATITUDE-LONGITUDE | |
| NORTH | N37° 43' 16.0625'' |
| WEST | W90° 10' 31.0749'' |

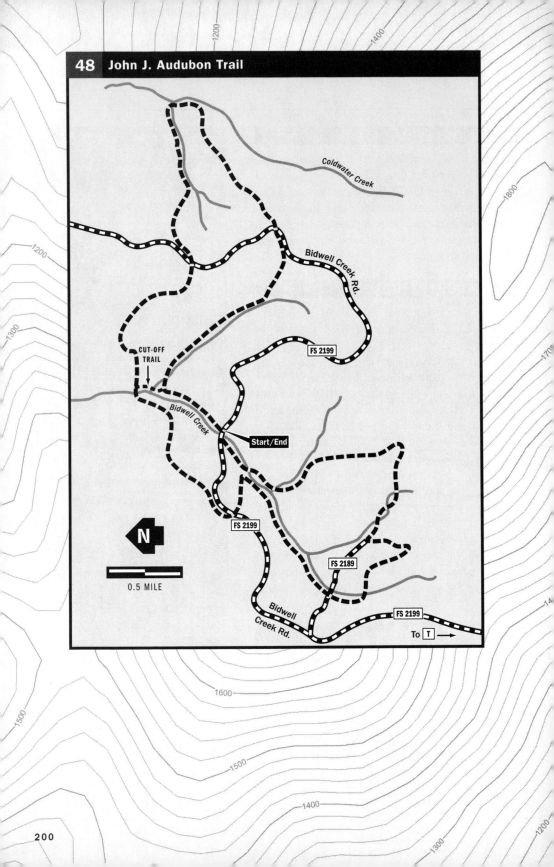

Coldwater Creek

Bidwell Creek Rd.

FS 2199

CUT-OFF TRAIL

Bidwell Creek

Start/End

N

0.5 MILE

FS 2199

FS 2189

FS 2199

Bidwell Creek Rd.

To T →

on the trail. No matter when you come here, this lonesome patch of the Mark Twain National Forest has a wonderful isolated feel. You'll hear few sounds of humans while hiking the Audubon.

The trail's rating, "difficult," is a little deceptive. While there are 3,000 feet of vertical gain and loss on the Audubon and the grades are steep and rugged, these challenging climbs aren't very long. They'll work you hard for short distances, but once you get them out of the way you'll have easy pleasant stretches along ridges or next to streams. You don't need to hike the whole trail, either: A shortcut along Bidwell Creek lets you divide the trail into two loops. Both loops cross FS 2199, so you could further shorten your hike by following from one of these crossings back to your car.

Don't judge the Audubon by its trailhead. There really is no trailhead, just parking areas next to FS 2199 where it fords Bidwell Creek. There's not even a sign marking the trail. You'll know you're there when you splash through Bidwell Creek on a concrete slab ford. The trail heads south along the west side of Bidwell Creek and returns from the north on its east side. Markings on the loop are clearer when hiking clockwise. The trail is blazed with white rectangles painted on trees. Double blazes mark all turns, sometimes supplemented with painted arrows. The Scouts do a good job marking the trail— except for a few tangly places, you're seldom out of sight of a white blaze.

The trail follows old roads used by four-wheelers, but not so used that the trail is abused. I've hiked the trail several times and have yet to see a four-wheeler, so don't let their possible presence keep you away. Because of its width, the Audubon Trail is a wonderful place to hike with a friend. You can hike side by side on much of the trail, talking and walking your way through the forest. For much of its length it could be a decent trail-running path, but the steep and rocky climbs and descents would be an iffy proposition in running shoes.

Hiking clockwise, you'll head south from the Bidwell Creek Ford. It's an easy hike along streams for the first mile, going upstream on Bidwell Creek and veering southeast up one of its tributaries. You'll splash through streams twice in this stretch, then turn south to start the first of the Audubon Trail's five climbs. You'll top out on a ridge, follow it south for a short way, then break west and descend into another tributary hollow of Bidwell Creek. You'll follow this stream for a short way until you reach the end of a road. The trail breaks south here and starts the steepest climb on the loop. Thankfully, it's the shortest, quickly topping out on a ridge above Bidwell Creek.

The trail breaks west to follow this ridge a short way, then descends to Bidwell Creek, crosses to its western side, and heads north along the stream. The next 1.5 miles are a delightful run along Bidwell Creek, sometimes next to the stream, other times slightly above it on benches. Much of this stretch is gentle down, broken by occasional quick climbs around side hollows. A road crossing (FS 2189) in this hollow marks the 3.5-mile mark of your hike.

At the end of this pleasant stretch of trail you'll turn west, climb steeply onto a ridge, and cross FS 2199. Leaving the trail here and following the road down to Bidwell Creek Ford would give you a 5.5-mile hike. The trail crosses the road and follows a high ridge heading northeast. In winter you'll have views in both directions along this ridge. Hills march away to your right, and a farm valley opens to the left. That's Crown Farm, and you'll see their property line several times over the next 2 miles. The trail follows this ridge for 0.75 miles, then makes a rugged and steep descent to Bidwell Creek.

It's a little tangled with overgrowth in this part of Bidwell Creek's bottomland, so it's hard to spot the markers. Luckily, Crown Farm's fenced property line is 100 yards downstream, so you can't stray off that way. Just pick the easiest place to cross the creek, then cross the narrow bottomland to the slope on the other side. You'll soon spot the markers heading straight east up the opposite slope. You're only 50 yards from the other side of the loop here. If you walk south up Bidwell Creek you'll soon find the other side of the trail. You could cross the loop here and hike back to your car, ending up with a 7-mile hike.

The main trail continues east, paralleling the property line for Crown Farms for much of the way. This climb on a piney hillside is the only single-track stretch of trail on the loop. It tops out on a ridge, joining a two-track road. An old logging cut took place years ago on the northern slope of this ridge, opening up the best vistas on the loop. The trail follows this two-track road southeast for the next 0.75 miles, doing little ups and downs on a ridge, until it hits FS 2199 at a primitive campsite. There you'll turn left, follow FS 2199 north for a short way, then break east off the road.

After leaving FS 2199 it's a nice 0.75-mile downgrade to Coldwater Creek, following a beautiful side stream with exquisite pools and cascades for the last half of the descent. Just before you reach Coldwater Creek, the trail breaks right off the four-wheeler path and goes steeply over a little hummock. I'm lazy, so I found an easier way. If Coldwater Creek isn't running deep, walk across it on the four-wheeler path. You'll T into another four-wheeler path on the other side. Turn right to follow it. You'll immediately cross the creek again, rejoining the trail 100 yards to the south and avoiding a rocky, steep climb in the process.

The trail leaves Coldwater Creek almost immediately, heading uphill and westward on another four-wheeler path. You'll climb steadily on a packed-earth road for 1 mile to FS 2199, then turn left to follow the road a quarter mile. The trail leaves the road (right) at another primitive campsite and heads downhill northwest. You'll soon land in a deep hollow bottom and begin hiking along yet another pretty stream. This creek has still more entrancing rocky-bottom cascades. One of these pours into a deep, wide pool with steep, slick-rock sides. I once surprised a heron in this pool. It startled me, too, when it flew through the trees, beating its way up through the forest canopy. I hadn't expected to see one of these long-legged birds in such deep woods!

A quarter mile after the pool, you'll reach Bidwell Creek at a point just upstream from the opposite side of the loop. Here you'll veer southwest and hike an easy half mile along Bidwell Creek back to the trailhead.

# BUFORD MOUNTAIN STATE FOREST

## ▶ IN BRIEF

Buford Mountain is a wild, unknown gem in southeast Missouri. It's a wonderful hike along forested ridges and rocky glades scattered along the 3-mile summit ridge of Buford Mountain.

## ▶ DESCRIPTION

How many times have you driven to Elephant Rocks, Johnson Shut-Ins, or Taum Sauk Mountain for hiking, canoeing, or swimming, and cruised past Buford Mountain? Lots of times, if you're like me. Before MO 21 was rerouted, there was even a highway sign pointing to it, making me wonder what was on that mountain. I always admired the long, hulking ridge to the east, and said I'd go there one day to check it out. For some reason I always opted for the better-known, proven-spectacular places down the road, telling myself I'd come back to Buford another day.

Well, a few years ago another day finally came, and I fell in love with the place. True, it's not Taum Sauk Mountain, and it doesn't have a reassuring, perfectly graded, clearly marked single-track trail—but that's what I like about it. Following a poorly marked route on rugged, washed-out woods roads, it's an undeveloped, undiscovered, wild hike on the spine of Buford Mountain. Rocky glades scattered along the mountain's backbone are your reward for the mile-long climb to the ridge. One of the glades is covered with a mantle of solid, lumpy rock like the back of a dinosaur,

## ▶ DIRECTIONS

Drive southwest from St. Louis on MO 21 through Caledonia. Six miles past Caledonia, turn left on MO U, and drive 2 miles east to Buford Mountain State Forest entrance on the left. If the gate is locked, start your hike here, heading north on the gravel road beyond. If it's unlocked, drive another half mile north to the trailhead.

## ⓘ KEY AT-A-GLANCE INFORMATION

**LENGTH:** 10 miles

**CONFIGURATION:** Loop, with spur access

**DIFFICULTY:** Very hard

**SCENERY:** Forested mountain ridges with high, rocky glades

**EXPOSURE:** Shady throughout, with open skies in glade areas

**TRAFFIC:** Light

**TRAIL SURFACE:** Rocky, rugged, abandoned double-track roads

**HIKING TIME:** 5–7 hours for entire loop; 2–3 hours for out-and-back to Bald Knob

**ACCESS:** Open 4 a.m.–10 p.m.

**MAPS:** Graniteville and Banner USGS topos; forest map available from Department of Conservation

**FACILITIES:** Trailhead parking

**SPECIAL COMMENTS:** Pets must be leashed. Due to past rowdy parties and vandalism at the upper trailhead, the entrance gate is sometimes locked. If it is, park in the small lot by the gate and hike the gravel road a half mile north to the old parking area, where the trail begins.

For such a small town, Caledonia is a neat place. It has a couple of restaurants and an ice-cream shop or two. Just a little further south are Elephant Rocks and Johnson's Shut-Ins (page 157) state parks.

**GPS TRAILHEAD COORDINATES (GATE)**

| UTM ZONE (WGS84) | 15S |
| --- | --- |
| EASTING | 703467 |
| NORTHING | 4172894 |

| LATITUDE–LONGITUDE | |
| --- | --- |
| NORTH | N37° 40' 50.5280'' |
| WEST | W90° 41' 33.5952'' |

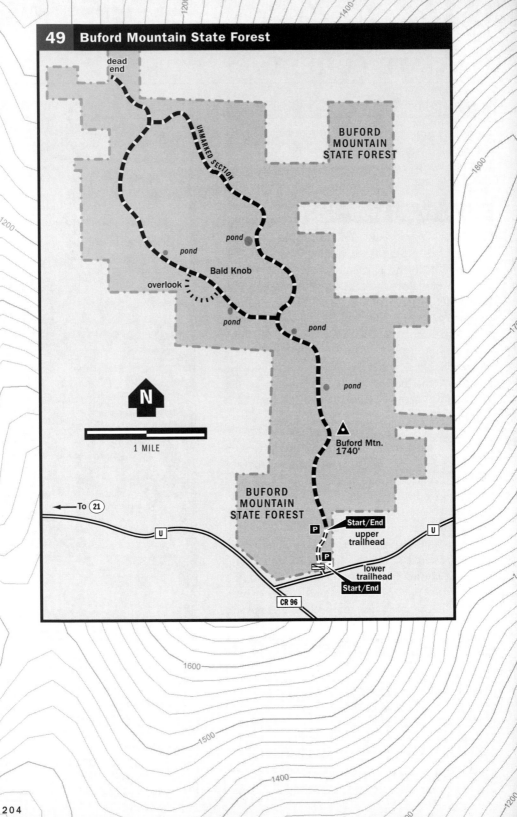

dead
end

UNMARKED SECTION

BUFORD
MOUNTAIN
STATE FOREST

pond

pond

Bald Knob

overlook

pond

pond

pond

N

1 MILE

Buford Mtn.
1740'

To 21

BUFORD
MOUNTAIN
STATE FOREST

P

Start/End
upper
trailhead

U

U

P

lower
trailhead
Start/End

CR 96

100 yards long and 100 feet wide. Another is the spectacular Bald Knob, where you'll admire 10 miles of the Belleview Valley. Both the glades and the rocky roads followed on the hike are speckled with bright wildflowers in spring, and in autumn fall colors set the mountain afire.

The trailhead is a half mile up a gravel road from MO U, but the gate is often locked to keep local teens from having beer parties there. If it's locked, you'll have to park in the lower trailhead by MO U and hoof it up the gravel road to the trailhead. This is a wild trail that receives little maintenance. Markings are poor and sometimes confusing. Occasional placards with hiker symbols mark the route inconsistently, and intersections aren't signed. Bring a map and consult it often, especially when hiking off the mountain's spine. It's a rocky and rugged climb to Buford's backbone, so wear good boots. You might like your walking stick on this rugged old road, too. Bring plenty of water—most of the time you'll be high on the mountain where no streams flow. The only water available on Buford is in scummy stock ponds in saddles connecting the mountain's five summits.

At 1,740 feet, Buford Mountain is only a little lower than Missouri's highest peak, Taum Sauk Mountain. Since the first summit on the hike is Buford's high point, from the trailhead you immediately climb. And climb, and climb some more. It's a steady, rugged, mile-long ascent to the peak. Halfway up you'll pass through an old stone wall, and wonder how anyone could have ever farmed this rough mountainside. Once on top you'll enjoy a relatively easy 4-mile stretch of Buford's spine, doing ups and downs over the mountain's five summits and the saddles between them. It's often breezy on the mountaintop, making this a nice hike on hot summer days. In winter the sun warms you through the bare trees, and on rainy days you're often hiking through the clouds on Buford's lofty ridge.

Just past the first summit there's a wide rock glade a few yards left of the trail. In winter you can see out into the Belleview Valley, but in summer the view is obscured. Like all the glades on Buford, it's a great place to stargaze if you're here at night. After the glade, the trail descends to a saddle with a stock pond on the right, then begins climbing to the second summit. Just before topping out, you'll pop out of the woods and cross one of the most rugged glades you'll ever see; almost all rugged and uneven rock, it stretches 50 yards to each side. The trail cuts straight across it and back into the woods on the summit. Though a few flowers, grasses, and shrubs cling to scattered patches of soil in the glade, most of its impressive expanse is a rock-strewn moonscape.

A short ways past the glade you'll top the second summit, descend to another saddle with a stock pond. Next you'll climb quickly to the third summit, just over 2 miles from the trailhead. There's no glade at this summit, but a path forks to the right with a trail marker a short way down its track. This is a confusing place. The right fork isn't shown on the map, but it's marked; the trail along Buford's spine—the one shown on the map—is not marked. For now, take the unmarked left fork to veer northwest and continue along Buford's ridge. If you decide to follow the entire loop you'll return on the other trail later in the day.

Leaving the fork, you'll descend for a while, then climb steadily to beautiful Bald Knob, Buford's fourth summit, located 3 miles from the trailhead. Here a grassy, rock-studded glade opens on the left side of the trail and extends to the edge of the

Vista from Buford Mountain's
fourth summit

mountainside—the views are breathtaking. The Belleview Valley opens up before you. Farms, fields, pastures, and a town or two, connected by hedges and the thin ribbon of MO 21, are scattered up and down the valley.

The St. Francois Mountains march away to the west, and cooling highland breezes blow as you admire the panorama below. Pick a comfortable boulder, stretch out in the sun, and relax awhile. This is the most spectacular place on Buford Mountain.

At this point you'll have seen the best of Buford Mountain and could return to the trailhead for a 6-mile out-and-back hike. If you keep going along the ridge, you'll finish with a 10-mile loop hike. There'll be the uncertainty of an unmarked intersection or two, but you'll get to see the wild backside of Buford. Continuing northwest on the loop route, the trail drops off Bald Knob, descends nearly a half mile, passes another stock pond in the saddle, then climbs 0.4 miles to a small glade on Buford's fifth and final summit. From there it's an easy 1-mile descent to a fork in the trail. The right fork is the one you want. If you miss the turn and go straight, the old roadbed hits a private property fence 1.25 miles later. You'll quickly know you missed the turn if you see a stone wall on your right that parallels the trail for several hundred yards. The turn was 0.2 miles behind you.

From the fork, the trail heads east, cuts through another rock wall, and begins descending into a hollow. It swings south and follows the hollow downhill, finally leveling out in a deep, brushy hollow bottom a mile after the fork. You'll wander south in the hollow for a while, then begin a 1.25-mile climb back up onto Buford Mountain. There are several level breaks in the climb, one near a stock pond, and another near the rusting carcass of a 1930s-vintage automobile. I love finding these relics in the woods, wondering who lived out here, and how they persuaded the old wrecks to jounce over these rugged mountains.

Finally, almost 3 miles from the fork, the climb tops out and rejoins the ridge trail at Buford's third summit. From there it's just over 2 miles backtracking to the trailhead.

# CRANE LAKE TRAIL

## ▶ IN BRIEF

Crane Lake is a clear, blue, 100-acre pool nestled in the rugged St. Francois Mountains. You can wander the lakeshore and admire the gorge below the dam on the 5-mile Crane Lake Trail. For more Ozark scenery, hike another 7 miles on the Marble Creek Section of the Ozark Trail, ending with a dip in the swimming hole at Marble Creek Campground.

## ▶ DESCRIPTION

The idyllic Crane Lake Recreation Area was acquired by the Mark Twain National Forest in 1973. The lake as it appears today was built in the early 1970s, when a failed dam was replaced with the concrete structure you'll see on your hike. Built in the mid-1970s by the Youth Conservation Corps, the Crane Lake Trail explores the lakeshore and wanders along the rugged gorge and hillsides below the dam. Anglers come to Crane Lake to fish for bass, catfish, and sunfish. Their boats are limited to electric trolling motors only. This, coupled with the low number of visitors to this out-of-the-way scenic spot, means Crane Lake is always an uncrowded and peaceful place.

The trail around the lake is a pretty one. In many places you'll hike the shoreline, while in others the path meanders through the woods. On the south loop you'll explore hillside glades with views

## ▶ DIRECTIONS

From US 67 just south of Fredericktown, drive west on MO E. At 16 miles you'll pass Marble Creek Campground, the northeast trailhead for the Marble Creek Section of the Ozark Trail. To get to Crane Lake, drive 3 miles farther on MO E to Iron County Road 124, where a sign points left to Crane Lake. Turn left and follow CR 124 for 3 miles to CR 131, where another sign points 2 miles left to Crane Lake. The road ends at the lake.

## ⓘ KEY AT-A-GLANCE INFORMATION

**LENGTH:** 5 miles; 7 optional miles on Marble Creek Section of the Ozark Trail

**CONFIGURATION:** Loop, with Ozark Trail spur

**DIFFICULTY:** Easy-moderate

**SCENERY:** Forested hills, clear streams, granite rock formations, hillside glades, and a deep blue Ozark lake

**EXPOSURE:** Shady, with numerous exposed areas in glades and fields

**TRAFFIC:** Light

**TRAIL SURFACE:** Packed earth, gravel, and buried rock; many rugged sections on south loop and Ozark Trail option

**HIKING TIME:** 3-5 hours

**ACCESS:** $2 per car day-use fee

**MAPS:** Des Arc NE USGS topo; Crane Lake Trail map posted at trailhead; Marble Creek Section of Ozark Trail

**FACILITIES:** Toilets, picnic sites; no water available at trailhead

**SPECIAL COMMENTS:** Be cautious on cliffs and rocks near the dam

**GPS TRAILHEAD COORDINATES (TRAILHEAD)**

UTM ZONE (WGS84)   15S
EASTING   710313
NORTHING   4144480

LATITUDE-LONGITUDE
NORTH   N37° 25' 23.7689"
WEST   W90° 37' 23.6417"

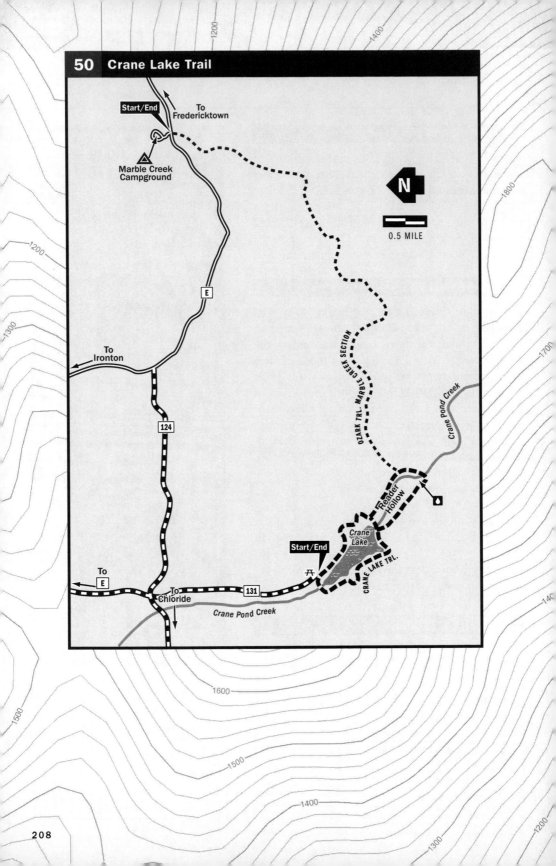

Start/End
To
Fredericktown

Marble Creek
Campground

N

0.5 MILE

E

To
Ironton

OZARK TRL. MARBLE CREEK SECTION

Crane Pond Creek

124

Reader
Hollow

Crane
Lake

Start/End

CRANE LAKE TRL.

To
E

To
Chloride

131

Crane Pond Creek

1200

1400

1800

1700

1600

1500

1400

1300

1200

1300

1400

1500

across Reader Hollow, the deep ravine carved below the dam by Crane Pond Creek. The trail descends into Reader Hollow, where granite shut-ins, waterfalls, and cascades in the creek will enthrall you. At the loop's southeastern end you'll hike past a spring that pours into Crane Pond Creek. In fall the hills above the lake are beautiful, and lots of pines and cedars scattered throughout the forest add a splash of color during the otherwise-gray winter season.

A map of the trail is posted on the trailhead signboard. Most of the route is marked with white plastic diamonds. The northeast side is a shared path with the Ozark Trail, so it'll have Ozark Trail markers. The OT markers also blaze the 7-mile route from the lake trail to Marble Creek Campground. In a couple of rocky glades the plastic markers are supplemented with rock cairns or white dashes painted on rocks in the treadway. The pathway gets hard to follow in a couple of rugged places and areas with confusing intersections, but it's hard to get lost with Crane Lake and Crane Pond Creek as reference points. Some stretches are very rugged and covered with loose rock, so wear proper footwear. This isn't a tennis-shoe or sandal trail.

The 5-mile Crane Lake Trail is portioned into a 3-mile north loop and a 2-mile south loop, with a cutoff trail running across the rugged gorge just southeast of the dam. The optional Marble Creek Section of the Ozark Trail runs northeast from the far end of the southern loop. If you hike the trail clockwise you'll handle the steepest, most rugged slope as a descent, and will finish the loop with an easy mile-long stretch on an old road next to the lake.

Traveling clockwise, follow the trail southeast through the picnic area and along the lake for a quarter mile to a small cove. There you'll veer east away from the water and hike in forest for nearly 1 mile, bouncing over side hollows draining into the lake. About 1 mile from the picnic area you'll break into an incredibly rugged glade. Look to the right for a beautiful view of the lake, framed by rocks and bright green cedars and pines. It's one of the best views of the lake on the entire trail.

The trail wanders through this glade, over and among several huge rocks, then makes an incredibly steep, rugged descent into Reader Hollow, a landscape of shut-ins below the dam. Don't just skip by this place: take some time to explore this exquisite hollow. Make your way out onto the granite ledges to admire huge boulders, entrancing waterfalls, and noisy cascades. Look upstream—in spring or after rain the dam's outflow chute can't keep up with the flow, and you'll see a foamy white curtain roaring over Crane Lake's concrete dam. Lots of pines shade the creek here, rising majestically above Crane Pond Creek.

The loop's cutoff trail crosses the creek just below the dam, but it's hard to find. If you try the cutoff, just cross the creek on a granite ledge and angle uphill to the southwest end of the dam and you'll find the other side of the loop. Otherwise, the main trail continues downstream, veering away from Crane Pond Creek into the woods and rolling up and down across side hollows. After a quarter mile, you'll break into a narrow open field, cross its lower end, and meet up with the Marble Creek Section of the Ozark Trail at a T intersection. Heading left, it's 7 miles to Marble Creek Campground.

To continue on the Crane Lake Trail, turn right on the old road and head south-southwest, ignoring old roads going left into fields. After a quarter mile, the road angles over to Crane Pond Creek and disappears out in the creek's flood wash. Markings are

View of Crane Lake from one of its rocky glades

poor here. Look at the opposite creek bank and you'll see the old road climbing out on the other side. That's the trail, and just a few feet after crossing the creek you'll see a little spring pool on your right, boiling gently as it wells up and flows a few feet into Crane Pond Creek.

After the spring and creek crossing, markings are poor for the next quarter mile. A few yards after the spring you'll break into an open field. Turn left and follow its edge for only a few yards, until you see another old track going left into the forest. Take it, and follow this old road for a couple hundred yards as it parallels the field. At the upper end of the field the trail breaks right off the old road, becomes single-track, and markings get better.

Once on the single-track path you'll climb steadily for the next quarter mile, topping out in a series of rocky glades edged with cedars. This is one of my favorite spots on the trail. You'll meander through these glades for several hundred yards, with spellbinding views across Reader Hollow and down the valley of Crane Pond Creek. At the end of this pretty glade walk you'll descend quickly to the dam, where you'll enjoy awesome views up the length of Crane Lake. From the dam it's an easy hike along the lakeshore back to the picnic area, often on an old road that once traveled the southwest side of the lake.

The extra 7 miles on the Ozark Trail to Marble Creek Campground, while not as scenic as the loop around Crane Lake, are a wonderful hike through deep hollows and along breezy ridges. Few signs of humankind mar the trail as it wanders over the hills and hollows. My favorite stretch is the first mile from the Crane Lake Trail junction, where the Ozark Trail runs through abandoned farm fields. Grasses there are three to five feet tall, accented with bright wildflowers in spring and summer, red patches of sumac bush in fall, and a scattering of scrub cedar year-round.

When you reach Marble Creek an inviting swimming hole awaits, and you can check out crumbling foundations left from a dam and water-powered mill that once operated at Marble Creek campground.

### ▶ NEARBY ACTIVITIES

For a panoramic view of the countryside from the highest point in Missouri, drive to Taum Sauk Mountain State Park (page 190) after your hike. It's just south of Ironton on MO 21. An old fire lookout tower offers 360-degree vistas of the St. Francois Mountains.

# HAWN STATE PARK

## ▶ IN BRIEF

Though the Whispering Pine Trail in Hawn State Park is a favorite trek for hikers in eastern Missouri, this spectacular 15-mile trail system rarely feels crowded. On your hike you'll enjoy panoramic vistas from windswept overlooks, admire impressive sandstone bluffs, relax beside waterfalls and cascades on Pickle Creek, and be calmed by the trail's namesake majestic stands of pines sighing in the breeze as you wander in their cooling shade. Hikers looking for something different at Hawn can explore the White Oaks Trail, opened in 2002.

## ▶ DESCRIPTION

Home to one of the most popular trails in Missouri, Hawn State Park is a hiker's dream. The park is named for Helen Coffer Hawn, a Ste. Genevieve teacher who in 1952 donated the first 1,459 acres of this 4,953-acre treasure. Hawn contains the 2,880-acre Whispering Pine Wild Area and the spectacular Whispering Pine and Pickle Creek trails. Built in the late 1970s with the help of the Sierra Club, the 10-mile Whispering Pine Trail is everything a great hike should be. You'll wander through thick stands of the trail's namesake shortleaf pines, meander along clear, quiet streams, admire rushing waterfalls and cascades, and be awed by spectacular vistas. When the weather is hot, the crossings of Pickle Creek

## ▶ DIRECTIONS

Drive south on Interstate 55 to Exit 154, Ste. Genevieve, Rocky Ridge, and MO O. Turn right 6 miles on MO O to MO 32. Turn right 5.5 miles on MO 32 to MO 144. Turn left and follow MO 144 4 miles to its end in Hawn State Park. The White Oaks trailhead will be on your right as you enter the park. The Whispering Pines trailhead is in the picnic area at the bottom of the long hill after the park office.

## ⓘ KEY AT-A-GLANCE INFORMATION

**LENGTH:** 15 miles; loop options of 2, 4, 6, and 10 miles

**CONFIGURATION:** Loops

**DIFFICULTY:** Moderate–hard on Whispering Pine Trail; easy on White Oaks Trail; very easy on Pickle Creek Loop

**SCENERY:** Rushing streams, waterfalls, panoramic bluff overlooks

**EXPOSURE:** Mostly shaded

**TRAFFIC:** Heavy on Pickle Creek Loop; medium on White Oaks Trail and North Loop of Whispering Pine; light on South Loop

**TRAIL SURFACE:** Packed earth and gravel with rocky and rugged sections

**HIKING TIME:** 1 hour on Pickle Creek Trail; 2 hours on White Oaks Trail; 3–4 hours on south loop of Whispering Pine Trail; 5–7 hours on both loops of Whispering Pine

**ACCESS:** Open 7:30 a.m.–sunset November 15–March 14; open 7:30 a.m.–9 p.m., March 15–November 14

**MAPS:** Coffman USGS topo; park and trail maps available at trailhead

**FACILITIES:** Water, picnic area, playground, restrooms, showers, laundry; naturalist talks during summer

**SPECIAL COMMENTS:** Pets must be leashed; no removal of artifacts

**GPS TRAILHEAD COORDINATES (PARK ENTRANCE)**

| | | |
|---|---|---|
| UTM ZONE (WGS84) | 15S | |
| | EASTING | 742850 |
| | NORTHING | 4190975 |
| LATITUDE-LONGITUDE | | |
| | NORTH | N37° 50' 2.0373'' |
| | WEST | W90° 14' 25.6394'' |

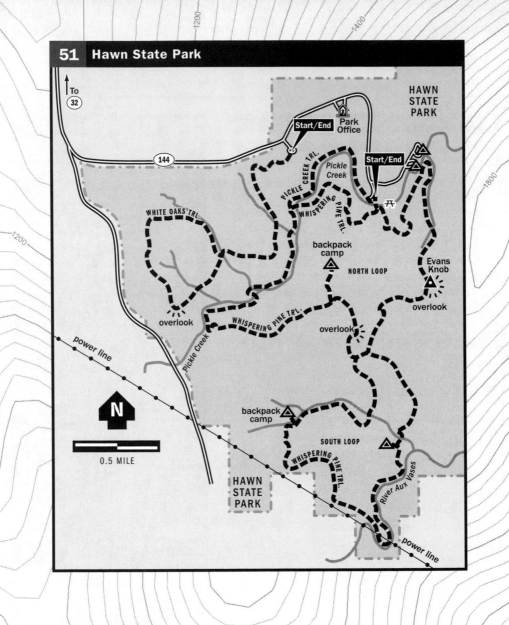

To
32

HAWN
STATE
PARK

144

Start/End Park
Office

Pickle
Creek

Start/End

PICKLE CREEK TRL.

WHITE OAKS TRL.

WHISPERING PINE TRL.

backpack
camp

NORTH LOOP

Evans
Knob

overlook

overlook

WHISPERING PINE TRL.

overlook

Pickle Creek

power line

N

0.5 MILE

backpack
camp

SOUTH LOOP

WHISPERING PINE TRL.

River Aux Vases

HAWN
STATE
PARK

power line

and the River Aux Vases are soothing splashes, and good swimming holes can be found on both streams. If you like overnighting in the woods, the Whispering Pine is an excellent backpacking route with three backcountry camps.

The trails at Hawn wind through a variety of habitats, so they're wonderful hikes for birding and wildlife spotting. Pickle Creek, River Aux Vases, and their tributaries flow through moist valleys and past steep bluffs. Dry highlands swell above the cool, damp stream valleys, and deciduous forests alternate with groves of pine and cedar to shade the landscape. Beavers work the creek bottoms, and rock overhangs sculpted by the park's streams harbor cool moss and fern gardens that make wonderful sheltered rest stops on hot or rainy days. You'll often tramp through burn areas in Hawn's forest—evidence of the park's ongoing pine-savanna-restoration project. If this project is successful, the park will one day be restored to its prehuman condition, where large, well-spaced trees protect an open understory.

Hawn State Park is a wonderful hike in any season. In spring the place is lousy with wildflowers, and the early-season runoff makes all the streams come alive. Pickle Creek really muscles its way through its cascades, and all the intermittent waterfalls are roaring. Autumn's cool temperatures, fantastic colors, and lower water levels make it a favorite time for most Missouri hikers to visit the park. My favorite is winter, and the colder the better: Pickle Creek gurgles unseen beneath its frozen cover, and the ice formations on the cliff seeps are otherworldly. You'll see ice towers that dwarf you, and the frozen sculptures in the cascades are amazing. Best of all, you'll probably have the place to yourself!

The new 4.4-mile White Oaks Trail is a good hike for beginners. It starts near the park entrance and explores the landscape in the western end of Hawn. Grades are gentle, and numerous stream crossings will add spice to your hike. You'll reach its main loop via a 1.25-mile spur, skirting grasslands and following a small ridge. The loop is marked for counterclockwise travel, and its grades are gentle. On the southern end of the loop there's a nice vista to the south overlooking a trickling stream and a hillside covered with impressive rock outcroppings. Ledgy rock layers for sitting or napping make this the ideal spot for a midhike picnic.

The 10-mile Whispering Pine Trail, the more popular trail at Hawn, is broken into a 6-mile north loop and a 4-mile south loop. If 10 miles is a bit much, simply use the cutoff trail and hike only the north loop. For an even shorter hike, combine the 1-mile Pickle Creek Trail with the northernmost segment of the Whispering Pine for a short but challenging 2-mile loop along both sides of the spectacular cascades, waterfalls, and shut-ins carved by Pickle Creek. The park's excellent "Trail and Wild Area Guide," available at the trailhead, picnic area, park office, and campground, is ideal for choosing your loop and finding your way around the trail system. Whichever option you choose, plan for wet feet in spring or after rain—all loops cross Pickle Creek at least once. Rocky and rugged sections are frequent, so wear solid boots and consider bringing a walking stick when trekking in Hawn State Park.

I like traveling the Whispering Pine Trail in a counterclockwise manner. The trail is marked for travel in that direction, I cover the most rugged terrain first, and it gets the deeper stream crossings out of the way early in my hike. All trail intersections are well marked. The North Loop is blazed with red arrows and red plastic squares, and the South Loop with blue ones. The Pickle Creek Trail, which can be part of your Whispering Pine loop if you choose, is blazed with green plastic squares. I usually start my hike on the Whispering Pine using the Pickle Creek Trail, because I like hiking next to its impressive cascades, waterfalls, and shut-ins for the first mile. Mile 1 of the Whispering Pine is pretty cool, too—it climbs to the highlands above Pickle Creek and has several spectacular rock-ledge overlooks of the stream. During high water the Pickle Creek route is best, because it avoids a rocky and fast-moving crossing of Pickle Creek near its junction with the Whispering Pine Trail.

River Aux Vases, from the south loop of the Whispering Pine Trail

After its junction with the Pickle Creek Trail on the network's west side, the Whispering Pine continues upstream along the creek. It immediately passes the best waterfall in the park, where you'll find rock ledges that make natural benches for picnicking or lying in the sun. Beyond these falls the stream becomes placid and the trail levels in a widening bottomland, meandering through several groves of huge pines. Half a mile south of the junction the creek has eroded the base of a low bluff for 150 feet, leaving a deep shelter cave. Huge icicles form here during cold and wet winters.

Just past the shelter cave you'll splash across Pickle Creek to its eastern side and continue south through more streamside pine stands for a half mile. Next, the trail climbs a rocky bluff face to an overlook, then heads east from Pickle Creek through yet another stand of pines on a very peaceful stretch of the trail. The stream noise is gone, the pine needles feel soft underfoot, and it's a gentle ascent in the quiet grove for the next 0.75 miles to the first backpack camp. From the camp the trail climbs on rugged terrain to a ridge, then follows its spine a quarter mile to one of the best overlooks on the trail. On this rocky, rugged promontory at the south end of the ridge you'll find panoramic views and rock ledges perfect for a rest break or picnic.

From the promontory, the trail makes a steep, rugged descent to the well-marked loop junction. A left turn on the cutoff trail leads 100 yards to the Whispering Pine Trail's far side, putting you on the 6-mile north loop. Ten-mile hikers should continue on the south loop, following blue markers. The trail on the south loop is nice for the next mile or so, descending gently to a stream crossing, then climbing the opposite hillside and veering west to parallel this tributary of the River Aux Vases. After a half mile, the trail swings south next to a stream fork where each branch gushes over an exquisite waterfall to form a single creek. This is the halfway point of the 10-mile loop, and it's the perfect rest stop. Two beautiful cascades pour into a wide, clear, pool that's just the right depth for cooling your feet, surrounded on all sides by shady, picturesque rock ledges. It's one of the most inviting places along the Whispering Pine. You'll feel like staying a long time, and lucky you—100 yards down the trail, next to the south fork of the stream, is the second backpack camp. What a great place to hang out for a day or two!

After leaving the camp, the trail trends southeast for the next mile. It ascends gradually to a ridge, follows it for a while on an old road, then descends to another small creek. After the creek crossing it climbs, then breaks left off the old road to wind through a fantastic boulder field for 100 yards. Just beyond the boulders the trail begins descending gently and soon hits a pretty bluff overlook of the River Aux Vases, where a surprisingly unobtrusive power line cuts through the area.

Descending beyond the overlook, you'll see a rushing stream downslope on both sides, and realize you're walking on a rocky spine dividing a horseshoe bend of the River Aux Vases. Don't cut across to the trail below to your left. If you do, you'll miss the towering bluffs on the outside curve of the horseshoe. The river has carved an overhang cave from the bluff, and huge boulders broken from the cliff wall guard a deep pool at the bluff's base. The flat slick-rock stream bottom in the river's bend is perfect for barefoot wading or sliding downstream on your derriere. As the trail and river make the hairpin to go north, you'll have to pick your way along rock ledges edging several inviting chutes and pools in the streambed.

The trail follows the River Aux Vases for the next 0.75 miles, usually on benches directly above the stream. Just before leaving the river, you'll hike opposite a 150-foot-long overhanging cliff on the outside curve of the river.

If it's rained recently, a waterfall will shower noisily from the overhang 15 feet to the river below. Shortly after this picturesque spot the trail breaks west away from the river, climbs over a hump (where the third backpack camp is), crosses a tributary of the River Aux Vases, and breaks northwest to parallel it upstream. This creek flows from the double-waterfall near the second backpack camp. After a short jaunt along the stream the trail breaks north on an old road, climbs into a pine grove, and tops out next to a pond and abandoned well a quarter mile up the hill. From there it's a peaceful 0.5-mile walk to the trail junction, where the path rejoins the south loop.

The next mile follows an old road for much of its run, culminating in a short, steep climb onto Evans Knob and its pretty views through the pines. From the knob, the trail descends for a mile down to Pickle Creek, ending with a pleasant run along a tiny stream flowing over an enchanting series of overhanging ledge waterfalls. Across Pickle Creek you'll see the campground, but you aren't done yet. The trail makes a hard turn west, climbs steeply to the top of a majestic bluff overlooking the campground, Pickle Creek, and the hills beyond, then climbs into the woods south of camp. After topping out on this last tough climb it's a nice descent back to Pickle Creek, across the stream on a picturesque wooden bridge, and back to the trailhead.

This has been only a "tip of the iceberg" rendition of the many pretty sights at Hawn State Park. To really enjoy the beauty of the Whispering Pine Wild Area, load up your pack and hit the trail for a leisurely two-day jaunt on this excellent backpack route.

# HICKORY CANYONS NATURAL AREA

## KEY AT-A-GLANCE INFORMATION

**LENGTH:** 1.5 miles

**CONFIGURATION:** 1-mile loop with 0.25-mile spur

**DIFFICULTY:** Easy

**SCENERY:** Shady, secluded canyons with intermittent streams and layer-cake rock bluffs

**EXPOSURE:** Shady throughout

**TRAFFIC:** Light

**TRAIL SURFACE:** Mixture of packed earth and gravel with numerous rugged and rocky stretches; wooden stairs cover the roughest section

**HIKING TIME:** 1-2 hours

**ACCESS:** Open daily 4 a.m.–10 p.m.; no permits or fees required

**MAPS:** USGS topo; interpretive trail map available at trailhead

**FACILITIES:** None

**SPECIAL COMMENTS:** Pets must be leashed; no collection of rocks or vegetation; no rock climbing; watch children closely where trails approach steep cliffs

### GPS TRAILHEAD COORDINATES (TRAILHEAD)

| UTM ZONE (WGS84) | 15S |
| --- | --- |
| EASTING | 737438 |
| NORTHING | 4195327 |
| LATITUDE–LONGITUDE | |
| NORTH | N37° 52' 28.2285'' |
| WEST | W90° 18' 1.6319'' |

## IN BRIEF

Hickory Canyons Natural Area, a little-known gem in southeast Missouri, offers one of the best short hikes in the St. Louis region. Its trail follows the spine of a rocky ridge, wanders past steep cliff edges, skirts towering bluffs, descends into deep hollows, and meanders along intermittent streams with enchanting seasonal waterfalls.

## DESCRIPTION

In more than 20 years of living in and hiking around Missouri and working in outdoor stores in St. Louis, I'd never heard any of my outdoors acquaintances mention this place. Perhaps it's overshadowed by its more spectacular neighbors, Hawn State Park and Pickle Springs Natural Area, but it sure shouldn't be. I first learned of Hickory Canyons while hiking at Pickle Springs. The trailhead signboard there blandly refers hikers to this nearby 280-acre landscape with no hint of how pretty it is. Once I explored the area, I couldn't believe I'd not heard hikers raving about Hickory Canyons. Hidden in this little-known natural area are box canyons, deep moist hollows, sandstone bluffs festooned with dripping seeps and ferns, intermittent streams with beautiful cascades and waterfalls, and thick forests of oaks and hickories

## DIRECTIONS

Take I-55 south to Exit 154, MO O. Turn right and follow MO O 6 miles to MO 32. Turn right 2.5 miles on MO 32 to MO C. Turn right 3 miles on MO C to Sprott Road. Turn left onto Sprott Road and follow this gravel track 1.5 miles to a trailhead parking area on the left side of Sprott Road. Watch closely for your turns—unlike most state parks and conservation areas in Missouri, there are no road signs to guide you to Hickory Canyons.

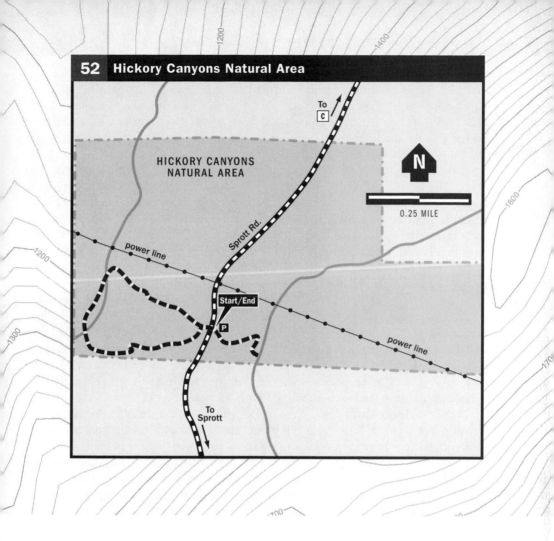

HICKORY CANYONS
NATURAL AREA

N

0.25 MILE

power line

Sprott Rd.

Start/End

P

power line

To
C

To
Sprott

with a scattering of pines and cedars that dash the landscape with color on dull winter days.

Hickory Canyons is owned by the LAD Foundation, a nonprofit organization founded by Leo Drey to protect unique and beautiful natural Missouri landscapes that might otherwise have been lost to development. Administered by the Department of Conservation, Hickory Canyons can be explored via two scenic trails—a 0.5-mile out-and-back path leading east from the trailhead and a 1-mile loop across Sprott Road to the west. Signboards painted with maps of the route are found at the beginning of each trail, complete with boxes of interpretive trail maps. While the short and easy-to-follow east trail is unmarked, the 1-mile west loop is well signed with white placards bearing a hiker silhouette. Though Hickory Canyons Natural Area's natural features make it an exciting hike for children, signs on both trails warn you to keep them on a tight leash near the beautiful but dangerous trailside cliffs.

Both trails begin on the dry ridge followed by Sprott Road, then descend into moist hollows. For a spectacular introduction to the area, take the short east trail first. Descending for most of its 0.25-mile length, this path begins as a rather nondescript walk in the woods until, 0.1 mile into the hike, it makes a hard right into a spectacular horseshoe-shaped box canyon. Here nature has eroded the canyon's sandstone layers into countless ledges, overhangs, shallow caves, and grottos. Moss and ferns paint bright-green patches on the walls, and tall trees stretch to reach the sunlight far above the canyon floor. The canyon is most captivating on rainy days, when a noisy waterfall cascades over six rock-layer steps before splashing into a clear, sand-bottomed pool nestled in the horseshoe curve of the sandstone cliffs. Dripping seeps in the canyon walls water lush fern gardens and form thousands of icicle mustaches on the rock layers during cold snaps. One sunny day after a winter rainstorm I spent an hour in this magical place, resting under an overhanging ledge and listening to the splash of the falls, the trickle of the seeps, and the occasional crash of icicles cracking loose and shattering on the canyon floor below.

The 1-mile west loop at Hickory Canyons isn't as spectacular as the east trail. It has more variety, though, and is best hiked in a counterclockwise direction, saving the best scenery for the latter part of your walk. From the ridge on Sprott Road the trail drops steadily for the first quarter mile. It squeezes through a gap at the head of a deep hollow, then descends along the hollow wall on a rocky trail with rock layers, outcroppings, and small boulders scattered all around. It levels where the hollow opens into a bottomland with a creek running north and south.

The trail breaks left to follow the creek, crossing it four times in the next quarter mile. It's a pretty little creek, with enchanting cascades on its predominantly slick-rock bottom offering several inviting spots for wading or dangling your feet in the water on a hot summer day. Just before the fourth crossing the trail splashes across a tiny creek flowing in from the left. A look up its course will show you an attractive box canyon. Don't clamber up this tight canyon and ruin the vegetation, though—you'll get a much better look at it a short way down the trail. Immediately after the fourth creek crossing the path breaks left and climbs through a set of eroded rocky layers, topping out on a pine-studded ridge spine that overlooks the hollow. The trail follows this narrow, flat-rock spine for 150 feet, passing several pedestal-like rock overlooks with wonderful views into the box canyon below. It's a spectacular spot, topped off with a set of wooden steps and landings with great views of the craggy rock layers at the head of the canyon.

The remainder of the trail is a gentle uphill back to the trailhead. It's a nice little hike in the woods, but nothing as impressive as what you've seen, so take time to enjoy the beautiful spots on this short hike. For more fun exploration of this area's spectacular scenery, head a few miles farther southwest and hike the trails of nearby Hawn State Park (page 211) and Pickle Springs Natural Area (see following profile).

## ▶ NEARBY ACTIVITIES

To the east is Ste. Genevieve, a French village founded in the 1700s. Many of Ste. Gen's fascinating old buildings are open for tours, and you can sample local wines at the Ste. Genevieve Winery. Visit **www.ste-genevieve.com/index.htm** for more information.

# PICKLE SPRINGS NATURAL AREA: TRAIL THROUGH TIME

## ▶ IN BRIEF

This trail has more smiles per mile than any other trail in Missouri. It's loaded with incredible natural wonders. And with its short length and well-designed treadway, it's a wonderful hike for kids and adults of all ages and skill levels.

## ▶ DESCRIPTION

The Trail through Time at Pickle Springs is one of the most spectacular hikes in Missouri. What the trail lacks in length is more than made up for with its incredible scenery. Pickle Springs Natural Area was named a National Natural Landmark by the National Park Service in 1974, and a short distance into your hike you'll find out why.

The trail begins at the back of the parking lot, where a short spur leads to the beginning of the loop. At the junction you'll find a nice touch—a little stand loosely packed with walking sticks to help you along your hike and a signboard with interpretive guides describing the beauty you'll be admiring. To follow the guidebook, go left at the junction. You'll descend through a rock layer and immediately arrive at The Slot, the first of many "oohs" and "ahhs" on the Trail through Time. The trail descends into a narrow gap in the rock layer and follows it for 250 feet. Shallow caves and rock nooks pockmark the mossy rock walls towering 10 to 15 feet on each side of the trail, and a large tree shades The Slot.

## ⓘ KEY AT-A-GLANCE INFORMATION

**LENGTH:** 2 miles

**CONFIGURATION:** Loop

**DIFFICULTY:** Easy

**SCENERY:** Wooded hills and hollows with incredible rock formations, overlooks, a canyon, and an enchanting spring

**EXPOSURE:** Shady throughout, with a few open exposures

**TRAFFIC:** Light to moderate

**TRAIL SURFACE:** Natural surface mix of packed earth; some rock ledges and roots; occasional bridges and wooden steps

**HIKING TIME:** 1–2 hours

**ACCESS:** Open daily 4 a.m.–10 p.m.; no fees or permits required

**MAPS:** Sprott USGS topo; interpretive booklet and map at trailhead

**FACILITIES:** None

**SPECIAL COMMENTS:** Pets must be leashed. Allow plenty of time for admiring rock formation, bluffs, and other natural features.

## ▶ DIRECTIONS

Drive south on I-55 to Exit 154, MO O. Turn right and follow MO O 6 miles southwest to MO 32. Turn right on MO 32 and follow it 11 miles west to MO AA. Go 0.75 miles left on MO AA to Dorlac Road. Turn left onto Dorlac and follow it a quarter mile to the trailhead on the right side of the road.

### GPS TRAILHEAD COORDINATES (TRAILHEAD)

| UTM ZONE (WGS84) | 15S |
| EASTING | 737564 |
| NORTHING | 4187003 |
| LATITUDE-LONGITUDE | |
| NORTH | N37° 47' 58.3253'' |
| WEST | W90° 18' 6.3260'' |

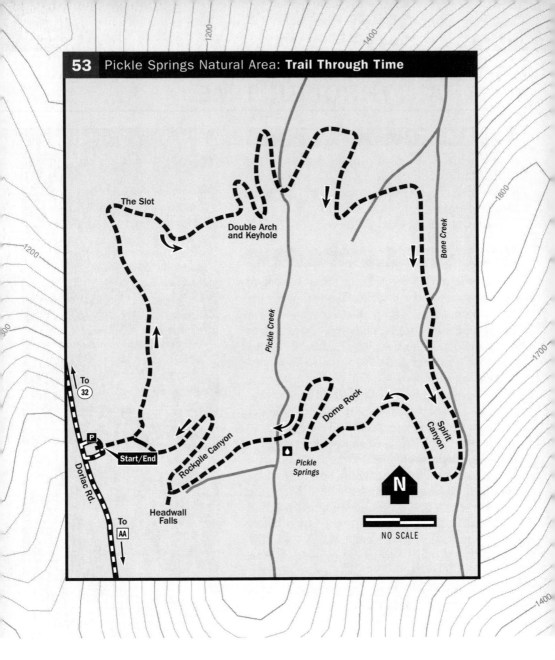

The Slot

Double Arch and Keyhole

Bone Creek

To 32

Pickle Creek

To AA

Doriac Rd.

P

Start/End

Rockpile Canyon

Dome Rock

Spirit Canyon

Pickle Springs

Headwall Falls

**N**

NO SCALE

After you exit The Slot you'll curve left past a low bluff that's covered with icicles in winter and dripping seeps in spring, then clamber over the Cauliflower Rocks, one of the most awesome landscapes on the trail. Here, erosion has carved amazing shapes and formations from the rock layer. One giant rock protrudes off the wall like a ship's prow, with the trail passing beneath it through Double Arch. Shortly after the arches you'll squeeze through The Keyhole, another arch in the rock layer, and skirt Terrapin Rock, a round-backed boulder with a protrusion that exactly mimics a turtle's head and neck. While you're admiring these formations, you'll be serenaded by the splashing flow of Pickle Creek in the hollow just below this otherworldly rock garden.

Shortly after Terrapin Rock, the trail descends into the hollow and crosses Pickle Creek. Beneath the bridge, rock ledges and logs lying across the creek form beautiful little waterfalls in the stream. Look uphill from the bridge and you'll see Double Arch, The Keyhole, and Terrapin Rock from below. Beneath the bridge is a three-foot waterfall—a perfect place to rest and dangle your feet in the water.

After crossing Pickle Creek, you'll climb gradually to a ridgetop, then drop into the hollow drained by Bone Creek. The trail parallels the creek, with an outcropping overlooking a little cascade on the stream's rock bottom. A little farther upstream, the trail crosses Bone Creek twice on twin bridges, with Mossy Falls, the halfway point of the loop, just above the second crossing. Here Bone Creek pours off a 20-foot-wide, overhanging, moss-covered rock layer and splashes into a cool, deep pool.

After Mossy Falls the trail climbs gently, with small outcroppings hinting of the wonders ahead. As the trail ascends over the next several hundred feet, Owl's Den Bluff appears to rise from the earth ahead of you as you hike toward it. Its wide, ledge-and-moss-covered face grows wider and taller until it fills the sky before you, then the trail breaks hard right to follow its base. This broad, towering bluff is a fascinating series of cross-bedded strata left by ancient seas and streams, decorated by scattered seeps, mossy patches, and, in winter, fascinating ice formations. Following the trail along the bluff base, you next come to Spirit Canyon, an overhang protecting a cool, moist shelter where the sun never shines. This alcove is cool on the hottest summer day, and water always drips from its ceiling.

After Spirit Canyon you'll climb along the cliff face to leave the Bone Creek drainage, then cross a ridge to reenter the hollow of Pickle Creek. As you work your way up and over the low ridge, you'll hike through impressive boulder gardens. A quarter mile after leaving the canyon you'll reach the panoramic view of Dome Rock. Dome Rock's wide stone terrace, with pines scattered over its surface, is the perfect place to soak up some sun and admire the vista up and down the Pickle Creek drainage. To the north you can see the Cauliflower Rocks and from below hear the trickling rush of Pickle Creek as it leaves its namesake spring. On winter days when the leaves are gone, you can see the spring pool below. The rock texture on top of Dome Rock resembles frozen ocean swells and offers a couple of sheltered nooks for warming up on a sunny winter day. If you like to picnic on your hikes, this is the place to spread your tablecloth.

From Dome Rock the Trail through Time swings north, then switchbacks south and descends to Pickle Springs. On the way you'll pass directly under the escarpment of Dome Rock, looking straight up at the overlook you so enjoyed only a few moments ago. The descent ends at Pickle Springs, where an exquisite little waterfall pours over the ledge that hides the spring. A bridge spanning Pickle Creek below the spring is the perfect vantage point to admire the spring, the falls, and the crystal clear pool they feed. During midsummer droughts in the old days, this tiny spring was often the only reliable water source for locals scratching out their living in these rugged hills and hollows. The spring was named for William Pickles, who owned the land in the mid-1800s.

Ice Sculptures at Pickle Springs

You'll begin climbing when you leave the spring, and after a fairly steep ascent the trail climbs into my favorite part—Rockpile Canyon and Headwall Falls. Hiking next to a huge jumble of giant rocks, you can see where they used to fit into the rock wall to your left before they fell away. This rock fall is relatively recent, having happened in 1959. Local residents remember hearing the thunderous sound when this portion of the wall tumbled to the canyon floor below. At one point you can hike out onto one of the behemoth boulders. The trail skirts the edges of these massive fallen rocks, then makes a switchback to climb up out of the canyon.

Don't be too anxious to get out, though—take the spur trail at the switchback and follow it 100 feet to Headwall Falls in the upper end of this hidden canyon. The rock formations here are incredible. Two shallow caves stacked on top of one another form inaccessible shelters high in the opposite wall of the canyon. More huge boulders from the rock fall dot the canyon floor. If there's been rain lately, a stream trickles over several steps high in the escarpment before tumbling off an overhang in the canyon's tall, rugged face. Here in this deep canyon, the trees seem unbelievably tall and straight, stretching high into the sky to reach the sunlight above the canyon wall. One long-dead snag leans over the fallen chunks of rock to rest against the towering walls of Rockpile Canyon.

The trail continues to climb from Headwall Falls, angling across the hillside with nice views down the hollow of Pickle Creek. You're on the final climb to the trailhead at this point, and, as you ascend through the rock layer that forms the top of Headwall Falls, you'll spot a delightful little grassy, pine-studded open space to your left. This is Pine Glade—a perfect place to warm up on a sunny winter day. The trailhead is only a few steps uphill from the glade, so stretch out under the sky for a while here, listen to the sounds of the forest, and relive all the natural wandering you just enjoyed.

## ▶ NEARBY ACTIVITIES

Ste. Genevieve, a French village founded in the 1700s showcasing beautiful colonial architecture, is 20 miles east of Pickle Springs. Many of these fascinating old buildings are open for tours, and you can enjoy a posthike libation at the Ste. Genevieve Winery (**www.ste-genevieve.com/index.htm**).

# ROCK PILE MOUNTAIN WILDERNESS AREA

## ▶ IN BRIEF

Start on one mountain, then hike to another ... pretty nice! Few people come to Rock Pile, so you'll likely have the place to yourself. While puzzling over the intriguing circular pile of rocks that gave the mountain its name, you'll hike miles and miles of ridges in this wilderness before descending into Cave Branch Hollow to soak your feet in a cooling stream.

## ▶ DESCRIPTION

At 4,131 acres, Rock Pile Mountain is the Mark Twain National Forest's smallest wilderness area, but it's big enough for splendid solitude. Surprisingly few people come to this secluded wildland. Hiking here is incredibly peaceful—you'll seldom hear anything but the sounds of nature while you explore Rock Pile's scenic ridges. Designated a wilderness area in 1980, Rock Pile Mountain Wilderness is named for a mysterious circular pile of rocks on its southern peak. No one knows who made this intriguing structure, or why.

You'll spend lots of time at altitude in this wilderness area. The trail starts at its high point, 1,306 feet on Little Grass Mountain, and follows ridges for much of its length. There's a steep and rugged half-mile grade off Little Grass that'll make you huff and puff on your return. If you hike around the loop, you'll descend to Cave Branch

## ⓘ KEY AT-A-GLANCE INFORMATION

**LENGTH:** 12.5 miles

**CONFIGURATION:** Loop with spur

**DIFFICULTY:** Moderate–difficult

**SCENERY:** Open glades, piney ridges, rocky streams, and immense stone outcroppings

**EXPOSURE:** Shaded with several exposed places in glades

**TRAFFIC:** Light

**TRAIL SURFACE:** Very rugged 0.5-mile descent off of Little Grass Mountain, otherwise packed earth and gravel with occasional rocky stretches

**HIKING TIME:** 4 hours to Rock Pile Mountain and back; allow 6–8 hours for entire loop

**ACCESS:** No permits or fees; open 24 hours

**MAPS:** Rock Pile Mountain USGS topo; Rock Pile Wilderness map available from Mark Twain National Forest

**FACILITIES:** None

**SPECIAL COMMENTS:** No water available. Bring map and compass to this unmarked trail.

## ▶ DIRECTIONS

From Fredericktown, drive 6 miles south on US 67 to Cherokee Pass. Go 5 miles west from Cherokee Pass on MO C to CR 406. There used to be a Rock Pile Wilderness sign here, but it was gone last time I was there. Go 2.5 miles north on CR 406 to FS 2124, where a sign points left to Rock Pile Mountain Wilderness. Turn left and drive 1.1 miles on FS 2124 until it ends at the trailhead on Little Grass Mountain.

**GPS TRAILHEAD COORDINATES (TRAILHEAD)**

| | |
|---|---|
| UTM ZONE (WGS84) | 15S |
| EASTING | 729444 |
| NORTHING | 4149437 |
| LATITUDE-LONGITUDE | |
| NORTH | N37° 27' 48.0868'' |
| WEST | W90° 24' 20.4967'' |

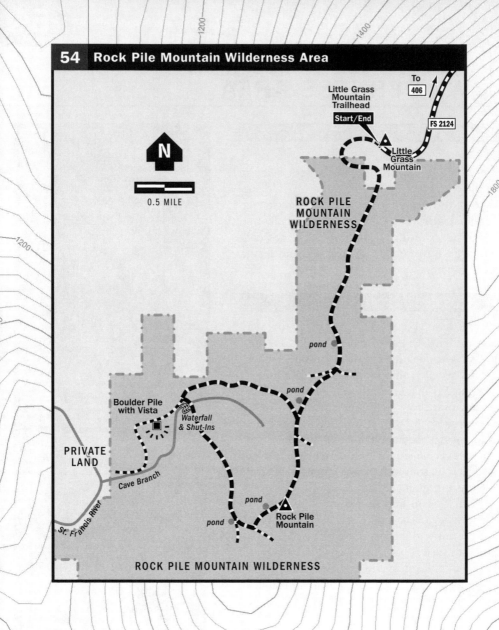

Little Grass
Mountain
Trailhead
**Start/End**

To
**406**

**FS 2124**

Little
Grass
Mountain

N

0.5 MILE

**ROCK PILE
MOUNTAIN
WILDERNESS**

*pond*

*pond*

**Boulder Pile
with Vista**

*Waterfall
& Shut-Ins*

**PRIVATE
LAND**

*Cave Branch*

*St. Francis River*

*pond*

*pond*

Rock Pile
Mountain

**ROCK PILE MOUNTAIN WILDERNESS**

and face a second long climb back to the ridges, but it's not as steep and rough as the rocky path off Little Grass. The rest of the hike is gentle undulation on ridge spines and the saddles between them, making for fast hiking. The only bummer is facing your toughest climb at the end, when you ascend back to the trailhead on Little Grass Mountain.

The best hiking at Rock Pile is between fall and late spring. In fall you'll enjoy the colors, and through winter and into spring the bare trees let you admire constant ridgetop vistas that would be obscured in summer. Lots of pines and cedars dot the forest, adding welcome color to gray winter landscapes. These evergreens are especially pretty after snowstorms, when they glow bright green against the white landscape. With the leaves gone, you can often pick out Rock Pile and Little Grass mountains, giving you excellent reference points for route finding in the wilderness.

There are two highlights to plan your hike around in Rock Pile Mountain Wilderness. One is the mountain itself, where the mysterious rock pile is located. The other is a pretty cascade on Cave Branch, and a huge boulder outcropping with views across Cave Branch Hollow. The cascade and boulder pile are on the west side of the loop. The easiest and fastest hike is a quick hitter to Rock Pile Mountain and back. It involves the smallest altitude change and totals 8 miles round-trip. Another option is a 9-mile jaunt to Cave Branch and back. You'll descend from 1,306 feet at Little Grass Mountain to 580 feet at Cave Branch, then climb back up to Little Grass. The third option is hiking the whole loop and seeing everything on a 12.6-mile hike. Once you're off Little Grass Mountain, the grades are relatively gentle, so it's pretty easy to do this even on the shortest winter day.

To find the trail from the parking area, go to the boulder with "ROCK PILE MTN WILDERNESS" carved in its face and look west. You'll see concrete footings from the old Little Grass fire-lookout tower, and beyond them a four-wheeler path heading west off the mountain, marked with white plastic diamonds. These plastic blazes last until you're on the ridge heading south toward Rock Pile Mountain, then they disappear, but that's all right—with the forest-service map and a compass, it's easy to find your way around the old road loop in the wilderness area. A quarter mile down the four-wheeler path, the diamonds lead left onto single-track, then along a rugged stretch curving around the side of the mountain to the ridge running south from Little Grass.

Once on this north–south ridge, the hiking gets easy. It's still single-track, but follows the undulations of the ridge for almost 2 miles, winding through several boulder fields and a rocky glade. Two miles from the trailhead you'll cross a saddle with a stock pond nestled in it, and the old road trail begins. A half mile later you'll T into another old road. The trail to the left leaves the wilderness area. Another goes hard right, and a third angles to the right and stays on the ridge southbound. That's the one you want. A half mile farther on you'll T into another road, where a couple of rocks are stacked up on the side of the path. This is the loop in the heart of the wilderness area.

Turn left to head for Rock Pile Mountain. The trail starts out east, but soon veers south again and begins climbing steadily. You'll go through and over several rocky stretches, topping out on Rock Pile Mountain about 1 mile from the start of the loop. When the trail veers west and levels out, look for the rock pile immediately to the right of the trail. It's a circular pile of small, gray rocks wrapping around a couple of small boulders and a cedar tree. A few feet farther down the trail is a wide, rocky glade.

The trail continues west, passing another stock pond just past the summit, begins a gentle descent, and slowly veers to the northwest. A quarter mile past the summit, another old road leads south, but white diamonds direct you to continue northwest. A half mile past the summit, you'll pass another stock pond, level out, veer to straight north, and wander through an impressive boulder field. You'll soon begin descending into a grove of majestic pines, dropping off the ridge nose into the hollow of Cave Branch. This is a place where the trail gets faint, so pay attention. When you bottom out in the hollow you'll cross Cave Branch, follow it downstream for a few hundred yards, then T into another old road.

A right turn leads back to the trailhead, but first go left to check out the highlights of this part of the wilderness. Note that the wilderness area map isn't accurate here—it shows this side trail beginning on a ridge and dropping down to Cave Branch, but it actually follows the stream from this point and leaves it just west of here—exactly opposite what the map shows. A hundred yards west down this trail you'll see a small set of shut-ins in Cave Branch, with a little cascade rushing into a green pool. Just downstream is an ideal campsite that'll draw you back here if you're a backpacker. It's an idyllic place to hang out for a while, soaking your feet and enjoying the music of the cascade.

The old road continues west along Cave Branch for another few hundred yards, then the creek bends to the south. The old road veers northwest, climbs over a low ridge, and descends into another hollow. You'll slowly bend to the south, and to your left you'll spot an immense boulder outcropping rising 50 feet from a pine grove east of the old road. It's a bit of a climb to get up on it, but worth the effort—you'll have impressive views south into a wide, forested amphitheater, framed by bright-green shortleaf pines. It's a great place to enjoy the sunshine on a cool fall or winter day. The old road continues on down hollow toward the St. Francis River, slowly narrowing to single-track and winding through tight cedar groves. Unfortunately, you'll hit the property boundary just before reaching the river, and the signs telling you to keep out are very firm.

Back on the loop near the shut-ins, the trail jumps up onto an ascending ridge and begins climbing. This ascent lasts for a half mile, followed by another half mile of little rollers on the ridge. A mile after leaving Cave Branch you'll reach the loop junction, turn north, and follow the ridges back to the trailhead on Little Grass Mountain.

## ▶ NEARBY ACTIVITIES

Visit Dog and Suds in Cherokee Pass (6748 Highway 67) after your day on the trail. It's an old-school drive-in—you don't have to get your tired tail out of the car to get some grub. Can't beat that after a long hike, can you? Great shakes at Dog and Suds . . . especially after 12 miles in the wilderness!

# SILVER MINES–MILLSTREAM GARDENS TRAIL

## ▶ IN BRIEF

The St. Francis River thunders through a rugged canyon cut through granite bluffs overlooking its course through the St. Francois Mountains. At Millstream Gardens the river crashes through the Tiemann Shut-Ins, forming rapids that attract river runners from throughout the Midwest.

## ▶ DESCRIPTION

The St. Francis River's 4-mile reach through Millstream Gardens Conservation Area and the Silver Mines Recreation Area is one of the loveliest places in Missouri. The Tiemann Shut-Ins in Millstream Gardens, a Missouri Natural Area, is an especially idyllic setting. Majestic pines overlook the St. Francis, and huge granite boulders and bluffs on the riverbanks make wonderful spots to kick back and admire the white water roaring through the shut-ins.

Missouri's only white water, these rapids draw river runners from all over the Midwest. The Missouri Whitewater Championships are held here in mid-March, attracting crowds of 1,000 or more spectators. It's a blast to hang out in this natural-rock amphitheater and watch kayakers

## ▶ DIRECTIONS

To reach the Silver Mines trailhead, drive south on US 67 to MO 72–Fredericktown. Turn right and go west 4.3 miles to MO D, where a sign directs you to Silver Mines. Turn left and continue 3 miles to Silver Mines Recreation Area. Trailhead parking is on either side of the river, next to the old MO D low-water bridge.

To reach the Millstream Garden trailhead: From US 67, drive 8.4 miles west on MO 72. From 72 you'll see a Millstream Gardens sign at an intersection. Turn left on the gravel road and drive 1 mile south. Hikes can start from three points (see map and hike description).

## ① KEY AT-A-GLANCE INFORMATION

**LENGTH:** 5 miles

**CONFIGURATION:** Point-to-point

**DIFFICULTY:** Moderate

**SCENERY:** Bluff overlooks, granite boulders, white-water rapids on the St. Francis River, pine forests

**EXPOSURE:** Shaded, with several exposed areas

**TRAFFIC:** Light, except during the MO Whitewater Championships

**TRAIL SURFACE:** Rocky single-track paths

**HIKING TIME:** 3-5 hours

**ACCESS:** Millstream Gardens section open 4 a.m.–10 p.m.; no limits on Silver Mines section

**MAPS:** USGS topo Rhodes Mountain; Silver Mines Recreation Area map from Mark Twain National Forest; Millstream Gardens Recreation Area map from Department of Conservation

**FACILITIES:** Parking, toilets, picnic shelter at Millstream Gardens; parking, toilets, picnicking at Silver Mines Recreation Area; toilets, picnic sites at Turkey Creek Picnic area at trail's midpoint; water available at Silver Mines and Turkey Creek during camping season

**SPECIAL COMMENTS:** Pets must be leashed; $2 fee per car at Silver Mines trailhead

### GPS TRAILHEAD COORDINATES (PARK ENTRANCE)

| UTM ZONE (WGS84) | 15S |
|---|---|
| EASTING | 723882 |
| NORTHING | 4162593 |
| LATITUDE-LONGITUDE | |
| NORTH | N37° 34' 59.4761'' |
| WEST | W90° 27' 52.2445'' |

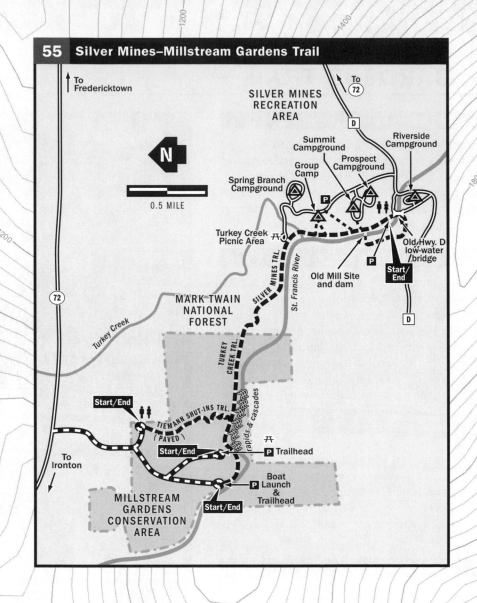

## 55  Silver Mines–Millstream Gardens Trail

To Fredericktown

SILVER MINES
RECREATION
AREA

To
72

D

**N**

0.5 MILE

Summit
Campground

Riverside
Campground

Group
Camp

Prospect
Campground

Spring Branch
Campground

P

Turkey Creek
Picnic Area

Old Hwy. D
low-water
bridge

P

Old Mill Site
and dam

Start/
End

MARK TWAIN
NATIONAL
FOREST

D

Start/End

TIEMANN SHUT-INS TRL.
( PAVED )

Start/End

Trailhead
P

Boat
Launch
&
Trailhead
P

Start/End

MILLSTREAM
GARDENS
CONSERVATION
AREA

To
Ironton

72

Turkey Creek

St. Francis River

SILVER MINES TRL.

TURKEY CREEK TRL.

rapids & cascades

1200

1400

1800

1700

1400

1200

shoot the rapids below. The races take in only a few of the river's rapids. Hiking downriver, you'll admire boiling, frothy stretches with names like Cat's Paw, Shark's Fin, Double-Drop, and Rickety Rack.

Two miles downstream from Millstream Gardens is a man-made rapid—a 125-year-old stone dam across the St. Francis. This relic was built in 1879 by the Einstein Mining Company to power a silver mine that once operated in this serene valley. Mining was once lucrative enough for Einstein to build a company town near the dam. Named Silver Mountain, the village was home to more than 800 people, and had a post office, a school, and several stores. All that's left of the mine and town are the breached dam and a few foundations.

This hike is three trails rolled into one. The Department of Conservation's Millstream Gardens Conservation Area includes the paved Tiemann Shut-Ins Trail and the natural-surface Turkey Creek Trail. The Tiemann Shut-Ins Trail is a 1-mile spur from the upper trailhead. It joins the Turkey Creek Trail at the Cat's Paw Rapid overlook. The Turkey Creek Trail runs downstream from the boat launch, through the shut-ins, and out of conservation department property about a mile later. There the path enters Mark Twain National Forest property and becomes the Silver Mines Trail. It reaches the Silver Mines trailhead 3.5 miles downstream from the Millstream Gardens boat launch, crosses the river, and heads back upstream 0.7 miles to the stone dam.

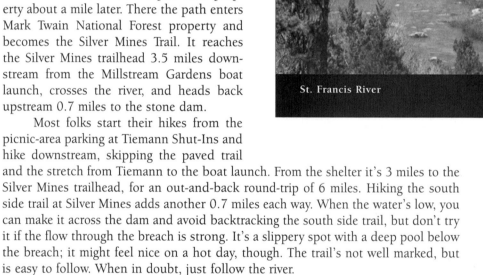

St. Francis River

Most folks start their hikes from the picnic-area parking at Tiemann Shut-Ins and hike downstream, skipping the paved trail and the stretch from Tiemann to the boat launch. From the shelter it's 3 miles to the Silver Mines trailhead, for an out-and-back round-trip of 6 miles. Hiking the south side trail at Silver Mines adds another 0.7 miles each way. When the water's low, you can make it across the dam and avoid backtracking the south side trail, but don't try it if the flow through the breach is strong. It's a slippery spot with a deep pool below the breach; it might feel nice on a hot day, though. The trail's not well marked, but is easy to follow. When in doubt, just follow the river.

Hiking east from the shelter, you'll start passing overlooks within a quarter mile. Cat's Paw Overlook has a viewing platform with vistas up and down the river's noisy rapids. My favorite is Pine Rock overlook, where a spur leads to a rocky point jutting out from the riverside cliffs. Just past Pine Rock the trail veers away from the river and heads into the woods. It follows an old road for a while, crosses a stream or two, and does some ups and downs in the forest before descending back to the St. Francis about 1 mile later.

You'll strike the river next to an old foundation. A spur trail heads upstream here, going 100 yards to a set of small rapids. The main route follows the river's edge for the next half mile to the national-forest picnic area at Turkey Creek. After leaving Turkey Creek, the trail climbs and soon gets rugged and beautiful. You'll walk on a tall, craggy bluff—sometimes on its edge, sometimes on shelf trails cut across its face. The river roars right below you, and pines shade the route. It's rough, rocky, and challenging—and it's spectacular. Along this stretch you'll see several side trails going east into the woods. They lead to the campgrounds in Silver Mines Recreation Area.

After a half mile of incredible cliff hiking, you'll spot the old stone dam. Side trails scramble down to it, and the monstrous, gently sloping granite rock faces anchoring its eastern end are great spots to soak up sunshine or dangle your feet in the water. From the dam, the trail descends for the next half mile, staying rocky and rugged until it reaches the Silver Mines Recreation Area trailhead.

Though it's not as spectacular, the 0.7-mile trail on the opposite bank is definitely worth a look. Cross the St. Francis on the old MO D low-water bridge near the trailhead, walk to the picnic area, and look for the trail heading upstream on the right. It passes through a couple of impressive rock gardens, and halfway to the dam a spur leads to scenic overlooks high above the St. Francis. Downstream you'll see the MO D low-water bridge, and upriver is an excellent vista of the old dam.

Next to the dam on this side of the St. Francis are haunting remnants of the old mining operation. Crumbling foundations stair-step up the rugged hillside. An eight-inch pine grows on the crumbling surface of an old concrete floor, roots curling to the earth below. Monstrous piles of leftover rock litter the place. The St. Francis roars through the old dam just upstream, and deep woods shade the old work site. Check out the tiny, open-ended shack below the foundations. Known locally as the "Air Conditioner," it covers an old mine shaft. Cool breezes from the shaft drift through the shack, and benches line its sides—a great escape on a hot summer day.

## ▶ NEARBY ACTIVITIES

Amidon Memorial Conservation Area (page 196), home of the Castor River Shut-Ins, is 8 miles east of Fredericktown.

# ST. FRANCOIS STATE PARK

## ▶ IN BRIEF

Legend has it that Civil War outlaws took cover in the hills and hollows of St. Francois State Park, which is known as "Yesterday's Hideout, Today's Retreat." Later, moonshiners concealed stills along the banks of Coonville Creek in Mooner's Hollow and secretively worked their trade. Today, you can explore the park on 17 miles of trail.

## ▶ DESCRIPTION

The history of St. Francois State Park began in the early 1960s, when residents of St. Francois County, hoping to preserve part of their landscape in its natural state, ran a door-to-door campaign for donations to buy land for the proposed park. From their first acreage purchase in 1964, St. Francois State Park has grown to its present 2,735 acres. The park contains the 2,101-acre Coonville Creek Wild Area, scenic bluffs over Big River, and the entrancing waterfalls, cascades, and springs in Mooner's Hollow.

You can explore St. Francois State Park on three excellent hikes. One of these combines the Missouri and Swimming Deer trails for a total distance of 4 miles. You'll use the point-to-point Missouri Trail, marked with orange blazes, to access the 3-mile loop of the Swimming Deer Trail. The Missouri Trail starts next to the amphitheater behind the shower house in the campground, and runs 0.35 miles to the Swimming Deer. Along the way it passes through the open area between the basic and electric campgrounds, then drops through a neat set of rock formations to intersect with the Swimming Deer. The campground will be

## ▶ DIRECTIONS

From the intersection of US 67 and I-55 in Festus, drive 20 miles south on US 67. The entrance is on the eastern side of the highway. Look for brown signs a half mile before the turnoff.

## ⓘ KEY AT-A-GLANCE INFORMATION

**LENGTH:** 17 miles on 4 separate trails

**CONFIGURATION:** The Pike Run, Swimming Deer, and Mooner's Hollow Trail are loops; the Missouri Trail is point-to-point

**DIFFICULTY:** Moderate–hard on Pike Run Trail; all others easy

**SCENERY:** Wooded ridges, deep hollows with rocky-bottom streams, mossy rock outcroppings, river-bluff views

**EXPOSURE:** Shaded

**TRAFFIC:** Light on Pike Run Trail, medium on all others

**TRAIL SURFACE:** Packed earth and gravel with many rocky stretches

**HIKING TIME:** 3–7 hours on Pike Run Trail; 1 hour on Mooner's Hollow and Swimming Deer trails; 15 minutes on Missouri Trail

**ACCESS:** Park open 8 a.m.–9 p.m., November–March; 7 a.m.–10 p.m., April–October

**MAPS:** Bonne Terre USGS topo; St. Francois State Park Trail Map

**FACILITIES:** Water, restrooms, camping, showers, phone, picnic areas, shelters

**SPECIAL COMMENTS:** Pets must be leashed

### GPS TRAILHEAD COORDINATES (PARK ENTRANCE)

| UTM ZONE (WGS84) | 15S |
| --- | --- |
| EASTING | 716345 |
| NORTHING | 4205729 |
| LATITUDE–LONGITUDE | |
| NORTH | N37° 58' 24.3400'' |
| WEST | W90° 32' 12.9436'' |

## 56 St. Francois State Park

N
0.5 MILE
To
St. Louis
Coonville Creek
67
NORTH LOOP
PIKE RUN TRL.
MOONER'S HOLLOW TRL.
Start/End
To
Bonne
Terre
Park
Office
SOUTH LOOP
PIKE RUN TRL.
backpack
camp
Start/End
MISSOURI
TRL.
SWIMMING DEER TRL.
overlook
Big River
Start/End
Campground Loops

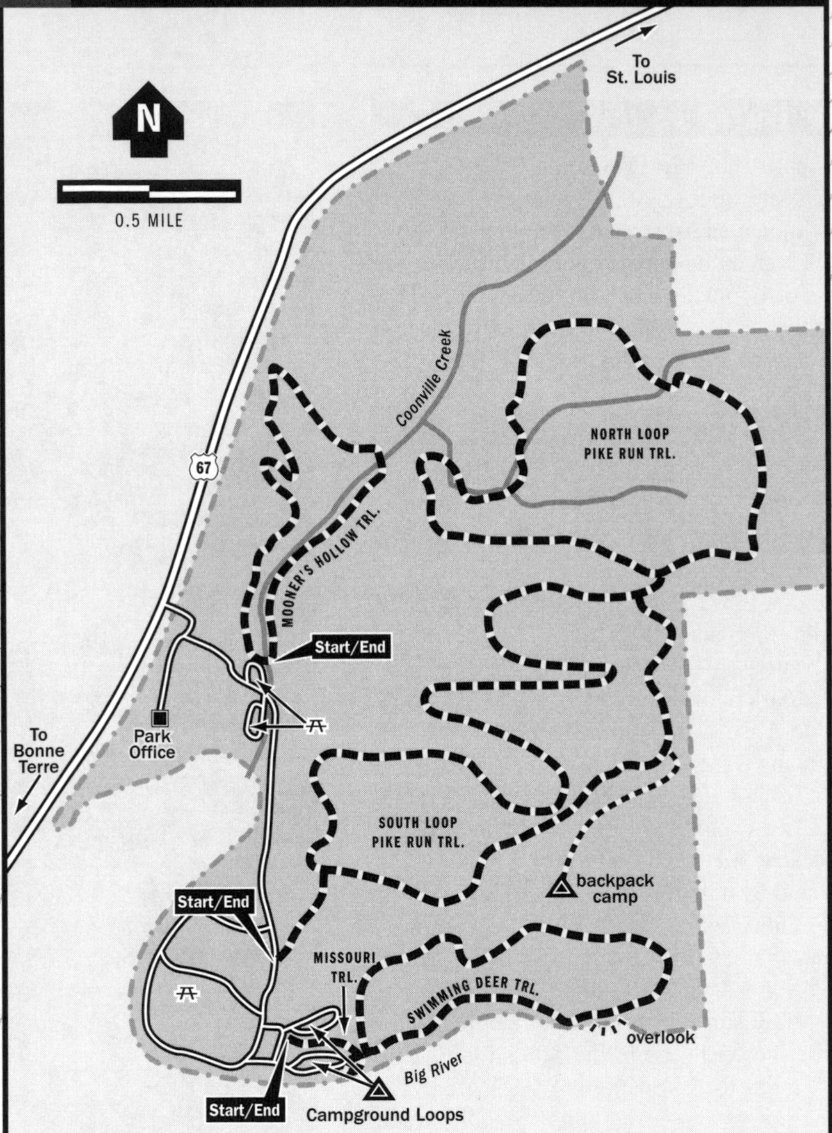

a few yards to the right, and the Swimming Deer loop to the left. Straight ahead goes the last bit of the Missouri Trail—it'll take you back to the campground after hiking the Swimming Deer Trail.

Go left at this intersection, and you'll reach the start of the Swimming Deer loop, marked with green hiker symbols. Bear right, cross a little wash, and you'll be next to Big River. The trail follows the river for a while, and there's a nice gravel bar for swimming or wading. A rock-layer bluff rises to your left, squeezing you against the river. At a gap in the wall, the trail breaks left and climbs steeply up through the cliff on natural rock steps. Follow the cliff for a short way, and watch for a side trail to the right; it leads to an overlook of Big River. From the overlook, the trail follows the descending cliff back to river level, crosses a side hollow on a footbridge, and immediately climbs back onto the riverside bluff.

Once on the bluff, you'll T into an old road. The trail continues east down the road, but first follow the road a short way to the right. It soon ends at a stupendous bluff overlook on an outside bend of Big River. Continuing east on the trail, you'll make a big arc to go west, then begin descending. As you near the hollow bottom, look for an abandoned barn in the woods to your right—a remnant of the days before this landscape was preserved by the park. You lose the old road in the hollow, spend the next quarter mile bouncing over incredibly rough and beautiful mossy rock gardens, then turn north and hike a gentle quarter mile uphill that ends next to a vertical cave entrance. The cave's mouth is fenced off, but it's intriguing to peer down into this interesting hole in the ground.

The last mile of the loop bounces through more rugged rock gardens, then finishes with a half-mile run along an old road back to the Missouri Trail. There's only 0.1 mile left on the Missouri Trail, but don't blow it off—it goes past some 250-year-old sycamores. They're huge! I once heard a tall tale, or so I thought at the time, that pioneers hollowed out immense sycamores in Ozark river bottoms and lived in them. After seeing these leftover monsters of the old days, I believe it. After the sycamores the Missouri Trail bends back to the campground and enters it behind site 30; follow the road back to the shower house.

The Swimming Deer Trail is a good one, but my favorite hike in St. Francois State Park is the 2.7-mile Mooner's Hollow Trail. Crystal-clear, spring-fed Coonville Creek winds along the bottom of this scenic hollow, flowing over ledges to form pretty waterfalls and cascades. The clear water and hidden quality of the hollow made this a favorite place for moonshiners, who, according to the park brochure, believed "It seemed to work out better if concocted in the night under the light of an Ozark moon."

The Mooner's Hollow Trail starts from the picnic area at the bottom of the hill near the park entrance. Park by the footbridge in the picnic area, cross it, and you're on the trail. Marked with blue arrows and hiker symbols, the path turns north at the end of the bridge and heads upstream along the creek. It parallels Coonville Creek for the next mile, sometimes next to the stream, other times climbing to the hillsides above. Huge mossy rocks cover the slope, and the trail winds over and through them. One mile from the trailhead you'll break west and cross the stream at a tantalizing spot. A quiet pool lies just upstream, and beyond its calm surface a series of cascades and waterfalls extends 50 yards up Coonville Creek. There's even a rock to sit on while you contemplate this exquisite scene.

After the crossing, you'll angle steadily away from Coonville Creek, bounce over several side hollows, and eventually climb to the ridge west of Mooner's Hollow. You'll be close to US 67 on the ridge, but the noise isn't overpowering. Once on the ridge you'll head south to follow it on an old road. It's a descending ridge, and when you drop off its nose you'll walk through a glade with beautiful views to the south before dropping back into Mooner's Hollow. The hike finishes with another run along the creek, with more mossy outcroppings, boulders, and overhanging rock ledges scattered up the hillside.

The longest hike in St. Francois is the Pike Run Trail. Since it follows old logging roads for parts of its length, it used to be called the Old Logger's Trail. Renamed the Pike Run Trail after the local Pike Run Hills through which it winds, this 11-mile trail is divided into a 4.3-mile northern loop and a 6.7-mile southern loop. Marked with yellow blazes and arrows, its trailhead is just north of the campground on the eastern side of the park road. While it has less scenery than the Mooner's Hollow and Swimming Deer trails, it's the wildest hike in the park, offering the most solitude—it's farther from the highway and the park amenities, and its distance shakes out the less energetic.

A 0.35-mile spur leads to the southern loop. Whether hiking only the southern loop or the entire trail, I prefer taking the left fork and hiking the trail clockwise. Most of the climbs are on the western side, and it's good to get those out of the way while you're fresh. The 3 miles on the western side of the southern loop explore three hollows and the ridges between them. You'll climb to a ridge, follow it for a while, then drop steeply into a hollow, only to climb up onto the next ridge. In the last hollow before the north loop connector, there's a deep pool tucked beneath a 3-foot-thick, 50-foot-long rock ledge. In fall the pool is especially attractive. Full of red and yellow floating leaves, it reflects the mossy rock ledge that guards it.

The connector to the north loop is only 0.1 mile long and is marked with white arrows. Taking the left fork of the north loop, you'll hike level or gently downhill for the first 0.75 miles, then break north and descend steeply off a ridge nose into a side hollow of Coonville Creek. You'll bottom out in the hollow, then turn east along a trickling stream. Just a few yards upstream is the coolest place on the Pike Run Trail. First you'll hike past a series of pools and trickling cascades, leading to a massive rock wall with a spring trickling from its base. If you're backpacking the northern loop, there's an ideal campsite on a bench land overlooking the spring and bluff.

After the spring the trail winds up-hollow for a quarter mile, then climbs steeply onto a ridge to the north. You'll follow this gentle ridge for a half mile as it swings slowly east. There'll be one more steep descent and climb as you cross the upper end of the hollow that hides the spring, then it's a winding hike back to the connector with the southern loop. Heading home on the eastern side of the south loop, you'll have three short, steep hollow crossings, then join an old logging road along the ridge. When you pass the spur to the backpack camp you have 1.6 miles to go. Except for one short climb, it's an easy hike from the backpack spur to the trailhead.

# ST. JOE STATE PARK

## ▶ IN BRIEF

St. Joe State Park, with an 11-mile paved loop trail, is the place to go if you like easy walking without the noise of city streets. It's also good for rugged hiking—the 6.5-mile Pine Ridge Loop on the park's equestrian trail system has enough rocky terrain to challenge the toughest outdoor enthusiast.

## ▶ DESCRIPTION

The land around St. Joe State Park, known as Missouri's "Old Lead Belt," once held the world's most abundant deposits of its namesake mineral. More than 1,000 miles of abandoned mine tunnel and 300 miles of underground railroad tracks, left to slowly fill with water when the mines closed, underlay the region. As you wander the park you'll spot an occasional foundation, or pipes left over from test holes drilled to search out deposits of lead.

The park is named for the St. Joe Lead Company, which closed its operations here in 1972 and in 1976 donated its land to the state-park system. With 8,238 acres, St. Joe is the third largest park in Missouri. In addition to the usual camping and hiking, the park offers excellent mountain biking; a paved path suitable for hiking, biking, and cross-country skiing; and four lakes stocked with bass, catfish, and crappie. Two lakes are open for swimming, complete with sandy beaches and changing houses. Two thousand acres of this old mine property, where wide expanses of mine tailings cover the landscape, are set aside for off-road-vehicle use.

The Missouri Mines Historic Site, a massive structure visible from several points in the park, was

## ▶ DIRECTIONS

Drive south from Festus–Crystal City on US 67 to the Leadington–Park Hills–MO 32 West exit. Go 3.5 miles west on MO 32 to Pimville Road. Turn left into the park and then follow Pimville Road to the trailhead of your choice.

##  KEY AT-A-GLANCE INFORMATION

**LENGTH:** 29 miles on 4 loop trails

**CONFIGURATION:** System of connected loops with shortcut options

**DIFFICULTY:** Easy to moderate on paved trails; moderate on natural surface paths

**SCENERY:** Forests, rugged rock formations, small patches of prairie, historical evidence of lead mining operations

**EXPOSURE:** Mix of shady and exposed

**TRAFFIC:** Medium

**TRAIL SURFACE:** 13.8 miles paved; remainder natural surface of gravel and rock with rugged sections

**HIKING TIME:** 1 hour–all day, depending on route choices

**ACCESS:** Trailheads open 7 a.m.–sunset

**MAPS:** Farmington and Flat River USGS topos; trail map available at park office

**FACILITIES:** Water, restrooms, campground, picnic sites, beaches, four-wheeler area, phone

**SPECIAL COMMENTS:** Pets on 10-foot leash; no cans or bottles in beach area

### GPS TRAILHEAD COORDINATES (PARK ENTRANCE)

| UTM ZONE (WGS84) | 15S |
| EASTING | 716724 |
| NORTHING | 4189274 |
| LATITUDE-LONGITUDE | |
| NORTH | N37° 49' 30.5782'' |
| WEST | W90° 32' 15.2541'' |

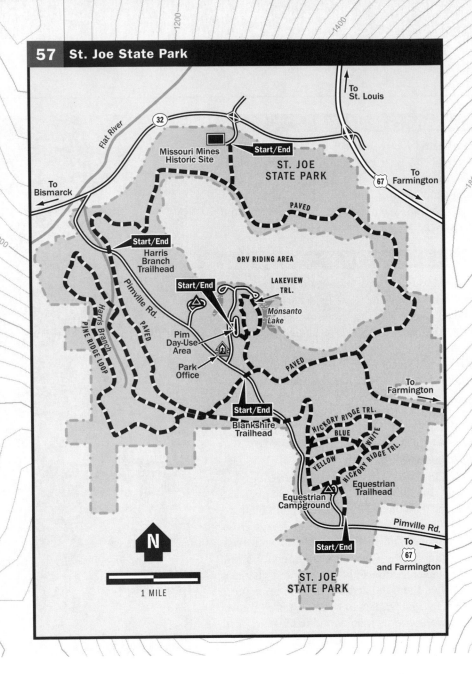

To St. Louis

Flat River

32

Missouri Mines Historic Site

Start/End

ST. JOE STATE PARK

67

To Farmington

To Bismarck

1200

Start/End
Harris Branch Trailhead

PAVED

ORV RIDING AREA

LAKEVIEW TRL.

Start/End

Monsanto Lake

Pim Day-Use Area

Pimville Rd.

PAVED

Harris Branch
PINE RIDGE LOOP

Park Office

PAVED

To Farmington

Start/End
Blankshire Trailhead

HICKORY RIDGE TRL.

BLUE

YELLOW

WHITE

HICKORY RIDGE TRL.

Equestrian Trailhead

Equestrian Campground

Pimville Rd.

To 67
and Farmington

N

1 MILE

Start/End

ST. JOE STATE PARK

another of the company's donations to the state-park system. Formerly St. Joe's operations center for many of the area's mines, it consists of more than 20 buildings, some dating back to the late 1800s. The 19,000-square-foot power house has been turned into a museum commemorating the region's lead-mining history. There you'll find geological information, mineral collections, and mining tools, including locomotives that pulled ore cars from the mine.

The paved loop trail is an excellent way to explore the park. Two of its five access points, the Blankshire and the Harris Branch trailheads, are on Pimville Road. The Blankshire trailhead on the south part of the loop has water, picnic sites, and toilets. The Harris Branch is the loop's west trailhead, and has picnic sites and toilets. Connected to the loop by a half-mile spur, the Missouri Mines Historic Site is the north trailhead. It has the largest parking area, and water and restrooms are available in the museum. The loop's eastern trailhead, accessed via a 1.7-mile spur, is in a subdivision at the park's boundary with Farmington. It has no amenities. To find it, exit US 67 by the Days Inn, go west to Bray Road, and follow the bike-path signs to the trailhead. The fifth trailhead is the Pim Day-Use Area, where a 0.6-mile spur leads to the loop.

The paved loop is hilly on its north side, with several vistas of Park Hills and the monstrous mill-mine complex at the Missouri Mines Historic Site. It's a wonderful trail-running path and is excellent for cross-country skiing. On the stretch of trail south of Pimville Road, the path follows an old rail bed for a while. This abandoned rail line once carried ore trains bound for the mill complex. The gentle grades on this 3-mile section of trail make it the easiest part of the paved loop.

The paved trail can get busy on nice weekends. To escape the crowds, take off on the equestrian trails. The Pine Ridge Loop, the most rugged at St. Joe, is in the western part of the park. The Hickory Ridge Trail, a 5.25-mile trail network north of the equestrian campground, is in the southeast corner of the park. A 2-mile connector stretches between the two, completing St. Joe's 14-mile equestrian trail system. The trailhead at the equestrian campground has water and toilets; if you're overnighting at St. Joe, it's the place to be. The main campground is where the four-wheelers hang out, so it's a noisier place. Check out the "headframe" across the road from the camp and trailhead. Built above a mine shaft to lift ore out of the ground, it had to be abandoned after only nine months because the miners struck an underground lake.

The Hickory Ridge Trail, marked with green blazes and green arrows on carsonite posts, is a 3-mile loop accessed via a half-mile spur from the equestrian trailhead. Connector trails, marked with yellow, blue, and white blazes, cut across the loop. These official trails combine with many side trails cut by equestrians to keep you exploring these forests, ridges, and hollows for hours. You'll not see many vistas, but will pass old foundations, a culvert, and several test-well pipes leftover from mining days.

Using the 2-mile connector, you could hike the Pine Ridge Loop from the equestrian trailhead—but that'd be a really long day. Easier access starts from the Blankshire trailhead on Pimville Road. Hike the bike trail 0.65 miles downhill to the old railbed. There you'll see a trail with the Pine Ridge Loop's red markings angling west into the forest. The Pine Ridge Loop begins a short way down that path. The western side of this long, skinny loop follows ridges on old road for most of its length and is an easy 3.5-mile hike. At the north end of the loop a power line cut opens up nice views to the north. When the trail breaks south, it becomes rugged single-track, and stays that way for most of the 3 miles to the loop's southern end. There's a pretty stream ford on Harris Branch, where slick ledges extend up and down the creek bottom, and an unbelievably rugged rock garden near the end of the Pine Ridge Loop.

The shortest hike at St. Joe is the Lakeview Trail. This 1.3-mile loop connects Pim Day-Use Area with the beach at Monsanto Lake, and can be hiked from either place. It's a natural-surface trail, with one long descent and one long climb. On the Lakeview Trail you might see a heron standing in one of the lake's coves. Near the beach you'll find a bench with nice views over the water, and you can end your hiking day at St. Joe with a dip in Monsanto Lake.

# TRAIL OF TEARS STATE PARK

 **KEY AT-A-GLANCE INFORMATION**

**LENGTH:** 13 miles on 4 trails

**CONFIGURATION:** 4 separate loops

**DIFFICULTY:** Nature Trail, very easy; Sheppard Point Trail, easy; Lake Trail, easy; Peewah Trail, moderate–hard

**SCENERY:** Scenic overlooks of Mississippi River, razorback ridges, quiet hollows

**EXPOSURE:** Shaded

**TRAFFIC:** Light on Peewah Trail, medium on all others

**TRAIL SURFACE:** Packed earth and gravel, many rocky and rugged sections

**HIKING TIME:** 1 hour or less on the Sheppard Point, Lake, and Nature trails; 2–6 hours on Peewah Trail, depending upon route choices

**ACCESS:** Park open 7 a.m.–10 p.m., April–October; 7 a.m.–9 p.m., November and March; 7 a.m.–6 p.m., December–February

**MAPS:** Ware, Cape Girardeau NE USGS topos; Trail of Tears State Park Trail and Wild Area map available at visitor center

**FACILITIES:** Water, camping, picnic shelters, phone, restrooms, swimming beach, visitor center

**SPECIAL COMMENTS:** Pets on leash; old quarry below Peewah Trail overlook off-limits

**GPS TRAILHEAD COORDINATES (VISITOR CENTER)**

| | |
|---|---|
| UTM ZONE (WGS84) | 16S |
| EASTING | 280301 |
| NORTHING | 4146233 |
| LATITUDE-LONGITUDE | |
| NORTH | N37° 26' 12.7246'' |
| WEST | W89° 28' 59.7765'' |

## IN BRIEF

Trail of Tears State Park is a beautiful place named for a tragic event. Thousands of Native Americans forcibly removed from their lands in the southeast crossed the Mississippi River, in or near this state park, during their 800-mile trek to Indian Territory in Oklahoma. Now you can explore the scenic landscape named for their memory on trails that overlook the wide river and wander among the mazelike ridges and hollows to its west.

## DESCRIPTION

Trail of Tears State Park is fascinating both for its natural beauty and its human history. The park's name evokes the forced relocation of Native Americans from their lands in the southeastern states. Called "Nunahi-Duna-Dlu-Hilu-I," or "Trail Where They Cried," by natives, this 800-mile trek passed by and through the park. In the hard winter of 1838–39, ice jammed the Mississippi and made crossing impossible, forcing thousands of Native Americans to camp near today's Trail of Tears Park. An estimated 4,000 Native Americans died during the trek to Indian Territory in what is now eastern Oklahoma. In 1987 Congress designated the Trail of Tears a National Historic Trail.

You can learn more about the Trail of Tears at the park's visitor center. Its hours vary widely from season to season, so check the state-park Web site (**www.mostateparks.com/trailoftears.htm**) before you go. The visitor center splits its exhibits between Trail of Tears history and the natural features of the park. Maps of the Trail of Tears's two

## DIRECTIONS

Drive south on I-55 to Exit 105 for Fruitland, Jackson, and US 61. From the ramp, all intersections are signed for the park. Turn left on US 61 and drive 1 mile to MO 177. Turn right and follow 177 11 miles to the park.

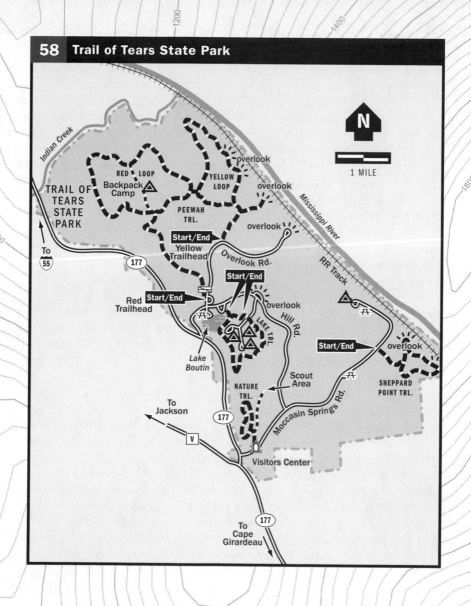

routes are displayed, along with bios of principal figures, both native and set-
tler. Panels with paintings, drawings, and participants' accounts of the sad trek
cover the walls. Other displays describe trees, plants, and animals you'll see in
the park; a large relief map shows the terrain you'll cross while hiking on the
Peewah Trail in the north end of Trail of Tears.

Trail of Tears State Park overlays a 3,415-acre mazelike landscape of bluffs,
razorback ridges, and deep hollows next to the Mississippi River. Both the hiking
trails and the park road feature overlooks with expansive views over the river and
far into Illinois. Bring your binoculars—the view is wonderful, and you may spot

an eagle roosting above the Mississippi in winter. During warmer months you'll see lots of wildflowers in the park's moist bottomlands and on its dry ridges.

Four scenic trails explore Trail of Tears State Park. The half-mile Nature Trail starts from the amphitheater behind the visitor center and explores a little hollow and low ridge. There's not much to it, but it's a nice hike for children, or for freezing winter days when a short hike to admire white landscapes or the glitter of ice-encrusted trees is all you need. The 2-mile Lake Trail, marked with green arrows and green plastic blazes, is more interesting. It wanders along Lake Boutin and around Lake Boutin campground. It starts next to the campground's bathhouse and descends to the lake, where a spur trail leads to the beach parking area—another possible starting point for the loop. From the spur, you'll follow the lakeshore a half mile to the dam, walking along the water's edge all the way. At the dam you can cross over to the picnic area. After leaving the dam, the Lake Trail winds up and down over deep hollows west of the campground on a challenging trail.

The 2-mile Sheppard Point Trail starts from the road leading to the Mississippi River campground. It's a 1.5-mile loop with a quarter-mile spur from the trailhead, marked with yellow arrows and yellow plastic blazes. The spur is a pretty ascent up a steep, deep hollow, topping out to join the loop at a beautiful spot where two ridges cross. You can see the Mississippi River through the trees to the northwest, and narrow ridge spines run in several directions. While the trail is marked for clockwise travel, I prefer hiking it counterclockwise—the climbs are a bit less steep that way. You'll bounce over one of the ridges and drop steeply into a deep hollow, cross it, then climb onto the riverside knob called Sheppard's Point. From the knob you'll descend back to the hollow, climb onto the nose of a ridge with more views of the river, and follow the ridge back to the trailhead spur.

The park's feature hike is the Peewah Trail, which explores the 1,300-acre Indian Creek Wild Area. (*Peewah* is a Native American word meaning "walk in this direction.") The Peewah is divided into a red loop and a yellow loop, joined by a 50-yard connector trail. Each loop has its own trailhead and spur access trail.

The park map says the Peewah is a 10-mile trail, but total mileage is closer to 8. Ten miles is the distance you'd cover if you hiked each spur out to its loop, around the loop, and back to the trailhead, including a side hike to the Mississippi River overlook. A map posted at the yellow trailhead shows mileage for each segment of the trail, and helps you choose a hike to match your time and abilities.

With its short half-mile spur trail, the yellow trailhead is the preferred starting point for hikes on the Peewah. It's a 3.4-mile hike around the yellow loop from this trailhead, a 4.5-mile hike around the red loop, and a 6-mile hike to do both. Hiking to the Mississippi River overlook and back is an easy 1.25-mile jaunt. The drawback to the yellow trailhead is its location on Overlook Road, which closes before the rest of the park. November through March, Overlook Road is open from 7 a.m. to 5 p.m. April through October, it's open from 7 a.m. to 7 p.m. If your hike might last longer than that, use the red trailhead located next to Overlook Road's gate. The spur from this trailhead is 1.6 miles.

Here's what you'll find on the Peewah Trail—starting from the yellow trailhead and hiking both loops clockwise, red loop first. The spur trail is an easy hike along a ridge. Along the way you'll pass a side trail marked with green arrows. It leads to the

Mississippi River overlook. The overlook is a beautiful place, but you'll see better views on the northeast side of the yellow loop. Half a mile from the trailhead the loop begins. Turn left to hike 0.4 miles to the red loop, winding up and down along a ridge with winter views left and right. This nice ridgetop hike continues for another 0.7 miles on the red loop. There you'll see the spur to the red trailhead, and the cutoff trail on the red loop. It leads downhill to the backpack camp, then on to the far side of the loop a half mile to the north.

Just past the cutoff trail, you'll descend steeply into a hollow. You'll stay level for the next mile to the other end of the cutoff trail, going gradually down this hollow, then veering east to go gently up another. After reaching the north end of the cutoff trail you'll climb for a quarter mile, topping out on a knob with views of the Mississippi through the trees to the north. The trail breaks south from the knob and follows a ridge for 0.75 miles, making short, steep climbs and descents all the way to the junction with the yellow loop.

Back on the yellow loop you'll break north and descend a quarter mile into a hollow, level out, and wind back and forth across its stream for a while. Just before reaching the confluence of Indian Creek and the Mississippi River, you'll break right and climb steeply onto a ridge above the river. The view is beautiful here, and it keeps getting better as you hike southeast along the Mississippi. Judging the trail by the park map's topo lines, it looks like the next couple of miles to the trailhead will be easy, but steep ups and downs on the ridge spine will keep you breathing deeply. The payback is in the views—for more than a mile you'll be walking on this ridge above the Mississippi.

After a mile along the river, the trail veers northwest and away from the cliff. Take the side trail going left here. It leads to the prettiest view on the Peewah Trail. This spur dead-ends on a bluff overlooking an old quarry, and you can see for miles down the Mississippi's wide valley. On sunny days, the river is blue and the abandoned quarry's pool is deep green. Monstrous steplike ledges tower over the quarry below you, and straight south is the Mississippi River overlook at the end of Overlook Road.

After leaving this overlook, the trail veers away from the river. It's 0.4 miles to the end of the loop, then another 0.45 miles to the trailhead. You can enjoy one last look at the river from the 0.3-mile side trail leading east from the trailhead spur.

## ▶ NEARBY ACTIVITIES

Isn't ice cream related to hiking? For me it is, so I always stop at the Dairy Queen, located at I-55 Exit 105. You'll see it on your way to the park.

# VALLEY VIEW GLADES

## KEY AT-A-GLANCE INFORMATION

**LENGTH:** 3 miles

**CONFIGURATION:** Loop

**DIFFICULTY:** Easy

**SCENERY:** A breathtaking combination of secluded forest hollows and wide, open glades offering expansive vistas of the surrounding hills

**EXPOSURE:** Moderately shady, long stretches of wooded hiking with numerous open stretches while crossing or hiking edges of glades

**TRAFFIC:** Light

**TRAIL SURFACE:** Mostly single-track over packed dirt or gravel; several short rocky sections where trail crosses rock layers; two short stretches on old forest roads

**HIKING TIME:** 1.5–2 hours

**ACCESS:** Open daily 4 a.m.–10 p.m.; no permits or fees required

**MAPS:** Valley View Glades map and brochure available at trailhead

**FACILITIES:** None

**SPECIAL COMMENTS:** Pets must be leashed; no collection of flowers, wild plant foods, or other vegetation

### GPS TRAILHEAD COORDINATES (TRAILHEAD)

| | | |
|---|---|---|
| UTM ZONE (WGS84) | 15S | |
| EASTING | 707739 | |
| NORTHING | 4236792 | |
| LATITUDE–LONGITUDE | | |
| NORTH | N38° 15' 18.5626'' | |
| WEST | W90° 37' 32.8324'' | |

## IN BRIEF

In the undiscovered beauty of Valley View Glades you'll find hidden waterfalls in wooded hollows, hillside vistas from expansive glades, and carpets of spring wildflowers—all accessible from an easy 3-mile loop hike.

## DESCRIPTION

Valley View Glades is a hidden gem less than an hour from downtown St. Louis. Few people come here, overlooking this hideaway in favor of better-known and supposedly more-spectacular trails in the St. Louis area. Well, now you have no excuse for making the same mistake—grab your boots and head for Valley View for an enchanting 3-mile wander through forested hollows and windswept grassy glades.

Of Valley View's 225 acres, 125 are woodland, and 100 are wide-open, prairielike glades. Usually found on south and southwest-facing slopes, glades are open spaces in otherwise-wooded landscapes. Valley View Glades is part of a long, narrow band of these forest openings scattered across the landscape stretching from Morse Mill all the way to the Mississippi River. The thin and rocky soil of these glades isn't well suited for trees, but grasses and wildflowers thrive here. Come to Valley View in spring, when the normally dry, sun-burned soil is moist from seasonal rains, and you'll find the place lousy with wildflowers, especially coneflowers and black-eyed Susans, liberally scattered across a grassy expanse.

Spring also brings to life a pleasant surprise hidden in the wooded hollows of Valley View—

## DIRECTIONS

From the southwest edge of Hillsboro, turn north off MO 21 onto MO B. Drive 4.7 miles northwest on MO B to Valley View Glades trailhead on the right.

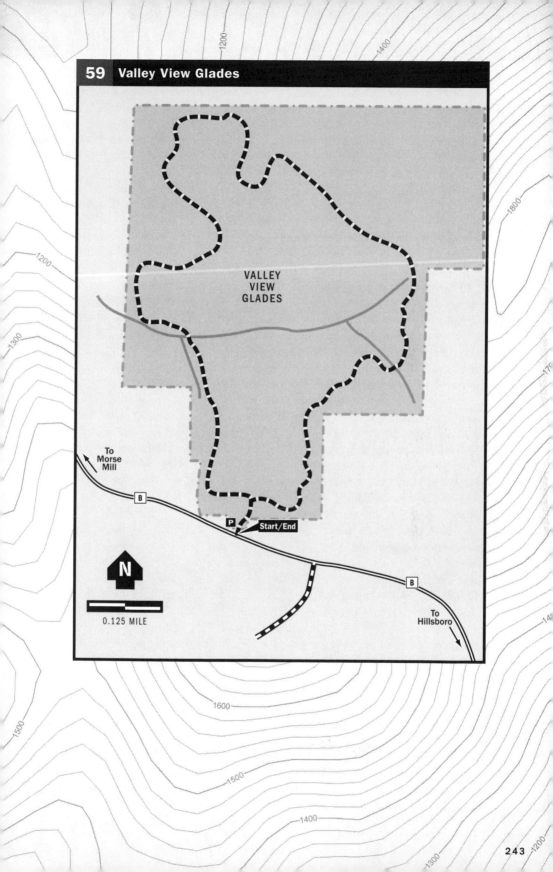

exquisite little waterfalls and cascades of the intermittent streams that wind through the valley. Come enjoy these secret jewels during so-called bad weather. The little cascades trickling over streambed rock outcroppings are always enchanting, but they really come alive during rainstorms. These falls are intriguing in winter, too, when they create unbelievable ice formations at pour-offs, and long ranks of icicles grow where seeps occur in the rock strata.

Any season is a good time to hike Valley View. Summer heat is offset by shade in the woods and cooling breezes in the glades. In autumn Missouri's glorious fall colors contrast brightly with the rusty-brown, dormant grasses in the glades. Since so much sunshine can brighten and warm the open glades, even snowy winter days are wonderful for exploring Valley View.

The trail itself is incredible. It's as if the designer surveyed the landscape here, noted the most enchanting waterfalls, rock gardens, and scenic vistas, and then constructed the trail to meander past every one. The first highlight comes after the 0.1-mile spur hike from the parking lot to the loop's beginning, where you break out of the woods and immediately see how Valley View got its name. Opening before you is a huge glade covering both sides of an expansive valley of grass, with forests on the ridges and a strip of timber in the ravine below. Take a good look—you can see almost all the landscape you'll explore on your hike.

The trail is marked for travel in a clockwise direction, with carsonite posts sporting hiker silhouettes, along with an occasional signpost with "Trail" emblazoned on it. After you turn left at the junction and descend from the trailhead ridge, you immediately enter the woods and stay in them for much of the first mile. At 0.2 miles into the hike there's a ledge to your left with a six-foot waterfall, a hint of things to come. A hundred yards farther is another rock ledge, this one stretching 40 feet across the hollow, creating a waterfall as tall as you, with a deep overhang. You can actually get behind the waterfall and look downstream through the falls.

You'll pass several more waterfalls in the next half mile, admire a stone overhang stretching 150 feet along a pool in the creek, and traverse a couple of small glades. At 0.75 miles into the hike you'll see a couple of trails cutting to the left. These are shortcuts across a bend in the trail, but don't take them. If you do, you'll miss breaking into a huge glade just ahead with beautiful vistas of the valley you just crossed. Upon reaching the glade, the trail steps onto a low rock ledge and follows it for a while, beginning the second mile of the trail. This middle part of the hike alternates between stretches of forest and open glades, with very nice views of the surrounding countryside. It descends into the hollow again at mile 1.2, where you'll admire the most impressive rock formation and waterfall in Valley View Glades. At this scenic break, the stream flows over slick rock and splashes five feet into a clear, deep pool, with overhanging ledges stretching downstream on both sides of the creek. The trail then turns hard right away from the stream, climbs through a pretty rock garden, and heads back to the glades.

About halfway through the hike the trail joins an old road, follows it for a short distance, then breaks downhill to the right. It's all right if you miss this turn, because the trail comes back to the old road shortly. Try not to miss it, though, because after you make this turn and push through just enough overgrowth to make you wonder if you've lost the trail, you'll break out of the brush to see an awesome view of the glade, framed by a cedar and a maple. From this vantage point you're looking across the valley to where your hike began. From this vista the trail turns to follow the edge of the glade on a low rock ledge for a short distance, with four or five similar rock layers spaced 15 to 20 feet apart marching down the slope of the glade like waves on a grassy beach.

The trail soon leaves the glade, pushes through the brush to the old road, and continues to the right. After a quarter mile, the trail breaks off the old road to the right. Look sharp here—the turnoff isn't well marked, and the old road looks like the logical way to go. There is a trail marker 50 feet down the proper route, so keep an eye out for that.

The last mile of the hike is spent mostly on ridges or side hills, with a few short descents and ascents to cross heads of draws (large gullies) feeding into the main valley and glade. You'll ramble along the forest edge, breaking in and out of the glade, often with wonderful views of distant hills to the north framed by the woods edging the glade. Though several rocky draws make the last mile a bit more difficult to hike, you'll see the most wildflowers there, and the numerous vistas are breathtaking.

You'll end your hike in Valley View Glades with one final little waterfall, a rocky and steep wash crossing, a good look at a gnarled old cedar leaning over the trail, and a last look at the grand vastness of Valley View Glades from the overlook at the trail junction.

# WASHINGTON STATE PARK

## KEY AT-A-GLANCE INFORMATION

**LENGTH:** 11.25 miles on 3 trails

**CONFIGURATION:** Network of interconnecting loops

**DIFFICULTY:** Easy on 1,000 Steps and Opossum trails; moderate on Rockywood Trail

**SCENERY:** Panoramic vistas, grassy glades, deep forests, rugged rock outcroppings and ledges, prehistoric Native American petroglyphs, and historic CCC buildings

**EXPOSURE:** Shady, with several exposed areas in glades

**TRAFFIC:** Medium-heavy on 1,000 Steps Trail; light-medium on Opossum and Rockywood trails

**TRAIL SURFACE:** Predominantly packed earth and gravel, with rocky, rugged stretches; extremely rugged rock-step sections on 1,000 Steps Trail

**HIKING TIME:** 1-2 hours on 1,000 Steps and Opossum Trails; 3-5 hours on Rockywood Trail

**ACCESS:** Park open sunrise-sunset

**MAPS:** Tiff USGS topo; trail map available at nature center building

**FACILITIES:** Water, restrooms, cabins, store, pool, picnic area, shelters, nature center, campgrounds

**SPECIAL COMMENTS:** Pets must be leashed

### GPS TRAILHEAD COORDINATES (THUNDERBIRD LODGE)

| | |
|---|---|
| UTM ZONE (WGS84) | 15S |
| EASTING | 703115 |
| NORTHING | 4217900 |
| LATITUDE-LONGITUDE | |
| NORTH | N38° 5' 9.9187'' |
| WEST | W90° 41' 2.3601'' |

## ▶ IN BRIEF

On top of the beautiful rivers, bluffs, glades, forested ridges, and deep hollows you find on Missouri hikes, Washington State Park has fascinating petroglyph displays etched into its rock outcroppings. Two-thirds of Missouri's known petroglyphs are found here, and the park's trails lead past the two best groupings of these haunting relics.

## ▶ DESCRIPTION

Do you think the Four Corners region is the only place to view prehistoric Native American rock art? Well, think again, and head south to Washington State Park. Two-thirds of Missouri's known petroglyphs are carved in the rock outcroppings of the 1,875-acre park, and you'll walk right past them on the Rockywood and 1,000 Steps trails. Interpretive displays help you find these timeworn etchings, and explain their possible meanings.

More-recent man-made attractions are the shelters, cabins, park lodge, and headquarters buildings built by the Civilian Conservation Corps (CCC) in the 1930s. The CCC boys must have been everywhere in Missouri—almost every state park I hike through is enhanced by their rustic log-and-stone architecture. I never tire of admiring it. You'll appreciate their labor as much as I do when you hike the 1,000 Steps Trail. There you'll climb a steep hillside on hundreds of massive rock steps manhandled into place by these hardworking men.

The CCC also did the stonework along the park's north entrance road, but their most interesting work is in the park store next to the trailhead. In keeping with the theme of several petroglyph

## ▶ DIRECTIONS

Drive south from St. Louis on MO 21. Eight miles past De Soto, turn right into the park on MO 104. Drive 1.3 miles to the Thunderbird Lodge. All three trails start from the parking area.

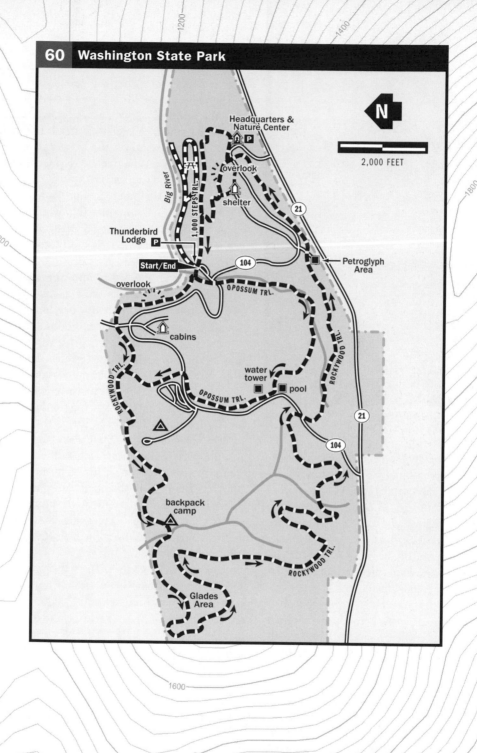

N

2,000 FEET

Headquarters &
Nature Center

overlook

shelter

Big River

1,000 STEPS TRL.

Thunderbird
Lodge

Start/End

overlook

104

21

Petroglyph
Area

OPOSSUM TRL.

cabins

water
tower

pool

OPOSSUM TRL.

ROCKYWOOD TRL.

ROCKYWOOD TRL.

21

104

backpack
camp

ROCKYWOOD TRL.

Glades
Area

Big River Overlook, Washington State Park

images, they named it the Thunderbird Lodge and worked thunderbird symbols into the structure's stone chimney and door hinges. The lodge is located on top of a creek flowing to the nearby river, with a huge masonry-lined channel guiding the creek beneath the building. You can stand on the lodge's porch and see the creek rushing below to pour into the Big River a few yards away.

While Washington State Park's petroglyphs and CCC workmanship won its place on the National Register of Historic Places, the natural beauty here is pretty snazzy, too. The park's heart is a wide, grassy valley between the Big River and the dolomite bluffs towering to the west and south. All three trails pass stupendous overlooks of the valley, wander among deep hollows, explore groves of pine, cedar, and hardwoods, and cross grassy, rock-studded glades. The place is full of the rock outcroppings and ledges that attracted the prehistoric carvers to Washington State Park's rugged landscape. The 1.5-mile 1,000 Steps Trail is the shortest hike in Washington State Park, and shares treadway with the Rockywood Trail up to the park headquarters. Marked with yellow arrows and blazes for travel in a counterclockwise direction, it leaves from the trailhead parking lot's northeast corner. Following the edge of the open valley, it stays in the fringe of moist bottomland woods for its first 200 yards. At that point the loop begins, and you'll start climbing on the CCC-built steps. The grade is steep, but when it tops out you travel along the cliff's edge to another gift from the CCC— a trail shelter with incredible views of the river valley below.

From the overlook you'll hike uphill a short way to a fork. The right fork goes to a picnic shelter, and the trail heads left, angling east and gently uphill toward park headquarters. Near the stone restroom, the Rockywood Trail leaves the 1,000 Steps and heads south across the park road. The 1,000 Steps continues east past the headquarters, where a spur trail leads to the nature center and petroglyph site. Next, you'll turn north and make a 0.2-mile descent back to the river valley, bouncing over still more steps and rock layers. From the end of the descent it's an easy walk through moist bottomland with wildflowers, moss-covered deadfall, and mature forest to the trailhead.

The 3-mile Opossum Trail is marked with blue arrows and blazes for travel in a clockwise direction. It starts in the picnic area across the road from Thunderbird Lodge and heads south along the small creek that flows beneath the lodge. You'll hike gently uphill, slowly bending westward with the stream, passing cascades and streamside cedar groves. At a half mile into the hike the trail breaks north and climbs steeply for 0.2 miles, topping out behind the park swimming pool. This might be a nice place for a break on a hot summer day.

The next half mile is an easy ridgetop hike, roughly paralleling the park road to the campground. Just past the campground the trail turns left across the road and heads north behind one of the camping loops. You'll soon swing northeast away from the campground, make a short and steep descent to join the Rockywood Trail, and turn right to follow it. The Opossum Trail shares the path with the Rockywood on its last mile back to the trailhead.

A pretty mile it is! Right after the junction you'll do a couple of switchbacks through a series of rock layers, then cut across an old burn area that's a glade under restoration. After leaving the glade you'll cross a road, head back into the woods, and then run smack into the edge of a cliff. This is the most spectacular stretch of trail in the park. You'll turn right and follow the cliff for the next 200 yards, with the Big River directly below. Rock layers make natural benches that are perfect for admiring the view, and a second CCC shelter sits at the apex of the bluff. From the overlook it's a half-mile descent back to the park lodge, passing over and through still more rock layers and cliffs above the river.

The Rockywood Trail is the wildest hike in the park. It explores the undeveloped western end of Washington State Park, and is a nice loop for backpackers. Marked with orange arrows and blazes for travel in a counterclockwise direction, its stated length is 10 miles, but it measures only 7. For the first mile of the trek you'll cover the path just described on the Opossum Trail.

Upon leaving the Opossum Trail, the Rockywood goes level or gently up for a quarter mile, then passes a spur trail leading to the north campground loop. Next, you'll go gently downhill for a quarter mile, bottoming out in a little hollow with pretty outcroppings scattered all around, then wander through cedars edging a glade-restoration area for another quarter mile. After a little up-and-down hiking through the burned-off glade restoration you'll come to an old homesite. In spring you'll spot daffodils here—a common indicator of an old farm in the woods. There's an old foundation in the brush, and next to the trail is a pretty watercress-filled spring that probably attracted settlers to this spot. The Rockywood's backpack camp is up the spur trail next to the spring. Beyond the spring, the trail wanders several hundred yards in a peaceful cedar grove, then breaks into a long glade.

For nearly a mile the trail winds through a grassy glade fringed with cedars, easing up and down through rock layers and around scattered boulders. You'll leave the last glade on an old road and swing south into the woods, climb gently for a quarter mile, then top out on another old road and turn to follow it east.

After a short way you'll turn north off the road and run into one of the park's more haunting spots—the old stone chimneys and concrete foundations of an abandoned CCC camp. Two large foundations sit on either side of a smaller one, all overlooked by their massive stone chimneys. I love finding these old chimneys in the woods, and marvel at the excellent construction that keeps them standing straight and tall after so many years. A smaller chimney and foundation nearby appears to have been the camp's cooking pit. It's fascinating to imagine this now-peaceful hilltop once being a rowdy CCC camp.

The next 1.25 miles is an easy ramble to the park road, rolling over gentle ups and downs through hardwood and cedar groves. You'll descend for a quarter mile after crossing the road, finding yourself in a deep, steep-sided hollow with slabby and rugged outcroppings scattered everywhere. This canyonlike hollow is the headwaters for the creek flowing along the Opossum Trail and under Thunderbird Lodge. After crossing the hollow bottom you'll ascend gently for a half mile, walk along and through a beautiful set of rock layers for several hundred yards, then break into a rocky glade with wonderful views to the north. Just beyond the glade is the park's largest petroglyph display—an expanse of rock protected by a roof, with signs explaining the glyphs' possible meanings.

From the petroglyph site it's an easy half-mile walk to the park headquarters. This stretch of trail parallels MO 21, so it's a noisy hike. You could take advantage of the highway's close proximity and bushwhack 100 yards through the woods to the E&T Convenience store for a cold drink. When you reach the park headquarters, the Rockywood joins with the 1,000 Steps Trail, follows it to the overlook shelter for the second panoramic vista on the Rockywood Trail, then ends with a descent to Thunderbird Lodge.

### ▶ NEARBY ACTIVITIES

Nearby Big River is a popular canoeing river. Canoe rentals are available at Thunderbird Lodge. Call (636) 586-0322 or visit **www.mostateparks.com/washington/ canoe.htm** for more detailed information.

# 60 Hikes
*within* **60 MILES**

## ST. LOUIS
### INCLUDING SULLIVAN, POTOSI, AND FARMINGTON

## APPENDIXES
## & INDEX

# APPENDIX A:
# OUTDOOR SHOPS

## ▶ NAME/LOCATION

**The Alpine Shop**
440 North Kirkwood Road
Kirkwood, MO 63122
(314) 962-7715
**www.alpineshop.com**

**The Alpine Shop**
1729 Clarkson Road
Chesterfield, MO 63017
(636) 532-7499
**www.alpineshop.com**

**Bass Pro Shops**
1365 South Fifth Street
St. Charles, MO 63301
(636) 688-2500
**www.basspro-shops.com**

**Dick's Sporting Goods**
200 West County Centre
Des Peres, MO 63131
(314) 649-1400
**www.dickssportinggoods.com**

**Outdoors Inc.**
9755 Clayton Road
Ladue, MO 63124
(314) 997-5866

**Recreational Equipment Inc.**
1703 South Brentwood Boulevard
St. Louis, MO 63144
(314) 918-1004
**www.rei.com**

# APPENDIX B:
# PLACES TO BUY MAPS

## ▶ NAME/LOCATION

These businesses sell USGS topographic maps. Free trail maps may be available from agencies listed in Appendix D. Stores listed in Appendix A sell CD-ROM topographic-map programs.

**The Alpine Shop**
440 North Kirkwood Road
Kirkwood, MO 63122
(314) 962-7715
**www.alpineshop.com**

**Mark Twain National Forest**
(MTNF Territory only)
Highway 8 West
Potosi, MO 63664
(573) 438-5427

**Missouri Department of Natural
  Resources**
Division of Geology and Land
P.O. Box 250
Rolla, MO 65402
(573) 368-2125

**Outdoors, Inc.**
9755 Clayton Road
Ladue, MO 63124
(314) 997-5866

# APPENDIX C:
# HIKING CLUBS AND EVENTS

## ▶ NAME/LOCATION

**American Youth Hostels**
7187 Manchester Road
St. Louis, MO 63143
(314) 644-4660
www.gatewayhiayh.org

**Ozark Trail Association**
483 S. Kirkwood Road #40
Kirkwood, MO 63122
(573) 786-2065
www.ozarktrail.com

**Sierra Club, Eastern Missouri Group**
7164 Manchester Avenue
St. Louis, MO 63143
(314) 644-0890
missouri.sierraclub.org/emg

**St. Louis County Parks Hiking Club**
550 Weidman Road
Ballwin, MO 63011
(636) 391-0922

# APPENDIX D:
# AGENCY LIST

## ▶ NAME/LOCATION

**Illinois Department of Natural Resources**
Region IV Office
4521 Alton Commerce Parkway
Alton, IL 62002
(618) 462-1181
dnr.state.il.us

**Mark Twain National Forest**
www.fs.fed.us/r9/marktwain
   **Fredericktown Ranger District**
   1501 Madison County Road 212
   Highways 72 and O
   Fredericktown, MO 63645
   (573) 783-7225
**Potosi Ranger District**
   Highway 8 West
   Potosi, MO 63664
   (573) 438-5427

**Missouri Department of Conservation**
www.mdc.mo.gov
   **East Central Regional Office**
   375 South Highway 185
   Sullivan, MO 63080
   (573) 468-3335
   **St. Louis Regional Office**
   2360 Highway D
   St. Charles, MO 63304
   (636) 441-4554
   **Southeast Regional Office**
   2302 County Park Drive
   Cape Girardeau, MO 63701
   (573) 290-5730

**Missouri State Parks**
Department of Natural Resources
P.O. Box 176
Jefferson City, MO 65102
(800) 334-6946
www.mostateparks.com

**Ozark Trail Association**
483 South Kirkwood Road, Suite 40
Kirkwood, MO 63122
(573) 786-2065
www.ozarktrail.com

**St. Charles County Parks**
201 North Second Street, Suite 510
St. Charles, MO 63301
(636) 949-7535
www.saintcharlescounty.org

**St. Louis County Parks**
41 South Central
Clayton, MO 63105
(314) 615-5000
www.stlouisco.com/parks

**Shawnee National Forest**
Murphysboro Ranger District
2221 Walnut Street
Murphysboro, IL 62966
(618) 687-1731
www.fs.fed.us/r9/Shawnee

# INDEX

# INDEX

# INDEX

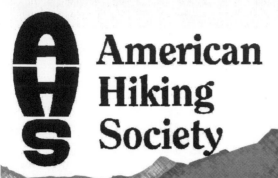